Health Psychology

Topics in Applied Psychology

Charles Abraham

Mark Conner

Fiona Jones

Daryl O'Connor

HODDER
EDUCATION
PART OF HACHETTE LIVRE UK

First published in Great Britain in 2008 by
Hodder Education, part of Hachette Livre UK,
338 Euston Road, London NW1 3BH

www.hoddereducation.com

Hachette Livre UK's policy is to use papers that are natural, renewable and
recyclable products and made from wood grown in sustainable forests.
The logging and manufacturing processes are expected to conform to the
environmental regulations of the country of origin.

The advice and information in this book are believed to be true and
accurate at the date of going to press, but neither the authors nor the publisher
can accept any legal responsibility or liability for any errors or omissions.

ﾟD OS673947

Every effort has been made to trace and acknowledge the owners of copyright.
The publishers will be glad to make suitable arrangements with any
copyright holders whom it has not been possible to contact.

British Library Cataloguing in Publication Data
A catalogue record for this book is available from the British Library

Library of Congress Cataloging-in-Publication Data
A catalog record for this book is available from the Library of Congress

ISBN 978 0 340 92890 5

1 2 3 4 5 6 7 8 9 10

Cover & section opener © Peter Dazeley/Stone/Getty Images

Figures 2.1 and 2.2 by Oxford Designers and Illustrators.

Typeset in 10pt Berling Roman by Servis Filmsetting Ltd, Stockport, Cheshire
Printed and bound in Malta

What do you think about this book? Or any other Hodder
Education title? Please send your comments to the
feedback section on www.hoddereducation.com.

Contents

Series Preface   vii
Preface   ix

Chapter 1: Introduction   1

Section 1: Biological bases of health and illness   13

Chapter 2: Biopsychosocial pathways to health and illness   15

Section 2: Stress and health   39

Chapter 3: Stress theory and research   41

Chapter 4: Stress and health in context   65

Section 3: Coping resources: Social support and individual differences   85

Chapter 5: Coping and social support   87

Chapter 6: Personality and health   109

Section 4: Motivation and behaviour   133

Chapter 7: Health cognitions and health behaviours   135

Chapter 8: Changing motivation   157

Chapter 9: Changing behaviour   179

Section 5: Relating to patients   207

Chapter 10: Relating to patients   209

Chapter 11: Future directions, roles and competencies   233

References   243
Index   277

Series preface

Psychology is still one of the most popular subjects for study at undergraduate degree level. As well as providing the student with a range of academic and applied skills that are valued by a broad range of employers, a psychology degree also serves as the basis for subsequent training and a career in professional psychology. A substantial proportion of students entering a degree programme in Psychology do so with a subsequent career in applied psychology firmly in mind, and as a result the number of applied psychology courses available at undergraduate level has significantly increased over recent years. In some cases these courses supplement core academic areas and in others they provide the student with a flavour of what they might experience as a professional psychologist.

Topics in Applied Psychology represents a series of six textbooks designed to provide a comprehensive academic and professional insight into specific areas of professional psychology. The texts cover the areas of **Clinical Psychology, Criminal Psychology, Educational Psychology, Health Psychology, Sport and Exercise Psychology**, and **Organizational and Work Psychology**, and each text is written and edited by the foremost professional and academic figures in each of these areas.

Each textbook is based on a similar academic formula which combines a comprehensive review of cutting-edge research and professional knowledge with accessible teaching and learning features. The books are also structured so they can be used as an integrated teaching support for a one-term or one-semester course in each of their relevant areas of applied psychology. Given the increasing importance of applying psychological knowledge across a growing range of areas of practice, we feel this series is timely and comprehensive. We hope you find each book in the series readable, enlightening, accessible and instructive.

Graham Davey
University of Sussex, Brighton, UK
September 2007

Preface

Health Psychology is an area of applied psychological research and a profession. Psychological research has established how perceptions and behaviour affect physiological processes such as those constituting the cardiovascular and immune systems. These processes, in turn, determine morbidity and mortality. Health psychology research has also helped discriminate between health promotion and health care practices which do and do not effectively promote health behaviours, quality of life and longevity.

Health psychology research examines the determinants and consequences of physical rather than mental health and illness (which is the focus of Clinical Psychology). This area of research is becoming increasingly important since it has become clear that 1) health behaviours are critical to health, and 2) without effective promotion of health-preserving lifestyles, it will become impossible to fund the treatment of those with ill health and chronic illness. Consequently, there is an increasing need to provide health care professionals with health-psychology-based skills (e.g. in relation to stress reduction or health behaviour change) and to employ health psychologists in health care services.

Inevitably, then, health psychology is now making an important contribution to undergraduate degree programmes (at all levels) and a substantial proportion of undergraduate students reading psychology study health psychology. The purpose of this book is to introduce undergraduate psychology students to health psychology research and to illustrate the links between such research and health psychology practice (e.g. in relation to health behaviour change). The book will prepare students for final examinations in health psychology at undergraduate level and provide a solid foundation for students wishing to pursue graduate studies in health psychology. The book has a UK and European perspective but is relevant to any health care system. It is divided into five sections, namely, 1) the biological basis of health and illness, 2) stress and health, 3) coping resources: social support and individual differences, 4) motivation and behaviour and 5) relating to patients. Throughout the book, we discuss health-related perceptions and behaviours and explain how psychological processes, e.g. emotional responses, shape heath-related behaviours and affect physiological systems such as the immune and cardiovascular systems. These relationships provide the foundation for psychological interventions which can change cognition, perception and behaviour and thereby improve health.

As with all the books in the *Topics in Applied Psychology* series, this text is written as a support for a one-term or one-semester course in Health Psychology, and contains a range of teaching and learning features such as focus boxes, research methods boxes, activity boxes (encouraging the student to engage actively with presented material) as well as consideration of issues of contemporary interest (including developments within the UK National Health Service [NHS], the National Institute for Health and Clinical Excellence [NICE] and the Health and Safety Executive [HSE]). Each chapter also ends with support for further reading, including relevant journal articles and books which will enable the interested student to engage with key topics in more depth.

The aim of this book is to provide the undergraduate psychology student with a concise, readable, structured introduction to health psychology. We have focused on core topics which define the sub-discipline and linked these together so that the text can be read as a continuous course. All of the authors teach health psychology to undergraduates and postgraduates and we hope that, like us, readers will be inspired by the findings of health psychology research and the impact of health psychology practice.

Charles Abraham
University of Sussex, Brighton, UK
February 2008

1 Introduction

This book provides a concise, one-term course covering core topics in health psychology suitable for final year undergraduate study. We discuss the origins and definition of the sub-discipline as well as considering available evidence identifying psychological processes which affect psychological well-being, physiological functioning, health behaviours, behaviour change, the usage of health services and response to health services.

In this first chapter we discuss definitions of health psychology as an academic discipline and as a profession. We also look back on academic traditions that have contributed to the development of health psychology illustrating the rich mix of theories, methodologies and practice which make health psychology what it is today. In addition, we offer guidance on using the book and studying health psychology generally, including introducing the structure and topic order used in this book. This chapter has four sections: 1) what is health psychology?; 2) foundations of health psychology; 3) using this book effectively; 4) the structure and content of this book.

Learning outcomes

When you have completed this chapter you should be able to:

1. Define and describe the discipline and profession of health psychology.
2. Identify psychological sub-disciplines which contribute to health psychology research and practice.
3. Explain what is meant by the biopsychosocial model of health and illness.
4. Understand how this book is structured and how to study it effectively.

What is health psychology?

The **World Health Organization** (WHO) (1948) defines health as:

a state of complete physical, mental and social well-being and not merely the absence of disease or infirmity.

This definition, which has not been amended since 1948, challenges psychologists to define and assess the determinants of 'physical, mental and social well being'. Within UK psychology there has been a division between health psychology, which focuses on physical health, and clinical psychology which focuses on mental health. The two sub-disciplines overlap because some of the psychological processes that affect physical health are also important to mental health. For example, anxiety and stress responses have important consequences for both physical and mental health and the broader social well-being of an individual.

The following broad definition of health psychology was provided by Matarazzo (1980: 815):

> *Health psychology is an aggregate of the educational, scientific and professional contributions of the discipline of psychology to the promotion and maintenance of health, the prevention and treatment of illness, the identification of etiologic and diagnostic correlates of health, illness and related dysfunction and the improvement of the health care system and health policy formation.*

This much-cited definition is usefully inclusive and highlights: 1) the overarching aims of the sub-discipline, namely, promoting health and preventing illness; 2) the scientific focus of research in health psychology, that is, understanding **aetiological and diagnostic correlates of health**; and 3) key priorities of *professional practice* in health psychology, that is, improving health care by focusing on delivery systems and policy.

Health psychologists seek to understand the processes which link individual perceptions, beliefs and behaviours to biological processes which, in turn, result in physical health problems. For example, how a person perceives work demands and copes with them will determine his or her stress levels (see Chapter 3) which, in turn, may affect the functioning of the cardiovascular and immune systems (see Chapter 2). Health psychologists also study social processes including the effect of wider social structure (such as socio-economic status) and face-to-face interactions with others (e.g. work colleagues) because these social processes shape perceptions, beliefs and behaviour (see Chapter 4). In addition, health psychologists explore individual processes that shape health outcomes and *health behaviours* (see Chapters 6 and 7) and social processes which influence the effectiveness of health care delivery. For example, the way health care professionals communicate with their patients influences patient behaviour, including patients' willingness to take medication and adopt health-enhancing behaviours (see Chapters 8 and 10). Since most health and medical interventions depend both on the behaviour of health care professionals and, critically, on the behaviour of patients, *behaviour change* processes limit the potential of health service delivery.

When research allows us to develop good models of underlying causal processes this establishes the evidence base for the design of interventions that will change those processes and, thereby, change health outcomes. Thus professional health psychologists use research findings to assess individuals and design and evaluate interventions which change perceptions, beliefs, behaviours and social relationships which affect health-related behaviour, quality of life and measures of health and disease. These interventions operate at different levels ranging from those focusing on the individual to those designed to change society, i.e. targeting, on the one hand, individual health and, on the other, public health (see Chapter 9).

We will examine the determinants of health behaviours, highlight the impact they have on health and health care delivery and consider how we can change such behaviour. Health behaviours have a crucial impact on individual and public health. The Alameda County study which followed nearly 7000 people over 10 years revealed that sleep, exercise, drinking alcohol and eating habits predict mortality (Belloc and Breslow, 1972). Moreover, the leading causes of death in the USA in 2000 were tobacco use (18.1 per cent), poor diet and physical inactivity (16.6 per cent), and alcohol consumption (3.5 per cent), accounting collectively for almost 40 per cent of all deaths (Mokdad et al, 2004). Similar findings emerge from other population studies. For example, in the UK, Khaw et al (2008) measured four key health behaviours among people with no known cardiovascular disease or cancer. These behaviours were: 1) not smoking; 2) being physically active; 3) only drinking alcohol moderately; and 4) plasma vitamins indicating consumption of five portions of fruit and vegetables a day. Eleven years later more than 20,000 people were followed up. Results showed that, controlling for age, gender, body mass index and socio-economic status, those engaging in none of the four behaviours were more than four times more likely to have died than those engaging in all four. The researchers note that this effect is equivalent to those who engaged in four behaviours having the health of someone 14 years younger than those who engaged in none! Health behaviours are not just relevant to our early and middle years but to older people as well. Yates et al (2008) studied a sample of 2357 healthy men aged 70 and examined the predictors of mortality over the next 20 years. A healthy 70-year-old had a 54 per cent chance of living to be 90 but this reduced to 44 per cent if he had a sedentary lifestyle, 36 per cent if he had hypertension, 26 per cent if he was obese, and only 22 per cent if he smoked. The percentage living to be 90 dropped to only 14 per cent if three of these factors were present. So promoting health behaviours among 70-year-olds is important because of the years of life that can be gained.

It is not surprising, therefore, that a review of the UK National Health Service concluded that its long-term effectiveness and economic viability depended on more successful disease prevention strategies and high levels of public engagement in health care and maintenance (Wanless, 2002). The economic implications of promoting preventive health behaviours, minimizing demands on health services and supporting people coping with chronic illness are substantial (e.g. see Chapters 8 and 10). For example, sick leave cost the UK economy £11.6 billion in 2002, an average of £476 per worker, with approximately 40 per cent of absence costs arising from long-term sickness (Choosing Health, 2004). Consequently, research-based interventions to prevent illness, enhance coping with chronic illness and reduce health service demand have the potential to make a substantial difference to public health and the efficiency of health services (Friedman et al, 1995).

Psychological processes can have **direct and indirect effects on health** and illness. The indirect effects are frequently referred to as behavioural pathways because they provide an explanation as to how psychological factors such as stress can indirectly influence health by producing positive or negative changes in health behaviours (e.g. exercise, diet and smoking). Direct effects are often referred to as *psychophysiological pathways* because they help us understand how psychological factors can directly impact on the body's physical systems such as the immune or cardiovascular systems (see Chapter 2). Feeling anxious or stressed changes physiological processes, and cumulatively these effects can damage physical systems and so compromise health. A number of studies have found that people who frequently have relatively large physiological responses to stress are more likely to develop serious illnesses in the future. For example, the Kuopio Heart Study, which has been following over 2500 men for the last 25 years in Finland, found that men who had large increases in blood pressure or heart rate when they felt stressed at the beginning of the study were more likely to have had a stroke or to have developed hypertension many years later (Everson et al, 1996a, 2001). These researchers suggested that the experience of frequent daily stressors over time leads to excessive wear and tear to the cardiovascular system and ultimately to poorer health and earlier death of these 'reactive' individuals.

Foundations of health psychology

Hippocrates is credited with the establishment of the medical profession and the Hippocratic Oath. He was born around 460 BC on the Greek island of Kos and sought to understand the processes which cause different illnesses. While this search for causal processes seems self-evident to us it was a formative step in the development of scientific medicine. Hippocrates also linked behaviour, including diet, to health and emphasized the healing power of the doctor–patient relationship. These topics remain key areas of health psychology research today.

More than half a millenium later, in the second century AD, the Greek leader Diogenes commissioned a wall etched with core messages taken from the teachings of the philosopher Epicurus in the city of Oenoanda in Lycia. The wall included 25,000 words written over 260 square metres and emphasized the importance of quality of life, self-reflection and self-regulation (see Chapter 9). This wall can be viewed as one of the first *public health campaigns* designed to enhance the lifestyle and quality of life of the general population. Nearly 2000 years later, we are still designing and evaluating such interventions (see Chapters 8 and 9), although we have more accessible and interactive media now, including leaflets and websites! Thus the questions and concerns which define health psychology are millennia old and intricately interwoven into the development of medicine.

Modern medicine is founded on basic research that revealed the biological processes which constitute health and illness. Painstaking studies of human physiology over many centuries, together with key scientific breakthroughs, provided the foundation for understanding how the body's systems work. Breakthroughs included understanding the nature of respiration, clarifying that specific bacteria cause particular illnesses, discovering compounds that kill bacteria, and showing how vaccination works. Such research continues today but we already have good models of how physiological systems (such as the immune and cardiovascular system) operate. It is these models that allow effective medical intervention through diagnosis and treatment. The science of health psychology has important contributions to make because we now know that our psychological processes and behaviour affect the operation of these bodily systems and are, therefore, important determinants of health and illness. Thus a key strand of health psychology research focuses on clarifying how psychological responses and behaviour impact on the body's physiological systems (see Chapter 2).

Health psychology also has its origins in early cognitive and social psychology as well as behaviourism. Wundt established the first experimental psychological laboratory at the University of Leipzig in 1879 and he is credited with establishing psychology as a research discipline. In the early part of the twentieth century, learning theorists including Pavlov, Watson and Skinner established the behaviourist school of psychology which focused on observable behaviour and on learning (e.g. through **classical and operant conditioning**; Skinner, 1974). The success of behaviourism in explaining behaviour and providing tools with which to change behaviour was critical to the recognition that professional psychology had an important contribution to make to the management of behaviour relevant to mental and physical health. The role of learning theory in health behaviour change interventions is still under investigation by health psychologists today (e.g. Hegel et al, 1992; and see Chapter 9).

Wundt had studied internal individual processes including attention and use of imagery and later it became evident that even when explaining how rats learn to run mazes we require a psychology of internal representation. Tolman (1948) found that rats learned mazes even when the behaviour was not reinforced and concluded that they had developed internal **cognitive maps**. This was an important development in what we now think of as cognitive psychology which seeks to understand the kind of representations of reality that are necessary to explain people's behaviour and how we process information (cf. Neisser, 1967). Developing models of how people perceive and understand their reality is central to health psychology research (see Chapters 7 and 8).

The sub-discipline of social psychology became established when researchers focused on the effects of others on our behaviour (e.g. Tripplett, 1898). Social psychologists applied experimental methods to understanding how we perceive and represent others, how others influence us, and how our position in wider society shapes our beliefs, attitudes and behaviour (cf. Allport, 1924; Sherif, 1936). These processes are important to health psychologists because health-relevant perceptions and behaviours are affected by others. For example, interactions with work colleagues may cause stress and interactions with health care professionals may change beliefs and motivations relevant to taking medication (see Chapters 4 and 10).

Thus health psychology draws upon the methods and theories of a range of sub-disciplines within psychology including learning theory, psychobiology, cognitive psychology and social psychology. More recently collaboration between health psychologists and neuroscientists has generated new insights (e.g. into the processing of health promotion messages – Ruiter et al, 2006). Health psychology applies these various theories and methods in order to better understand how our perceptions, beliefs and behaviour can maintain health or cause illness. The recognition that health (or illness) results from the interaction of biological characteristics and processes (including genetic predispositions and physiological mechanisms), psychological processes (including perceptions, beliefs and behaviours) and social processes and contexts (including social structure, cultural influences and interpersonal relationships) is what is meant by adopting a **biopsychosocial model** (Schwartz, 1980) of health and illness. This biopsychosocial perspective is central to current health psychology research and practice.

The profession of health psychology was institutionalized in 1978 when the Division of Health Psychology of the *American Psychology Association* (APA) was established. The *European Health Psychology Society* (EHPS) was established in 1986 in Tilberg and, in the UK, the Division of Health Psychology of the *British Psychology Society* (BPS) first met in January 1998. The establishment of these organizational structures recognized the profession of health psychology and allowed research-based training courses to be set up to train professional health psychologists worldwide (see Chapter 11). These organizations also provided a focus for research by arranging conferences and sponsoring academic journals. For example, the journal *Health Psychology* is published by the APA, *Psychology and Health* is the journal of the EHPS and the *British Journal of Health Psychology* is published by the BPS. Other journals publishing health psychology research include: *Journal of Behavioral Medicine, Preventive Medicine, Social Science and Medicine, Health Psychology Review, Journal of Health Psychology, Health Education Research, Patient Education and Counselling, Annals of Behavioral Medicine,* and *Psychology, Health and Medicine.*

Using this book effectively

In each chapter of this book we have included brief introductory chapter plans, learning outcomes, lists of key terms introduced, individual and/or group exercises and short lists of recommended additional reading. These are designed to help you actively learn as you proceed through the course. In Chapter 8, we note that lasting cognitive change depends on *systematic processing* of incoming messages involving active engagement with the content. This includes linking content to prior knowledge and critically evaluating it in terms of pre-existing standards and principles. In building your expertise in health psychology you are managing your own cognitive development. So how can you facilitate systematic processing of the material in this book?

It is important to read the chapter plans and learning outcomes before reading the chapters to develop an overview of the material. Then at the end of each chapter check that you understand the terms introduced and that you can now do whatever is specified in the learning outcomes. *Testing* yourself by checking through previous learning outcomes and planning essays is also important.

Research has found that testing improves retention compared to studying without testing and that this is true even if the test is never marked! (Roediger and Karpicke, 2006). Testing is a central part of learning. It is not just an assessment tool. Testing can also work well when groups of students study together in a study group.

You should read papers from our additional reading lists and make your own notes on these papers and the chapters in this book. Research has shown that *making notes* enhances learning and the transfer of learning from one topic to another (e.g. Wittrock and Alesandrini, 1990). Your notes are not just useful for revision. Making them will enhance your learning even if you do not consult them later!

When reading empirical papers it may be helpful to think of them as boxes that contain things you want rather than stories that need to be read from beginning to end. You might try reading the abstract first and then the first couple of paragraphs of the discussion to get a good overview of the paper before you decide what else you need to know about it. When reading a paper reporting an empirical study it is useful to check that you can answer the questions highlighted in Activity box 1.1.

Activity 1.1

Reading empirical papers

Try reading an empirical paper and answering the questions below. For example, you could try reading the following paper which is highlighted as additional reading in Chapter 9.

Luszczynska, A., Sobczyk, A., and Abraham, C. (2007). Planning to lose weight: RCT of an implementation intention prompt to enhance weight reduction among overweight and obese women. Health Psychology, *26, 507–512.*

- What kind of study is reported? For example is it an experiment, a correlational study (cross-sectional or longitudinal), a qualitative analysis of text or interview data, or a review (narrative, systematic or meta-analysis)?
- What are the independent variables and which are the dependent variables (or outcome measures)? Are there any mediating or moderating variables (see Research methods box 3.1)?
- How do the measures used relate to measures of these (or similar) constructs in other studies? Are the measures reliable? Do they have good construct and predictive validity?
- Are there any confounding variables? Have these been controlled for?
- What population is studied? How does this relate to other populations studied in this area?

... Continued

... Continued

- What are the key findings?
- Is the sample size adequate? Is the sample representative? Can we generalize from these findings? If so, what are the limits to this generalization?
- Does the study suggest any new theoretical development/s? What further research should be undertaken to explore questions arising from the results or problems with the study's methodology?
- Does the study have practice and/or policy implications?
- Does the study need to be replicated?

Planning and writing essays are also effective ways to test and develop your understanding of a topic. You may have a well-developed approach to writing essays but it may be useful to revise the points in Focus box 1.1 when thinking about your next health psychology essay.

Focus 1.1

Essay writing

First make sure you understand the question. The question will direct you towards particular readings and research and perhaps ask you to treat these in a particular way – e.g. 'discuss' – 'contrast', etc. Make sure you have a good plan which sets out a clear structure for your essay that corresponds to what the questions ask. Also try to ensure that you know how your arguments link together (e.g. using a diagram).

In the opening sections ensure your title makes sense to the reader by providing any necessary definitions and explanations. Also outline and explain your objectives in writing the essay – what do you intend to argue and achieve in the essay – how is this linked to previous research? Use appropriate references to anchor your essay to previous research findings.

The main body of your essay will convey your core arguments, which have been outlined in the introduction. Think about the following points.

You should be able to summarize your essay as a series of core arguments or points. It is often helpful to state these explicitly early on in the relevant paragraph. For example, 'I will highlight one strength and two weaknesses in this theory. First...' Then for each of these (three) arguments, consider what evidence and illustrations you need.

Be precise about theoretical distinctions and definitions and avoid lapsing into lay psychology.

Know the data you are discussing. Be specific about measures and methods used and illustrate measures where this clarifies a construct or a methodological critique. Support your arguments with data (e.g. means, correlations or effect sizes). This can emphasize the strength or weakness of an association or the effect of an intervention and, thereby, strengthen an argument or critique. However, it is uninformative to provide '*p*' values alone without references to statistics that convey size of associations, differences or effects.

Note also that, sometimes, an anecdote or case study can illustrate a point in a concrete way.

Reference claims you make about previous findings using author names and dates. Your essay is about research findings so avoid unsupported claims. Use American Psychological Association (APA) referencing rules unless told otherwise by your tutor.

Link your arguments. Each paragraph should lead onto the next and the introduction should link clearly to the conclusion. You may want to make this explicit, e.g. 'The study by Brown (2003) outlined above also emphasizes . . .'

Make links across the reading you have completed for the course.

Provide a short conclusion at the end of the essay. This should summarize your main points and highlight connections between them. In many essays this will also be the opportunity to succinctly state what you think needs to be done next, in terms of further research, intervention, adoption or policy changes (including implications for health care practice and social policy).

You may have been told correctly that your psychology essays are not about your opinion but about research findings. However, a good essay will involve a personal synthesis of research, including your evaluations of findings and your evidence-based conclusions (e.g. the weight of the evidence suggests . . .). Do not be afraid to draw your conclusions – it is your essay.

Finally, make sure you provide a complete set of references (i.e. all papers, books, etc. that you have referred to in your text in APA format).

The structure and content of this book

The book is divided into five sections: 1) biological bases of health and illness; 2) stress and health; 3) coping resources – social support and individual differences; 4) motivation and behaviour; and, finally, 5) relating to and caring for patients.

Chapter 2 deals with the body's physical systems such as the central nervous system, the endocrine system and the immune system. We then consider how these basic biological processes may be influenced by psychological factors such as stress. A brief overview of the role of psychological processes in the experience of pain is also provided. This chapter finishes by introducing important developments linking psychological factors to immune function.

In Chapters 3 and 4 we review and critically appraise research into the nature of stress. We introduce key theories and methodologies used in researching stress and examine its impacts on health. In Chapter 3 we introduce early approaches, including theories which viewed stress primarily as a physiological phenomenon, before moving on to more contemporary approaches looking at the impact of major life events and day-to-day hassles on health. We also consider possible pathways for links between stress and disease. In Chapter 4 we focus on specific environmental or contextual factors which have been prominent in stress research and have been shown to affect health, in particular social inequality and employment factors. Models of work stress are discussed and evidence relating work stress to disease is considered. We conclude by examining the role of organizational change and worksite interventions in reducing stress, foreshadowing our focus on behaviour change in Chapter 9.

In Chapters 5 and 6 we focus on key individual differences between people that affect the way in which environmental factors (such as stress or social inequality) impact on health. These factors are said to 'moderate' the relationships between the environment and an outcome such as stress. In Chapter 5 the focus is on individual differences in the ways that people cope and in the types of social support they have. We first consider types of coping strategies that individuals use and whether these are consistent across situations (i.e. whether people have their own coping style). We review the effect that such styles have on health. We then consider different types of social support and their value for preventing illness. In Chapter 6 we review work on how personality factors influence health. Much of this research focuses on the big five dimensions of personality: openness, conscientiousness, extraversion, agreeableness and neuroticism. Several of these personality dimensions have important consequences for health including how long we can expect to live. A key issue addressed in this chapter is the nature of mechanisms by which personality factors affect health outcomes. So, for example, the personality trait of conscientiousness appears to exert effects on health outcomes by influencing the extent to which individuals will engage in health behaviours.

In Chapters 7–9 we focus on motivation and behaviour. In Chapter 7 we examine models which identify beliefs, attitudes and intentions (that is *cognitions*) which predict behaviour. We note the success of these models in predicting behaviour using prospective surveys and objective measures of behaviour. These models help us identify potentially modifiable determinants of behaviour (e.g. attitudes) which, if changed, would lead to changes in health behaviours. In Chapter 8 we discuss methods used to change these cognitions including use of information provision and *social influence* and note some of the pitfalls that health educators must avoid in using these methods. We highlight how best to change attitudes using persuasive methods and also discuss how self-efficacy can be enhanced. This leads directly into approaches to behaviour change and we consider how behaviour change interventions need to be carefully planned, implemented and evaluated if they are to contribute to health promotion. We identify key features of behaviour change interventions and highlight a range of behaviour change techniques that may be employed in such interventions.

In Chapter 10 we focus on interactions between health care professionals and patients, examining the processes which prompt medical help seeking and the reasons why some patients follow advice given by health care professionals while others do not. We consider consultation management in some detail and discuss the particular needs of people with long-term illness. We explore the role of complementary therapies in health care and explain why people may show health benefit even when they have only received a placebo treatment such as a sugar pill. Research in these areas clearly highlights the importance of consultation management to patients' satisfaction and health. Cognitive and emotional care is likely to impact on health behaviour and health over and above the pharmacological effects of medication. Psychological interventions are especially important to patients with long-term illnesses and have been shown to be effective in pain management.

We draw to a close in Chapter 11 by reflecting on future developments in health psychology research, the professional roles health psychologists may occupy and the competencies required to practise in those roles.

Summary

Health psychology aims to promote health and prevent illness through scientific research that elucidates psychological processes linked to health. Good causal models provide the basis for effective interventions that may enhance health by changing psychological processes. Interventions designed to change demand for health services can have substantial effects on the cost effectiveness of services. Emotional responses and health behaviours have been shown to have important measurable effects on morbidity and mortality. Behavioural effects are referred to as indirect effects whereas psychological processes which affect health through psychophysiological pathways are referred to as direct effects.

The origins of health psychology research can be seen in the teaching of ancient Greek philosophers and more recently in the application of learning theory, cognitive theories and social psychological theories to health and health behaviour. The biopsychosocial model incorporates biological, psychological and social processes.

You will learn more effectively if you: 1) read the learning outcomes before reading chapters; and 2) check that you understand the terms introduced and that you can do what is specified in the learning outcomes. Taking notes, reading recommended additional readings and writing essays will also consolidate your learning.

Key concepts and terms

Aetiological and diagnostic
  correlates of health
Biopsychosocial model
Classical and operant
  conditioning

Cognitive maps
Direct and indirect effects on
  health
World Health Organization

2 Biopsychosocial pathways to health and illness

In Chapter 1, we introduced health psychology as a discipline, the biopsychosocial model of health and illness, the context in which health psychology research takes place and areas studied. In this chapter we consider the main psychophysiological pathways through which psychological factors impact on physical health and illness.

We discuss the body's physical systems including the central nervous system, the endocrine system, the cardiovascular system and the immune system. We then consider how these basic biological processes may be influenced by psychological factors such as stress. In particular, we will describe how activation of the hypothalamic–pituitary–adrenal (HPA) axis and the sympathetic adrenal medullary (SAM) system are linked to increased cardiovascular disease. Next, we present a brief overview of the role of psychological factors in the experience of pain and gate-control theory. Finally, we introduce important developments in the area of psychoneuroimmunology and discuss how psychological factors can affect the immune system within the context of susceptibility to upper respiratory illness and the speed of wound healing.

The chapter is composed of five sections: 1) basic features of the nervous system; 2) the stress response; 3) biopsychosocial aspects of pain; 4) psychoneuroimmunology; 5) stress and the immune system.

Learning outcomes

When you have completed this chapter you should be able to:

1. Describe the basic features of the central nervous system.
2. Explain how activation of the hypothalamic–pituitary–adrenal (HPA) axis and the sympathetic adrenal medullary (SAM) system links to stress and health.
3. Understand the role of psychological factors in the experience of pain.
4. Discuss how psychoneuroimmunology (PNI) plays a role in illness processes.
5. Design an experiment to examine the effects of psychological stress on health outcomes within a laboratory setting.

What is the biopsychosocial perspective on health and illness?

As outlined in Chapter 1, the biopsychosocial model postulates that health and illness are influenced by psychological factors (e.g. cognition, emotion, personality), social factors (e.g. people in your social world, social class, ethnicity) and biological factors (e.g. viruses, lesions, bacteria). Within this context, there is increasing evidence that psychological factors such as stress affect health directly, through autonomic and neuroendocrine responses (e.g. blood pressure and hormonal changes), but also indirectly, through changes to health behaviours (e.g. exercise, diet, smoking). The direct effects of stress on health are often referred to as **psychophysiological pathways** because they help us understand how psychological factors can directly impact on physiological disease-related processes. The indirect effects are frequently referred to as the *behavioural pathways* as they provide an explanation as to how psychological factors can indirectly influence disease-related processes by producing negative changes in health behaviours. This chapter describes the main psychophysiological pathways that may influence health and illness, while the key behavioural pathways are considered in Chapter 3. Before the direct effects are considered in more detail, we introduce you to the basic features of the nervous system. It is paramount that you understand some of the basic biological processes constituting the human body in order to gain a good understanding of the psychophysiology of health and illness. Throughout this book we use activity boxes to consolidate your learning, and there is one just beyond the next section so read carefully!

Basic features of the nervous system

The role of the nervous system is to allow us to adapt to changes within our body and environment by using our five senses (touch, sight, smell, taste, sound) to understand, interpret and respond to internal and external changes quickly and appropriately. The nervous system consists of the *brain*, the *spinal cord* and the *nerves* (bundles of fibres that transmit information in and out of the nervous system). The brain is the central part of the nervous system and it helps control our behaviour. It receives and sends messages for the rest of the body through the spinal cord. The brain has three major anatomic components: the *forebrain*, the *midbrain* and the *hindbrain*.

The anatomy of the brain

The forebrain consists of dense, elaborate masses of tissue and has two main subdivisions:

1. The *telencephalon*, which is composed of the cerebrum and limbic system.
2. The *diencephalon*, which comprises the thalamus and hypothalamus.

The *cerebrum* is the largest part of the human brain and is divided into the two halves – the left and right cerebral hemispheres – that are connected in the middle by a bundle of nerve fibres called the *corpus callosum*. The upper part of

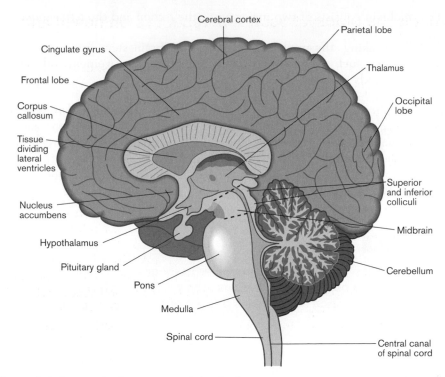

Figure 2.1 Anatomical structure of the brain.

the cerebrum is the *cerebral cortex* (its outermost area). This is subdivided into the frontal, parietal, occipital and temporal lobes and controls higher processes such as speaking, reasoning, memory, etc. (see Figure 2.1). More specifically, the frontal lobe (located towards the front of the cerebrum) is involved in speech, thought and emotion. Behind this is the parietal lobe which perceives and interprets sensations like touch, temperature and pain. The occipital lobe is at the centre back of the cerebrum and detects and interprets visual images. Finally, the temporal lobes located on either side are involved in hearing and aspects of memory storage. The **limbic system** is evolutionarily older than other parts of the brain and consists of the amygdala and hippocampus among other structures (not shown above). This system interacts with the endocrine system (a network of glands that secrete hormones throughout the body described later) and the autonomic nervous system (ANS) and plays an important role in motivational and emotional aspects of behaviours such as sex, eating, drinking and aggression. It is also involved in aspects of memory processes.

The second major division of the forebrain is the diencephalon. Its two most important structures are the thalamus and the hypothalamus (see Figure 2.1). The *thalamus* is thought to have multiple functions and plays an important role in regulating states of sleep, arousal and consciousness. The *hypothalamus* is located below the thalamus and although it is a relatively small structure it is very important as it regulates the ANS and the endocrine system and, as we will see later in this chapter, it controls how individuals respond to stressful encounters. In short, it oversees the basic behaviours associated with the survival of the species: fighting, feeding, fleeing and mating, often referred to as the four Fs!

The midbrain consists of two major parts: the *tectum* and the *tegmentum*.

Broadly speaking, the midbrain, including the brain stem, regulates critical bodily functions such as breathing, swallowing, posture, movement and the rate at which the body metabolizes foods.

The hindbrain has two major divisions: the *metencephalon* and the *myelencephalon*. The former comprises the cerebellum and the pons and the latter contains one major structure, the medulla oblongata (usually referred to simply as the medulla). The cerebellum is involved in coordinating the body's movements and the pons has been implicated in sleep and arousal. The medulla controls vital functions linked to the regulation of the cardiovascular system and respiration.

Activity 2.1

You have just read that the brain has three major anatomical components and each has a number of subdivisions. Can you list them? If not, it might be useful as a revision aid to draw a diagram of each component and its subdivisions.

The spinal cord and nerve cells

The spinal cord is a long, delicate structure that begins at the end of the brain stem and continues down to the bottom of the spine. It carries incoming and outgoing messages between the brain and the rest of the body. The brain communicates with much of the body through nerves that run up and down the spinal cord. As you will see later, the spinal cord plays an important role in responding to pain stimuli. The nervous system contains 100 billion or more nerve cells that run throughout the body. A nerve cell, called a neuron, is made up of a large cell body and a single, elongated extension (axon) for sending messages. Neurons usually have many branches (dendrites) for receiving messages. Nerves transmit messages electrically from the axon of one neuron to the dendrite of another (at the synapse) by secreting tiny amounts of chemicals called *neurotransmitters*. These substances trigger the receptors on the next neuron's dendrite to start up a new electrical impulse.

Central nervous system and peripheral nervous system

The nervous system is classified into various different subsystems and subdivisions but these different components are all part of an integrated system and do *not* operate independently.

The nervous system has two distinct parts:

1. The **central nervous system**.
2. The **peripheral nervous system**.

The central nervous system (CNS) comprises the brain and spinal cord and is protected by bone. The brain is encased in the cranial subcavity within the skull

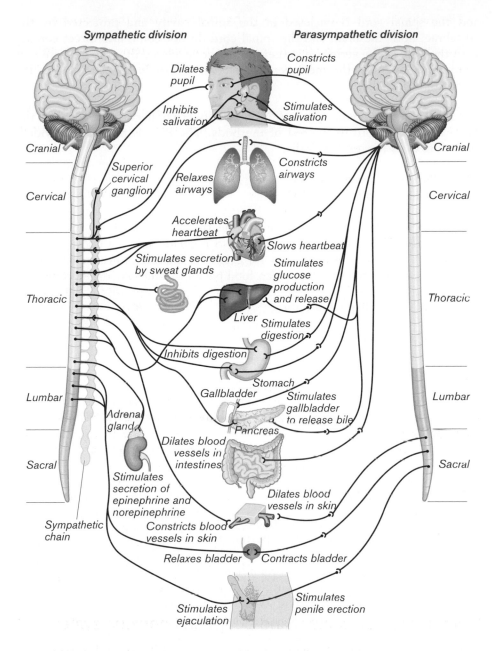

Figure 2.2 The sympathetic nervous system (solid lines) and the parasympathetic nervous system (broken lines).

and the spinal cord is enclosed in the spinal cavity and protected by the vertebrae. Both the brain and the spinal cord do not come into direct contact with the skull or the vertebrae as they are further enclosed by a three-layered set of membranes called the meninges. Instead, they float in a clear liquid called cerebrospinal fluid.

The peripheral nervous system (PNS) is a network of nerves that connects the brain and spinal cord to the rest of the body. The PNS is further subdivided, according to its function, into the:

1. **somatic nervous system** (SNS).
2. **autonomic nervous system** (ANS).

The SNS is concerned with coordinating the 'voluntary' body movements controlled by the skeletal muscles. The ANS regulates internal body processes that require no conscious awareness, for example, the rate of heart contractions and breathing, and the speed at which food passes through the digestive tract.

The ANS is subdivided into the:

1. **sympathetic division**.
2. **parasympathetic division**.

As shown in Figure 2.2, the sympathetic division mobilizes the body by increasing heart rate and blood pressure among other physiological changes, whereas the parasympathetic division generally restores the body's energy by reducing heart rate and respiration while increasing the rate of digestion. The changes in each of the divisions occur when the ANS triggers the endocrine system to react in the face of stress.

Endocrine system

The **endocrine system** is an integrated system of small glands that work closely with the ANS and are extremely important for everything we do! In particular, *endocrine glands*, which secrete their chemicals into the bloodstream to be carried to their point of use, are most important here. Similar to the nervous system, the endocrine system communicates with many different parts of the body, however, it uses a different 'signalling system'. Whereas the nervous system uses nerves to send electrical and chemical messages, the endocrine system only uses blood vessels to send chemical messages. In particular, each of the endocrine glands, once activated, secretes chemical substances called *hormones* into the bloodstream which carry messages to different parts of the body. There are a number of endocrine glands located throughout the human body such as the adrenal glands, gonads, pancreas, thyroid, thymus and pituitary gland (see Figure 2.2). Within the context of understanding the influence of psychological factors, such as stress, on the development of disease, the most important glands to consider are the adrenal and pituitary glands. Moreover, the endocrine system is linked to the nervous system by connections between the hypothalamus and the pituitary gland, the latter of which is discussed next.

The pituitary gland

The *pituitary gland* is located just below the hypothalamus and is considered the 'master' gland because it regulates the endocrine gland secretions. It has two parts: the anterior pituitary and the posterior pituitary. The former secretes growth hormone (GH), adrenocorticotrophic hormone (ACTH), thyroid stimulating hormone (TSH), follicle stimulating hormone (FSH) and luteinizing hormone (LH). The latter component releases oxytocin and vasopressin. Overall the pituitary gland plays an important role in the regulation of the growth of body tissues (through release of GH), the development of the gonads, ovum and sperm (through the release of FSH and LH) as well as stimulating lactation (through the release of oxytocin) and maintaining blood pressure (through the release of vasopressin). However, it also releases ACTH (after stimulation by the hypothalamus) which stimulates the adrenal cortex – this is known as the hypothalamic–pituitary–adrenal (HPA) axis response. This is a most important response system which we consider in some detail shortly.

The adrenal glands

There are two *adrenal glands* located on the top of each kidney (see Figure 2.2). The adrenal glands are best considered as being two glands within one. Each has a central core, called the *adrenal medulla*, which secretes the hormones *adrenaline* and *noradrenaline* (also known as epinephrine and norepinephrine), which act on the visceral organs in the same way as neurons in the nervous system. In other words, they increase heart rate and mobilize glucose into the blood among other things. Collectively, adrenaline and noradrenaline (and dopamine) are known as *catecholamines*. The outer portion of the adrenal gland, called the adrenal cortex, produces *mineralocorticoids* and *glucocorticoids*. The former hormones act on the kidneys to conserve salt and water by returning them to the blood during urine formation. The latter are secreted when we encounter stressors in order to help the body respond appropriately. One of the most important glucocorticoids is cortisol *(corticosterone in rodents)* and as such it is frequently referred to as the 'stress hormone' and measured in studies of psychological stress.

Cardiovascular system

The central function of the **cardiovascular system** is to ensure that oxygen (with other nutrients) is transported to all the organs of the body and that carbon dioxide (as well as other waste products) is removed from each of the body's cells. The blood is the vehicle that transports the oxygen with the heart and blood vessels allowing the blood to be carried around the body. The heart, the centre of the cardiovascular system, is made of muscle and 'beats' or 'pumps' approximately 100,000 times per day. The main muscular outer part of the heart, which contains the cardiac *veins* and *arteries*, is called the *myocardium*. The heart has four chambers: the two upper chambers are known as *atriums* and the two lower ones are called *ventricles*. In the cardiovascular system, veins carry blood *to* the heart and myocardium and the arteries carry blood *from* the heart and myocardium.

We can follow the journey of blood flow by considering where it enters the heart. Blood enters the right atrium deficient of oxygen and full of waste products (carbon dioxide) and is bluish in colour. Once the atrium is full, the blood is pushed into the right ventricle, which then contracts, thus pumping the blood from the heart towards the lungs, where it becomes oxygenated (and red in colour). Once oxygenated, the blood travels to the left atrium in the heart and is passed into the left ventricle before it is pumped into the general circulation via the *aorta* (a large artery). Before returning to the heart, some of the blood is cleansed of waste products by passing through the kidneys (where the waste products are filtered out and excreted in urine) and the liver (where nutrients, e.g. simple sugars, are stored and harmful bacteria are removed).

The cardiovascular system is a closed system and therefore it always contains some pressure. Blood pressure is the force exerted by the blood on the artery walls and has two components:

1. *Diastolic blood pressure* is the resting level in the arteries in between contractions.
2. *Systolic blood pressure* is the maximum pressure in the arteries when the heart pumps.

An individual's blood pressure is described using two numbers representing both the systolic and diastolic components and is expressed in units known as millimetres of mercury (mmHg; e.g. 126 over 70 or 126/70 mmHg). A number of factors increase blood pressure including temperature, weight, posture and food intake. Psychological factors, such as chronic stress, have also been found to be associated with the development of high blood pressure (or hypertension), which is known to damage the heart and the arteries. We will consider the links between stress, blood pressure and cardiovascular disease in more detail later.

The stress response

What happens when you experience stress? Two systems are activated. The first and easiest to activate is the **sympathetic adrenal medullary (SAM) system**; the second is the **hypothalamic–pituitary–adrenal (HPA) axis**. To borrow an analogy from Clow (2001: 53) activating the SAM system 'can be likened to lighting a match whereas activating the HPA axis is like lighting a fire. Lighting a match is easy, has an instant effect and the effect does not last long, whereas lighting a fire takes a lot more effort and its effects last much longer. The HPA axis is only activated in extreme circumstances'. Each of these systems is considered in more detail in the following sections. In addition, later we consider how researchers induce the stress response in the laboratory using the **Trier Social Stress Test** (see Research methods box 2.1).

The sympathetic adrenal medullary (SAM) response system

When an individual is suddenly under threat or frightened, their brain instantly sends a message to the adrenal glands which quickly release noradrenaline that in turn activates the internal organs. This is the basic ANS

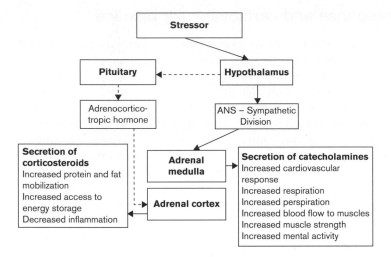

Figure 2.3 Stress response. Hypothalamic–pituitary–adrenal (HPA) axis response system (dashed line) and the sympathetic adrenal medullary system (SAM) response system (solid line).

sympathetic division response to threat. However, at the same time, the adrenal medulla releases adrenaline which is rapidly transported through the bloodstream in order to further prepare the body for its response. This system is known as the sympathetic adrenal medullary (SAM) system (see Figure 2.3). Within moments adrenaline and noradrenaline have the entire body on alert, a response sometimes called the fight or flight response. As outlined earlier, as a result breathing quickens, the heart beats more rapidly and powerfully, the eyes dilate to allow more light in, and the activity of the digestive system decreases to permit more blood to go to the muscles. This effect is both rapid and intense.

The hypothalamic–pituitary–adrenal (HPA) axis response system

In addition to the SAM response, when an individual experiences an unpleasant event in their environment that they perceive as stressful, the hypothalamus (the H in HPA) releases a chemical messenger called *corticotrophin releasing factor* (CRF). Once released, CRF is transported in the blood supply to the pituitary gland (the P) where it stimulates the release of *adrenocorticotrophic hormone* (ACTH). Subsequently, the latter hormone travels through the circulatory system to the adrenal (the A) cortex where it stimulates production of the glucocorticoid *cortisol* – known as the 'stress hormone' (see Figure 2.3).

Why is cortisol released in response to stress? One of the central functions of cortisol is to increase access to energy stores, increase protein and fat mobilization, and decrease inflammation. Therefore, when an individual experiences stress, the release of cortisol triggers excess energy stored in the muscle and liver as glycogen to be liberated and broken down into glucose ready for utilization by the muscles and brain.

The stress response and cardiovascular disease

In evolutionary terms, these stress response processes are adaptive and help ensure survival. Nevertheless, they are only adaptive in so much as they are short lived and the body's systems swiftly return to normal. Our ancestors may well have encountered *acute* stressors in the form of wild animals while hunting which made such 'flight or fight' responses adaptive. The SAM and HPA response systems would prepare the body appropriately. However, the stress of modern day life rarely affords such infrequent, acute, life-threatening stressful encounters. Instead, we are exposed to frequent daily hassles as well as long-lasting, chronic stressors. As a result, the stress response system is repeatedly activated and the cardiovascular system is potentially exposed to excessive wear and tear. Overtime, such repetitive activation may contribute to future ill health by increasing cardiovascular disease risk.

This may result in the development of *atherosclerosis*, that is, the build-up of fatty plaques in the inner lining of the blood vessels which leads to the occlusion (narrowing) of the arteries. The increase in blood pressure as a result of the repeated activation of the SAM system may cause damage to the lining of the blood vessels, thus allowing access to fatty acids and glucose. At the same time, activation of the HPA axis leads to the release of cortisol which increases the liberation of glucose from glycogen stores. These processes taken together increase the likelihood that chronic stress may lead to a build-up of plaque. The development of plaque can have serious health consequences. The first symptom of a narrowing artery may be pain or cramps at times when the blood flow cannot keep up with the body's demands for oxygen. During exercise, an individual may feel chest pain (angina) because of the lack of oxygen reaching the heart. In addition, this person may experience leg cramps because of lack of oxygen to the legs. However, more seriously, if the coronary arteries supplying the heart become 'blocked', which may happen if increased blood pressure in a narrowed artery sheers off a section of plaque, this can lead to a *myocardial infarction* (or heart attack) where part of the heart muscle (deprived of oxygen) dies. If blood flow to the brain is obstructed, this can result in a stroke where part of the brain dies.

We will consider evidence linking stress with cardiovascular disease in more detail in Chapter 3. Research has found that acute (i.e. short-lived) and chronic (long-lasting) stress are both associated with the development of cardiovascular disease. For example, Matthews and Gump (2002) examined the impact of different work stressors and marital breakdown (a major stressor in its own right) on coronary heart disease mortality during a nine-year follow-up period. These researchers found that an increasing number of different work stressors and being divorced were associated with an increased risk of cardiovascular-related deaths during the study. Another study investigating the impact of an acute stressor found that admissions to hospitals in England increased on the day following England losing to Argentina in a penalty shoot-out in the 1998 Football World Cup (Carroll et al, 2002). The authors argue that their results suggest myocardial infarction can be triggered by emotional upset, such as watching your football team lose an important match!

How to induce stress in the laboratory: The Trier Social Stress Test (TSST)

The Trier Social Stress Test (TSST) was developed in 1993 by Kirschbaum, Pirke and Helhammer at the University of Trier. The aim was to develop a stress paradigm which would reliably stimulate the HPA axis. Previous techniques had yielded inconsistent results, therefore a standardized protocol was deemed necessary.

After arriving in the laboratory (room A), participants rest for between 10 and 30 minutes depending on whether hormones are being measured in saliva (using salivettes) or in blood (using an intravenous catheter). Participants are then taken to a different room (room B) where they are introduced to three individuals sitting in a panel and asked to stand by a microphone. Next the investigator explains that the participant is to take the role of a job applicant who will be interviewed by the panel. As part of the interview process, the participants are given 10 minutes to prepare a 5 minute free speech in which they must convince the interview panel that they are the perfect applicant for the vacant position. The participant is informed that the presentation will be video-taped and evaluated for non-verbal behaviour and voice frequency and that a video analysis of the participant's performance will also be conducted. The anticipation of giving such a presentation is the stressor that stimulates the HPA axis. Following receipt of the instructions, participants return to room A to prepare a speech with the aid of paper and a pen. After 10 minutes, the participant returns to room B to deliver the speech in front of the panel. If the speech falls short of 5 minutes, the participant is told 'You still have some time left. Please continue!'. After 15 minutes, the panel asks the participant to start to serially substract the number 13 from 1022 as quickly and accurately as possible. If an error is made, one of the panel requests that the participant start again at 1022. After 20 minutes, the task is ended and the participant returns to

Figure 2.4 Typical cortisol profile following the TSST.

room A to rest and be debriefed about the nature of the experiment and be informed that no voice and video analysis of their performance will be conducted. The rest period may last between 30 and 70 minutes depending on which hormones are being monitored.

The TSST has been widely used by health psychologists because it is simple to administer and researchers can easily monitor changes in a wide range of cardiovascular (e.g. heart rate, blood pressure) and neuroendocrine (e.g. cortisol, ACTH) parameters during the paradigm. Changes in salivary and serum (in the blood) cortisol levels have probably received the most attention in the literature. A typical cortisol profile (using salivettes) in response to the TSST is shown in Figure 2.4. Two characteristics of the profile are worth noting: the extent to which cortisol increases in response to the stressor (i.e. *stress reactivity*) and the length of time it takes for cortisol levels to return to baseline (*stress recovery*). Stress reactivity and stress recovery are discussed further in Chapter 3.

Biopsychosocial aspects of pain

Psychological factors have been found to affect many different biological processes too numerous to describe here. However, one area in which psychology has made a substantial impact is in understanding the experience of pain and the management of pain.

Early theories of pain did not incorporate a role for psychological factors in explaining how we experience pain. This is surprising given that we can all think of episodes when someone's perception of pain has been influenced by cognitive, emotional or social factors. For example, we are less likely to experience pain when we are distracted by the demands of taking part in a competitive sporting event.

The role of meaning in pain

The meaning an individual attributes to pain has been found to affect their experience of it. Beecher (1956) provided striking evidence of the important role of the meaning of pain during the Second World War. As a physician he treated many soldiers who had been badly wounded and found that 49 per cent reported being in 'moderate' or 'severe' pain with only 32 per cent requesting medication when it was offered. However, several years later when he was treating civilians with similar if not less severe wounds after having undergone surgery, he found that 75 per cent of the civilians reported being in 'moderate' or 'severe' pain with 83 per cent requesting medication. Beecher accounted for these stark differences in terms of the meaning the injuries had for the soldiers compared to the civilian surgical patients. For the soldiers their injuries represented the end of their war and they could look forward to resuming their lives away from the dangerous battleground. In contrast, for the civilians, the surgery represented the beginning of a long and challenging disruption to their lives.

Two of the early dominant theories of pain perception are *specificity theory* and *pattern theory*. The former theory takes a very mechanistic view and assumes that we have a separate sensory system for perceiving pain similar to hearing and vision. Moreover, specificity theory posits that the 'pain system' has its own set of special pain receptors for detecting pain stimuli and its own peripheral nerves which communicates via a separate pathway to a designated area in the brain for the processing of pain signals.

Pattern theory offers a competing view. It suggests that a separate sensory system does not exist but instead receptors for pain are shared with the other senses. Central to this view is the notion that an individual will only experience pain when a certain pattern of neural activity reaches a critical level in the brain. Moreover, given that mild and strong pain stimulation uses the same sense modality, this theory suggests that only intense stimulation will produce a pattern of neural activity that will result in pain.

Nevertheless, as outlined above, none of these early theories can explain the role of psychological factors in pain perception. For example, they cannot account for how cognitive, emotional and social factors such as the meaning of pain can influence the experience of pain.

Gate-control theory of pain

In 1965, Melzack and Wall introduced the **gate-control theory** of pain perception. This theory was innovative as it incorporated important aspects of earlier theories but at the same time provided a detailed description of the physiological mechanisms through which psychological factors could influence an individual's experience of pain. In a nutshell, gate-control theory proposes that a *neural gate* in the spinal cord can modulate incoming pain signals and that a number of factors influence the opening and closing of the gate. Broadly speaking, these are:

1. The amount of activity in pain fibres.
2. The amount of activity in other peripheral fibres.
3. Messages that descend from the brain (or central nervous system).

When the neural gate receives information from each of these sources it decides whether to open or close the gate. When the gate is open, pain is experienced.

The theory postulates that the gating mechanism is located in the *substantia gelatinosa* (i.e. the grey matter that extends along the length of the spinal cord) of the *dorsal horns* in the spinal cord. When we are exposed to a painful stimulus the gating mechanism receives signals from *pain fibres (A-delta and C- fibres)* located at the site of the injury, other *peripheral fibres (A-beta fibres)* which transmit information about harmless stimuli, and the brain (or central nervous system) to open the gate. The pain fibres then release a neurotransmitter called *substance P* that passes through the gating mechanism (substantia gelatinosa) and stimulates *transmission cells* that in turn transmit impulses to specific locations in the brain (e.g. thalamus, limbic system, hypothalamus). When the activity of the transmission cells reaches a critical threshold level we experience pain with greater pain intensity associated with greater activity. Once the pain centres in the brain have been activated, we are able to respond quickly to remove ourselves from danger. It is worth noting that the brain produces its own pain-relieving chemicals in the form of *endorphins* (i.e. a chemical similar to opiates) that inhibits the pain fibres from releasing substance P which subsequently reduces the experience of pain. This is why endorphins are often described as being associated with a 'jogger's high'.

As outlined above, pain sensations from the injury site are transmitted to the gating mechanism by pain fibres (or nerves) known as *nociceptors*. This is known as an *afferent pathway* because it indicates information is travelling towards the CNS. In addition to A-beta fibres two other key fibre types have been identified:

- A-delta fibres (types I and II)
  - Transmit information about sharp, brief pain
  - Wrapped in layers of 'fatty' cell membranes (i.e. myelinated) which increases the speed of action

- C-fibres
  - Transmit information about dull, throbbing pain
  - Not wrapped in 'fatty' cell membranes, therefore they have a slower speed of action.

Each of the three types of nociceptors is important as stated by Melzack and Wall (1965: 222) 'The degree to which the gate increases or decreases sensory transmission is determined by the relative activity in large diameter (A-beta) and small diameter (A-delta and C) fibres and by descending influences from the brain'. The other group of nerves that transmit information to the gating mechanism are the other peripheral fibres. In particular, A-beta fibres carry information about harmless stimulation or mild irritation, such as gentle touch or stroking or lightly scratching the skin, to the spinal cord. When A-beta fibres are stimulated the gate is likely to close and pain perception is inhibited, explaining why people experience a reduction in pain during a gentle massage or when heat is applied to aching limbs.

The final factor that influences the opening and closing of the gate is the impact of messages descending from the brain. Neurons in different parts of the brain send impulses, via what are known as *efferent pathways* (i.e. indicating they lead away from the CNS or are descending from the brain), to the spinal cord. Various brain processes such as anxiety, distraction, hypnosis and excitement have the capacity to influence this neural activity by releasing chemicals such as endorphins and therefore the opening and closing of the gate. From a biopsychosocial point of view, this is the most important component of gate-control theory as it provides a clear route through which cognitive, emotional and social factors can influence pain perception. Focus box 2.1 provides an overview of various conditions that individuals may experience that may open and close the gate. Since the introduction of this theory, researchers have been inspired to investigate the efficacy of psychological and behavioural approaches to pain management. We will consider these approaches in Chapter 10.

Focus 2.1

Conditions that can open and close the pain gate

Conditions that open the gate

Physical conditions
   – Extent of the injury
   – Inappropriate activity level

Emotional conditions
   – Anxiety or worry
   – Tension
   – Depression

Mental conditions
   – Focusing on the pain
   – Boredom; little involvement in life activities

Conditions that close the gate

Physical conditions
   – Medication
   – Counterstimulation (e.g. heat or massage)

Emotional conditions
   – Positive emotions (e.g. happiness or optimism)
   – Relaxation
   – Rest

Mental conditions
   – Intense concentration or distraction
   – Involvement and interest in life activities

Source: Adapted from Sarafino (2008); based on material by Karol et al, cited in Turk, Meichenbaum and Genest (1983).

Neuromatrix theory of pain

Melzack (1999) extended his gate-control theory of pain during the 1980s and 1990s. The primary reason for this was the original theory's inability to explain the phenomenon known as phantom limb pain (i.e. experiencing pain in a limb that no longer exists). This new model has suggested a stronger and more dominant role for the brain. The central tenets of the theory are:

1. The areas of the brain linked to particular parts of the body continue to be active and receive inputs even if a body part no longer exists.
2. We can still experience the qualities of the human condition, including pain, without receiving input from the body, indicating that the origins of the

Figure 2.5 Anxiety and worry can open the gate leading to the experience of greater pain.
Source: © ACE STOCK LIMITED/Alamy.

    patterns of activation that bring about these qualities of experience must be located in neural networks in the brain.

3. Conscious awareness of 'body' and 'self' is generated in the brain via patterns of input that can be modified by different perceptual inputs.
4. A network of neurons, known as the *neuromatrix*, is distributed throughout the brain to process all incoming sensory information including pain signals (known as the *body-self neuromatrix*). This neural network consists of cyclical, feedback loops between three of the brain's main neural circuits: the thalamus, limbic system and the cortex. The neuromatrix can process 'experiences' such as pain without receiving direct input from the body.
5. When the neuromatrix receives sensory inputs, they are processed (synthesized) and become imprinted on the matrix creating what is known as a *neurosignature*. The neurosignature is projected to areas of the brain – *the sentient neural hub* – where the flow of nerve impulses is transformed into a constantly changing stream of awareness.
6. An action neuromatrix is then activated to signal appropriate movements when pain is experienced (e.g. remove hand from hot iron).
7. The neuromatrix is genetically determined, however, it is modified through sensory inputs such as pain experiences.

As you will have gathered, this is a complicated theory and further work is required before researchers fully understand phantom limb pain, nevertheless, the developments presented by Melzack's **neuromatrix theory of pain** have provided valuable insights into the mechanisms underlying this phenomenon (Giummarra et al, 2007).

Psychoneuroimmunology

Have you ever wondered why a relatively large number of students report having the common cold around the time of important examinations? Is this simply bad luck, all in the mind, or is there a biological explanation? A growing body of evidence indicates that there is a link between social and psychological factors and susceptibility to respiratory infectious illness. This is noteworthy given that historically these two realms were considered quite distinct (i.e. the mind versus body debate).

The term **psychoneuroimmunology** or PNI was coined by Robert Ader and Nicholas Cohen of the University of Rochester in the USA to describe this new area of science that explored the interaction between psychological processes and the nervous and immune systems. Ader and Cohen were at the forefront of this area and demonstrated the link between the brain and the immune system early on (Ader and Cohen, 1975). Using a paradigm called *conditioned immunosuppression*, based upon Pavlov's classical conditioning, they discovered that the immune system of rats could be conditioned to respond to external stimuli unrelated to immune function. They found that after an artificially flavoured drink was paired with an immune suppressive drug in rats, the presentation of the drink alone was sufficient to suppress immune functioning. Studies such as this one have provided the starting point for researchers to examine the effects of various psychological factors on human immunity. Over the last 20 years or so, a large amount of research effort has concentrated on exploring the extent to which psychological stress may influence different aspects of the immune system. Two areas that have received particular attention are respiratory infectious illness and wound healing (cf., Kiecolt-Glaser et al, 1998; Cohen, 2005). However, in order to understand the link between stress, the common cold and wound healing, we need to appreciate how the immune system works. Therefore, the next section provides a basic introduction to the immune system.

The immune system

The function of the *immune system* is to defend the body against invaders. Microbes (germs or microorganisms), cancer cells and transplanted tissues or organs are all interpreted by the immune system as 'non-self' against which the body must be defended. Although the immune system is incredibly complex, its basic strategy is straightforward: to recognize the enemy, mobilize forces and attack. Amazingly, the immune system can distinguish between 'self' and 'non-self' and learns to remember the distinctive cellular features of invaders. Moreover, it is able to form an immunological memory of infectious agents and so mount a more effective response the next time the invader attacks. It is this process that is exploited when a person is vaccinated with a mild dose of an infectious agent – the body becomes primed for a real invasion.

What are the basic features of the immune system? Broadly speaking, the human body has the capacity to mount two types of immune defence:

Table 2.1 Comparison of the roles of T and B cells

Cell-mediated immunity: T cells	Antibody-mediated immunity: B cells
Work directly at cell level	Work via the bloodstream
A type of lymphocyte (white blood cell)	A type of lymphocyte (white blood cell)
Formed in the bone marrow, but matured in thymus (T)	Formed and matured in the bone (B) marrow
Attack and destroy infectious agents by triggering release of cytotoxic killer cells	Attack and destroy infectious agents by stimulating the release of antibodies

1. **Cell-mediated immunity**.
2. **Antibody-mediated immunity**.

In both cases, the basic immune response is brought about by the actions of two types of *white blood cells* known as *lymphocytes* and *monocytes*. Importantly, there are two types of lymphocytes with different functions: T (for thymus) cells and B (for bone) cells. Both types are formed in the bone marrow, but the *T cells* migrate to the thymus to mature while the *B cells* remain in the marrow. B cells produce *antibodies* (i.e. large proteins that will recognize and bind to invading infectious agents), whereas T cells do not. It is also worth noting that there are a number of different kinds of T cells including T helper cells, natural killer cells, T suppressor cells and cytotoxic killer cells.

T and B cells operate very differently when attacking infectious agents. The former bring about cell-mediated immunity while the latter bring about antibody-mediated immunity (see Table 2.1 for an overview of the roles of T and B cells). In the former case, when an infectious agent enters the body, it is recognized by a type of monocyte called a *macrophage*, which presents the infectious agent to a *T helper cell* and releases *interleukin-1* (IL-1; a type of *cytokine* released from cells to influence the activity of other cells), this in turn stimulates T-helper cell activity. As a result, the T helper cells then release *interleukin-2* (another cytokine) which triggers the proliferation of T cells and eventually the release of *cytotoxic killer cells* which attack and destroy the infectious agent.

In antibody-mediated immunity, the initial stages are similar, such that there is collaboration between macrophages and T helper cells. However, in this case, the T helper cells stimulate the proliferation of B cells leading to the secretion of antibodies which identify and bind to specific features of the infectious agent. The antibodies then immobilize and destroy the pathogen.

Stress and the immune system

Can stress alter immune functioning? There is evidence to show that stress can suppress cell-mediated immunity, although the data relating to the antibody response and B cell function in particular are less clear (cf., Rabin, 1999; Cohen et al, 2001). For example, many studies have shown that increased secretion of stress hormones such as cortisol can alter the production of cytokines. As we already know, cytokines are important in the activation of T cells as well as in mediating the pro-inflammatory response (this process is explained further in a later section). Therefore, stress-induced changes in the production of cytokines may represent an important mechanism through which stress compromises the body's response to infectious illness. Recently, Kunz-Ebrecht and colleagues (2003) showed that cortisol responses to psychological stress were inversely associated with the production of two cytokines (IL-6 and IL-1ra), indicating that psychological factors can influence important components of immune functioning.

Stress and respiratory infectious illness

Over the last 25 years, Sheldon Cohen, a psychologist at Carnegie Mellon University in the USA, has explored the extent to which psychological and social factors influence susceptibility to infectious illnesses such as the common cold (see Cohen, 2005, for a review). As part of this work, Cohen and his colleagues have developed a unique prospective study design in which healthy participants are exposed to a virus that causes the common cold. Participants are then monitored following exposure in order to determine who develops a respiratory illness and reports cold-like symptoms. At baseline, participants also normally complete a range of psychological measures to assess their current level of perceived stress, their mood and any recent stressful life events.

In 1991, Cohen and his colleagues published a seminal paper, in the prestigious journal, the *New England Journal of Medicine*, in which they demonstrated for the first time that increases in psychological stress are associated with increases in risk for developing a cold after exposure to a cold virus. If this is not impressive enough, they also demonstrated that this association was independent of the participants' baseline levels of specific antibody, age, sex, education, allergic status and body mass index, and the season of the year. In addition, they also explored whether the increased susceptibility was related to changes in stress-related health behaviours such as smoking, exercise and diet. None of these variables explained the relationship.

In a subsequent study, Cohen and colleagues (1998) concentrated on identifying the *types* of stressful life events that were most predictive of increased susceptibility to infectious illness. In order to do this, these researchers conducted detailed interviews with each of the participants who took part in their standard prospective design and found two types of stressful life events were most strongly related to susceptibility. The first type of event was enduring (1 month or longer) interpersonal problems with family and friends. The second type were enduring problems associated with work (such as under- or unemployment). They also found that the longer the stressful event had lasted, the greater was the risk of developing an infectious illness.

Similar to their earlier study, the authors again examined which psychological and biological factors may be mediating the effects of psychological stress on increased susceptibility (see Research methods box 5.2). Interestingly, they found that regular exercise, non-smoking and greater sleep efficacy (percent of time in bed sleeping) were associated with lower susceptibility to developing a common cold. In addition, they also found that higher levels of adrenaline and noradrenaline (in the urine in the past 24 hours) were related to greater susceptibility. However, surprisingly, the effects of these factors were independent of the relationship between psychological stress and risk of developing a cold.

More recently, research has turned its attention to exploring the role of pro-inflammatory cytokine regulation in explaining the mediating pathways between psychological stress and the common cold. You will recall from earlier that cytokines are produced in response to infection. They are also believed to trigger symptoms associated with upper respiratory infections such as the common cold and the influenza virus (Cohen, 2005). Therefore, using a more complex study design, Cohen, Doyle and Skoner (1999) investigated whether psychological stress influenced cytokine production in participants after receiving an influenza virus. Specifically, they tested whether stress had the capacity to interfere with the body's ability to regulate cytokine production. Normally, when a virus is detected, the body produces enough cytokines to remove the virus. However, Cohen et al found that stress short-circuited the body's ability to switch off the cytokine response. Individuals who had previously experienced high stress prior to receiving the virus were found to have higher IL-6 (cytokine) levels and greater symptom scores in response to the viral challenge. In a subsequent study, these researchers replicated their findings and demonstrated that prolonged stress influences susceptibility to infectious illness by decreasing cortisol's effectiveness in regulating the pro-inflammatory cytokine response, leading to increased production of IL-6 and greater illness expression (Miller et al, 2002). Taken together, these findings bring us to a surprising conclusion: Psychological stress does not influence upper respiratory illness by suppressing the immune system. On the contrary, stress experienced over an extended period of time results in the immune system over-responding, which in turn activates and extends the symptoms of upper respiratory infections.

Stress and wound healing

In 1995, Janice Kiecolt-Glaser and colleagues from Ohio State University published a seminal study that provided evidence, for the first time, that psychological stress slowed wound healing. Similar to Cohen and his co-investigators, Kiecolt-Glaser and her colleagues developed an unusual research design to investigate the links between stress and immune functioning. Using a punch biopsy, a 3.5 mm full thickness wound was created on the non-dominant forearm, approximately 4 cm below the elbow, in each of the study participants. Levels of perceived stress were then measured using questionnaires and the wound was photographed every day until it completely healed. A wound was considered fully healed when it no longer foamed after hydrogen peroxide was applied! In this study the researchers were interested in the effects of chronic stress on immune function and wound healing. Therefore, participants who were caring for a relative with Alzheimer's disease (high stress group) were compared to control participants (low stress group) matched for age and family income. The results of the study showed that complete wound healing took an average of nine days or 24 per cent longer in the caregiver group compared to the controls. They also found differences between the groups in the production of an important cytokine (interleukin-1ß) suggesting this as one of the immunological mechanisms underlying the observed effects.

Next this research group investigated whether a relatively minor, commonplace stressful event such as an examination had the potential to similarly influence wound healing. In this study, Marucha et al (1998) placed a 3.5 mm punch biopsy wound in the mouths (i.e. on the hard palate) of a sample of dental students, once during the summer vacation and again three days before a major examination. This repeated measures design allowed the participants to act as their own controls. Again, two independent methods assessed wound healing (daily photographs and a foaming response to hydrogen peroxide). Surprisingly, all students took longer to heal in the examination condition compared to control conditions with complete healing taking an average of three days (or 40 per cent) longer in the examination condition. These data suggest that even short-lived, predictable and relatively benign stressors can have significant consequences for wound healing. More importantly, these findings have important implications for understanding recovery from surgery. Evidence suggests that a more negative psychological response to surgery is associated with a slower and more complicated post-operative recovery, greater pain, longer hospital stay and worse treatment adherence (for more detailed discussion see Kiecolt-Glaser et al, 1998). Moreover, these results indicate that if patients are psychologically better prepared for surgery they are likely to experience significant health benefits.

Psychological influences on recovery from surgery

Using this work as a starting point, Kiecolt-Glaser and colleagues (1998: 1209) have developed a model of psychological influences on surgical recovery. They suggest that psychological factors can impact wound healing, a key variable in short-term post surgical recovery, via three key pathways:

1. Emotions have direct effects on 'stress' hormones, and they can modulate immune function.
2. The patient's emotional response to surgery can influence the type and amount of anaesthetic, and anaesthetics vary in their effects on the immune and endocrine system.
3. Individuals who are more anxious are also more likely to experience greater post-surgical pain, and pain can suppress immune functioning.

Summary

In this chapter we have considered several of the key psychophysiological pathways through which psychological factors (and particularly stress) may influence health and illness processes. Chapter 3 describes the key theoretical approaches to stress and evaluates the research evidence concerning the links between stressors and illness and between stressors and health behaviour. Psychological factors such as stress can affect health directly, through autonomic and neuroendocrine changes but also indirectly, through changes in health behaviours. The direct effects of stress on health outcomes are known as psychophysiological pathways, while the indirect effects are known as behavioural pathways.

The role of the nervous system is to allow us to adapt to changes both within our body and our environment. It consists of the brain, the spinal cord and billions of nerves. The brain is the central part of the nervous system and consists of three major components: the forebrain, the midbrain and the hindbrain. The forebrain is divided into two main subdivisions: 1) the telencephalon which comprises the cerebrum and the limbic system; and 2) the diencephalon which is composed of the thalamus and hypothalamus. The midbrain consists of two major parts: the tectum and the tegmentum. Similarly, the hindbrain has two major divisions: the metencephalon and the myelencephalon.

The nervous system is divided into the central nervous system (CNS) and the peripheral nervous system (PNS). The CNS comprises the brain and spinal cord whereas the PNS is a network of nerves that connects the brain and spinal cord to the rest of the body. An important part of the PNS is the autonomic nervous system (ANS) that has a sympathetic division and a parasympathetic division. The former mobilizes bodily processes (e.g. increases heart rate), whereas the latter restores the body's energy resources.

Two response systems are activated when we experience stress. The first and easiest to activate is the sympathetic adrenal medullary (SAM) system; the second is the hypothalamic–pituitary–adrenal (HPA) axis response system. The SAM system leads to the release of the adrenaline and noradrenaline that put the body on alert; the HPA axis response system leads to the release of the stress hormone, cortisol. The stress response has been found to impact negatively on a number of health outcomes such as cardiovascular disease. Excessive wear and tear of the cardiovascular system through repeated activation of the stress response may increase the development of atherosclerosis and increase the likelihood of myocardial infarction and stroke.

Psychological factors can play a role in the perception of pain. Early theories of pain were mechanistic and did not account for the influence of cognitive, emotional and social factors. Gate-control theory, introduced by Melzack and Wall (1965), proposes that a neural gate in the spinal cord receives signals from pain fibres at the site of injury, other peripheral fibres and messages descending from the brain. The degree to which the gate opens (leading to experience of pain) is determined by the combined effects of these three factors. Gate-control theory was extended by Melzack and is known as the neuromatrix theory of pain. This theory contends that the pain experience is governed by the body-self neuromatrix.

The human body has the capacity to mount two types of defence known as cell-mediated immunity and antibody-mediated immunity. Psychological factors such as stress have been found to influence these immune functions. A number of researchers have shown stress to be associated with increased susceptibility to infectious illnesses and the slowing down of wound healing.

Key concepts and terms

Antibody-mediated immunity	Neuromatrix theory of pain
Autonomic nervous system	Parasympathetic nervous system
Cardiovascular system	Peripheral nervous system
Cell-mediated immunity	Psychoneuroimmunology
Central nervous system	Psychophysiological pathways
Endocrine system	Somatic nervous system
Gate-control theory	Sympathetic adrenal medullary
Hypothalamic–pituitary–adrenal	(SAM) response system
(HPA) axis response system	Sympathetic nervous system
Limbic system	Trier Social Stress Test

Sample essay titles

- To what extent can psychological factors influence health and illness processes?

- Cognitive, emotional and social factors affect pain. Discuss this statement with reference to recent psychological theory.

- Social and psychological factors are linked to susceptibility and respiratory infectious illness. Discuss.

- What are the pathways through which stress can alter immune functioning?

Further reading

Books

Horn, S., and Munafo, M. (1997). *Pain: Theory, Research and Intervention*. Milton Keynes: Open University Press.

Kalat, J.W. (2004). *Biological Psychology*. New York: Thomson Wadsworth.

Lovallo, W.R. (2005). *Stress and Health: Biological and Psychological Interactions*. Thousand Oaks, CA: Sage.

Sapolsky, R.M. (1998). *Why Zebras Don't Get Ulcers*. New York: W.H. Freeman.

Vedhara, K., and Irwin, M. (2005). *Human Psychoneuroimmunology*. Oxford: Oxford University Press.

Journal articles

Cohen, S. (2005). The Pittsburgh common cold studies: psychosocial predictors of susceptibility to respiratory infectious illness. *International Journal of Behavioral Medicine*, 12, 123–131.

Eccleston, C., Morley, S., Williams, A., Yorke, L., and Mastroyannopoulou, K. (2002). Systematic review of randomized controlled trials of psychological therapy for chronic pain in children and adolescents, with a subset meta-analysis of pain relief. *Pain*, 99, 157–165.

Kiecolt-Glaser, J.K., McGuire, L., Robles, T., and Glaser, R. (2002a). Emotions, morbidity, and mortality: New perspectives from psychoneuroimmunology. *Annual Review of Psychology*, 53, 83–107.

Steptoe, A., Hamer, M., Chida, Y. (2007). The effects of acute psychological stress on circulating inflammatory factors in humans: A review and meta-analysis. *Brain Behavior and Immunity*, 21, 901–912.

2 | Stress and health

3 Stress theory and research

Stress is widespread and media coverage suggests that it causes illness. In this chapter we will examine how stress is studied and how it is linked to disease. We will consider evolutionary perspectives on stress in preparing humans for fight or flight as well as more contemporary views. Building on Chapter 2, we discuss a model of physiological responses to stress leading to the long-term health impact of stress, known as allostatic load. We then explore different measures of stress including **life events** such as marriage, divorce or bereavement and daily hassles such as losing one's keys. We discuss these in terms of Lazarus' Transactional Theory of Stress (1966, 1999, Lazarus and Folkman, 1984). Finally, we discuss Conservation of Resources theory (Hobfoll, 1989, 2001).

We highlight the pathways by which stress impacts on health. Stress affects health through biological processes (e.g. blood pressure, release of stress hormones, immune functioning) and (indirectly) through health behaviours (e.g. exercise, diet, smoking). We consider evidence for both pathways when discussing the impact of life events and daily stressors on health outcomes. In the final section of this chapter we consider why some people become ill in response to stressful situations and others do not.

The chapter has five sections: 1) what is stress?; 2) early approaches to stress; 3) contemporary approaches to stress – allostatic load and health; 4) contemporary psychological approaches; 5) why do some people get ill in response to stressors and others do not?

Learning outcomes

When you have completed this chapter you should be able to:

1. Describe what is meant by stress. Discuss whether stress is a growing problem.
2. Describe and evaluate key theoretical approaches to stress.
3. Describe and evaluate key ways in which stress has been measured.
4. Discuss and evaluate research evidence concerning the links between stressors and a) illness, and b) health behaviour.
5. Describe the impact of individual differences in responses to stressors.

What is stress?

The increase in press and television coverage of stress over two decades has corresponded to a growth in research and public awareness. We can all empathize with feeling stressed. However, it is not always clear what we mean by 'stress'. Over centuries, 'stress' has come to mean pressure or strain (e.g. Cooper and Dewe, 2004). Scientific interest dates back to the early part of the twentieth century. For example, First World War concerns about industrial efficiency led to studies of fatigue in wartime munitions factories and the war focused attention on 'shellshock' which was subsequently acknowledged as a manifestation of post-traumatic stress disorder (Lazarus, 1999).

There have been three different approaches to the study of stress: the *stimulus-based* or engineering approach; the *response-based* or *medico-physiological* approach; and the psychological *'interactional-appraisal'* approach (Cox, 1978). The engineering approach views stress as a demand on an individual from their environment which produces a strain reaction: the greater the strain, the larger the reaction. This approach assumes that undemanding situations are not stressful. However, monotonous undemanding work environments very often are stressful. The engineering analogy is also problematic because it makes the assumption that individuals function both unconsciously and automatically; no consideration is given to the mediating psychological processes (e.g. cognitive appraisal) but such processes are very important. The response-based approach mainly considers stress in terms of the general physiological reaction to noxious events in a person's environment such as changes in blood pressure, heart rate and stress hormones. Again this approach does not account for individual psychological processes. More recent work has adopted an interactional-appraisal (or transactional) approach in order to explain the stress process. Such theories have contributed to our understanding of the variation in responses to similar noxious (or stressful) stimuli by emphasizing the importance of the intervening psychological processes.

The development of the transactional approach owes much to the work of Richard Lazarus and his colleague Susan Folkman (Lazarus, 1966; Lazarus and Folkman, 1984). They define stress as 'a particular relationship between the person and the environment that is appraised by the person as taxing or exceeding his or her resources and endangering his or her well-being' (Lazarus and Folkman, 1984: 19). This means that researchers need to look at the environment, the individual's reaction to the environment and the outcome (which might be in terms of physiological or psychological well-being). Perhaps because of the breadth of issues encompassed within this concept of stress, Lazarus also suggested that the most useful approach would be to regard stress not as a single variable but as a 'rubric consisting of many variables and processes' (Lazarus and Folkman, 1984: 12). Thus stress may be viewed as an umbrella term covering a general field of study. Within this field there are many diverse areas of research which look at relationships between objective or perceived antecedents (or stressors) and a range of physiological, psychological or behavioural outcomes (often referred to as strains). The latter may include the kind of physiological measures (e.g. cortisol, blood pressure) discussed in

Chapter 2, as well as illness outcomes (like the occurrence of cancer or heart disease), measures of work performance or health behaviours or, perhaps most frequently, self-ratings of satisfaction or anxiety.

Perhaps because of the vagueness of the concept there is sometimes disagreement about basic issues such as whether a certain amount of stress is good for you. This clearly depends on the definition you use. For example, taking a stimulus-based approach, up to a certain point, stimuli such as work pressures may certainly be motivating and beneficial. However, using Lazarus' popular definition given above, which views stress in terms of a process involving threats to our well-being, it is harder to see how this can be construed as beneficial! A number of different approaches to stress are considered in the following sections.

Activity 3.1

Is stress increasing?

There is a widespread view, often reflected in the media, that the amount of stress in society, both within the family and the workplace, has increased greatly in recent decades. This has been attributed to the breakdown of the nuclear family, the loosening of extended family bonds caused by the widespread mobility in the community and the rapid changes in the workplace. What do you think? Is life really much more stressful than it was 50 years ago? Discuss this topic in groups, taking into account the increased public awareness of psychological responses to stressors and changes in people's expectations.

Consider also what variables you would need to consider in making an assessment of whether stress had increased. This could include increases in stressors such as wars, poverty, unemployment or work stressors. It could also include increases in outcomes such as psychiatric illness or stress-related disease.

Early approaches to stress

Two theorists who had a great influence in terms of popularizing the concept of stress were both physiologists: Walter Cannon and Hans Selye. Cannon (1932) wrote about the 'fight-or-flight' reaction to describe the human response to threats. Cannon believed that when faced with danger, such as a predator, the human being feels the emotions of fear or anger, the former being linked to an instinct to run away and the latter with the urge to fight. These reactions served to prepare the body for action as outlined in Chapter 2.

Hans Selye built on Cannon's work and described a reaction pattern called the **general adaptation syndrome** (GAS; Selye, 1956). Selye wrote that 'Adaptability and resistance to stress are fundamental prerequisites for life, and every vital organ participates in them' (Selye, 1950: 1383). He believed that the basic physiological reaction was always the same regardless of the stressor and that an understanding of this phenomenon depended on many branches of physiology, biochemistry and medicine. He even stated that the phenomenon would never be really understood 'since the complete comprehension of life is beyond the limits of the human mind' (Selye, 1950: 1383). It is difficult to do justice to this complex theory in a brief paragraph! However, in essence it comprises three stages:

- *Alarm*. This is the immediate reaction whereby stress hormones are released to prepare the body for action (fight or flight).

- *Resistance*. If stress is prolonged, levels of stress hormones remain high. However, during this period the individual seems superficially to adapt to the stressor but will still have heightened susceptibility to disease.

- *Exhaustion*. If the stress continues long enough the body's defensive resources are used up leading to illness and, ultimately, death.

In summary, according to Selye, prolonged exposure to a strong stressor will increase an individual's risk of developing health problems which he described as **diseases of adaptation** (e.g. ulcers, high blood pressure). Moreover, he suggested that repeated and long-term exposure to stress will lead to dysfunction of a number of the body's basic systems such as the immune and metabolic systems.

Selye's early approach focused on stress as a physiological reaction and his theory influenced many subsequent researchers. However, Mason (1971) questioned the generality of this approach, arguing that some noxious (stressful) physical conditions do not produce the predicted three-stage alarm, resistance and ultimately exhaustion responses (e.g. exercise, fasting, heat). More recent approaches have tended to emphasize psychological process and impacts and have recognized that individuals may respond differently to the same stressful events.

Contemporary physiological approaches to stress – allostatic load and health

Building on the work of Selye is an important contemporary approach to stress, introduced by McEwen and Stellar (1993), that helps us understand how stress can cause illness over a lifetime. This approach attempts to provide a complete physiological account of the various bodily systems which may be affected by stress and how different stressful situations may impact on health. McEwen (1998) proposed that the long-term impact of stress, known as **allostatic load** affects the body at cardiovascular, metabolic, neural, behavioural and cellular levels. Similar to basic homeostatic systems such as body temperature, the HPA axis, the autonomic nervous system and the cardiovascular, metabolic and immune systems protect the body by adapting to internal and external stress. This is known as allostasis. However, if the activation of these systems is repeated and prolonged, allostatic load will be experienced in the form of increased release of stress hormones, immune cells, brain activity and cardiovascular response. It is suggested that if a person experiences allostatic load for a long time, they are at increased risk of developing disease because the bodily systems will stop working as effectively (for a full account see McEwen, 1998, 2007).

In terms of allostasis, when we encounter a psychological or physical stressor (e.g. giving a speech or encountering an infection or a physical threat), our body has a twofold response. First, it initiates an allostatic response that activates the stress response (as described in Chapter 2). Second, when the stressor has passed, the allostatic response is terminated. As you already know, activation of these systems leads to the release of several stress hormones including cortisol and changes in blood pressure and heart rate, which normally return to baseline levels when the stressful encounter has ended. However, if the allostatic response is not shut off but is maintained overtime, due to inadequate coping, this will result in allostatic load, thus placing excessive pressure on our bodily systems.

McEwen has suggested that four situations are associated with allostatic load. Each situation differs in terms of how often we encounter stressful situations and whether we can cope with them:

1. Repeated 'hits' from multiple stressors.
2. Lack of adaptation.
3. Prolonged response.
4. Inadequate response.

As shown in Figure 3.1, the first situation is when we experience frequent stressors. If these are sustained over long periods of time they can trigger repeated elevations in blood pressure thereby increasing the risk of having a heart attack or speeding up the early stages of heart disease. The second is where we are unable to cope with or to adapt to the same type of stressor, and as a result our body is exposed to stress hormones for a long period of time. The third condition is when our bodily systems are exposed to the stress response over an extended episode due to a delayed shutdown of the body's response. The fourth is when an inadequate stress response causes the body to release extra, unnecessary hormones and other chemical messengers which may be harmful to health. As you can see, this approach deals primarily with the physiological changes that accompany stress. Contemporary psychological approaches are considered in the next section.

Contemporary psychological approaches to stress

In parallel with the development of physiological explanations of the stress process, psychologists have focused on stress as a predominantly psychological phenomenon and produced definitions and theories which concentrate on the psychological precursors and processes. The three approaches described in this section have all been influential but approach the conceptualization and study of stress in different ways. For each approach the evidence linking them to disease is considered.

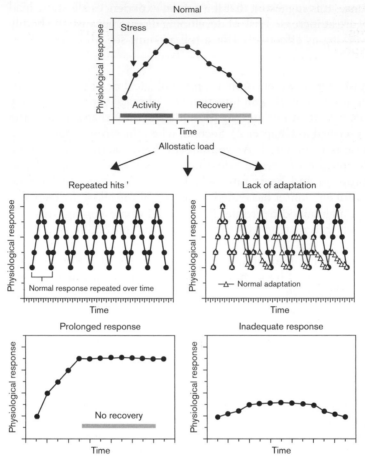

Figure 3.1 Four types of allostatic load. Top, the normal allostatic response in which a response is initiated by a stressor, sustained for an appropriate interval, and then turned off. The other four panels illustrate four conditions that lead to allostatic load: repeated 'hits' from multiple stressors; lack of adaptation; prolonged response due to delayed shutdown; and inadequate response that leads to compensatory hyperactivity of other mediators (e.g. inadequate secretion of glucocorticoids, resulting in increased concentrations of cytokines that are normally counter-regulated by glucocorticoids).

Source: Protective and damaging effects of stress mediators. New England Journal of Medicine, 338, 171–179.

Life events

The study of major **life events** is perhaps the earliest, as well as most enduring, approach to measuring stressors. The idea that emotionally distressing events might be associated with disease and particularly cancer goes back at least as far as the nineteenth century where many anecdotal reports of links between negative events such as bereavement and cancer can be found in the medical literature (LeShan, 1959). The first statistical study of this association is attributed to Snow (1893) who studied 250 cancer patients in London and found that in over 60 per cent of them there had been some problem before the onset of the disease. Frequently this was the death of a close relative.

Table 3.1 Social Readjustment Rating Scale (Holmes & Rahe, 1967)

Rank	Life events	LCU* score
1	Death of spouse	100
2	Divorce	73
3	Marital separation	65
4	Jail term	63
5	Death of close family member	63
6	Personal illness or injury	53
7	Marriage	50
8	Fired at work	47
9	Marital reconciliation	45
10	Retirement	45
11	Change in health of a family member	44
12	Pregnancy	40
13	Sex difficulties	39
14	Gain of a new family member	39
15	Business readjustment	39
16	Change in financial state	38
17	Death of a close friend	37
18	Change to a different line of work	36
19	Change in number of arguments with spouse	35
20	Mortgage over $10,000	31
21	Forcclosure of mortgage or loan	30
22	Change in responsibilities at work	29
23	Son or daughter leaving home	29
24	Trouble with in-laws	29
25	Outstanding personal achievement	28
26	Wife begin or stop work	26
27	Begin or end school	26
28	Change in living conditions	25
29	Revision of personal habits	24
30	Trouble with boss	23
31	Change in work hours or conditions	20
32	Change in residence	20
33	Change in schools	20
34	Change in recreation	19
35	Change in church activities	19
36	Change in social activities	18
37	Mortgage or loan less than $10,000	17
38	Change in sleeping habits	16
39	Change in number of family get-togethers	15
40	Change in eating habits	15
41	Vacation	13
42	Christmas	12
43	Minor violations of the law	11

*LCU = Life change unit

Source: Reprinted from Journal of Psychosomatic Research, 11, 213–218. Holmes, T.H., and Rahe, R.H. (1967). The social readjustment rating scale, with permission from Elsevier.

More formal measurement approaches to studying life events originated in the 1960s when Holmes and Rahe (1967) published a checklist of life events called the **Social Readjustment Rating Scale** which is reproduced in Table 3.1. The idea of a change being stressful and requiring adaptation is central to the approach. Thus life events were changes rather than persistent states. Furthermore, they were objectively verifiable events.

In the initial research to establish this measure, Holmes and Rahe drew on their clinical experience to list 43 events. A sample of 394 people were asked to rate these for the degree of 'social readjustment' they required. Marriage was given an arbitrary value (50 in the final scale) and they were asked to assign numeric values to all the other events based on how much more (or less) adjustment the event required than marriage. The sum of ratings for events an individual experiences in the last year is known as their *life change unit* (LCU) score. Holmes and Masuda (1974) described an LCU score of over 150 in one year as a life crisis, (150–199 is a mild crisis, 200–299 a moderate crisis and over 300 a major crisis). They also reported an early study which indicated that life crises were linked to deterioration in health. For example, 37 per cent of those whose scores indicated they had experienced a minor crisis, and 79 per cent of those with a major crisis, reported changes in health. Further studies in the 1970s by Rahe and colleagues suggested that high LCU scores were linked with heart disease (Rahe and Paasikivi, 1971; Theorell and Rahe, 1971). However, as the methodology has improved, and more longitudinal studies have been conducted, results have tended to be less consistent.

Activity 3.2

Look at Table 3.1 and work out your own LCU score for the past year. Do you think this is a reasonable indication of the stress you have experienced in the last year? Before you read on, write down any problems you can see with this approach to measuring stress.

There have been a number of criticisms of the life events approach highlighting limitations which may account for the large number of positive findings in the early literature. Some critics have commented on the fact that where two people both have the same score their subjective experience may actually be very different. In one study, researchers interviewed people about their responses and found that, for some people, the death of a close friend involved the death of a childhood friend who they had not seen for a long time whereas for others it was a much more significant loss (Dohrenwend et al, 1990). This has been labelled the problem of 'intracategory variability' (Dohrenwend, 2006).

A further criticism, which you may have identified, is that the Social Readjustment Rating Scale does not discriminate between positive and negative events (Jones and Kinman, 2001). However, most people would assume that only negative events would be harmful for health, while positive events might even be beneficial (but see Research methods box 3.1). Because of this criticism many more recent approaches to life events measurement also take into account people's appraisals of each event.

Research methods 3.1

Are positive events always good for you? The unconscious cost of good fortune (Shimuzu and Pelham, 2004)

Some research suggests that positive events are good for health (e.g. Evans and Edgerton, 1991) whereas other studies have found they are bad (e.g. Evans et al, 1996). Brown and McGill (1989) have suggested that positive life events are only linked to improved health for people with high self-esteem. They suggest an '*identity disruption model*' to explain these findings. This suggests that for those high in self-esteem an accumulation of positive events merely confirms the positive views and expectations that such individuals hold about themselves, whereas for those low in self-esteem such events may disrupt their sense of self, making them question their negative self views and so undermine their sense of predictability and control over the environment. However, a subsequent study by Kaniasty and Norris (1993) failed to support this model. In a sample of older people they found no evidence that those with low self-esteem who experienced more positive life events suffered more illness. This study suggests that the different effects reported are dependent on whether people's self-esteem is assessed by self-reports (*explicit self-esteem*) or via measures which assess people's unconscious self-evaluations (*implicit self-esteem*). The research described here therefore aimed to examine the effect of both types of self-esteem on the impact of positive life events on health.

Method

A total of 171 students took part in the study. They completed explicit and implicit measures of self-esteem. They were then followed up five weeks later when they completed a survey of negative affectivity, life events and health. Explicit self-esteem was measured using a well-known self-report measure (Rosenberg, 1979). The measure of implicit self-esteem was based on research which has shown that people like the letters of their own names more than other people like those letters (the name-letter effect; e.g. Nuttin, 1987). Stronger name-letter preference is regarded as an indication of implicit self-esteem (Koole et al, 2001). The life events measure tapped events that were relevant to students including failing courses or getting good marks.

Results

The study found that, overall, *negative* (but not positive) life events were linked to increased illness. However, there were interaction effects between *positive* life events and both explicit and implicit self-esteem such that positive life events were only associated with illness for participants with low self-esteem (see Focus box 5.2 for further explanation of interaction effects). This was true for both the implicit and the explicit measure of self-esteem, but the effects were stronger when the implicit measure was used. Negative affectivity (or neuroticism – see Chapter 6) was controlled for in these analyses.

... Continued

... Continued

The study also found that the association between positive life events and increased illness was particularly strong in those with *both* low implicit and low explicit self-esteem. However, there were also some interesting findings for those who had a mismatch between implicit and explicit scores. For those who were *high in implicit but low in explicit self-esteem* there was no association between positive life events and illness. But for those who were *low in implicit, but high in explicit self-esteem* there was still a significant tendency to suffer more illness. Thus having low implicit self-esteem may dominate even when explicit self-esteem is high.

Discussion

The results provide support for Brown and McGill's identity disruption model. A number of possible explanations are offered. Individuals who are low in self-esteem may become unhealthy because they lose a sense of control over their lives, or because they must devote more resources to processing positive events. Alternatively, it is possible that they may engage in unhealthy behaviours such as drinking to reduce the anxiety caused by the identity disruption. The study is limited by its retrospective assessment of life events and illness and the authors suggest an improvement would be to collect daily reports of events and health. Nevertheless the study demonstrates the importance of individual differences in reactions to stressors. It further demonstrates the importance of unconscious mechanisms. The authors suggest that it may be hard for people to adjust to positive events simply because they do not have conscious access to why something that should feel good can feel so wrong.

Research on life events has also been criticized for the *reliability* and *validity* of measures (that is, do people produce the same scores if asked to complete the questionnaire after a time interval and do the measures actually measure what they are intended to measure). In the 1970s and 1980s researchers considered reliability over time (usually called test–retest reliability). One study found that, when people repeated the measure after 1–2 weeks, there was only 70 per cent agreement (Steele et al, 1980), and other research has indicated that reliability declines dramatically over longer periods (Dohrenwend, 2006). Related to this, there are concerns that retrospective reports may not be valid when, as is often the case, they are reported by people who are already diagnosed with a disease. In these circumstances people may be inclined to want to find an explanation for their illness, leading them to report more life events than those who have no illness (Brown, 1974). This factor may account for some of the positive relationships found in the early studies. Nowadays limited credence is given to studies unless they use longitudinal approaches which assess life events prior to the development (or at least the diagnosis) of disease.

Over the years there have been improvements to life events methodology and many different measures of stressful life events have been developed. Some have been established that are relevant to particular subgroups. For example, there are a range of scales specifically for use with children and adolescents (Grant et al, 2004). Others have tried to overcome the methodological limitations of the checklist approach by using the much more time-consuming approach of semi-structured interviews where people describe events which are then rated by trained individuals. The most well-known example of this is the *Life Events and Difficulties Schedule (LEDS)* developed by Brown and Harris (1978). This was used in an important study of life events, social support and depression which is described in more detail in Chapter 5 (Brown and Harris, 1978).

Over the past 40 years researchers have studied the relationship between life events and disease. Yet there is still controversy concerning whether major life events do cause disease. The early studies showed strong links but have been subject to criticism. Literature on breast cancer provides a good example of how some well-publicized studies find links between life events and cancer (e.g. Geyer, 1991; Chen et al, 1995) but other research fails to support the findings (e.g. Greer and Morris, 1975; Protheroe et al, 1999). Many studies have used what is known as a 'limited prospective design'. For example, Chen et al (1995) studied 119 women who were referred for biopsies for suspected breast cancer. They were interviewed and their experience of life events was assessed before they received a definitive diagnosis. The researchers found that 19 out of 41 women who were subsequently diagnosed with cancer had experienced threatening life events during the five years before diagnosis compared with 15 out of the 78 controls. While isolated studies such as this often get media publicity and strengthen public perceptions that there is a link, literature reviews and meta-analyses of the overall associations tend to conclude that there is little evidence to link life events and breast cancer (e.g. Petticrew et al, 1999).

Stressful life events may be more strongly linked to psychological outcomes. Research into life events in extreme situations such as wars and natural disasters suggests that exposure to such events is likely to lead to serious psychopathology (Dohrenwend, 2000). Evidence about the impact of life events in more normal situations is less conclusive (Kessler, 1997). This may be because, in less extreme circumstances, individual differences in people's susceptibility are more important. The idea that some people are genetically more susceptible to stressors is known as the **stress diathesis** model (the term 'diathesis' meaning a predisposition to illness). A number of studies now suggest that some people are indeed more genetically vulnerable to stressors than others (e.g. Kendler et al, 1995). Advances in genetics have now enabled researchers to identify specific genes which are associated with this susceptibility. For example, Caspi et al (2003) found a gene by environment interaction whereby only those with a specific genetic makeup exhibited more depressive symptoms in relation to stressful life events.

Overall, despite the many criticisms of life events research, it seems to be an approach that is here to stay with the number of studies increasing dramatically decade by decade (Dohrenwend, 2006). Furthermore, modifications in methodology have helped to improve reliability and validity of measurement.

Transactional theory and the daily hassles and uplifts approach

One of the most influential critics of life events research was Richard Lazarus who suggested that the focus on major life changes, which are comparatively rare, ignores the fact that a great deal of stress stems from recurrent day-to-day problems or chronic conditions which he describes as daily hassles. He also suggested that many of the other limitations of the approach (which are discussed above) stem from the fact that it is essentially atheoretical (Lazarus, 1990).

Lazarus (1966; Lazarus and Folkman, 1984) suggested a new approach to stress based on his own **transactional theory** of stress. Central to this theory and to his definition of stress (see above) is the notion of appraisal. Lazarus takes the view that stress is not a property of the environment (as suggested by the life events approach), nor is it a property of the individual (as implied by research into physiological markers discussed in Chapter 2), rather it is a transaction between the individual and the environment (Lazarus, 1990). The focus is therefore on the process of appraisal and coping. In any potentially stressful transaction or encounter, a person may appraise the situation as involving harm or threat of harm, or alternatively they may see it in a positive, optimistic light and view it as a challenge. The type of appraisal will then determine the person's coping processes, which will in turn determine subsequent appraisals (see Chapter 5 for further discussion of the role of coping in this theory). Lazarus is therefore describing a constantly changing relationship between the person and the environment. Furthermore, he suggests that stress is a complex phenomenon which involves many variables in terms of inputs, outputs and mediating factors associated with appraisal and coping.

This approach clearly has implications for the way stress is measured. In particular, Lazarus (1990) suggests that the search for a single satisfactory measure is 'doomed to failure'. He argues that stress needs to be assessed by a series of different measures which each capture different aspects of the stress process. Relevant measures therefore might include environmental inputs (e.g. daily stressors as well as life events), measures of individual differences, coping, and physiological and psychological responses. A critical feature of this approach is that, because stress is a process, assessments should be repeated over time. This theory led to the development of a measure of daily stressors known as the Hassles Scale (e.g. Kanner et al, 1981) and subsequently a shorter **Hassles and Uplifts Scale** (DeLongis et al, 1982). In this measure 53 items are listed, for example 'your children', 'your fellow workers', 'your health', and respondents are asked to rate separately the extent to which each item is a hassle or an uplift. A number of studies have examined the extent to which both daily hassles and major life events to predict ill health and these have tended to suggest that hassles are more predictive (e.g. Kanner et al, 1981; DeLongis et al, 1982). Research based on the transactional theory has been associated with a growth in daily assessment to tap the stress process. This typically uses 'daily diaries' which contain rating scales, such as the Hassles and Uplifts Scale. In addition, they may also offer scope to provide qualitative descriptions of daily events (see Research methods box 3.2).

Research methods 3.2

Using diaries in health psychology research

Approaches to studying stress differ in their focus. For example, compare the life events approach with the transactional approach. The life events approach has been criticized on methodological grounds and stress research, like other areas in health, social and clinical psychology, has been criticized for over-reliance on cross-sectional, 'snap-shot' methodologies (see Affleck et al, 1999; Nezlek, 2001 for further discussion). For example, research into the impact of stress on eating behaviour has tended to use laboratory-based methods which employ single measures of stress (e.g. life events over the previous year) or one-off retrospective measurements of stress in the short term (e.g. perceptions of stress over the past two weeks). Such research ignores the substantial evidence showing that changes in within-person stressful daily hassles are important in understanding stress-outcome processes (see Bolger et al, 2003).

We are often interested in investigating causal relationships between study variables and/or determining whether a particular psychological variable influences a later health outcome, e.g. on the following day or week (known as a lagged effect). Imagine we wanted to find out if negative mood was associated with the onset of pain episodes in arthritis patients or whether in psoriasis patients, stressful events on one day could trigger 'flare ups' the next day. Conventional cross-sectional or longitudinal study designs would not be very useful here because they miss the detailed daily variation driving the causal processes we are interested in. In these cases and others in health psychology research, the dependent variable under investigation is a *daily process*, that is, it changes from day to day and/or frequently within days. Therefore, in order to assess it we need to measure it repeatedly during and over several days. A diary approach is ideally suited to such research.

What are the advantages of using diary designs and measuring daily processes? Affleck and colleagues (1999: 747) argue that daily diary studies allow researchers '(a) to capture as closely as possible the "real-time" occurrences or moments of change (in study variables); (b) to reduce recall bias; (c) to mitigate some forms of confounding by using participants as their own controls, and (d) to establish temporal precedence to strengthen causal inferences'. In addition, using daily diaries permits researchers to use sophisticated statistical techniques (e.g. **hierarchical linear modeling**) to examine day-to-day within-person effects *together* with the impact of between-person factors such as personality or gender.

There are important procedural differences in the way daily diary studies are conducted. If we were designing a study, we would have to consider how frequently our participants completed their diaries. Three main methods exist:

1. *Interval-contingent*: the participant completes diary at end of each day (e.g. before going to bed).

... Continued

... Continued

2. *Event-contingent*: the participant completes diary each time a specific event happens (e.g. every time they experience a daily hassle).
3. *Signal-contingent*: the patient completes diary in response to random 'alarms' or 'beeps' from a palmtop computer or similar device.

Researchers also have to consider how participants actually record their responses. Typically researchers use either paper and pencil diaries or handheld computers. In fact, the issue of which method is best has recently sparked a lively debate within the research methods literature (see Stone et al, 2002; Green et al, 2006; Tennen et al, 2006). Both methods have their pros and cons. For example, using paper and pencil methods, the researcher cannot be certain that the participant has completed their diary when they claimed to have done so (this is known as '*compliance*'), whereas a computer will date and time stamp all diary entries. However, handheld computers are relatively expensive and they can malfunction resulting in loss of important data. Nevertheless, a recent study which compared paper and pencil with electronic techniques showed that both methods found a similar pattern of findings and yielded equivalent data (Green et al, 2006). In either case it is critical that the researcher designs the entry system so participants can easily and efficiently record the particular events under investigation.

Inevitably, Lazarus' approach has not been without critics. Criticisms have primarily focused upon the notion that by including appraisal of the stressful nature of transactions within measures of hassles, items may be inadvertently measuring psychological distress. If correct, this would inevitably lead to positive correlations between stressors and strains (Dohrenwend et al, 1984; Dohrenwend and Shrout, 1985). Dohrenwend et al suggested that while life events measures may also sometimes include items which are symptoms rather than causes of distress, this is much more of a problem for Lazarus' measures. Here the mere instruction to rate severity of hassles implies a level of distress. Thus all items are potentially confounded with psychological distress. Dohrenwend and Shrout (1985: 782) argue that environmental events should be measured 'uncontaminated by perceptions, appraisals or reactions'. While self-report measures are arguably always likely to be influenced by the individual's appraisal, the implication of this argument is that researchers should use items which ask about the existence of stressors (e.g. whether or not a particular event happened) rather than items which ask people to rate stress or hassles associated with the event. This more objective approach to stressors is commonly found in the work stress literature (see Chapter 4), where researchers (and employers) are primarily concerned with identifying the negative effects of work irrespective of individuals' idiosyncratic appraisal.

Within the current literature you may spot both relatively objective measures of stressors and measures which include elements of appraisal of distress. In your reading of research it is important to look out for instances where there is overlap between stressors and strains. It is likely to be a particular problem where, for example, individuals' ratings of hassles are correlated with a rating of anxiety or depression. The findings may not be very meaningful if both measures are essentially measuring anxiety! However, subjective ratings may not be a problem if ratings of hassles are correlated with a relatively more objective outcome such as a physiological measure or a rating of health behaviour (see Research methods box 3.3)

Nowadays, a range of different types of approach to measuring hassles and other daily stressors are used. For example, the study described in Research methods box 3.3 asked people to describe their own hassles which were then categorized by independent raters.

Research methods 3.3

Daily hassles and eating behaviour (O'Connor et al, 2008a)

Background

When under pressure we may be more likely to skip exercise sessions and replace nourishing meals with quick fast food snacks or indulge in comfort eating of sweets and other high fat foods. Such negative health behaviours may be one of the ways in which stress indirectly contributes to both cardiovascular disease and cancer risk. This study set out to explore the complex relationship between stress (assessed as daily hassles) and eating behaviour in a sample of employed men and women in a naturalistic setting using a multilevel prospective diary design.

The study also aimed to explore the different types of stressors that may affect changes in eating behaviour. A number of researchers have previously found that particular types of stress had different effects on eating. For example, in the laboratory, Heatherton and colleagues (1991, 1992) found stressors of an *ego-threatening* nature (e.g. where there is a fear of failure) were associated with an increase in eating whereas physical threats (e.g. fear of an electric shock) led to a decrease in eating. Therefore, the study described here looked at the effect of a range of different daily hassles, namely ego-threatening, interpersonal, physical and work-related stressors.

A final aim of the study was to investigate the influence of individual difference variables on the relationship between hassles and eating. Individual difference models of stress hypothesize that certain groups of individuals will show different responses to stress (e.g. the obese and non-obese; women and men; and those with certain eating styles such as *emotional eating*). In addition, few previous studies have explored multiple individual differences variables, therefore not allowing conclusions to be drawn about the relative importance of these different variables (e.g. Conner et al, 1999; O'Connor and O'Connor, 2004).

Design and methods

A total of 422 employees completed daily diaries over four weeks in which they recorded daily hassles and provided free response reports of

... Continued

Conservation of resources theory – a resource-based model of stress

A slightly more recent approach to stress, which poses a challenge to the transactional **model**, is the **conservation of resources** model (COR; Hobfoll, 1989, 2001). This represents a shift away from the emphasis placed on appraisal in the transactional model back towards a more objective approach. This model suggests that resources (not demands) are the key variables of importance and that people strive to 'retain, protect and build resources' (Hobfoll, 1989: 516). Stress is defined as a reaction to loss, a threatened loss, or a failure to gain resources following an investment of resources. This may include personal resources (such as sense of mastery) and social resources (such as social support) which have been well-studied outside of the context of this theory (see Chapter 5). However, they also include a range of other factors such as financial/material resources. The model predicts that when faced with stress people will seek to minimize the potential loss of resources. In the absence of stress, Hobfoll suggests they will seek to build resources as a hedge against future stressors. He argues that the association of social resources with positive well-being is an example of the benefits of resource building (e.g. Cohen and Wills, 1985).

A central principle of the theory is that 'resource loss is disproportionally more salient than resource gain' (Hobfoll, 2001: 343), so that in circumstances of equal resource loss and gain, the loss will have greater impact. Hobfoll suggests that this emphasis on resources differentiates this theory from transactional theory which emphasizes appraisals. In the COR approach, although stress processes may be assessed via people's appraisals, most are resources which are objectively observable. The model is also distinct from the transactional theory in its idea of building resources for prevention of, or protection against, future stressors. Thus it highlights the importance of proactive coping (see Chapter 5). It also introduced the notion of '*resource caravans*'. This is the idea that resources cluster together in groups so that if you have one major resource such as self-efficacy this is likely to be linked to a range of others such as social support and other positive coping styles. Over time these caravans travel with us such that resources at one time period tend to carry over into future times (Hobfoll, 2001). Hobfoll further suggests the notion of *loss or gain spirals* whereby initial resource gain leads to future gain, and loss leads to future loss. These principles seem intuitively sensible and Hobfoll supports them with examples, frequently drawing on studies of stress and coping in disaster areas.

The model is underpinned by its own questionnaire, the Conservation of Resources Evaluation (COR-E; Hobfoll, 2007). This consists of a list of 74 resources ranging from 'adequate income', 'support from coworkers' to 'adequate home furnishings' and 'positive feelings about myself'. Currently, there is little research using this model to predict major physical health outcomes, however resource loss has been linked to depression and other psychological strains. For example, Ennis, Hobfoll and Schroeder (2000) report that *lack* of resources such as low income or poor education was almost unrelated to depressed mood whereas *loss* of material resources (e.g. deterioration in finances) was highly related.

The model has produced a certain amount of controversy, particularly as it can be seen as a challenge to Lazarus' highly influential theory. It was hotly debated in a series of articles in *Applied Psychology: an International Review* (2001). Here Hobfoll describes the theory and a number of other experts, including Lazarus himself, debate the issues in a series of subsequent articles. Lazarus (2001) attacks the theory in no uncertain terms and states that all the elements of the COR theory can already be found in his transactional theory. For example, there are plenty of references to resources within his theory and resource loss is central to the idea of loss appraisal, for example in the grief process (e.g. Lazarus and Folkman, 1984; Lazarus, 1999). His view is therefore that the COR approach is 'fundamentally unsound and fails to advance us beyond what we know' (Lazarus, 2001: 381). Others take a more moderate view. For example, Schwarzer (2001) suggests that Hobfoll's and Lazarus' views differ in emphasis rather than in fundamental principles. He argues that the difference lies in the centrality of either objective or subjective resources. Thus Lazarus takes the view that objective resources are simply antecedents which lead to appraisals (subjective resources) which are the direct precursors of perceptions of stress. In contrast, Hobfoll examines both objective and subjective resources but emphasizes the former. Schwarzer further suggests that the inclusion of the notion of resource investment and proactive coping introduces a forward time perspective which opens up new research questions. Thus, he suggests that this theory represents an advance on the earlier theories rather than a major paradigm shift.

Why do some people get ill in response to stress and others do not?

It is often claimed that stress can cause all sorts of diseases including cancer. In fact consideration of the life events literature suggests that the evidence linking stress and many diseases is far from clear. Evidence is much clearer that experiencing certain stressors can have negative impacts in terms of increasing risk of coronary heart disease and can impact on immune functioning and day-to-day deterioration in health outcomes (e.g. Everson et al, 1996a, 2001; Cohen, 2005). However, not everyone who feels stressed becomes ill, distressed or experiences stress-related disruptions to their normal health behaviours. In fact, researchers now believe that certain individuals are more vulnerable to the effects of stress due to differences in their psychological as well as biological makeup. As you will see in Chapter 5, the effects of stress can be buffered by having a good social support network of friends and family and being well equipped to cope with different stressful situations. Personality also plays an important role in the stress process and will be covered in detail in Chapter 6. A number of personality traits have been found to predispose people to respond negatively to stress (e.g. type A personality, neuroticism, perfectionism). This is another example of the stress-diathesis paradigm. For example, individuals who have perfectionistic tendencies are more likely to experience serious psychological distress after each stressful encounter as it represents a chance for them to fail to meet their high standards (see O'Connor et al, 2007). Therefore, as you can imagine, people who are perfectionistic may be more vulnerable to suffering from the negative effects of stress in the future.

As well as psychological differences, researchers have identified biological differences in the way people respond to and recover from stressful situations. It has been proposed that certain individuals generally may have a large physiological response to stress (this process is known as **stress reactivity**), while for others the body may take much longer to return to normal once the stressor has passed (this process is known as **stress recovery**). In both cases, over time, the body is likely to experience greater wear and tear. If such differences exist, then they may explain why some people are more likely to become ill as a result of stress and others do not. These exciting developments are considered in the next section.

Stress reactivity

The central idea linked to the 'stress reactivity hypothesis' is that individuals who have large emotional and physiological responses to stress may be more likely to develop health problems in the future (Kamarck and Lovallo, 2003). In particular, people who are prone to having dramatic increases in heart rate and/or blood pressure after stressful situations may be at greater risk of developing high blood pressure and cardiovascular disease. Over the last 25 years, evidence has accumulated in support of this hypothesis from animal as well as human studies. In a sample of monkeys, Manuck, Kaplan and Clarkson (1983) found greater evidence of heart disease in monkeys who were previously identified as being high reactors to stress compared to the low reactors. The high reactors were also found to be more aggressive than the low reactors. In a human study, the results from the Kuopio Heart Study in Finland showed that men who had a greater cardiovascular response to stress were more likely to develop hypertension (i.e. high blood pressure) and stroke (Everson et al, 1996a, 2001). In another longitudinal study known as the Coronary Artery Risk Development in Young Adults (CARDIA) study, Matthews et al (2004) found that cardiovascular reactivity to stress at the beginning of the study was associated with higher blood pressure levels 13 years later!

However, not all studies have been supportive with several researchers suggesting that the mixed findings may be associated with methodological inconsistencies (e.g. using different laboratory stress challenges; time of testing, Nebel et al, 1996; Linden et al, 1998; Kamarck and Lovallo, 2003) and with individual differences (e.g. cynical hostility (see Chapter 6), morningness-eveningness; Kamarck and Lovallo, 2003; Willis et al, 2005) which may obscure the effects. For example, Willis et al (2005) found that stress reactivity levels were moderated by morningness-eveningness (i.e. the extent to which you are a 'lark', who prefers doing tasks in the morning, or an 'owl' who prefers the evening). They found that 'owls' had higher heart rate generally and in response to stress in the afternoon compared to the morning. Therefore, it seems that the research into the impact of stress reactivity is far from clear-cut, nevertheless, there is fairly strong evidence showing that some people at least who have large physiological responses to stress may be at greater risk of becoming ill following the long-term effects of stress.

Stress recovery

More recently, researchers have turned their attention to exploring the impact on health outcomes of the amount of time it takes the body to return to normal after stress. This is known as stress recovery and it is proposed that people who take longer to recover may be more vulnerable to future ill health (e.g. Schuler and O'Brien, 1997; Schneider et al, 2003). For example, in a study by Steptoe and Marmot (2005) in which the effects of stress reactivity and post-stress recovery on blood pressure three years later were investigated, they showed that increases in blood pressure levels three years later were most strongly associated with longer post-stress recovery. More impressively, these effects were independent of all the other risk factors measured (e.g. age, gender, body mass index, socio-economic status, smoking status, hypertension medication, etc.). Steptoe and Marmot (2005) also suggested that post-stress recovery may become more important as we get older. When we are young our recovery from stress tends to be swift and efficient, whereas, as we age, it may become less well controlled. One reason for this may be linked to McEwen's concept of allostatic load – longer post-stress recovery may develop as a result of wear and tear to the cardiovascular system caused by the body having to frequently respond to stress over several decades. This area of research is relatively new, therefore we cannot draw firm conclusions about the importance of stress recovery; however, the initial findings are promising.

Conclusions

We have presented a range of perspectives on stress and its relationship with health. These have included research which has sought to establish links between the existence of objective stressors (such as measures of major life events) and physical health outcomes, research which has focused on the appraisal of stress (e.g. drawing on transactional theory), and research which has shed light on physiological processes. Across this research gradually stronger links are emerging between stressors, the processes whereby stressors lead to disease (e.g. impaired immune functioning) and actual disease outcomes. However, we are still a long way from knowing for sure the extent to which stress is implicated in most diseases.

At the start of this chapter we asked you to consider whether stress has increased in recent years. It is of course not possible to give a definitive answer to this question. Clearly the types of stressors we experience have changed over the last 50 years. For most in western society, standards of living, working conditions, life expectancy and health have improved. Thus it might seem we have little to complain about. However, the pace of life seems to be ever increasing and the rate of change in technology and employment (for example) imposes new stressors. It is certainly the case that people are more aware of stress due to the work of psychologists and social scientists and the publicity that this has generated. Some have even suggested that stress is produced, or at least exacerbated by the increased awareness and expectation of stress in society (e.g. Pollock, 1988). While this may be a negative impact of our increased knowledge of stress, information about the impacts of psychological (as well as physiological) processes is essential for improving individual health and well-being.

Summary

References to 'stress' are widespread in society but the term is used in different ways in different contexts. Lazarus suggested that stress is best regarded as a rubric or umbrella term which covers a wide range of variables (including stressors such as life events or hassles, and strain outcomes, such as physical symptoms or depression). Historically, stress has been variously viewed as a stimulus, a response or in terms of an interaction between the two. Selye's influential work on the general adaptation syndrome focused particularly on the physiological response. More recent approaches to research on allostatic load, which build on Selye's work, have helped to explain the ways in which stressors lead to disease.

Psychologists have developed a range of different perspectives on stress. Life events researchers claim that major life events are a key predictor of disease. Transactional researchers have focused on appraisals of stress and specifically the impacts of appraisals of minor day-to-day hassles and uplifts. Conservation of resource theorists focus on the impact of loss of resources as the main predictor of stressors. These approaches are sometimes seen as in conflict but can also be viewed as all contributing a useful perspective on a complex phenomenon. All have had some success in predicting negative health and psychological outcomes. However, links between stressors and major physical health outcomes such as breast cancer have not been established.

People do clearly differ in their individual responses to stress, so some will get ill in response to stressors while others will not. For example, it is likely that some people are physiologically more reactive to stressors and/or take longer to recover.

Key concepts and terms

Allostatic load
Conservation of resources
  (COR) model
Diseases of adaptation
General adaptation syndrome
  (GAS)
Hassles and uplifts scale
Hierarchical linear modelling

Life events
Social Readjustment Rating
  Scale
Stress
Stress diathesis
Stress reactivity
Stress recovery
Transactional theory

Sample essay titles

- 'Having a stressful life increases the likelihood of contracting disease.' Evaluate this statement with reference to examples from the psychological literature.

- Compare and contrast the transactional approach and the conservation of resources approach to stress.

- Why do some people get ill in response to stress and others do not? Discuss.

- Critically evaluate two approaches to measuring the effects of stress on health.

Further reading

Journal articles

Dohrenwend, B.P. (2000). The role of adversity and stress in psychopathology: some evidence and its implications for theory and research. *Journal of Health and Social Behaviour*, 41, 1–19.

Hobfoll, S. (2001). The influence of culture, community, and the nested-self in the stress process: advancing conservation of resources theory. *Applied Psychology: An International Review*, 50, 337–421. (See also the subsequent articles in this journal by Lazarus, Schwarzer and others.)

Kamarck, T.W., and Lovallo, W.R. (2003). Cardiovascular reactivity to psychological challenge: Conceptual and measurement considerations. *Psychosomatic Medicine*, 65, 9–21.

Lazarus, R.S. (1990). Theory-based stress measurement. *Psychological Inquiry*, 1, 3–13.

McEwen, B.S. (1998). Protective and damaging effects of stress mediators. *New England Journal of Medicine*, 338, 171–179.

4 Stress and health in context

Chapter 3 examined a range of different approaches to stress and considered the links between stress and health. In this chapter we look at the effect of environmental or contextual factors on stress and their relationship to health.

In the first section, we consider the effect of **socio-economic status** (SES) and **social inequality** on stress and health. It is well established worldwide that poverty and deprivation are associated with poor health and that even within affluent societies lower SES is linked to poorer health. We consider the role of stress in this relationship.

We then consider stress at work in a subsequent section. For most people, their job determines their income and therefore their SES. Indeed, researchers typically classify individuals into social classes based on their occupation using formal classification systems such as the UK National Statistics Socio-Economic Classification (NS-SEC; National Statistics, 2002). Most people spend a significant proportion of their lives at work and evidence suggests that many people feel that it is a major source of stress (Smith et al, 2000). *Work stress* is also of great interest to employers who need to have healthy and productive workforces.

Work stress is also known to have implications beyond the work environment. If we feel stress at work this cannot always be easily switched off when we go home, and similarly major problems in our personal lives may affect our work. Work stressors may impact even more on our home lives if we work long hours and take work home with us. Increasingly, the barriers between work and home are being eroded by new technology and changing working patterns (Major and Germano, 2006). Therefore, researchers have examined the relationships between work and home lives, looking at such concepts as work–family conflict, work–home spillover and work–life balance.

In the final section of the chapter we discuss ways to intervene to reduce stress, with a particular focus on work stress. This includes what governments, organizations and individuals themselves can do to reduce stress. Thus there are four sections to this chapter: 1) socio-economic status, stress and health; 2) work stress and *occupational health psychology*; 3) stressors in work and home life; 4) preventing and reducing stress at work.

Learning outcomes

When you have completed this chapter you should be able to:

1. Discuss the impact and the causes of social inequality on health.
2. Describe and evaluate key theories of work stress.
3. Describe the impacts on well-being of a range of different types of stressor, e.g. family stressors, conflict between home and family, etc.
4. Discuss the ways stress can be reduced in the workplace.

Socio-economic status, stress and health

Poverty is linked to poorer health *within* most countries. It is easy to think of reasons why this might be the case. Poorer housing conditions, inadequate diet and reduced access to health care services are just a few potential explanations. However, there is a difference between the relationship found within each country and what we observe when we compare one country with another (i.e. comparisons *between* countries).

We might expect that, even in the western world, relatively more prosperous countries would have relatively lower mortality than poorer countries. However, comparing countries, we find that in poor countries increases in gross national product (and average income) over time are correlated with life expectancy but above a certain threshold this correlation disappears, that is, there is no further increase in longevity as people become richer. Wilkinson (1996: 29) calls this the '*epidemiological transition*'. Yet within these countries there remains a strong link between income and mortality.

Wilkinson suggested that in affluent societies (beyond the epidemiological transition), health is affected less by changes in material standards and more by **relative poverty** (Wilkinson, 1992, 1996, 1997). Wilkinson argues that it is our position in this hierarchy, including our feelings of relative advantage/ disadvantage within society, that causes stress and poorer health. He considered England and Japan to illustrate this phenomenon. In 1970 England and Japan had very similar life expectancies and similar income distribution. However, between 1970 and the 1990s Japan's income distribution shifted to become much narrower (that is, people had more similar incomes clustered around the mean), while in England the distribution became much wider (with increasing differences between the richest and poorest). At the same time, Japan's life expectancy increased dramatically while the UK moved down the international longevity league tables. Wilkinson argues that this phenomenon is not easily explained by factors such as health policies or nutrition.

Potential explanations of this effect include the role of psychological factors associated with the stress of relatively low social status in an affluent society. This explanation is bolstered by animal studies. For example, Wilkinson (1996) draws on Sapolsky's (1993) work showing that baboons lower in dominance hierarchies show higher levels of glucocorticoids indicating more frequent stress responses that could be detrimental to immunological functioning. In addition these lower dominance animals have higher resting blood pressure and their blood pressure returns more slowly to resting levels following stressful encounters. High status animals also show changes in hormonal and cardiovascular functioning indicative of stress when their position in the hierarchy changes, for example, when a larger male is introduced into their group. Similar correspondence between such physiological indices of stress response and social position is observed in people, e.g. among civil servants working at different levels within government (Marmot et al, 1991; Wilkinson, 1996).

A further puzzling finding is that, while SES is strongly linked to mortality in men (when their SES is determined by their occupation) this is not the case for women. In fact, women's mortality is more strongly affected by socio-economic class when they are classified according to their husband's job and not their own (Bartley et al, 1994). One explanation is that, traditionally, a husband has been the main breadwinner and his participation in the workforce was often more enduring. Thus men's occupation has more influence on the overall living standards of the family and so determined family members' positions within the societal hierarchy.

Traditionally, it has been hypothesized that inequalities in health are due to material/structural and cultural/behavioural differences between socio-economic groups. However, researchers debated whether social inequality *causes* ill health or ill health *causes* social inequality (Carroll et al, 1993). This has given rise to two opposing explanations. The first is known as the **social causation hypothesis** which states that low SES causes ill health. In other words, factors associated with occupying a low socio-economic position negatively impact on health. The alternative explanation is known as the **social drift hypothesis** which states that ill health causes low SES, that is, when an individual becomes ill, they drift down the socio-economic hierarchy because they may be unable to hold down a job. In general, more evidence supports the former explanation. In longitudinal studies following large samples of individuals over time, baseline measures of SES have been found to be good predictors of subsequent health status, whereas health status has been found to be a weaker predictor of SES. Moreover, if ill health caused SES decline one might expect to see differences between fast-acting fatal illnesses (e.g. lung cancer) where there is usually little time to change SES and chronic illnesses (e.g. chronic bronchitis). Yet the SES gradient is seen equally strongly in both types of illness (Carroll et al, 1993).

Stress and social inequality

Cardiovascular disease has been found to be associated with SES and this relationship is not eliminated after conventional risk factors such as smoking are taken into account. This has led researchers to search for additional factors that explain these social inequalities. Two hypotheses have been suggested relating to the role of stress in contributing to social inequality (e.g. Adler et al, 1994). First, the differential exposure hypothesis maintains that the higher prevalence of health problems in low socio-economic groups may be associated with a greater exposure to psychological stressors in these groups. Second, the differential vulnerability hypothesis suggests that individuals in lower socio-economic groups are less well equipped to cope with stressors due to having fewer resources (e.g.

having less money to buy healthy foods, choosing less effective coping strategies, and having limited social support networks) and as such their impact is much greater in these groups. Evidence supporting both hypotheses has been found, although the most consistent findings relate to the differential vulnerability hypothesis. However, Stronks et al (1998) have suggested that the importance of the differential exposure hypothesis has been underestimated.

Cohen, Doyle and Baum (2006) investigated the link between SES and a number of stress hormones. After controlling for race, age, gender and body mass index, the results showed that lower SES was associated with higher levels of cortisol, adrenaline and noradrenaline, mirroring Sapolsky's work with baboons. More impressively, Cohen et al also showed that the effects of SES on these stress hormones were mediated via smoking status, not eating breakfast and having a less diverse social network. These findings emphasize the importance of psychological, biological and behavioural factors in understanding the effects of SES on health. They suggest that health behaviours and social resources, typifying lower SES, explain why those in lower SES positions suffer greater stress-related illness.

Work stress and occupational health psychology

Investigating and reducing work stress has become a major focus of a newly established field of psychology known as occupational health psychology. The US National Institute of Occupational Safety and Health (NIOSH) states that 'Occupational Health Psychology concerns the application of psychology to improving the quality of working life and to protecting and promoting the safety, health and wellbeing of workers' (NIOSH, 2004). The emphasis here is on reducing occupational stress, injuries and illness and there are now a number of postgraduate courses which are concerned with psychosocial and organizational issues relevant to occupational health and safety (see Chapter 11). The research literature on stress is vast but some key models of work stress can be identified.

Theories and models of work stress

A number of writers have produced useful frameworks and models summarizing key variables which might cause stress for individuals at work (Warr, 1987; Cooper et al, 1988). For example, Warr (1987) listed nine key stressors which are like vitamins, in that a certain amount is essential for good mental health. Thus, to minimize stress, a job needs to have: 1) appropriate levels of *personal control* over activities and events, and 2) the right amount of *opportunity to use existing skills* and develop new skills. The job also needs to provide 3) *opportunities to pursue goals or meet demands*, and have the right amount of 4) *variety*, 5) *clarity* and 6) *opportunity for interpersonal contact*. Like some vitamins (e.g. vitamins A and D), either too much or too little of these variables may be bad for well-being. However, the final three factors (like vitamins C and E), are only thought to be stressful if there is a shortage. These are 7) *money*, 8) *physical security* (e.g. job security or working conditions) and holding a 9) *valued social position*. This framework simply focuses on external environmental stressors. However, as we noted in Chapter 3, people vary in their perceptions of stressors and in their ability to cope, so what is a reasonable demand for one person will overload another.

Focus 4.1

What are theories and models? Why do we need them in health (and occupational health) psychology?

Theories are descriptions of how things, or people, are constructed and how they behave. Science is the process of generating theories and testing their capacity to account for observations of events. As scientists, psychologists use theory in their efforts to *describe, explain, predict* and *change* cognition, emotion and behaviour. In psychology, theory includes descriptions and categorizations that allow us to distinguish between types of people, for example in relation to cognition or personality, and between types of social situation, for example in terms of work demands or role relations. Identifying correlations between characterizations of people (e.g. personality) or jobs (e.g. work demands) and health or health-related outcomes is the first step in theory development which next proceeds to articulating processes which explain correlations. These causal explanations describe sequences of interconnected mechanisms underlying psychological responses and behavioural patterns. Once such processes are understood we can predict relationships between theorized variables and intervene to change such processes (Abraham, 2004). For example, see the development of psychological processes linking personality to coronary heart disease (as described in Chapter 6). Thus, developing and testing theory helps us explain *why* people behave differently and thereby facilitates prediction of the behaviour of particular types of people or people in particular roles and/or situations (Abraham, 2004).

The terms 'framework', 'model' and 'theory' are often used interchangeably in psychology and the distinctions are not clear-cut. However, generally speaking, a framework is a loose set of constructs that does not clearly specify linking mechanisms. Models may provide clearer links between constructs but theories should ideally specify interconnecting causal mechanisms which can be experimentally tested (see our discussion of testing social cognition models in Chapter 7).

In research in the area of occupational health psychology, many theoretical constructions are more accurately described by the term 'model' than 'theory' and we still have few theories to help us understand the processes whereby work stressors may damage health. Better theories would help us to design more effective interventions. Arguably, theoretical development is more advanced in other areas of health psychology such as predicting and changing motivation and health behaviour (see, e.g., Chapters 7–9).

The limitations of such frameworks have prompted some researchers to develop more complex models incorporating all possible stressors and influences (Beehr and Newman, 1978; Cooper et al, 1988). For example, the model developed by Beehr and Newman incorporated 150 variables. Unfortunately, such models are too complex to be easily testable or to provide practical guidance to those attempting to provide interventions to reduce stress (see Chapter 9 on sustainability of behaviour change interventions). The breadth of the concept of stress, and the large number of variables involved has undoubtedly rendered it challenging to develop concise and comprehensive theories of work stress.

Activity 4.1

Working in groups, make a list of all the things that you think are stressful about work (i.e. independent variables). Then note down individual characteristics that would allow some people to cope with these stressors better than others, for example, personality (see Chapter 6) or other resources they might have (i.e. moderators – see Research methods box 5.1). Then, finally, think of all the possible outcomes (i.e. physical, psychological and behavioural) that might result from high levels of stress (i.e. dependent variables).

Much has been written about the key elements of a good theory (e.g. Popper, 1963). Usually this includes that the theory should be falsifiable and concise (or parsimonious). Do you think it would be possible to produce a concise and falsifiable theory of the causes of work stress from your three lists of variables? Discuss why it might be difficult to produce a good theory of work stress.

Thus, most research has focused on more specific testable models focusing on a limited number of variables and potential interactions between them. Two such models have stimulated a great deal of research in recent years: the *job demand–control (JDC) model* (also known as the job strain model; Karasek, 1979; Karasek and Theorell, 1990) and Siegrist's *effort–reward imbalance model* (Siegrist, 1996).

Karasek's job demand–control model

In its original form this model focused on two key aspects of work – demands and control – as suggested by the name of the model (Karasek, 1979). A high demand job is a job with heavy workload, fast pace of work and conflicting demand (see Figure 4.1). A high control job means the employee has a say in decisions relating to their job. The model predicts that jobs which have a combination of high demand and low levels of control would result in high levels of psychological and physical strain for employees, i.e. they would be 'high strain' jobs (see Figure 4.2). Typical jobs of this type might include call centre work or being a junior doctor or nurse in a busy casualty department. The opposite combination, low levels of demand and high levels of control would result in low levels of strain. While there is a common view that it is senior executives in a company who are likely to experience stress, it is in fact the case that those lower

Figure 4.1 A high demand job is a job with heavy workload.
Source: Corbis Premium RF/Alamy.

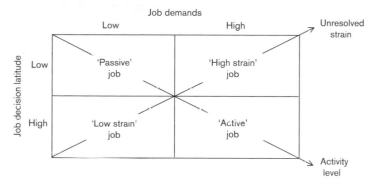

Figure 4.2 The job strain model.

Source: Karasek, R.A. (1979). Job demands, job decision latitude and metal strain: Implications for job design. Administrative Science Quarterly, 24, 285–308.

down an organization suffer the most heart disease (e.g. Marmot et al, 1991). The JDC model suggests that this is because executives are able to exercise greater control and therefore reduce the effects of demands.

The JDC model also describes two further job types. Active jobs are those with high levels of demand and high control. These are hypothesized to be less stressful than high strain jobs because they offer the individual opportunities to develop protective behaviours, encourage active learning and motivate engagement in new behaviours (Karasek, 1979). Thus, for example, a high level manager might have high job demands, but may also be in a position to delegate some of the work. By contrast, passive jobs, that is, those with low demands and low control (for example, an assistant in a seaside cafe out of season) are essentially boring and are suggested to result in learned helplessness and reduced activity. The original conceptualization of the model (Karasek, 1979) emphasized the importance of the interaction between the two variables in predicting strain. In those with low efforts and high rewards. Research is rather more mixed where studies have looked at the effects of an imbalance between efforts and rewards. A number of studies have found that effort–reward imbalance also increases the risk of physical symptoms, psychological distress and emotional exhaustion over and above that associated with efforts and rewards separately (e.g. Pikhart et al, 2001; Niedhammer et al, 2004) but some have failed to find this effect (e.g. Siegrist et al, 1997; Kudielka et al, 2004).

Siegrist (2005) suggests that the model may be useful for designing worksite interventions. For example, improving leadership skills of supervisors and increasing their awareness of the need for recognition and constructive feedback may help increase perceptions of rewards among employees. He also suggests that structural interventions designed to increase non-monetary incentives, e.g. flexible working time, job security and increasing contractual fairness, may also reduce imbalance.

While the ERI model focuses primarily on the workplace, van dem Knesebeck and Siegrist (2003) suggest that the model may be relevant in other social contexts. For example, they found that elderly men and women who reported non-reciprocal social exchange in social relationships (e.g. in marital, parental and other social roles) were twice as likely to experience depressive symptoms.

Comparing the JDC and ERI

There is some overlap between these two models. Specifically, the concept of effort is similar to that of demands in the JDC. However, there are also differences between the two models. First, only the ERI incorporates a measure of individual difference (i.e. overcommitment). Second, the models differ in their approach to control. JDC focuses on control over tasks, a feature which is not included in the ERI despite clear evidence of its importance in predicting health outcomes. Some researchers have combined the JDC and ERI to predict psychological and physical health outcomes (e.g. Bosma et al, 1998; van Vegchel et al, 2005). Studies have typically indicated that variables from the ERI, i.e. effort–reward imbalance (and in some cases overcommitment), together with low job control (from the JDC model), predict negative health outcomes.

Overall, research based on both these models has told us a great deal about the range of factors that are stressful at work and how they impact on our health. They also suggest ways in which work can be structured and organized to reduce stress. A limitation of both models is that they focus on work in isolation, failing to take into account how work and other roles are interlinked. Stressors in home and family life cannot be clearly separated from those in work life.

Stressors in work and home life

How does work life or university life affect you during your leisure time? If you are stressed during the day do you worry in the evening and feel low, or do you switch off and make sure you do something pleasant to compensate for the hard day you have had? These kinds of questions have interested researchers investigating the relationships between stressors in different domains of life and they are becoming increasingly important as the boundaries between work and home life are reduced. More women (including those with young children) are now working so both men and women occupy potentially conflicting roles. Furthermore, new technologies such as laptop computers, emails and mobile phones mean that employees can work anywhere. This is linked to a trend for work to be more flexible with more people working outside the traditional 9-to-5 day to cater for demands for 24-hour services (e.g. supermarkets, call centres) as well as to facilitate working in global organizations operating across time zones. This has led to an increasing concern among employees about lack of *work–life balance* (Major and Germano, 2006).

Three types of relationships between work and home life have been considered (Staines, 1980). First, the impact of work was hypothesized to **spillover** to affect the individual at home. For example, those experiencing negative emotions at work would take these to the home environment. However, this hypothesis has been extended beyond stressors and is assumed to also apply to activities and behaviour. So those with active and stimulating jobs would seek similar types of experience out of work. In contrast the **compensation** hypothesis, suggested that, for example, those with active stimulating jobs might seek calm and undemanding leisure activities and vice versa. A third hypothesis, the **segmentation** hypothesis, suggested no relationship, implying that work and non-work domains are independent (Staines, 1980). Studies have tended to support the spillover hypothesis. For example, Meissner (1971) found that individuals who were isolated at work were also isolated at home. However, most studies were cross-sectional leaving the direction of causation unclear. Did work stressors spillover to the home or were home stressors affecting people at work, or was a third variable (such as personality) responsible for the link? Longitudinal studies have helped clarify these relationships. For example, Williams and Alliger (1994) showed that spillover occurs in both directions, with moods experienced in one environment influencing those in the other. However, in common with most other studies, they found that work seems to interfere more with family life than vice versa.

These findings have been extended by examining *crossover* of stress. This is the idea that stressors in one environment (usually work) not only affect the individual directly experiencing them when that person is at home but also affect others who share the home environment. Support for this phenomenon has now been found in numerous studies (Westman, 2001). For example, a study of more than 2000 couples found striking evidence that workplace aggression experienced by one member of a couple was associated with an increase in psychological distress in their partner (Haines et al, 2006). Children have also been found to suffer from their parents' work stressors. Repetti and Wood (1997) studied working mothers and their pre-school children in a laboratory setting after work for five consecutive days. They found that on days when they reported heavier workloads, or where they had experienced interpersonal conflicts, the mothers were more withdrawn from their children. Repetti (1994) found similar effects when she studied men's interactions with older children.

Work–life conflict

Relationships between work and other aspects of life have been investigated in terms of role conflict, that is, when a person feels incompatible pressures from two separate roles. Most commonly this has focused on **work–family conflict** (Greenhaus and Beutell, 1985). For example, it may be that *time* spent at work prevents people from participating in family activities, or it may be that *strain* experienced at work affects people psychologically at home, or that particular *behaviours* found useful at work spillover and cause problems in the home environment. Thus, Greenhaus and Beutell introduced the concepts of *time-based*, *strain-based* and *behaviour-based conflict*. Like spillover, conflict can occur in two directions, work-to-family interference and family-to-work interference (O'Driscoll et al, 2006). Recently, there has been some criticism of the emphasis on 'family' implied by the term 'work–family conflict', as increasing numbers of people live alone but nevertheless may experience conflicts with personal life and leisure activity. Some researchers now prefer to look at 'work–life' conflict (e.g. Siegel et al, 2005).

Research suggests that in the past work-to-family conflict (i.e. work interfering with family) was typically higher among men than women, while family-to-work conflict was higher in women. However, research suggests that these effects are now levelling out (O'Driscoll et al, 2006). This is probably due to more equal roles in both work and home life. The negative effects of work–family conflict include increased work turnover and poorer work performance, reduced job satisfaction, increased distress and depression, poorer physical health and increased alcohol consumption.

Grandey and Cropanzano (1999) suggest that the effect of work and family stress can be explained by conservation of resources theory (Hobfoll, 1989; see Chapter 2). For example, conflict arising in the work role may result in fewer resources (such as time) being available to spend in the other role. However, those with additional resources such as marital partners may suffer less than those with fewer overall resources. Consistent with this, research has found that long work hours are linked to work–family conflict (e.g. Major et al, 2002) and that having a partner is linked to reduced conflict both from work to family and family to work (Brough and Kelling, 2002).

Work–family and family–work facilitation

Positive experiences at work may also spillover and lead to greater happiness at home and vice versa. However, until recently, the bulk of research has focused on stress and role conflict. With current trends towards a more positive psychology, however, researchers are looking at these beneficial impacts. A range of terms have been used to describe this process including *positive spillover, work–family (and family–work) facilitation, enhancement* or *enrichment* (O'Driscoll et al, 2006). These terms all broadly refer to the idea that engagement in work has beneficial impacts on engagement in the family and vice versa. For example, skills and knowledge gained in one domain may be beneficial in the other. Similarly, affective assets (positive moods or confidence) or capital assets (e.g. financial or social) acquired in one domain may help in the other (Carlson et al,

2006). Grzywacz and Bass (2003) have found that optimal adult mental health is found in conditions where both **work–family and family–work facilitation** is high and work–family conflict is low. We await further research to find out how we can achieve this optimal state. However the following sections will look at how interventions are currently used to reduce stress at work.

Preventing and reducing stress in the workplace

A number of different types of intervention have been used in the work setting. Organizational change and job design interventions reduce stress by modifying the job to remove stressors. Other types of intervention aim at modifying the individual's ability to cope with stress, for example, by training, counselling or by changing the individual's physical fitness. These are described in further detail in the following sections.

Preventing or reducing stress by changing the work environment

Removing or reducing stressors at source wherever possible seems both sensible and ethically desirable. Furthermore, the focus of the work stress models discussed above is to determine sources of stressors with, by implication, a view to intervening to change the nature of jobs. This may be done by, for example, changing task characteristics such as job control as suggested by the JDC model.

This type of intervention has gained in importance with the increased public and governmental pressure to reduce work stressors throughout Europe, Australia and North America. For example, in the UK, the Health and Safety at Work Act (1974: 2) states that employers have a duty 'to ensure as far as is reasonably practicable, the health, safety and welfare at work of all employees'. Since the 1990s this has been interpreted to include work demands, organization and work relationships (HSE, 1995). UK employers are now also required to assess the risk of stress-related ill health arising from work and to take steps to control such risks. This approach is now formalized within the Management Standards approach to work stress advocated by the UK Health and Safety Executive (see Table 4.1). For each of the standards listed there is the additional standard that 'systems are in place locally to respond to any individual concerns' (HSE, 2007). These standards are not legally enforced, rather they are recommendations to help employers meet legal obligations.

Interventions aimed at changing the workplace and thereby reducing or removing causes of stress are perhaps the most challenging type of stress management both to conduct and to evaluate rigorously and thus there is less research evidence in this area (Randall et al, 2005). For example, a meta-analysis (see Research methods box 8.1) by van der Klink et al (2001) considered 48 experimental evaluations of stress reduction interventions to be of sufficient rigor to be included (see too discussion of intervention evaluation in Chapter 9). However, only five of these were organizational interventions aimed at reducing stressors (the rest being interventions targeting the individual). These researchers

Table 4.1 UK Health and Safety Executive Management Standards (HSE, 2007)

Stressor area	Description	The standard
Demands	Includes workload, work patterns and work environment	Employees indicate that they are able to cope with the demands of their jobs
Control	How much say the person has in the way they do their work	Employees indicate that they have a say about the way they do their work
Support	Includes the encouragement, sponsorship and resources provided by the organization, line management and colleagues	Employees indicate that they receive adequate information and support from their colleagues and superiors
Relationship	Includes promoting positive working to avoid conflict and dealing with unacceptable behaviour	Employees indicate that they are not subjected to unacceptable behaviours, e.g. bullying at work
Role	Whether people understand their role within the organization and whether the organization ensures that the person does not have conflicting roles	Employees indicate that they understand their role and responsibilities
Change	How organizational change (large or small) is managed and communicated in the organization	Employees indicate that the organization engages them frequently when undergoing an organizational change

found no overall significant effect across the five studies. However, a study by Bond and Bunce (2001) found that increases in job control were related to improved well-being and sickness absence, offering some grounds for optimism. Such interventions face numerous challenges. For example, uncontrolled variables, such as changes in market conditions causing job insecurity, may undermine positive influences. Furthermore, organizational change can itself be stressful. Murphy (2003) suggests that simultaneous individual interventions may be needed to help people adjust to planned organizational change. Nevertheless, while evidence concerning such interventions is as yet limited, the pressure to reduce the causes of stress in the workplace remains high.

In recent years, the call for greater work–life balance has led to new organizational interventions aimed at helping people to manage the interface between home and work, for example the introduction of policies enabling employees to work more flexibly both in terms of working hours and work location. Such interventions might be expected to enhance employees' control and thereby reduce stress. As yet there is little evidence for such benefits (Grzywacz et al, in press) although one study has shown that perceived flexibility was linked to improved well-being and health behaviours (Grzywacz et al, 2007).

Reducing stress by stress management training

A common approach to reducing stress in the workplace is to offer employees **stress management training** courses, a form of intervention which is not unique to the workplace. There is no set format for these courses and they are likely to include information about the nature of stress and a series of emotion-focused and problem-focused coping strategies (see also Chapter 5).

Emotion-focused techniques typically involve some form of *relaxation* training. This frequently involves a technique known as *progressive muscle relaxation* in which individuals are typically instructed to focus on specific groups of muscles in turn and progressively tense them and then release the tension (e.g. 'Clench your fist as tight as you can, then let it go'). Finally, they aim to tense and release all muscles together. Relaxation may be accompanied by the use of music or visualization techniques (e.g. 'Imagine you are lying on a beach, you can hear the waves in the distance and feel the gentle breeze'). Tapes are also available for people to use these techniques at home. **Biofeedback** is also sometimes used as an adjunct to relaxation. This gives individuals continuous feedback throughout a relaxation session about physiological processes such as muscle tension or blood pressure.

Another emotion-focused technique which involves relaxation is meditation. The most well-known approach to meditation is transcendental meditation (TM) which was popular in the UK in the 1960s and 1970s after the Beatles went to India to train with the Maharishi Mahesh Yogi, the founder of the TM movement. However, a number of other forms of yoga have since developed which are simpler and more appropriate to the work setting, e.g. Benson's (1976) relaxation response. These methods rely on mental rather than physical calming by, for example, encouraging sitting in a relaxed comfortable position and breathing slowly while focusing on a word or phrase (such as 'peace' or 'mmmm' which is repeated silently with each exhalation). Like physical relaxation this aims to induce psychological and physical responses which are fundamentally incompatible with stress and tension.

Problem-focused techniques can include techniques such as assertiveness or teaching time management skills (see Chapter 9). However, the most commonly used techniques are derived from **cognitive behaviour therapy** (see also Chapter 11 on CBT competencies) which seek to alter people's appraisals of stressful situations, inhibit automatic thoughts and enhance coping skills. Some people exacerbate the stress they experience by negative cognitions. Thus, for example, when faced with a disagreement with a work colleague about how to do a piece of work, a typical thought might be 'he obviously does not like me, maybe no-one likes me'. This irrational response illustrates *personalizing* and *catastrophizing*. This would be explored with the individual and different responses considered, e.g. 'We obviously do not see eye to eye on this task. How can we resolve this difference?' This response is much less likely to generate stress and depression and more likely to lead to constructive problem solving. Stress management techniques which draw on cognitive behaviour therapy involve people examining their reactions and developing skills to stop what for many are automatic negative thoughts and to replace them with more constructive cognitions. This then leads to rehearsal of different appraisals and new coping skills. These kinds of techniques have been demonstrated to be effective in therapeutic interventions (e.g. DeRubeis and Crits-Christoph, 1998).

Stress management training courses vary greatly in the length of the course and the components used within the course. In the workplace they may consist of very brief one-off sessions for participants who are not particularly stressed at the outset. It is not surprising if evaluations of such interventions show little improvement. However, rigorous evaluations of longer training interventions for individuals with high levels of anxiety show significant improvements in well-being (e.g. Ganster et al, 1982). Identifying which components are responsible for benefits has proved more difficult (see Chapter 9). Comparisons between different methods often show all techniques to be equally successful. However, a meta-analytic review of workplace interventions has found that cognitive behavioural skills training was the most effective workplace intervention overall, although training which included a variety of methods was most effective for improving physiological symptoms (e.g. muscle tension; van der Klink et al, 2001).

Counselling

The provision of **counselling** services for distressed employees is now a popular form of intervention which aims to treat rather than prevent stress. Some companies provide their own in-house staff counselling service. However, frequently, services are provided by **employee assistance programmes** available to employees and (frequently) their families. Such services are provided by a specialist provider retained by companies. The level of service offered is variable and may range from telephone counselling and advice to the provision of a series of face-to-face counselling sessions. Typically employees are provided with a card offering a 24-hour telephone service. The best services offer a range of help which may include specialist legal and financial advice, relationship support and trauma counselling. Some are also providing online support and support for health behaviour change. It has proved difficult to rigorously evaluate these schemes because random allocation to treatment and control groups is not possible when individuals refer themselves for services. Furthermore, withholding treatment from distressed employees would be unethical. However, evaluations do suggest that employees find such services useful and they report improved well-being (e.g. McLeod and McLeod, 2001).

Worksite lifestyle change interventions

Physical fitness is the main lifestyle intervention which has clear benefits in terms of stress reduction. It can be seen as both an emotion-focused and a problem-focused strategy (Long and Flood, 1993). It can distract the individual from stressful emotions and invoke a relaxation response which is incompatible with stress. However, it can also increase people's confidence and self-esteem which may affect appraisal of their ability to cope with problems, that is, it may increase task-specific self-efficacy (see Chapter 8). Many workplaces now encourage physical activity by provision of sports facilities on site or negotiated rate reductions with local facilities. It is in an employer's interest to have a healthy workforce who will be less prone to sickness absence, and it may also have other organizational benefits in terms of employee relations. Exercise can be promoted at an individual or organizational level. While there is clear evidence for the effectiveness of exercise as a stress reduction strategy there is currently less research into the effectiveness of workplace exercise interventions (Taylor, 2000).

What type of intervention is most successful?

Removing stressors at source seems the most desirable and ethically acceptable approach but there have been relatively few successful interventions of this kind because **job redesign** operates in a complex context in which other factors can cancel out potential benefits. This weak evidence base is not a justification to abandon this type of intervention. Indeed, in the UK, any company that did so would be likely to fall foul of the Health and Safety at Work Act (1974). Instead Murphy (2003) advocates using a range of interventions. Many jobs are inherently stressful at times or include elements that will be stressful for some employees, while other employees will be suffering as a result of unavoidable stressors outside of work. The provision of a range of interventions which are based on the best possible evidence and which combine both organizational change and individual support would seem likely to offer the best chance of success.

Activity 4.2

Chris is a qualified social worker with a good track record. He is one of the most experienced workers in his team. He therefore has one of the heaviest caseloads including a number of children who are at risk of child abuse. He frequently works long hours and faces aggressive clients alone. He is feeling increasingly overloaded and most days can do little more than respond to crises. He often has to cancel routine visits and is unable to make constructive plans to work towards improving his clients' situations. Because he does not have time to get round to all his clients, he is anxious that one of the children in his care may be harmed before he has the chance to intervene. He feels that he does not get adequate support from his manager and gets little feedback about how well he is doing. Recently the situation has become so bad that Chris feels perpetually anxious and unable to sleep. He is beginning to feel that he can no longer cope with the job and is considering looking for alternative employment.

What do you think Chris' managers should do to alleviate the problem? Consider the role of each of the types of interventions described in this chapter.

Summary

Social inequality is linked to poorer health within countries around the world, even within affluent countries. In richer countries ill health and mortality are associated with relative poverty. Evidence suggests that it is low SES causing ill health rather than vice versa. Stress is implicated in this relationship. Those in lower SES positions are exposed to more stressors and tend to be more vulnerable to their effects.

The workplace has been a dominant focus of stress research and a number of models of work stress have been proposed. The JDC and the ERI models have been particularly influential. Together these models highlight the importance of having a manageable level of work demands (or efforts) and the need for these to be balanced by appropriate rewards, including recognition and status, and the importance of adequate levels of control over your job as well as adequate support from colleagues and management. There is evidence that a lack of these components is related to increased coronary heart disease.

Changes in the nature of work have led to an increase in concern about poor work–life balance. When work and family demands conflict or when work spills over into home life it can have negative impacts on individuals and on other family members. However work can also bring psychological benefits which may have positive effects on home life.

There are a range of interventions to reduce stress which include removing stressors by organizational interventions such as job redesign, reducing the impacts of stressors by stress management training, treating stressed individuals by counselling and changing aspects of lifestyle to help people to be able to resist or cope with stress. All can play a useful part in reducing the effects of stress at work as well as in other environments.

Key concepts and terms

Biofeedback
Cognitive behaviour therapy
Compensation
Counselling
Employee assistance
  programmes
Job redesign
Relative poverty
Segmentation
Social causation hypothesis

Social drift hypothesis
Social inequality
Socio-economic status
Spillover
Stress management
  training
Work–family and family–work
  facilitation
Work–family conflict
Workplace counselling

Sample essay titles

- Does being poor make people less healthy? Discuss with reference to psychological research.

- Evaluate current theoretical approaches to work stress. How useful have they been for guiding interventions to improve the work environment?

- 'Work stress is unpleasant for employees but it has no real implications beyond the workplace.' Discuss.

- Imagine you have been asked by a company management team to advise on how they should reduce stress amongst their employees. What evidence-based advice would you offer?

Further reading

Books

HSE (2007). The Management Standards. www.hse.gov.uk/stress/ standards/ standards.htm

Jones, F and Bright, J. (2001). Stress: Myth, Theory and Research. Pearson Education.

Journal articles

Bosma, H., Peter, R., Siegrist, J., and Marmot, M. (1998). Two alternative job stress models and the risk of coronary heart disease. *American Journal of Public Health*, 88, 68–74.

Karasek, R.A. (1979). Job demands, job decision latitude and mental strain: Implications for job design. *Administrative Science Quarterly*, 24, 285–308.

van der Klink, J.L., Blonk, R.W.B., Schene, A.H., and van Dijk, F.J.H. (2001). The benefits of interventions for work-related stress. *American Journal of Public Health*, 91, 270–276.

Wilkinson, R.G. (1997). Health inequalities: relative or absolute material standards? *British Medical Journal*, 314, 591–595.

5 Coping and social support

Chapters 3 and 4 examined a range of theories relating stress to health outcomes. However, not everyone reacts in the same way to the pressures of life. This chapter explores ways in which different approaches to coping and the availability of social support can affect health.

In the course of normal life we are all faced with a range of stressors and challenges. When faced with a threat such as failing an important exam or having an argument with a friend, how do you cope? Do you try to think calmly about how you can address the problem, do you feel angry and distressed and express your feelings, do you talk to a friend or do you go for a drink or cigarette? Perhaps you use several of these strategies? These are just a few of the many ways of coping that have been identified by researchers in a range of different typologies of **coping strategies**. Does the way you cope depend on the circumstances or do you behave consistently across different situations? For example, do you tend to adopt a problem-solving approach or, alternatively, deny the threat? Consistent coping tendencies are known as **coping styles** which are related to personality. How we cope affects the outcomes we experience. In this chapter we will consider a range of coping approaches and their implications for health.

Friends, family and work colleagues are, for most people, particularly important in times of stress. We may seek out our friends to listen to us express our feelings, distract us from insoluble problems or help us to find solutions. Thus, for many people, using **social support** is an important coping strategy and most measures of coping ask people about the extent to which they use social supports. Of course, social support depends on having a friend or network of friends who we can call on. Thus friends and family are regarded as **coping resources**. The availability of these resources seems to be important for our well-being regardless of whether they are providing social support in times of stress or whether we deliberately draw on them as a coping strategy. The chapter is divided into two sections: 1) coping; 2) social support.

Coping

Coping is a key element of Lazarus and Folkman's (1984) transactional theory of stress, described in Chapter 2. In this theory, coping is viewed as part of the stress process, defined as 'constantly changing cognitive and behavioural efforts to manage specific external and/or internal demands that are appraised as taxing or exceeding the resources of the person' (Lazarus and Folkman, 1984: 141). You may recall the two types of appraisal. **Primary appraisal** involves the individual assessing the potential harm, loss, threat or challenge imposed by the stressor, that is, what's at stake. This leads to **secondary appraisal** in which the individual evaluates the coping options and resources available. In the case of potentially failing an exam, primary appraisals might range from 'this does not matter too much, it's just a setback' to 'this means I am hopeless and my future is bleak'. Secondary appraisals will depend partially on the primary appraisal but also on the resources the individual feels they have (including their confidence, their intellectual resources, financial resources, etc.). In relation to the exam threat, secondary appraisals could include investigating the possibility of re-sitting the exam and planning how to do more work in future or eliciting the support of others to go out and 'drown your sorrows'. Thus appraisal provides the basis for coping and so leads finally to the outcome which may involve emotional responses, behaviour and health. Arranging to re-sit the exam and/or planning to do more work would be described as **problem-focused** strategies. These are strategies which involve trying to obtain information and formulate actions which will change the situation, e.g. to reduce or remove the impact of the stressor. However, 'drowning your sorrows' would be an example of an **emotion-focused** strategy which simply aims to regulate the emotions generated by the stressor, in this case, by avoiding thinking about it. An alternative emotion-focused approach would be to think about the problem in a different light (i.e. appraising it more positively, e.g., 'this has taught me a lesson I won't forget'). Thus coping is a *mediator* between the stress appraisal and the final outcome (see Focus box 5.2 for a further discussion of mediation).

To assess how people cope, Folkman and Lazarus (1988) developed a measure called the Ways of Coping (WOC) Questionnaire. They used factor analysis of responses to a range of coping items to produce eight overall measures. These are: 1) confrontative coping, 2) distancing, 3) self-controlling, 4) seeking social support, 5) accepting responsibility, 6) escape avoidance, 7) planful problem solving, and 8) positive reappraisal. Some subsequent researchers have criticized these measures on the grounds that other studies have failed to replicate these eight factors. For example, in a review of coping measures, Skinner et al (2003) argue that eight studies that used the WOC produced eight different sets of categories based on factor analyses with the number of categories ranging from two to nine. Carver, Scheier and Weintraub (1989) also criticized the model for its lack of comprehensive coverage of coping methods.

To overcome this problem, Carver et al (1989) produced an alternative, theory-based questionnaire called the *COPE*. This is based on both Lazarus' theory and their own model of behavioural self-regulation. The strategies measured by this questionnaire are shown in Research methods box 5.1. The measure includes more distinct types of strategies than the WOC questionnaire. However, there is considerable overlap between these two measures and both have proved popular and have been widely used in coping research over the last 20 years.

Research methods 5.1

Measuring coping using the COPE (adapted from Carver et al, 1989)

The COPE questionnaire consists of sub-scales to assess each of the following types of coping. The response scale can be adjusted to apply to a particular situation or to assess dispositional coping.

Primarily problem-focused coping

- *Active coping*, e.g. 'I take direct action to get around the problem'
- *Planning*, e.g. 'I make a plan of action'
- *Suppression of competing activities*, e.g. 'I put aside other activities in order to concentrate on this'
- *Restraint coping*, e.g. 'I hold off doing anything about it until the situation permits'
- *Seeking instrumental social support*, e.g. 'I try to get advice from someone about what to do'

Primarily emotion-focused coping

- *Seeking emotional social support*, e.g. 'I discuss my feelings with someone'
- *Focus on and venting emotion*, e.g. 'I get upset and let my emotions out'
- *Behavioural disengagement*, e.g. 'I give up the attempt to get what I want'
- *Mental disengagement*, e.g. 'I go to the cinema or watch television, to think about it less'
- *Positive reinterpretation and growth*, e.g. 'I learn something from the experience'
- *Denial*, e.g. 'I act as though it hasn't even happened'

... Continued

... Continued

- *Acceptance*, e.g. 'I learn to live with it'
- *Turn to religion*, e.g. 'I try to find comfort in my religion'
- *Alcohol/drug use*, e.g. 'I use alcohol and drugs to help me get through it'
- *Humour*, e.g. 'I make jokes about it'

Lazarus (1999) argues that there is no universally effective (or ineffective) coping strategy. What works in one situation will not work in another. Furthermore, Lazarus suggests that the effectiveness of coping strategies will depend on the type of person and the outcome you are considering. Different coping strategies may also be useful at different stages of dealing with a stressor. Folkman and Lazarus (1985) found that just before an exam, problem-focused coping strategies are used most, whereas in the period waiting for results emotion-focused strategies predominate. Emotion-focused approaches, such as denial, are often unhelpful because they leave the threat unchanged. However, in some situations, they may be useful in the short term. For example, when experiencing the symptoms of a heart attack, denial is likely to be dangerous and even life-threatening because it may lead to delay in seeking treatment. However, once in hospital, denial may be helpful in reducing the anxiety which is likely to exacerbate the medical condition. Once the patient is discharged from hospital denial again may be dangerous as it may lead to resistance to modifying health behaviours. Lazarus (1999) suggests that when there is nothing that can be done to alter the stressor or reduce the harm (i.e. when there is little control) then denial can be beneficial. Emotion-focused coping may also be important for people with high trait anxiety who are more likely to become anxious when faced by potential stressors. In a prospective study, Sultan et al (2008) found that emotion-focused coping enhanced glycaemic control among diabetics high in trait anxiety (so that trait anxiety moderated the emotion-focused coping–health outcome relationship). However, problem-focused coping was also found to reduce trait anxiety, suggesting that for this highly anxious group of patients both coping strategies were important.

Critical evaluation of coping research

The literature on coping is extensive and complex and has been much criticized, not least because it has provided limited information on which to base interventions (e.g. Somerfield, 1997). The limitations of classification systems and the over-reliance on questionnaires are key problems.

In this chapter we have considered two well-established classification systems but many others have been proposed. In a review, Skinner et al (2003) found over 100 different classification systems which, collectively, generated more than 400 ways of coping. Typically, these are classified into a range of higher order categories. The three most common higher level categories were a) problem-focused versus emotion-focused, b) approach versus avoidance, c) cognitive versus behavioural. Skinner et al suggest that this range of diverse classifications has made it difficult to make progress. They argue that many systems such as the two discussed above are based on exploratory factor analyses and, as a result, have a number of flaws. First, there is often a lack of clarity or distinctiveness in the different categories. Second, it is difficult to ensure that the categories are comprehensive and, finally, even where items do load onto a single category they may still represent more than one underlying category, which perhaps have a single underlying emotional tone. For example, both rumination and avoidance coping may load on to a single factor because worrying is common to both, even though the response is very different. Skinner et al (2003: 248) suggest that there is a need for a comprehensive list of ways of coping which can then be classified into 'conceptually clear and mutually exclusive action types'. They identify 13 families of coping which fit this description. They are problem solving (e.g. direct action); support seeking; escape (e.g. avoidance, disengagement and denial); distraction; cognitive restructuring (e.g. positive thinking); rumination (e.g. worry and self-blame); helplessness (e.g. giving up); social withdrawal; emotional regulation (e.g. by emotional expression or self-calming); information seeking; negotiation (e.g. compromise or prioritizing); opposition (aggression or blaming others) and delegation (e.g. maladaptive help seeking).

Do we have consistent styles of coping across different situations?

When faced with a stressful situation, we do not all adopt the same coping strategy. Thus we need to consider individual differences or the ways personality affects choice of coping strategy. However, the extent to which coping is determined by stable factors, rather than varying across situations, has been a source of debate among researchers. Those such as Lazarus who are interested in the different strategies used in different circumstances take a situational view, while those who focus on consistency across different situations take a dispositional (or trait) approach to coping.

Carver and Scheier (1994) argue that there are dispositional tendencies to use emotion-focused or problem-focused coping. The COPE is designed to be used as either a dispositional or a situational measure depending on whether the individual is asked to complete it in relation to specific situations or in relation to general tendencies. Some researchers are sceptical about the accuracy of people's reports of their general coping tendencies (e.g. Coyne and Gottlieb, 1996). Lazarus (1993) suggested that dispositional tendencies to use particular coping strategies are better obtained by looking at the individual in a range of different situations. One study that compared people's ratings of how they generally coped with their average coping across a number of specific episodes found that asking people how they generally coped was a poor predictor of what they did in a specific situation, although the tendency to use escape-avoidance or religious coping showed more consistency across situations (Schwartz J.E. et al, 1999). The tendency to use avoidance (versus approach) coping is a key feature of two coping trait classifications, namely, repressive coping and monitoring (versus blunting) coping.

Repressive coping

People who have a **repressive coping** style direct attention away from threatening information or stimuli or interpret such information in a non-threatening manner (Derakshan and Eysenck, 1997). This has clear links to the Freudian notion of repression and was originally contrasted with 'sensitizing', a form of approach coping. A 'repressive' person will avert attention from negative feelings to the extent of being unaware that they feel anxious or depressed. However, this is different from intentional suppression of disturbing thoughts or feelings (Myers et al, 2004). A characteristic of repressors is that, when faced with stressful tasks, there is a discrepancy between their self-reports of anxiety (which are low) and their scores on physiological indicators of anxiety (which tend to be high). This has been demonstrated in experimental studies where people have been asked to perform anxiety-provoking tasks such as public speaking (e.g. Newton and Contrada, 1992).

Focus 5.1

The alexithymic personality

A personality trait often considered alongside repressive coping is alexithymia. The term alexithymia, when literally translated, means 'lacking words for feelings' and relates explicitly to an individual's capacity to process and express emotion. Alexithymia can be assessed using the Toronto Alexithymia Scale which measures the extent to which respondents have difficulty in identifying, labelling and understanding emotions, thereby identifying individuals who show impaired capacity for emotional expression (Bagby et al, 1994). However, unlike people with a repressive coping style who are unconsciously motivated not to recognize negative emotions such as anger, fear and stress, individuals with an alexithymic personality experience negative emotional states but are unable to identify, label and understand the emotion. Interestingly, the term alexithymia was introduced in the 1970s by psychodynamically-oriented clinicians who noticed that many clients who presented with stress-related or psychosomatic illnesses exhibited little insight into the causes of their stressful experiences or negative moods (see Lumley et al, 1999). Typically when an individual with an alexithymic personality is asked about a significant relationship or an emotionally charged situation, they will be unable to answer (e.g. 'I don't know'), or they will provide simple and non-specific responses (e.g. 'I felt bad').

It has been suggested that this emotional deficit may negatively impact on an individual's ability to cope with stressful and traumatic events. Evidence indicates that the alexithymic personality is associated with mortality and morbidity from all causes. In particular, research has shown a link between alexithymia and increased risk of developing cardiovascular disease (e.g. Waldstein et al, 2002). More recently, the alexithymic personality has been found to be associated with cancer pain (Porcelli et al, 2007). These findings suggest that alexithymic individuals may be more likely to use maladaptive coping and engage in more health risk behaviours.

Measuring repression is problematic because repressive copers will, by definition, be unaware of their feelings of anxiety. In most cases they will not even know that they have tendencies to repress feelings. An early self-report measure of repression (the repression–sensitization scale, Byrne, 1961) was found to correlate so highly with measures of trait anxiety that repression was effectively equivalent to low anxiety (Eysenck and Matthews, 1987). However, for a measure of repression to be useful, repressors need to be distinguishable from those who are simply not anxious. Fortunately, Weinberger, Schwarz and Davidson (1979) have developed a method of measuring repression using a measure of anxiety together with a measure of defensiveness. To be defined as a repressor a person must have a low score on anxiety and a high score on defensiveness. The measure of defensiveness often used is the Marlowe–Crowne measure of social desirability (Crowne and Marlowe, 1960). A more recent measure capitalizes on the finding that self-reports and physiological measures are discrepant in repressors. Thus they are identified by their high levels of physiological reactivity and low self-reports of anxiety. This form of repressive coping has been termed affective–autonomic response discrepancy (Coifman et al, 2007).

Is repressive coping beneficial because it leads to low awareness of anxiety? Findings are inconsistent. Repression has been linked to poorer immune functioning (e.g. Esterling et al, 1993) and to increased coronary heart disease risk factors such as high cholesterol (Niaura et al, 1992). However, more recent research suggests that repressive coping may be associated with enhanced well-being and fewer symptoms in the long term, particularly in the face of extremely stressful events such as bereavement (e.g. Coifman et al, 2007).

Monitoring and blunting

Monitoring and blunting coping styles refer to the information-processing style of people facing threats. It has typically been studied in medical situations with a view to ascertaining the appropriate type of information to give to patients to help them cope with impending medical or surgical interventions. Those with a monitoring style will tend to seek out information about the impending threat and amplify or worry about it (e.g. Miller et al, 1988) whereas those with a predominantly blunting style will actively avoid it. Typically, these two dimensions are treated as independent (rather than being opposite poles of a single dimension) so that individuals are divided into high and low **monitors** and high and low **blunters**.

Research suggests that monitors and blunters react differently to medical stressors. For example, high monitors go to the doctor with less severe medical problems and demand more tests and information than low monitors (Miller et al, 1988). Miller et al suggests that this is not accompanied by any greater wish for control, rather it is to reduce uncertainty and lower arousal.

Miller and Mangan (1983) suggested that a patient's level of arousal was lower if the level of information given was matched to their coping style (i.e. monitors require much more detailed information). This theory has been used to inform the design of appropriate health messages (see also Chapter 8). Williams-Piehota et al (2005) matched messages about mammography to women's coping styles. They hypothesized that matched messages would be more effective in persuading women to attend for mammography. The leaflet designed for those classified as blunters was short and to the point. It gave basic facts such as 'the key to finding breast cancer is early detection and the key to early detection is getting regular screening mammograms'. In contrast, the leaflet for monitors gave details of symptoms and risk factors for cancer and explanations of mammography procedures, e.g. 'for some women early detection may prevent the need to remove the entire breast or to receive chemotherapy'. Both leaflets included information to reassure and address anxiety. Messages which were matched to monitoring style were more effective in promoting uptake of mammography during the following six months. However, the difference was only significant for blunters, for whom it may be particularly important to provide messages which are appropriate.

Personality, coping dispositions and situational coping

We have discussed situational and dispositional approaches to coping, separately. However, coping styles and strategies are interrelated and function within the context of general personality. Many studies have examined links between personality and coping strategies, especially neuroticism and optimism. Hewitt and Flett (1996) suggest that the relationship between personality and coping can be conceptualized in terms of the three types of relationships between variables shown in Focus box 5.2. Thus for the mediational model, personality would determine coping style or strategy which then determines adjustment. In the additive model, personality and coping have independent effects and in the interactive (or moderation) model coping may buffer the impact of personality on adjustment.

Focus 5.2

Direct effects, mediation and moderation

Researchers examining coping and social support have investigated the mechanisms by which these factors influence relationships between stressors and outcomes such as health and well-being. There are three main types of mechanisms that are examined in this research and in other areas of health psychology (see Figure 5.1).

1. *Direct effects*. In this case coping or social support has a direct impact on the outcome. For example, having good social support or a positive approach to coping could lead to better health irrespective of the amount of stress the person is experiencing. Figure 5.1a) illustrates a situation where a high level of stress and poor coping strategies would both independently act to decrease well-being (and vice versa). This is sometimes also described as an additive effect.

2. *Mediated effects*. This occurs when one variable has its effect on another via an intervening variable. In Figure 5.1b) coping acts as an

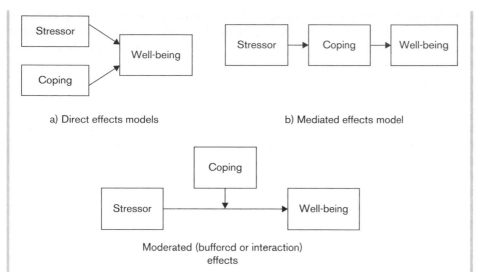

Figure 5.1 *Direct effects, mediation and moderation: Alternative models of mechanism.*

intervening variable through which the stressor exerts its effects on the level of strain. For example, the experience of stress could result in poor coping (e.g. use of alcohol or drugs) which leads to deteriorated well-being. Social support could be said to be a mediator in circumstances where, for example, a breast cancer diagnosis leads to someone joining a support group, which in turn reduces their anxiety or depression. Alternatively, a stressor such as marital breakdown may lead to a reduction in support (through loss of a previously supportive partner and perhaps the partner's family and friends) that may increase anxiety and depression.

3. *Moderated effects.* Moderators, unlike mediators, change the nature of the relationship between two variables, e.g. the stressor–strain relationship. Moderators may alter either the strength or direction of this relationship. Thus coping would be described as moderating the relationship between a stressor such as bereavement and an outcome such as well-being if, for example, bereavement led to poor health only for those who did not use social support or emotional expression as coping strategies. This kind of moderator is also referred to as a *buffer* because it reduces the impact of the stressor. This effect can be identified as an interaction effect (e.g. in a regression equation) because social support affects the association between stress and well-being. Other variables such as gender or personality may also act as moderators because, for example, some stressors may only result in strain for those scoring highly on a certain personality trait (e.g. neuroticism). Logically, however, fixed traits such as gender cannot act as mediators.

psychological well-being whereas benefit finding was not. They suggest that positive reappraisal coping involves 'more active, intentional attempts to pursue positive outcomes' (Sears et al, 2003: 494). Positive reappraisal, unlike benefit finding, was not related to optimism. They suggest that benefit finding may be more stable and less effortful. Teasing apart the processes whereby positive reappraisal and benefit finding have their separate beneficial effects requires further research. Benefit finding is sometimes examined within the context of emotional writing interventions (see Focus box 5.3).

Focus 5.3

Written emotional disclosure interventions

In 1986, James Pennebaker developed the 'emotional writing paradigm' in which he explored the effects of writing for 15–20 minutes on three consecutive days about stressful or traumatic events on a range of health outcomes. Typically, individuals in the experimental group are asked to write about their deepest emotions and thoughts about the most upsetting experience(s) in their life. They are encouraged to really let go and to link their writing to other aspects of their life such as relationships, their childhood, their careers and who they would like to become, who they were in the past and who they are now. In the control group, individuals are asked to write about what they have done the previous day and to describe their plans for the following day.

Research has found that emotional disclosure through expressive writing can produce clinically significant changes on a number of physiological and psychological health outcomes such as enhanced responses to hepatitis B vaccination in healthy adults, improvement in lung function in asthmatic patients and increased lymphocyte counts in HIV patients (Petrie et al, 1995; Smyth et al, 1999; Petrie et al, 2004). Emotional disclosure through writing has also been found to reduce physician visits at follow-up, increase exam performance, reduce psychological distress and increase re-employment following job loss (see Pennebaker, 1997).

Support for the benefits of emotional writing has also been found in meta-analyses (Smyth, 1998; Frisina et al, 2004). However, a more recent meta-analysis has shown that the effects of emotional disclosure are likely to be smaller than previously hoped and its impact is moderated by individual differences variables (e.g. personality and previous experience of trauma) and by the characteristics of the writing task (e.g. time spent writing) (Frattaroli, 2006).

How does emotional writing influence health? Several mechanisms have been suggested. For example, writing may reduce the cumulative physiological drain of not confronting upsetting experiences or facilitate cognitive processing of traumatic memories which in turn leads to affective and physiological change. The current mechanism proposed to account for the positive effects of emotional disclosure involves exposure and cognitive processing (Sloan and Marx, 2004). By accessing the emotions, feelings and cognitions linked to a stressful or traumatic event, memory begins to be restructured. Through such restructuring the individual assimilates the stressor into their own self-schema and beliefs system, becomes aware of the associated feelings and considers methods of coping with the traumatic or stressful encounter.

Recent work has concentrated on understanding the psychological processes associated with the beneficial effects of emotional disclosure. For example, Creswell and colleagues (2007) content analyzed the essays of early-stage cancer survivors and showed that essays that included self-affirmation writing (i.e. evidence that an important personal value was affirmed as a result of their cancer) were associated with fewer physical symptoms at three months' follow-up. In other work, O'Connor and Ashley (2008) have explored the importance of the emotional characteristics of disclosure essays together with the alexithymic personality trait. Using the computer programme, Linguistic Inquiry and Word Count (LIWC), they found that alexithymic participants who disclosed *more negative* emotion words compared to positive emotion words exhibited reduced blood pressure responses to stress two weeks after writing. Yet non-alexithymic participants who disclosed *more positive* and less negative emotion words displayed reduced blood pressure responses to stress.

Future-oriented or proactive coping

It has been argued that coping research has told us quite a lot about ineffective coping but too little about how to cope effectively (Jones and Bright, 2001). You can probably think of occasions where life has become stressful purely because of your own lack of forward planning, for example when you leave an essay to the very last minute. Whatever coping strategy you use at this late stage is unlikely to be as effective for your well-being as managing to avoid getting into that situation in the first place. If you cannot prevent facing a stressor you may be able to anticipate it and minimize its effect. This is what is meant by **proactive coping**. Aspinwall and Taylor (1997) describe the central elements of proactive coping. They highlight the importance of building resources (for example, financial or social resources) in a similar manner to Hobfoll's (1989) conservation of resources theory (see Chapter 3). Proactive coping also involves recognition and initial appraisals of potential stressors, preliminary coping efforts and obtaining and using feedback about coping success. Individual differences (such as personality or control beliefs), availability of social support and environmental factors (such as the presence of other demands) all influence the extent we are able to engage in proactive coping. Measures of proactive coping have been developed (e.g. Greenglass et al, 1999) and some research suggests that it may predict successful ageing (e.g. Greenglass et al, 2006; Ouwehand et al, 2007).

Aspinwall and Taylor have indicated that social support resources may be important in helping individuals to proactively cope. The importance of social support is explored in the next section.

Social support

What do we mean by social support? What should researchers be measuring when they look at social support? Is it important to be part of community networks with large numbers of social contacts, or is it more important to have one close relationship perhaps with a spouse, cohabiting partner or close friend? Maybe the crucial issue is not the nature of the relationship but whether people perform behaviours that help out in a stressful situation. These are key questions addressed by social support research.

Types of social support

Researchers have distinguished between *structural* and *functional* approaches to support (e.g. Uchino et al, 1996). Structural approaches examine the simple existence of networks and friendships, whereas functional approaches look at the actual function that such social contacts serve (e.g. providing practical help versus emotional support). Researchers have also assessed perceived social support, i.e. the cognitive appraisal of support (e.g. Barrera, 1986). Four categories of social support based on a classification by Winnubst, Buunk and Marcellissen (1988) are discussed below.

Social networks

In 1979, Berkman and Syme published what is now regarded as a classic study demonstrating the value of **social networks** for health. The study, conducted in the USA, followed up a random sample of almost 5000 adults (aged 30–69) for nine years from 1965. At the start of the study the researchers recorded the presence and the extent of four types of social ties – marriage, contact with the extended family and friends, church membership and other formal and informal group affiliations. These were combined to form a social network index. They found that both the individual ties and the combined index predicted mortality over the next nine years. Those with low scores on the index were about twice as likely to die as those with high scores, even after controlling for self-reports of social class, smoking, obesity and health at the outset. One limitation of this study was the use of self-reports of health in the initial measurements but findings have since been replicated using physical examinations. In a review of a range of such studies, House, Landis and Umberson (1988) concluded that evidence consistently supports the view that there is an increased risk associated with having few social relationships even after adjusting for other risk factors. However, there are gender differences. In particular, marriage has more health benefits for men than for women, and bereavement is more harmful for men.

Quality of relationships

Being part of a large social network does not guarantee that people will receive greater help when they need it. The correlation between the number of connections people have and the actual support they receive tends to be quite low, perhaps because one good relationship may provide better support than a large number of more superficial contacts (Cohen and Wills, 1985). The importance of quality rather than quantity of relationships is demonstrated by a well-known sociological study conducted by Brown and Harris (1978), who

Figure 5.2 Greater social support is associated with better health.
Source: © Purestock

studied the origins of depression in women. They interviewed 400 women about
the life events they had experienced in the past year. They also asked the
participants to name the people they were able to confide in about their worries.
Women were classified into one of the four following categories: a) those who
had a close relationship with someone in the same household, b) those without
such a relationship who had a friend or relative they saw at least weekly, c) those
with a close friend or relative they saw less than weekly, and d) those with none
of these relationships. The study found that having a confiding relationship
protected the women from depression following major life events. Among the
women who experienced a stressful life event, only one in ten of those in
category a developed depression, compared to one in four of those in category b
and one in 2.5 of those in categories c or d. This suggests that having confiding
social support buffered the impact of life stressors.

Perceived social support

Our cognitive appraisals of having reliable social support may affect coping
regardless of our actual social networks or the number of confiding relationships
we have. This emphasis on appraisal results in an approach to measuring social
support which is consistent with the transactional model of stress. It also allows
easy assessment using self-report questionnaires. Thus such measures are regularly
used, e.g. in studies of occupational stress. However, these measures have been
criticized for overlap with stress outcome measures. For example, a depressed
person is likely to be pessimistic about their social support, thus a correlation
between a measure of deprression and a measure of perceived lack of social
support may be higher then when more objective measure are used. Furthermore,
ratings of perceived social support are only moderately related to the ratings of
quality of specific relationships (Pierce et al, 1991). Pierce et al suggest that
people's general perceptions of support may reflect a stable characteristic or
personality style. They may therefore not be an accurate reflection of support
available in a crisis.

Enacted support

None of the above measures taps supportive behaviours. However, it is important to consider what types of behaviour may be most helpful if we wish to develop effective social support interventions (e.g. Dakof and Taylor, 1990). For example, what type of support would be most helpful when an individual received a diagnosis of cancer? Various types of specific social support have been assessed, including emotional support (helping the person to feel accepted or valued), instrumental support (that is practical support) and informational support (e.g. Cohen and Wills, 1985). The match between support provided and an individual's need may be crucial to effectiveness. For example, a study of support from family and friends provided for breast cancer sufferers (Reynolds and Perrin, 2004) compared a range of provided support with the support desired by the women. The study found that only two behaviours which were intended to be supportive were unwelcomed by over 90 per cent of the women. These both related to trying to find causes or explanations for the cancer. However, reactions to other types of support varied greatly between women. Using cluster analysis, a statistical technique which classifies people into groupings according to specified characteristics, they found four different patterns. Group 1 wanted many types of support which focused on reassurance that everything would be OK; group 2 wanted people to act normally and did not want to talk about cancer; group 3 wanted facts, information and general advice; group 4 wanted to talk but did not want advice. The four groups did not differ on measures of adjustment to breast cancer. However a mismatch of support was associated with poorer adjustment, particularly where people received support they had not wanted.

Health impact of social support

There is strong evidence for positive effects of social support. For example, a thorough review of 81 studies (Uchino et al, 1996) indicated that social support was related to beneficial effects on cardiovascular, endocrine and immune functioning. These researchers also found that interventions to improve social support had beneficial impacts on heart disease risk factors such as blood pressure.

The mechanisms whereby social support impacts on health have been discussed at length. Cohen and Wills (1985) suggested two alternative pathways. First, social support may have a direct effect on well-being and health, i.e. it is beneficial regardless of the presence of stressors. Second, social support may buffer or moderate the impact of stressors on health so that it only benefits those facing threats. In a review of early literature, Cohen and Wills found evidence of direct effects for structural supports (e.g. when measures of social networks are used), but buffering was sometimes found when studies focused on close relationships. Uchino et al (1996) confirmed this finding. Studies tend to find buffering effects when measures of enacted supports are used. It is perhaps not surprising that, when close family or friends provide specific supports in response to a particular stressful situation, this buffers the stress, while simply having a large social network may not have the same effect. Social support may also have a positive impact on health through its effect on health behaviour (i.e. the social support–health relationship is mediated by health behaviours). Finally, it is also possible that the level of social support available to an individual is a stable individual difference which is linked to personality traits (e.g. agreeableness or lack of hostility, see Chapter 6). However, Uchino et al concluded that relationships between social support and health occur even where personality variables are controlled for.

Negative effects of social support

In some situations social support can be unhelpful. We have seen that this is the case where there is a mismatch between our needs and the support provided. It is also not unusual for researchers to find that social support provided in the work situation is not beneficial (e.g. Uchino et al, 1996). Support at work, especially from a supervisor, may make the recipient feel incompetent and so is not experienced as helpful. This idea was tested in an experimental study by Deelstra et al (2003) which imposed instrumental support and found that negative affect was higher and self-esteem was lower when support was given, except when the problem could not have been solved without it. These effects were confirmed by physiological indicators (e.g. pulse rate).

Similarly, social networks may not always be supportive For example, in a study of widowed women (aged 60–69), Rook (1984) found a stronger relationship between problematic relationships and reduced well-being than between positive relationships and improved well-being. Furthermore, most of those relationships identified as 'problematic' were friends or relatives. The researchers suggested that many of these unhelpful relationships were not seen to be egalitarian, i.e. others were making decisions for them. There is also evidence from a meta-analysis that negative aspects of social relationships may have a negative impact on the immune system (Herbert and Cohen, 1993).

Finally, it is also worth considering the impact of social support on the provider of the support. We saw in Chapter 2 that carers of Alzheimer's patients showed slower wound-healing than matched controls (Kiecolt-Glaser et al, 1995), a clear instance of negative impact of offering social support. This may be an extreme example where giving support is damaging because it is extremely stressful. However, social psychologists researching *reciprocity* in social support have suggested that the feeling of giving more support than you receive is generally beneficial for health (e.g. Liang et al, 2001). However, there do seem to be gender differences. Vaananen et al (2005) examined the long-term effects of perceived reciprocity in intimate relationships on sickness absence and found that women who gave more support than they received were healthier (compared to those who received more than they gave), whereas men who received more than they gave were healthier. They suggested that giving support was associated with enhanced self-esteem for women.

In summary, many of the findings in studies discussed in this section emphasize the importance of providing social support in a way that does not undermine individuals' self-esteem and feelings of competence.

Focus 5.4

Can a socially supportive intervention save your life?

Providing social support interventions in health care settings for people with chronic or serious illnesses is quite common and seen to be generally beneficial. However, there is some debate about whether such interventions affect cancer survival. In 1989, Spiegel et al reported on one of the first randomized controlled trials which suggested that social support might increase longevity for women with metastatic breast cancer (i.e. where cancer has spread to other parts of the body). This study compared a group intervention with a control group who received normal cancer treatment only. The women in the intervention group met for 90 minutes a week over a period of one year in a group led by a psychiatrist or social worker with a therapist who had herself had breast cancer. The intervention was not originally intended to improve survival. Social support was one aspect of the intervention, which also included discussions related to pain control (including teaching self-hypnosis) and other coping strategies. The study found that women in the intervention group lived on average for 36.6 months compared to only 18.9 months in the control group. These findings were controversial and the study was criticized for having failed to control for differences in the intervention and control groups. Some subsequent studies failed to replicate this effect (e.g. Goodwin et al, 2001) but a 10-year follow-up study of malignant melanoma sufferers who had attended a supportive group compared to a control group found enhanced survival in the intervention group (Fawzy et al, 1993). It is difficult to compare findings of these studies as the nature of the illness and the intervention varies. Furthermore, most interventions contain a number of potentially therapeutic elements, not just social support. A meta-analysis examining 13 such controlled interventions concluded that it was premature to assume that psychosocial interventions can prolong cancer survival (Smedslund and Ringdal, 2004).

Social support in cyberspace

Over the past 50 years the nature of social networks has changed for many people. Greater social mobility means that many people work away from home and families are often dispersed around the world. At the same time new technologies have made it possible for people to maintain contact by cheap phone calls, e-mail and web camera. Opportunities to build new networks, often based on specific interests, are also offered via internet chat rooms or discussion forums.

Whether the internet has a positive or negative impact on social networks and individuals' well-being has proved controversial. Kraut et al (1998) studied 179 people in 73 households over the first year or two of their internet use. They found that greater use of the internet was linked to reductions in communication

Activity 5.1

It has been suggested that excessive internet use makes people isolated and withdrawn. Discuss whether you think this is the case. Do you think it is possible to improve your social support via the internet?

with others in their household, a decline in the size of their social circle and increases in feelings of depression and loneliness. This was true even though they used the internet predominantly for communication purposes. They labelled this phenomenon the 'internet paradox'. They followed up the same sample three years later (Kraut et al, 2002) and found that the negative effects had generally been replaced by positive effects in that more use of the internet was associated with improved psychological well-being and more social involvement, although, on the negative side, there was also an increase in stress. However, there were important individual differences in the long-term effects of internet use with better outcomes for extroverts and those who already had good social support but poorer outcomes for introverts and those lacking social support. Overall, they suggest that the internet may have improved in the three years of the study, offering better information and communication services (e.g. instant messaging) which help maintain social contacts. There are also gender differences in internet use such that women are more likely to use e-mail to keep in touch with family and friends who live far away (Boneva et al, 2001). It is clearly likely that the effects on social contacts are very dependent on type of use made of the internet and whether it is a replacement for social contact or for other individual activities.

For people who are perhaps isolated by illness or disability, the internet can provide a unique and invaluable source of support. It can provide informational support and can also put people in touch with others experiencing similar circumstances who may be able to provide emotional support. Researchers have examined internet social support for a range of illnesses, including breast cancer or strokes, as well as sites offering support for behaviour change such as quitting smoking or losing weight. For example, Fogel et al (2002) found that women with breast cancer who used the internet for information on breast health issues reported greater social support and less loneliness. This was true even when the use of the internet was less than one hour a week. Similarly, Kalichman et al (2003) reported greater perceptions of social support, as well as greater active coping, among HIV-positive people who used the internet for health-related information.

Researchers have also used qualitative methods to content analyze communications in internet social support groups. This sheds light on the types of social support available. For example, Coulson, Buchanan and Aubeeluck (2007) analyzed communications online in a support group for people affected by Huntington's disease (an inherited degenerative neurological disorder). They found that informational and emotional supports were most commonly offered. Just less than 10 per cent offered tangible help and this included indirect help such as advising someone of sources of direct help. Other studies confirm the finding that informational and emotional supports are the dominant forms of support in online communications.

Of course, in online support as in face-to-face interaction, there can be a downside. For example, there has been considerable concern in the media about pro-anorexia websites which provide support for life-threatening behaviour. In an experimental study of exposure to such websites, Bardone-Cone and Cass (2007) found evidence of negative effects on viewers' affect, self-esteem and perceived weight. Similarly, Whitlock et al (2006) analyzed self-injury message boards for adolescents and suggested that while they may provide valuable support they may also normalize and so encourage damaging behaviour.

Activity 5.2

Search for support groups online (e.g. type 'support group' into Google). Pick three support groups for physical or psychological disorders and evaluate them. What kind of support do they offer? How likely is it to fit the needs of the target group?

See Kiesler and Kraut (1999) for a discussion of the value of such groups.

Summary

Coping can be viewed both as a situational and dispositional variable. A wide range of coping strategies have been identified which are typically measured using standard coping questionnaires. These have been used to explore coping in response to particular situations and to examine dispositional tendencies to use particular coping strategies. These strategies are often further grouped into overarching categories, e.g. emotion-focused or problem-focused coping.

Repressive coping is a form of avoidant coping style which is linked to health outcomes. The distinction between monitoring and blunting coping styles addresses people's information processing preferences and is useful in helping to design strategies to communicate medical information to patients. General personality styles are also linked to coping strategies. Coping strategies can be seen as mediators of the relationship between personality and well-being outcomes.

A positive or optimistic approach to the experience of threat has coping benefits. People typically report feeling positive affect (as well as negative affect) even in the most stressful times. This is thought to provide respite and help build resources. Positive reappraisal and looking for benefits in stressful situations also benefits health. Proactive coping is a form of coping which helps to anticipate or minimize stressors.

Four main types of social support have been identified: belonging to a social network, having good quality close relationships, perceiving social support and being the recipient of supportive behaviours (enacted supports). These types of support have generally been linked to positive health outcomes. Both direct and stress buffering effects have been found depending on the type of support considered. There are also instances when social support may not be helpful. This may be particularly the case where social support is damaging to the self-esteem of the recipient. In some circumstances it may also be harmful to the support giver. Websites and internet forums may be useful in providing informational and emotional support.

Key concepts and terms

Benefit finding
Blunter
Coping resources
Coping strategies
Coping style
Emotional writing
Emotion-focused
Monitor

Primary appraisal
Proactive coping
Problem-focused
Repressive coping
Secondary appraisal
Social networks
Social support

Sample essay titles

- Moving house is generally considered to be a stressful experience. How does psychological theory and research help to explain why one person may cope with this experience better than another?

- 'Coping is personality in action under stress.' Evaluate this statement with reference to situational and dispositional approaches to coping.

- Are personal relationships helpful in reducing stress? Discuss with reference to the psychological evidence.

Further reading

Journal articles

Carver, C.S., Scheier, M.F., and Weintraub, J.K. (1989). Assessing coping strategies: A theoretically based approach. *Journal of Personality and Social Psychology*, 56, 267–283.

Cohen, S., and Wills, T.A. (1985). Stress, social support and the buffering hypothesis. *Psychological Bulletin*, 98, 310–357.

Folkman, S., and Moskowitz, J.T. (2004). Coping: Pitfalls and promise. *Annual Review of Psychology*, 55, 745–774.

Kiesler, S., and Kraut, R. (1999). Internet use and ties that bind. *American Psychologist* 54, 783–784.

Terry, D. (1994). Determinants of coping: the role of stable and situational factors. *Journal of Personality and Social Psychology*, 66, 895–910.

Uchino, B.N., Cacioppo, J.T., and Kiecolt-Glaser, J.K. (1996). The relationship between social support and physiological processes. A review with emphasis on underlying mechanisms and implications for health. *Psychological Bulletin*, 119, 488–531.

6 Personality and health

In this chapter we examine the way in which personality dimensions or traits can determine health outcomes. These effects of personality on health include direct effects through physiological mechanisms and indirect effects through health behaviours.

Personality traits refer to stable individual differences in thinking, feeling and behaving across a range of different situations. Research in the health domain has found that particular dimensions of personality are associated with poor health and reduced longevity while others are linked to good health and increased length of life. The magnitude of these effects can be similar to those of known biological risk factors such as cholesterol (Caspi et al, 2005). The personality dimensions associated with poor health outcomes include neuroticism (or negative affect), type A personality and hostility. The dimensions associated with good health outcomes include optimism, extraversion and conscientiousness. In this chapter we consider the evidence linking these personality variables to health outcomes and some of the mechanisms by which personality affects health. For example, personality traits might lead to greater exposure to stressful events, to a reduction in the effectiveness of coping strategies, or a change in coping resources such as social support. These explanations of the personality health link build on the discussion of the impact of personality on coping in Chapter 5. Other personality traits such as hostility may affect health through changing the intensity and duration of physiological reactions to stress, linking personality to the biopsychosocial pathways considered in Chapter 2.

In this chapter we will consider: 1) optimism and health; 2) type A behaviour and coronary heart disease; 3) hostility and coronary heart disease; 4) neuroticism and health; 5) extraversion and health; 6) conscientiousness and health.

Introduction

This chapter reviews evidence suggesting that stable individual differences in the way people think, feel and behave (i.e. personality) are predictive of various health outcomes. We explore how these stable individual differences can predispose individuals to respond to life challenges in a manner which, over time,

Learning outcomes

When you have completed this chapter you should be able to:

1. Explain how optimism is related to positive health outcomes and the role of attributional styles in this relationship.
2. Discuss the effects of type A personality and hostility on coronary heart disease and potential mediation of these effects through physiological reactions.
3. Describe the role of neuroticism (or negative affect) on poor health and the explanations of this effect through perceptions of stress, ability to cope and social support.
4. Describe the impact of extraversion on positive and negative health outcomes through effects on mood and health risk behaviours.
5. Describe the relationship between conscientiousness and positive health outcomes and the mediating effects of health behaviours.
6. Evaluate the different mechanisms through which personality variables affect health outcomes.

damages or protects their health. Much research on personality in recent years has focused on five broad personality types: **openness to experience** (or intellect), **conscientiousness**, **extraversion**, **agreeableness** and **neuroticism** (or emotional stability) (McCrae and Costa, 1987; Digman, 1990). This is often referred to as the Big Five Taxonomy or the OCEAN model of personality. A growing body of research now relates traits from the Big Five Taxonomy to various health behaviours and health outcomes. For example, Booth-Kewley and Vickers (1994) suggest that the **Big Five personality traits** may determine the extent to which people engage in general clusters of health-related behaviours such as substance use risk behaviours (e.g. smoking). However, there has been less research on how openness and agreeableness link to health outcomes so we will focus on extraversion, neuroticism and conscientiousness. The Big Five model is based on the assumption that a range of more specific personality traits can be understood as blends of the different Big Five traits. Some of the best evidence for the impacts of personality on health outcomes arises from work looking at more specific personality traits. So, for example, work has examined the impact of optimism or positive affect on health. We will consider work on optimism, type A behaviour pattern and hostility as important areas of research relating personality traits to health outcomes. Some research has also suggested a cancer or type C personality type (see Focus box 6.1) and a distressed or type D personality type (see Focus box 6.3).

Since the magnitude of personality effects on health outcomes can be comparable to known biological factors, these effects must be taken seriously by health psychologists (Hampson et al, 2006). In the western world the leading causes of morbidity and mortality in middle and later life are now various chronic diseases such as coronary heart disease, cancer and diabetes, while in children, adolescents and young adults unintentional injuries are the leading causes of death. Personality traits may have important roles to play in both these periods of life. In relation to the development of chronic diseases, personality traits may play an important role in the maintenance of behaviours that are health promoting or health damaging when engaged in over time (e.g. smoking and unhealthy eating).

Focus 6.1

Type C personality

This chapter reviews work on the 'type A' or coronary prone behaviour pattern. The type A individual appears to be hostile, easily angered, competitive and hard-driving. Research by oncologists interested in the behavioural causes of cancer has suggested a 'type C' or cancer risk pattern (Temoshok et al, 1985). Type C individuals are characterized by high levels of denial and suppression of various emotions, in particular anger. Type C includes a number of other features including 'pathological niceness', conflict avoidance, high social desirability, harmonizing behaviour, over-compliance, over-patience, as well as high rationality and a rigid control of emotional expression. It is suggested that the excessive denial, avoidance, suppression and repression of emotions that characterize type C over time weaken the individual's natural resistance to carcinogenic influences. Support for the link between type C personality and cancer is found in studies relating different immune parameters (natural killer cell activity, lymphocytes, serotonin uptake, mean platelet volume) to mood states, coping styles and personality traits (Cunningham, 1985). Alexithymia is a related personality type (a literal translation is the lack of words for emotions), characterized by difficulty identifying, labelling and understanding emotions, which is also found to be associated with negative health outcomes. Evidence exists to suggest that alexithymia is linked to an increased risk of developing cardiovascular disease (Waldstein et al, 2002). Recently, it has also been found to be associated with blood pressure reactivity following written emotional disclosure (O'Connor and Ashley, 2008; see also Focus box 5.1).

Similarly, accidents and unintentional injuries are usually a consequence of repeated exposure to risky situations rather than a single chance event. Personality traits may also have impacts on health outcomes through a variety of other mechanisms such as increasing perceptions of stress. A key theme in this chapter is the different mechanisms by which personality traits affect health outcomes. In considering each personality trait and its impact on health we discuss potential explanations and then in a final section consider these explanations collectively. Table 6.1 provides a summary of key explanations of the relationships between personality traits and health discussed in greater detail below.

Optimism

Optimism refers to the expectation that in the future good things will happen to you and bad things will not. While we all may be optimistic in some areas of our lives and pessimistic in others, optimism taps the extent to which an individual is optimistic in general across a range of domains and across time. A

Table 6.1 Explanations of the relationship between personality traits and health outcomes

Non-causal explanations	
Causal direction problem	Health outcome causes personality change (e.g. illness affects perceptions and behaviour)
Third variable problem	Both the personality trait and health outcome are caused by another underlying variable (e.g. disease)
Measurement artefact	The measurement of the health outcome is contaminated by the personality trait
Causal explanations	
Physiological changes	The personality trait causes physiological changes that in turn influence health outcomes
Tropisms	The personality trait means the individual is more likely to be exposed to risky situations
Health behaviours	The personality trait makes the individual more likely to engage in health-risk behaviours and less likely to engage in health-promoting behaviours
Effects of stress	The personality trait makes the individual more likely to experience stress and/or less likely to be protected from the effects of stress through coping mechanisms or social support

number of measures of optimism have been developed. Scheier and Carver (1992) developed a measure that focuses on optimistic expectations. This includes items such as 'In uncertain times, I usually expect the best' and 'I always look on the bright side of life'. Optimism has also been assessed using indices of an individual's sense of **hope**. A measure developed by Snyder et al (1996) focuses on the extent to which individuals pursue their goals and their beliefs that their goals can be realized. Items include 'I energetically pursue my goals' and 'There are lots of ways around any problem'. Other researchers have focused on how people explain the causes of bad events (Peterson, 2000). Such explanations or 'attributions' can be classified along a number of dimensions such as whether they are internal or external to the individual (e.g. whether the cause is something about the individual versus their environment), whether they are likely to be stable or unstable over time (e.g. the extent to which the cause will affect future outcomes or just this specific one), and whether they are general or specific causes (e.g. will the cause affect a range of life events for that individual or just this particular event). Optimists tend to attribute bad events to external, unstable and specific causes while pessimists see the same events as resulting from internal, stable and global causes (Peterson et al, 1988). For example, an optimist might believe that they got a minor illness because they were 'run down' after an unusually busy time at work. In contrast, a pessimist might believe they contracted a minor illness because they are always susceptible to such things no matter what they do.

The outcomes of optimism include increased psychological well-being, better physical health and even greater longevity. For example, in relation to psychological well-being, Litt et al (1992) found that optimistic individuals were less depressed after unsuccessful in vitro fertilization. Similarly, Carver et al (1993) reported that optimism in women with breast cancer was associated with less distress following surgery and that this effect persisted one year later. Alloy, Abrahamson and Francis (1999) found that students with a pessimistic explanatory style were more likely to subsequently experience depression.

Research also demonstrates that high levels of optimism are associated with better physical health. Those with high levels of optimism have fewer infectious illnesses and report fewer physical symptoms even during periods of stress (Peterson and Seligman, 1987). They are also more likely to recover from surgery more quickly and less likely to be re-hospitalized (Scheier et al, 1999). Peterson and colleagues provide an impressive demonstration of the effects of optimism on physical health. In a sample of men, attributional style measured at age 25 was found to predict health status 35 years later as assessed by doctors; the optimists were more likely to be in better health even when initial physical and mental health were statistically controlled for (Peterson et al, 1988).

Most impressively, those with high levels of optimism may even live longer. Danner, Snowdon and Friesen (2001) coded pieces of text that a sample of 180 Catholic nuns had written about themselves on entering the church as young women, for emotional content. The research then examined the survival rates of these same women when they were 75–95 years of age. Those who wrote sentences containing self-descriptions with the most positive emotions (e.g. happiness, pride, love) were more likely to live longer than those containing the fewest positive emotions. Comparison of the top and bottom 25 per cent (quartiles) indicated that 24 per cent of those in the top quartile had died compared to 54 per cent of those in the bottom quartile. Similar results have been reported for men. Everson et al (1996b) examined the relationship between hopelessness and health outcomes in a large sample of men. Comparing the top and bottom 33 per cent (tertiles) showed that those in the top tertile compared to the bottom tertile for hopelessness were 3.5 times more likely to die from all causes of death, 4 times more likely to die from cardiovascular disease, and 2.5 times more likely to die from cancer. Similarly, men with AIDS who are optimistic live twice as long as men who are pessimistic (Reed et al, 1994). More generally, among older individuals, those with positive attitudes towards ageing live an average of 7.5 years longer than those with more negative attitudes (Levy et al, 2002).

These studies on health outcomes highlight an important but subtle emerging distinction between optimism and **positive affect**. Whereas optimism refers to

Figure 6.1 We can all show different 'faces' to the world. Personality traits tap consistencies in how we respond. Such consistencies have been found to play important roles in the development of illness.

positive beliefs and feelings about the future, positive affect reflects a level of pleasurable engagement with the environment such as happiness, joy, excitement, enthusiasm and contentment. The two tendencies may overlap substantially as is shown in the Danner et al (2001) study. However, recent research has begun to examine the effects of positive affect independent of optimism (see Pressman and Cohen, 2005, for a review of positive affect and health). One important issue here is the extent to which positive affect is just the opposite of, or alternatively truly distinct from, negative affectivity, a personality trait we consider below. Currently there is evidence supporting both views.

The explanation for the relationship between optimism and various health outcomes is still unclear. One interesting suggestion is that those high in optimism may be more likely to avoid certain high risk situations. Some supporting evidence for this view comes from Peterson and colleagues (1988) who showed that those with an **optimistic attributional style** were less likely to die from accidental or violent causes than those with a pessimistic style, while the two groups did not differ in respect of mortality from cancer or cardiovascular disease. A further explanation for the relationship between optimism and health is through the effects of optimism on coping strategies. Those high in optimism are more likely to use adaptive and functional strategies for coping with problems such as acceptance, rational thinking, social support and positive reframing. For example, Scheier, Weintraub and Carver (1986) conducted a study in which students had to write about coping with stressful situations. Optimists were found to be more likely to use strategies such as making a plan and sticking to it, focusing intently on the problem, and seeking social support. Optimists were also less likely to distract themselves from thinking about the problem. Scheier et al (1989) reported similar differences between optimists and pessimists in the way they coped with recovery from surgery that resulted in faster recovery among the optimists. The use of more constructive coping strategies may lead to better health outcomes, partly by helping individuals to avoid negative life events and also by helping them to confront and deal with problems earlier and more effectively. A further explanation focuses on the effect of pessimism on physiological reactions to stress in terms of immune functioning and cardiovascular response (Scheier and Carver, 1987). Some support of this explanation can be found in studies that have shown immune responses to be lower in pessimists (Segerstrom et al, 1998).

Type A behaviour

Type A behaviour pattern is typified by a competitive drive, aggression, chronic impatience and a sense of time urgency (Rosenman et al, 1976). This type of behaviour is contrasted with the opposite cluster of characteristics, type B behaviour pattern, which leads to a more relaxed, laid-back approach to life. The concept of type A behaviour originated from the work of two cardiologists, Meyer Friedman and Ray Rosenman, who realized that their patients' disease was not fully explained by conventional risk factors such as dietary cholesterol and smoking. For years they failed to look beyond the physical symptoms and to consider the signs of stress in their patients, even though patients tended to sit on the edge of waiting room chairs to the extent that an upholsterer commented that the front edges of the waiting room chairs were unusually worn (Friedman and Rosenman, 1974). Eventually, however, they sent out a questionnaire asking 150 businessmen what they believed had precipitated a heart attack in a friend. Few thought it was due to diet or smoking and most felt it was due to 'excessive competitive drive and meeting deadlines' (Rosenman et al, 1964: 73). A subsequent study suggested that physicians agreed even though this was not a recognized cause in the medical literature of the time. This and subsequent research ultimately led to the identification of the constellation of characteristics described above, and its long-term investigation in a large prospective study known as the *Western Collaborative Group Study*. This examined risk factors for coronary heart disease (CHD) in a sample of over 3000 healthy middle-aged men. The study started in 1960 and followed participants for more than 27 years.

Rosenman and colleagues assessed the participants in the study using a structured interview. This interview involved the interviewer asking questions in a confrontational manner (including interrupting the participant) with the aim of provoking the participant in order to assess aggression and time urgency (Chesney et al, 1980). The men were then followed up at 8.5 and 22 years. The researchers found after 8.5 years that those men who were classified as type A had around twice the risk of developing CHD as those who were type B, even after controlling for other risk factors. At this stage it appeared that type A was a risk factor that was as important as smoking or high blood pressure for the development of CHD. However, on follow-up after 22 years, the researchers found that type A behaviour no longer showed a significant relationship with CHD (Ragland and Brand, 1985). Thus, after the initial enthusiasm about the importance of this risk factor, doubts began to be raised.

Many other research teams around the world were also conducting studies of type A behaviour during the 1960s and 1970s and in the early years (pre 1978) these tended to support the idea that type A was linked to CHD (Miller et al, 1991). However, after this time, the majority of subsequent studies, like that of the Western Collaborative Group itself, failed to support the original findings. As a result the role of type A in heart disease became quite a controversial issue. Some people even questioned whether type A was a risk factor at all (Ragland and Brand, 1985). In the 1980s and early 1990s a number of meta-analytic studies (see also Focus box 8.2) were conducted, sometimes with conflicting conclusions (Booth-Kewley and Friedman, 1987; Matthews, 1988; Miller et al, 1996). Miller et al suggested that the null findings were due to a range of methodological differences between the early studies and those conducted later. First, the more recent studies often looked at samples that were already at high risk of heart disease. Second, over time, questionnaire measures (e.g. the *Jenkins Activity Survey*; Jenkins et al, 1971) have been used rather than the structured interview which allows assessment of behaviour in interaction. The Jenkins Activity Survey contains items such as 'Would people who know you well agree that you tend to do most things in a hurry?' and 'Do you ever set deadlines of quotas for yourself at home or at work?'. Positive responses to these items indicate type A behaviour. Compared to the interview, such measures have limitations in terms of assessing behaviour and tend to be less effective in predicting CHD. Third, many of the later studies used mortality from the disease as their dependent variable. It is possible, however, that type A individuals may develop CHD when they are younger, but survive longer, than those who develop it later in life. Overall, Miller et al concluded that type A behaviour was a risk factor for heart disease as, across studies based on structured interviews, about 70 per cent of middle-aged males with CHD were type As, as opposed to 46 per cent of healthy males.

Two other meta-analytic reviews by Booth-Kewley and Friedman (1987) and Matthews (1988) raised the interesting possibility that not all aspects of type A behaviour are equally predictive of CHD. Booth-Kewley and Friedman (1987: 359) suggested that in fact the person who is prone to CHD is not the typical type A person, rather it is someone who is prone to negative emotions 'perhaps someone who is depressed, aggressively competitive, easily frustrated, anxious, angry or some combination'. Matthews, however, whose meta-analysis included several additional studies and used different inclusion criteria, focusing on prospective studies, found little to support the idea that negative emotions were predictive of CHD. However, both meta-analyses suggested that **hostility** (a component of the type A construct) predicts heart disease.

A number of studies have investigated the mechanisms whereby type A may lead to CHD, with most research focusing on the tendency for type A individuals to show particularly strong physiological reactivity in the face of environmental stressors (Krantz and Manuck, 1984). Thus, although the research discussed so far has focused on direct relationships between type A and health behaviour, the implication is that type A moderates the relationship between stressors and health. This has been investigated by researchers interested in relationships between work stress and health. Type A behaviour is important in the work environment because employers value some aspects of type A behaviour which lead to employees being more productive (Bluen et al, 1990). Most occupational stress researchers who now investigate type A consider each of the components that make up the trait separately. This is because of criticisms of the validity of the overall measure (e.g. Edwards et al, 1990). In so doing they have tended to find differential effects for different aspects of type A. So, for example, Jex et al (2002) found that job stressors were most predictive of ill health for those with high levels of **achievement-striving** (i.e. achievement-striving moderated the impact of job stressors on health), whereas the **impatience–irritability** dimension did not moderate the impact of job stressors.

A certain amount of research continues into the type A behaviour pattern and its individual components. However, following from the meta-analyses discussed above, the emphasis has shifted towards investigating hostility.

Hostility

Hostility, like type A, is a complex and multidimensional construct. It has been defined as 'a negative attitude towards others, consisting of enmity, denigration and ill will' (Smith, 1994: 26). Components of this characteristic are **cynicism** about others' motives, **mistrust** and **hostile attributional style**, i.e. a tendency to interpret other people's actions as aggressive (Smith et al, 2004). While this definition is primarily cognitive, the associated emotional and behavioural constructs of anger and aggression are often incorporated within the construct (Miller et al, 1996). The construct is measured using items such as 'Some of my family have habits that bother and annoy me very much' and 'It is safer to trust no-one'; with a response of 'true' indicating higher levels of hostility. These items are taken from the Cook–Medley hostility scale which is a commonly used measure (Cook and Medley, 1954). Hostility has been found to be correlated quite highly with the hard-driving component of type A behaviour ($r = .44$). It is also positively correlated with a range of measures of neuroticism ($r = .27$ to .54) and negatively with measures of extraversion ($r = 2.48$) (Carmody et al, 1989). Some authors discuss hostility as one (negative) expression of the Big Five personality trait agreeableness (Ozer and Benet-Martinez, 2006), i.e. hostility is low agreeableness.

Following from the tradition of research in type A behaviour, most research in this area has focused on the role of hostility in CHD. As for the research on type A, meta-analysis techniques have been used to assess the strength of effects (Miller et al, 1996). Miller et al included 45 studies in their review and concluded that hostility was an independent risk factor for CHD. As was the case with the research into type A, they found that the strongest relationships were found using structured interviews to assess hostility which emphasize the expressive component of hostility (i.e. verbally and physically aggressive behaviour). These studies suggested that the effects were at least similar in magnitude to those reported for traditional risk factors such as smoking, high blood pressure and cholesterol. Even among studies using self-report measures (the Cook–Medley scale: Cook and Medley, 1954), the review found small but consistent relationships with heart disease. It should be noted, however, that a more recent meta-analysis offers a less positive interpretation based on a smaller subset of papers (Myrtek, 2001), i.e. they suggest that while the effects are significant they are very small indeed. In the main, subsequent studies and reviews continue to suggest that hostility plays a role in causing CHD (e.g. Gallo and Matthews, 2003) and also hypertension (Rutledge and Hogan, 2002). Focus box 6.2 discusses how we can reduce hostility.

Focus 6.2

Interventions to reduce hostility

There is now evidence suggesting that a hostility-reduction intervention aimed at CHD patients with high levels of hostility may reduce risks for heart disease. Gidron, Davidson and Bata (1999) conducted a randomized controlled trial in which 22 hostile male patients were assigned to either a treatment or control group. Hostility was assessed by observation during a structured interview and by self-ratings. The hostility-reduction intervention involved eight 90-minute weekly group meetings using cognitive behaviour techniques. Participants were taught skills to reduce antagonism, cynicism and anger. They were also asked to rate their hostility in a daily log and to record their use of skills. The control group had a one-session group meeting giving information about the risks of hostility and about basic hostility-reduction skills. The participants were followed up immediately after the trial and again after two months. Those in the intervention group were observed to be, and rated themselves to be, less hostile at follow-up than the controls. They also had lower diastolic blood pressure. Furthermore, reductions in hostility were correlated with reductions in blood pressure.

In a subsequent paper, Davidson et al (2007) conducted secondary analysis of the data from the above study. They found that patients who received the intervention tended to have fewer hospital admissions in the six months following the intervention, and, importantly, had significantly fewer days in hospital (a mean of 0.38 days compared with a mean of 2.15 days for the control group). Consequently, their hospitalization costs were less. While more studies are needed with larger and more diverse groups, these findings suggest there may be potential to design efficacious and cost-effective hostility-reduction treatments.

The possible mechanisms underlying the effects of hostility have also been discussed in some detail. Smith et al (2004) discuss five possible models:

1. **Psychophysiological reactivity** model. This suggests that hostile individuals show exaggerated cardiovascular and neuroendocrine responses to stressors.
2. **Psychosocial vulnerability** model. This model suggests that hostile individuals experience more interpersonal conflict. Hostility may lead to more stress and also be associated with less social support.
3. Transactional model. This combines the above two models and suggests that hostile individuals experience more interpersonal conflict and also have greater physiological reactivity – a 'double whammy' effect.
4. Health behaviour model. This suggests that hostility affects health via the mediating impact of poorer health behaviours. For example, hostile people may be cynical about health warnings or resistant to medical advice.
5. Constitutional vulnerability model. This model raises the possibility that individual differences (which might be genetic) are associated with both the personality tendency and the disease risk, i.e. the association between hostility and CHD is due to a third variable.

Overall, Smith et al conclude that there is considerable support for a number of these models. Hostile people do display heightened physiological responses; they also experience increased levels of conflict and less social support. However, research has not yet established whether these tendencies mediate the relationship between hostility and health. There is some evidence that hostile people do display poorer health behaviours but it is also clear that this does not wholly account for the relationship between hostility and health. Finally, the development of molecular genetics offers opportunities to explore the constitutional vulnerability model. Further research is awaited on these mechanisms. However, it is possible that several mechanisms play a part in explaining the association between hostility and health.

An interesting possibility in relation to the development of hostility is suggested by the work of Matthews et al (1996). In this work, negative behaviours during parent–son discussions aimed at resolving disagreements were observed in 51 Caucasian adolescent (12–13 years of age) boys. Results showed that the frequency of negative behaviours in the family discussions predicted hostility and expressed anger assessed three years later even after controlling for baseline hostility. This would suggest that hostility may be nurtured within particular family backgrounds that are characterized by negative behaviours during interactions. In contrast, work by Caspi et al (1997) shows that measures of temperament taken at 3 years old predict later health-related risk behaviour in early adulthood and that this effect is mediated by personality measures taken in late adolescence. This would appear to be good evidence that personality traits are something we are born with or at least develop very early in life and remain stable throughout our lives (i.e. a nature explanation of personality). Together these studies suggest that, while certain aspects of personality may be stable from a very young age, other aspects change and develop over time as a result of our interaction with our environment. This would appear to suggest the relevance of both a nature and a nurture explanation of personality trait development.

Focus 6.3

Type D personality

Similar to type A, type D personality is a risk factor for coronary heart disease. The type D, or distressed, personality refers to individuals who experience high levels of negative emotions (negative affectivity) and inhibit the expression of these negative emotions in social interactions (social inhibition). The concept was introduced by Johan Denollet, of Tilburg University in the Netherlands.

Type D personality can be assessed by a self-report questionnaire containing items that tap negative affectivity (e.g. 'I often make a fuss about unimportant things' or 'I often feel unhappy') and social inhibition (e.g. 'I often feel inhibited in social interactions' or 'I find it hard to start a conversation'). A type D individual would be someone who scores highly on both of these dimensions. This is important because previous research has shown negative affectivity or neuroticism to be related to various negative health outcomes.

Denollet and colleagues have shown the type D personality to be a risk factor for adverse health outcomes in cardiac patients. So, for example, Denollet et al (1996) assessed type D in a sample of 286 cardiac patients who were receiving treatment. Approximately one-third of the sample were classified as type D. Approximately eight years later, the patients were followed up. Among those classified as type D a total of 27 per cent had died compared with a total of 7 per cent of the rest of the sample. A majority of the deaths were due to heart disease or stroke. This translates into an odds ratio of almost four (i.e. being four times more likely to die if classified as type D compared to those not classified as type D). These effects have been replicated in several studies. Type D is also related to various forms of psychological distress in cardiac patients including depression and anxiety.

The explanation for the relationship between type D and risk of death is not entirely clear. Those with type D personalities appear to have more highly activated immune systems and more inflammation (perhaps indicating more damage to blood vessels in the heart and throughout the body). They also show greater increases in blood pressure in reactions to stress. Recent research has suggested that type D individuals engage in fewer health behaviours and experience lower levels of social support and that these effects remain after controlling for neuroticism (Williams et al, 2008).

Neuroticism

Neuroticism is one of the Big Five personality traits. It refers to the tendency to commonly experience negative emotions such as distress, anxiety, fear, anger and guilt (Watson and Clark, 1984). Because of the focus on negative emotions it is sometimes referred to as **negative affect**. Those high in neuroticism or negative affect worry about the future, dwell on failures and shortcomings, and have less favourable views of themselves and others. There are a number of well-established measures of neuroticism. For example, the **International Personality Item Pool** (website: www.ipip.ori.org/ipip), which contains a set of public domain measures of the Big Five personality traits, includes statements such as 'Worry a lot', and 'Get upset easily'; those high in neuroticism are more likely to consider these statements as good self-descriptions. A variety of studies show that those high in neuroticism report themselves as experiencing more physical symptoms and that these symptoms are more intense (Affleck et al, 1992). For example, Costa and McCrae (1987) reported neuroticism to be related to frequency of illness, cardiovascular problems, digestive problems and fatigue across a sample of women with a wide variety of ages. These effects have been demonstrated in various cross-sectional and longitudinal studies.

Similar to the case for hostility, a number of mechanisms by which neuroticism might influence health outcomes have been suggested. One potential mechanism relating neuroticism to health outcomes might be through perceived or actual stress experienced. For example, those high in negative affect tend to perceive events as more stressful and difficult to cope with than those who are low in negative affect (Watson, 1988). In addition, those high in negative affect may experience more prolonged psychological distress after a negative event (Ormell and Wohlfarth, 1991). However, an important alternative suggestion in relation to neuroticism is that the reported impact on health symptoms may be attributable to the use of self-report measures of health. The hypothesis is that high levels of neuroticism lead to an individual noticing or complaining more about symptoms without this influencing the symptoms he or she experiences. Work that has objectively assessed physical health has indeed tended to report little association between such measures and neuroticism (Watson and Pennebaker, 1989). This importantly suggests the need to measure and control for the effects of neuroticism in any studies using symptom reports as outcome measures.

A further mechanism by which neuroticism may lead to negative health outcomes is through impact on coping mechanisms. Neuroticism might be related to maladaptive coping strategies in a similar way to pessimism. For example, Costa and McCrae (1990) showed that those high in neuroticism were more likely to engage in self-blame and less likely to engage in problem-solving in response to a scenario describing a nuclear accident. A related way in which neuroticism may impact on health outcomes is through influencing social support. It has been suggested that those high in neuroticism may have greater difficulties in forming and maintaining close relationships and may experience higher levels of interpersonal conflict. In support of this view those high in negative affect have been shown to have lower marital satisfaction (Burke et al, 1980). These effects of neuroticism may have the result that those high in neuroticism experience less social support and so are less likely to experience the health protective effects associated with social support (see Chapter 5).

Neuroticism may also influence an individual's health behaviours and in this way impact on health outcomes. Neuroticism has been shown to relate to more smoking and alcohol abuse, and less healthy eating and exercise (Booth-Kewley and Vickers, 1994). For example, in relation to smoking, longitudinal studies have found that those with higher neuroticism scores are more likely to take up smoking and maintain the habit (e.g. Canals et al, 1997). Here the negative outcomes associated with higher levels of neuroticism might be partly attributable to those with higher levels of neuroticism being more likely to smoke. Shipley et al (2007) recently reported the impact of neuroticism on mortality in a sample of over 5000 UK adults over a period of 21 years. High neuroticism was associated with mortality from all causes and with mortality from cardiovascular diseases. However, these effects became non-significant after controlling for age, gender, social class, education, smoking, alcohol consumption and physical activity. This would suggest that the effects of neuroticism on mortality may be explained by sociodemographic factors and health behaviours. A final mechanism by which neuroticism may impact on health is through physiological changes. Research has highlighted the impact of high levels of neuroticism on reduced immune function (Kiecolt-Glaser et al, 2002) suggesting another potential mechanism through which neuroticism impacts on various health outcomes.

Extraversion

Extraversion is a further Big Five personality trait where those with high levels of the trait are referred to as extraverts and those with low levels referred to as introverts. Extraverts tend to be outgoing, social, assertive and show high levels of energy; they also tend to seek stimulation and so enjoy new challenges but get easily bored. In contrast introverts tend to be more cautious, serious and avoid over-stimulating environments and activities (Eysenck, 1967; Costa and McCrae, 1992). There are a number of well-established measures of extraversion–introversion. For example, Eysenck and Eysenck's (1964) measure contains items such as 'Are you usually carefree?' and 'Do you enjoy wild parties?' with extroverts more likely to agree with these types of items (see Figure 6.2). Extraversion has been found to be associated with positive psychological well-being and better physical health. For example, extraverts report more positive moods and higher levels of pleasure and excitement. Costa and McCrae (1980) showed that extraversion measured at one time point significantly predicted happiness 10 years later. In terms of physical health, extraverts tend to report lower rates of coronary heart disease, ulcers, asthma and arthritis (Friedman and Booth-Kewley, 1987). Some research has reported effects for extraversion on mortality. For example, Shipley et al (2007), in addition to examining the impact of neuroticism on mortality, also examined the impact of extraversion. In their sample of over 5000 UK adults examined over a 21-year period, extraversion was found to be significantly associated with a reduced risk of respiratory disease.

The explanation for the relationship between extraversion and health is not entirely clear. Although it is possible that this relationship is attributable to extraverts experiencing lower levels of stress, better coping strategies or more social support compared to introverts, there is as yet no strong evidence to support these explanations. Similarly, in relation to impacts on health

Figure 6.2. The Rorschach ink blot test for personality. Most modern personality tests employ questionnaires to assess different personality traits. Earlier tests employed more projective tests such as the Rorschach ink blot test shown here where respondents were required to interpret ink blots and their responses used to classify their personality. Such tests however have low reliability and scores tend to vary depending on the psychologist doing the interpretation.
Source: © Science Museum.

behaviours, extraversion appears to be associated with both health-protective behaviours like exercise (Rhodes et al, 2002) and health-risking behaviours like smoking (Booth-Kewley and Vickers, 1994)!

Activity 6.1

The accident-prone personality?

Some research has addressed the idea that certain personality traits are precursors of accidents or unintentional injuries, i.e. the accident-prone personality. The best evidence supporting such a personality type comes from studies focusing on impulsivity. This research shows that childhood impulsivity predicts injuries both during childhood and later life (Caspi et al, 1997; Cooper et al, 2003).

What mechanisms might explain how impulsivity is related to injuries? Try reading these two articles and coming up with a list of potential mechanisms.

Conscientiousness

Conscientiousness refers to the ability to control one's behaviour and to complete tasks. Highly conscientious individuals are more organized, careful, dependable, self-disciplined and achievement-oriented than those low in conscientiousness (McCrae and Costa, 1987). High conscientiousness has also been associated with a greater use of problem-focused, positive reappraisal and support-seeking coping strategies (Watson and Hubbard, 1996), and a less

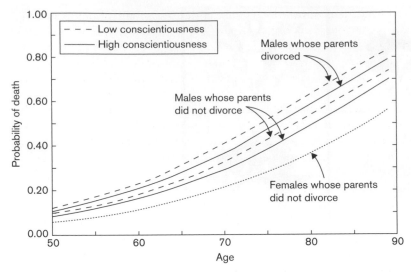

Figure 6.3 Probability of dying (survival curves) at different ages for the Terman sample for different groups of males in comparison to females.

Source: © 1993 Howard S. Friedman and Joseph E. Schwartz. Reprinted by permission. For further information about this project, see www.faculty.urc.edu/~friedman/.

frequent use of escape-avoidance and self-blame coping strategies (O'Brien and Delongis, 1996). Conscientiousness is also associated with a propensity to follow socially prescribed norms for impulse control (John and Srivastava, 1999; Bogg and Roberts, 2004). In the last few years measures of conscientiousness with good levels of reliability and validity have become available. For example, the International Personality Item Pool contains statements such as 'Am always prepared', and 'Am exacting in my work' in order to tap conscientiousness. Those high in conscientiousness are more likely to consider these statements as accurate self-descriptions. A growing body of research shows conscientiousness to have impacts on health behaviours, health outcomes and even longevity.

The key evidence for the impact of conscientiousness on longevity comes from the *Terman Life-Cycle personality cohort study*. In this highly regarded study, a sample of over 1000 children born around 1910 completed various measures every five to ten years from the age of 11. The original sample of children were selected to have above average IQ and were drawn from the area around the Californian cities of San Francisco and Los Angeles. The personality assessments included measures of conscientiousness, optimism, self-esteem, sociability, stability of mood and energy level. Friedman et al (1993) reported that of these variables only conscientiousness was significantly associated with lower mortality over time. The degree of association was such that those high in conscientiousness were more likely to live longer (by about two years) compared to those low in conscientiousness. Comparing the top and bottom 25 per cent (quartiles) on conscientiousness indicated that those in the bottom quartile were one and one half times more likely to die in any one year compared to those in the top quartile. Figure 6.3 shows the survival curves for participants in the Terman sample separately for males and females and for those with and without divorced parents among those with high and low levels of conscientiousness.

An important mechanism by which conscientiousness may influence health is through health behaviours. Friedman H.S. et al (1995) showed that the impact of conscientiousness on longevity in the Terman sample was partly accounted for by its effect on smoking and alcohol use, that is, conscientious children were less likely to become heavy smokers and drinkers. Consistent with these findings, Booth-Kewley and Vickers (1994) found that conscientiousness was more strongly correlated with clusters of health-related behaviours than the other Big Five traits, and was particularly strongly associated with health protection and accident control behaviours. Similarly, Courneya and Hellsten (1998) reported that, of the Big Five traits, conscientiousness was most strongly related to engaging in exercise behaviours, while Siegler, Feaganes and Rimer (1995) showed that regular mammography attendance was predicted by conscientiousness and extraversion. A comprehensive meta-analysis of work on the relationship between conscientiousness and behaviours (Bogg and Roberts, 2004) showed conscientiousness to be positively related to a range of protective health behaviours (e.g. exercise) and negatively related to a range of risky health behaviours (e.g. smoking). Table 6.2 shows the size of these effects for a range of different health behaviours (the impact of health behaviours on health is further considered in Chapter 7). A further way in which conscientiousness may impact on health outcomes is through modifying behaviour following illness. So, for example, some studies have demonstrated that individuals high in conscientiousness are more likely to follow health care advice and that this difference is particularly apparent when the advice is difficult or time consuming to follow (Christiansen and Smith, 1995; Schwartz J.E. et al, 1999).

Recent research has begun to examine how personality traits may produce changes in health behaviours through shaping the way in which individuals think about these behaviours. This work suggests that our thoughts and feelings about performing a particular health behaviour (e.g. exercising) are a primary determinant of whether we perform that behaviour. That is, we tend to engage in behaviours that we have positive thoughts and feelings about (see Chapter 7). In this view, conscientiousness might, for example, influence the amount of exercise we do as a result of shaping our thoughts and feelings about exercising (i.e. thoughts and feelings mediate the impact of conscientiousness on exercise). Such mediation effects have been demonstrated by Siegler et al (1995) who found that the effect of conscientiousness on mammography attendance was mediated by knowledge of breast cancer and the perceived costs of seeking mammography. Similarly, the impact of conscientiousness on the self-care activities of patients with type 1 diabetes has been found to be mediated by treatment beliefs (e.g. Christensen et al, 1999). However, other research has found both mediated and direct effects for conscientiousness when predicting health behaviour (Vollrath et al, 1999; Conner and Abraham, 2001).

In addition to mediation effects, conscientiousness might also operate as a moderator changing the relationship between health beliefs and health behaviour. A few studies have examined the moderating role of conscientiousness. For example, in a retrospective study, Schwartz M.D. et al (1999) found that conscientiousness moderated the relationship between breast-cancer-related distress and mammography uptake such that, among those with

Table 6.2 Relationship between conscientiousness and various health behaviours based on a meta-analysis of available studies

Behaviour	Effect size	Total sample size
Physical activity	.05	24,259
Excessive alcohol use	−.25	32,137
Drug use	−.28	36,573
Unhealthy eating	−.13	6,356
Risky driving	−.25	10,171
Risky sex	−.13	12,410
Suicide	−.12	6,087
Tobacco use	−.14	46,725
Violence	−.25	10,277

Note. Cohen (1992) suggests that $r = 0.1$ equates to a small effect size, 0.3 to a medium effect size, and 0.5 to a large effect size, so these effect sizes for conscientiousness are mostly in the small to medium range.
Source: Bogg and Roberts, 2004

high levels of distress, those with high conscientiousness scores were more likely to have attended mammography screening than those with low conscientiousness scores. Conscientiousness scores had no effect on attendance among those with low levels of distress. Hampson et al (2000) reported a similar significant interaction between conscientiousness and perceived risk in relation to changes in indoor smoking behaviour in response to the threat from radon gas. In relation to exercise, Rhodes et al (2002) reported conscientiousness to significantly moderate the intention–behaviour relationship, with higher levels of conscientiousness associated with stronger intention–behaviour relationships. Conner et al (2008) showed intentions to be stronger predictors of resisting initiating smoking for an adolescent sample with high rather than low levels of conscientiousness.

Conclusions

We have reviewed relationships between key personality traits and health outcomes and considered some of the explanations of this relationship. Out of the Big Five personality framework we noted that although there was as yet less evidence linking openness to health outcomes, there was more evidence in relation to conscientiousness, extraversion, neuroticism and agreeableness (when defined as high hostility), with better health outcomes associated with high conscientiousness, high extraversion, low neuroticism and high agreeableness (or low hostility). We also noted that a body of research supports a link between optimism and positive health outcomes. The negative impacts of type A behaviour pattern and hostility on health were also noted, particularly in relation to the risk of coronary heart disease.

While discussing the effects of individual personality traits on health outcomes we also noted a number of important explanations for the relationship between the two. Table 6.1 provides a summary of these explanations and is worth reviewing now.

Not all these explanations constitute true causal mechanisms. Indeed part of the problem in interpreting any relationship between personality and health is that the data obtained is usually correlational (see Research methods box 6.1).

A further explanation of the relationship between personality traits and health outcomes is a **measurement artefact** explanation. Here the suggestion is that the personality trait may cause differences in the way certain health outcomes (e.g. symptoms) are reported. For example, we noted that, at least in relation to neuroticism, some of the relationship between the personality trait and health outcomes may be artefactual, caused by a reliance on self-report measures of symptoms (see Chapter 4). This would account for the stronger relationship between neuroticism and symptom reports compared to the relationship between neuroticism and non-self-report health outcomes (e.g. illness).

The remaining explanations of the relationship between personality traits and health outcomes are more easily interpreted as causal relationships. A key explanation may be that personality traits can lead to health outcomes through physiological mechanisms. So, for example, hostility might cause damage to arteries which in turn leads to a greater likelihood of heart disease. Another explanation focuses on the idea that certain personality traits may be associated with approaching certain risky situations. Friedman (2000) has referred to this idea as **tropisms**. Drawing on the analogy of phototropic plants that move towards sources of light, the suggestion is that certain personality types are drawn to particular situations which then pose a risk to the individual's health. For example, extraverts might be more likely to seek out situations where the risk of accidental injury is higher or where health risk behaviours such as smoking or drug use are common. Relatedly, personality traits may lead to negative health outcomes through changing engagement in health-related behaviours. We noted that conscientious individuals appear to be less likely to engage in health-risking behaviours such as smoking and more likely to engage in health-protective behaviours such as exercise. As we have already suggested, this might be through exposure to such behaviours in situations individuals are drawn to. Alternatively, personality traits like conscientiousness might make some health behaviours more likely by changing the way conscientious individuals think about behaviours such as exercise (Conner and Abraham, 2001). Thus conscientious individuals might value health-protective behaviours more or might just be better at planning how best to engage in such behaviours. These cognitions about health behaviours are the focus of Chapter 7.

A final set of explanations for the relationship between personality traits and health outcomes relates to stress and the variables that protect against the effects of stress. So, for example, individuals high in neuroticism may perceive themselves as experiencing more stress. Such individuals may also be less likely to employ appropriate coping mechanisms or have access to coping resources such as social support to deal with this stress. In this case it may be the stress that causes the negative health outcomes, but it is high levels of neuroticism that cause the stress and the inability to cope appropriately with the stress. Penley and Tomaka (2002) provide an interesting discussion of the relationship between all of the Big Five personality traits and both stress and coping.

Research methods 6.1

Correlation and inferences of causation

When an independent (or predictor) variable (e.g. social support or attitude) is measured at the same time as a dependent (or outcome) variable (e.g. immune functioning or condom use) this is known as a cross-sectional study. When the dependent variable is measured at a later time then this is known as a longitudinal or prospective study. For example, if we measure job stress and then follow up our participants a year later this is a prospective study. Prospective studies offer more reassurance regarding the **direction of causation** because we know that the independent variable measure preceded the dependent variable measure in time. Prospective studies also allow us to control for levels of a dependent variable at time 1 so that we can predict change in the dependent variable from an independent variable. For example, we might find that lower reported social support (at time 1) predicts increases in stress over the following year. Thus while we might use analysis of variance (ANOVA) to test whether an association between an independent and dependent variable is likely to be replicable, we can use analysis of covariance (ANCOVA) to assess the degree to which an independent variable can predict change in a dependent variable over time by including a baseline measure of the dependent variable as a covariate.

The direction of causation is ideally assessed in an experimental study in which we manipulate (rather than measure) the independent variable. In health psychology, interventions such as behaviour change interventions provide good examples of experimental methodology. For example, one group may receive an intervention to change attitudes or reduce work stress while another (control) group receives no intervention. If participants are randomly allocated to these two groups (to try to distribute confounding factors across groups) or matched (to balance confounding factors) then any difference in the dependent variable following the manipulation (that is, the intervention) can be reasonably attributed to that manipulation. The classic use of experimental methodology in health psychology is the randomized controlled trial (RCT). It is of course worth noting that such experimental methods merely establish one causal determinant of the dependent variable, they do not necessarily demonstrate that this is the one and only causal determinant.

Unfortunately, we often cannot manipulate independent variables in health psychology and so must infer underlying causal mechanisms from correlational data. For example, in relation to smoking, the majority of the evidence supporting an impact of smoking on cancer and cardiovascular disease outcomes is correlational, at least for studies in humans. Similarly, the relationship between personality and health is based on correlational data.

There are well-known dangers in drawing causal inferences from correlational data. Two key issues are causal direction and the **third variable problem**. Causal direction refers to the issue of the direction of effect being unknown when two variables are correlated: did A cause B or B cause A? For example, in relation to personality and health this issue becomes one of whether a personality trait resulted in a health outcome or the health outcome produced the personality trait. So, for example, some patients with serious illnesses such as cancer may become anxious and neurotic. This might lead us to the erroneous conclusion that neuroticism played a role in causing the cancer when in fact the cancer had produced increased neuroticism.

Third variable problems refer to the possibility that a correlation between two variables might be due to both variables being caused by a third variable. So, for example, there is some evidence that a hyper-responsive nervous system is an underlying factor in both the development of an anxious personality (high neuroticism) and the development of heart disease. Here an anxious, reactive personality would be related to (that is, correlated with) heart disease without being a causal determinant of heart disease (McCabe et al, 2000). Similarly, Eysenck (1967) argued that extraversion relates to differences in the sensitivity of the nervous system that influences emotional reactions and reactions to socialization. Extraverts may also be more likely to seek stimulation through behaviours such as smoking. In both these cases it is not the personality trait itself which causes the health outcomes but an underlying biological mechanism that causes both the personality trait and the health outcome.

Summary

A number of personality traits show significant relationships with various health outcomes such as morbidity and mortality. Indeed some of these relationships are of a similar size to those reported for more well-known risk factors like blood cholesterol levels. Of the Big Five personality traits that form much of the focus in modern-day personality research there is good evidence relating low levels of neuroticism and high levels of extraversion and conscientiousness to health outcomes (e.g. lower levels of illness and greater longevity). Evidence also suggests that optimism is positively related to health outcomes, while type A behaviour and hostility (low agreeableness) are negatively related to health outcomes.

The explanations of these relationships between personality and health are many and varied. They range from artefactual explanations, through mediating mechanisms, to direct biological or physiological effects. So, for example, much of the observed impact of neuroticism on self-reported illness is probably attributable to those higher in neuroticism being more likely to report symptoms. In relation to conscientiousness and health, for example, there is evidence of a mediating mechanism through greater engagement in health-protective behaviours and less engagement in health-risking behaviours, whereas in relation to hostility there is evidence of a direct effect through damage to arteries cause by over-reactivity to stress among those high in hostility. Detailing the range of effects that different personality dimensions can have on health and assessing the explanations of these effects is an exciting area of current research in health psychology.

Key concepts and terms

Achievement-striving	Mistrust
Agreeableness	Negative affect
Big Five personality traits	Neuroticism
Conscientiousness	Openness to experience
Cynicism	Optimism
Direction of causation	Optimistic attributional style
Extraversion	Positive affect
Hope	Psychophysiological reactivity model
Hostile attributional style	
Hostility	Psychosocial vulnerability model
Impatience–irritability	
International Personality Item Pool	Third variable problem
	Tropisms
Measurement artefact	Type A behaviour pattern

Sample essay titles

■ Describe the evidence relating key personality traits to different kinds of health outcomes.

■ Critically evaluate the mechanisms by which personality traits might have impacts on health.

■ Do personality differences predict health? Discuss relevant findings and mechanisms.

Further reading

Journal articles

Caspi, A., Roberts, B.W., and Shiner, R.L. (2005). Personality development: Stability and change. *Annual Review of Psychology*, 56, 453–484.

Matthews, K.A., Woodall, K.L., Kenyon, K., and Jacob, T. (1996). Negative family environment as a predictor of boys' future status on measures of hostile attitudes, interview behavior and anger expression. *Health Psychology*, 14, 30–37.

Peterson, C., Vaillant, G.E., and Seligman, M.E.P. (1988). Pessimistic explanatory style is a risk factor for physical illness: A thirty-five-year longitudinal study. *Journal of Personality and Social Psychology*, 55, 23–27.

Pressman, S.D., and Cohen, S. (2005). Does positive affect influence health? *Psychological Bulletin*, 131, 925–971.

Smith, T.W., Glazer, K., Ruiz, J.M., and Gallo, L.C. (2004). Hostility, anger, aggressiveness, and coronary heart disease: An interpersonal perspective on personality, emotion, and health. *Journal of Personality*, 72, 1217–1270.

4 | Motivation and behaviour

7 Health cognitions and health behaviours

In Chapter 6 we examined the part that personality plays in determining health outcomes. In this chapter we examine health cognitions, foundational to motivation, which have been found to differentiate between people who do and do not perform **health behaviours**. This is followed by an examination of how health-related motivation can be changed in Chapter 8, and how health-related behaviours can be changed in Chapter 9.

The prevalence of health-related behaviours varies across social groups. For example, smoking is more prevalent among those from more economically deprived backgrounds. This would suggest that these factors might be the focus of interventions to change health-related behaviours. However, socio-demographic factors may be impossible to change or may require political intervention at national or international levels (such as changes in income distribution or taxation). For that reason a considerable body of research has examined more modifiable factors that may mediate (and explain) the relationship between socio-demographic factors and health-related behaviours. A particularly promising set of factors are the thoughts and feelings the individual associates with the particular health-related behaviour. These are known as health cognitions and are the focus of this chapter. We will consider: 1) predicting health behaviours; 2) social cognition models; 3) a critical appraisal of social cognition models; 4) the **intention–behaviour gap**.

Learning outcomes

When you have completed this chapter you should be able to:

1. Describe the key health cognitions associated with performing health behaviours.
2. Explain what the cognitive determinants of health behaviours are according to: a) the health belief model; b) protection motivation theory; c) theory of planned behaviour; and d) **social cognitive theory**.
3. Evaluate the contribution of stage models to the understanding of change in health behaviours.
4. Critically evaluate the contribution of social cognition models to understanding the determinants of health behaviours.
5. Describe the intention–behaviour gap in relation to health behaviours.

Predicting health behaviours

Can we predict who will perform health behaviours? Such knowledge might help us understand variations in the distribution of health across society and suggest targets for interventions designed to improve health through changing health behaviours. As you might expect, a range of differences exist between those who do and do not engage in health behaviours such as smoking or exercise. These include demographic factors, social factors, personality factors and cognitive factors (Conner and Norman, 2005).

Focus 7.1

What are health behaviours?

The range of behaviours influencing health is extremely varied, from health-enhancing behaviours such as exercise participation and healthy eating, to health-protective behaviours such as health screening clinic attendance, vaccination against disease, and condom use in response to the threat of AIDS, through to avoidance of health-harming behaviours such as smoking and excessive alcohol consumption, and sick role behaviours such as compliance with medical regimens. A unifying theme across these behaviours has been that they each have immediate or longer-term effects upon the individual's health and are at least partially within the individual's control.

A number of definitions of health behaviours have been suggested. For example, Kasl and Cobb (1966: 246) defined them as 'Any activity undertaken by a person believing himself to be healthy for the purpose of preventing disease or detecting it at an asymptomatic stage'. Can you see any problems with this definition? A more recent definition is offered by Conner and Norman (2005: 2), who define health behaviours as 'any activity undertaken for the purpose of preventing or detecting disease or for improving health and well-being'. Behaviours encompassed in such a definition include medical service usage (e.g. physician visits, vaccination, screening), compliance with medical regimens (e.g. dietary, diabetic, antihypertensive regimens), and self-directed health behaviours (e.g. diet, exercise, breast or testicular self-examination, brushing and flossing teeth, smoking, alcohol consumption and contraceptive use).

Demographic variables show reliable associations with the performance of various health behaviours. Age, for example, shows a curvilinear relationship with many health behaviours, with higher incidences of health-risk behaviours such as smoking in young adults and much lower incidences in children and older adults (Blaxter, 1990). Health behaviours also vary between genders, with women being generally less likely to smoke, consume large amounts of alcohol or engage in regular exercise, and more likely to monitor their diet, take vitamins and engage in dental care, although such patterns can change over time (Waldron, 1988). Differences predicted by economic and ethnic status are also apparent for behaviours such as diet, exercise, alcohol consumption and smoking (e.g. Blaxter, 1990). Generally, younger, wealthier, better educated individuals are more likely to practise health-enhancing behaviours and less likely to engage in health-risking behaviours. Social factors, such as parental models, are important in instilling health behaviours early in life. Peer influences are also important, for example, in the initiation of smoking (e.g. McNeil et al, 1988). Cultural values also appear to be influential, for instance in determining the exercise behaviour of women across cultural groups (e.g. Wardle and Steptoe, 1991). We noted in Chapter 6 that personality traits are fundamental determinants of behaviour and that there is now considerable evidence linking personality and health behaviours (see Vollrath, 2006). For example, H.S. Friedman and colleagues (1993, 1995) found that childhood conscientiousness predicted longevity and that this was partly accounted for by conscientious individuals being less likely to engage in smoking and alcohol use.

None of the correlates of health behaviours mentioned above can be easily modified and, therefore, they do not represent useful targets for interventions designed to change health behaviours. This is not the case for the cognitive antecedents of behaviour. A variety of cognitive factors distinguish between those who do and do not perform various health behaviours. For example, knowledge about behaviour–health links (or risk awareness) is an essential factor in an informed choice concerning a healthy lifestyle (see Chapter 8). The reduction of smoking over the past 20–30 years in the western world can be largely attributed to a growing awareness of the serious health risks posed by tobacco use brought about by widespread publicity. However, the fact that tobacco continues to be widely used among lower socio-economic status groups, and the growing uptake of smoking among adolescent girls in some countries, illustrate that knowledge of health risks is not a sufficient condition for avoidance of smoking by all individuals.

Knowledge is just one of a number of cognitive correlates of health behaviours. Others include perceptions of health risk, potential efficacy of behaviours in reducing this risk, perceived social pressures to perform a behaviour, and control over performance of the behaviour. The relative importance of individual cognitive factors in predicting performance of health behaviours has been the focus of numerous studies. For example, Cummings, Bekker and Maile (1980) had experts sort 109 variables associated with performing health behaviours and derived six distinguishable factors:

1. Accessibility of health care services.
2. Attitudes to health care (beliefs about quality and benefits of treatment).
3. Perceptions of disease threat.
4. Knowledge about disease.
5. Social network characteristics.
6. Demographic factors.

These six groups of correlates may not be independent. For example, there may be considerable overlap between perceptions of disease threat and knowledge of the disease. In order to account for such overlaps and describe the relationships between different influences on health behaviours a number of models have been developed. Such models have been labelled 'social cognition models' because of their use of a number of cognitive variables to predict and understand individual behaviours, including health behaviours. It is important to note at the outset that these models focus on behaviour-specific cognitions as determinants of the relevant behaviour. For example, on this view healthy eating is best understood in terms of cognitions about healthy eating rather than more general thoughts and feelings about health.

Focus 7.2

How do health behaviours impact on health outcomes?

A great many studies have now looked at the relationship between the performance of health behaviours and a variety of health outcomes (e.g. Doll et al, 1994). Large scale epidemiological studies have demonstrated the importance of a variety of health behaviours for both morbidity and mortality. For example, the Alameda County study, which followed nearly 7000 people over 10 years, found that seven key behaviours were associated with lower morbidity and longer life: not smoking, moderate alcohol intake, sleeping seven to eight hours per night, exercising regularly, maintaining a desirable body weight, avoiding snacks and eating breakfast regularly (Belloc and Breslow, 1972; Breslow and Enstrom, 1980).

Health behaviours are assumed to influence health through three major pathways (Baum and Posluszny, 1999): first, by generating direct biological changes such as when excessive alcohol consumption damages the liver; second, by changing exposure to health risks, as when the use of a condom protects against the spread of HIV; and third, by ensuring early detection and treatment of disease, as when testicular or breast self-examination leads to early detection of a cancer that can more easily be treated.

Can you think of further examples of the pathways through which health behaviours might exert their effects on health?

Social cognition models

Social cognition models describe the important cognitions that distinguish between those who do and do not perform health behaviours. This approach focuses on the cognitions or thought processes that intervene between observable stimuli and behaviour in real world situations (Fiske and Taylor, 1991). This 'social cognition' approach has been central to social psychology over the past quarter of a century. Unlike behaviourism, it is founded on the assumption that behaviour is best understood as a function of people's perceptions of reality, rather than objective characterizations of environmental stimuli.

Research into social cognition models can be seen as one part of what has been called 'self-regulation' research. Self-regulation processes are defined as those '... mental and behavioral processes by which people enact their self-conceptions, revise their behavior, or alter the environment so as to bring about outcomes in it in line with their self-perceptions and personal goals' (Fiske and Taylor, 1991: 181). Self-regulation research has emerged from a clinical tradition in psychology which views the individual as striving to eliminate dysfunctional patterns of thinking or behaviour and engage in adaptive patterns of thinking or behaviour (Bandura, 1982; Turk and Salovey, 1986). Self-regulation involves cognitive re-evaluation of beliefs, goal-setting and ongoing monitoring and evaluating of goal-directed behaviour. Two phases of self-regulation activities have been defined: motivational and volitional (Gollwitzer, 1990). In the *motivational phase* costs and benefits are considered in order to choose between goals and behaviours. This phase is assumed to conclude with a decision concerning which goals and actions to pursue at a particular time. In the subsequent *volitional phase*, planning and action directed towards achieving the set goal predominate.

Much of the research with health behaviours has focused on the important cognitions in the motivational phase, although recent research has begun to focus on the volitional phase. The key social cognition models in this area are:

1. The health belief model (HBM; e.g. Janz and Becker, 1984; Abraham and Sheeran, 2005).
2. Protection motivation theory (PMT; e.g. Maddux and Rogers, 1983; Norman et al, 2005).
3. The theory of reasoned action/theory of planned behaviour (TRA/TPB; e.g. Ajzen, 1991; Conner and Sparks, 2005).
4. Social cognitive theory (SCT; e.g. Bandura, 2000; Luszczynska and Schwarzer, 2005).

A distinct set of models focus on the idea that behaviour change occurs through a series of qualitatively different stages. These so-called 'stage' models (Sutton, 2005) importantly include the transtheoretical model of change (Prochaska and DiClemente, 1984; Prochaska et al, 1992). In the following sections we consider these different models and what they say about how cognitions help direct health behaviours. These **social cognition models** (SCMs) provide a basis for understanding the determinants of behaviour and also provide important targets which interventions designed to change behaviour should focus on if they are to change motivation (see Chapter 8) and, thereby, behaviour (see Chapter 9).

The health belief model

The **health belief model** (HBM) is the earliest and most widely used SCM in health psychology (see Abraham and Sheeran, 2005, for a review). For example, Hochbaum (1958) found that perceived susceptibility to tuberculosis and the belief that people with the disease could be asymptomatic (so that screening would be beneficial) distinguished between those who had and had not attended for chest X-rays. Haefner and Kirscht (1970) took this research further by

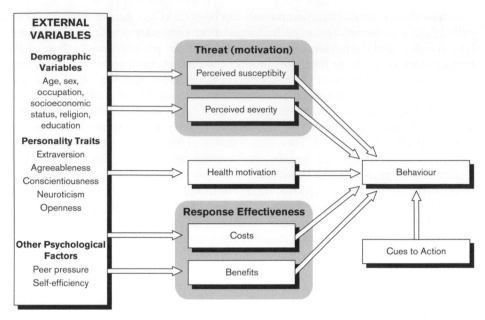

Figure 7.1 The health belief model.

demonstrating that health education interventions designed to increase participants' perceived susceptibility, perceived severity and anticipated benefits resulted in a greater number of check-up visits to the doctor compared to controls over the following eight months.

The HBM suggests that health behaviours are determined mainly by two aspects of individuals' representations of health behaviour: perceptions of illness threat and evaluation of behaviours to counteract this threat (see Figure 7.1). Threat perceptions are based on two beliefs: the perceived susceptibility of the individual to the illness ('Am I likely to get it?'); and the perceived severity of the consequences of the illness for the individual ('How bad would it be?'). Similarly, evaluation of possible responses involves consideration of both the potential benefits of, and barriers to action. Together these four beliefs are believed to determine the likelihood of the individual undertaking to perform a health behaviour. The particular action taken is determined by the evaluation of the available alternatives, focusing on the benefits or efficacy of the health behaviour and the perceived costs or barriers of performing the behaviour. Hence individuals are more likely to follow a particular health action if they believe themselves to be susceptible to a particular condition which they also consider to be serious, and believe that the benefits of the action taken to counteract the health threat outweigh the costs. For example, an individual is likely to quit smoking if he or she: believes him or herself to be susceptible to smoking-related illnesses; considers the illnesses to be serious; and that, of the alternative behaviours open to him/her, considers quitting smoking to be the most effective way to tackle his/her susceptibility to smoking-related illnesses.

Two other variables often included in the model are cues to action and health motivation. Cues to action are assumed to include a diverse range of triggers to the individual taking action which may be internal (e.g. physical symptom) or external (e.g. mass media campaign, advice from others) to the individual (Janz and Becker, 1984). An individual's perception of the presence of cues to action would be expected to prompt adoption of the health behaviour if the other key beliefs are already established in their mind. Health motivation refers to more stable differences between individuals in the value they attach to their health and their propensity to be motivated to look after their health. Individuals with a high motivation to look after their health should be more likely to adopt relevant health behaviours.

The HBM has provided a useful framework for investigating health behaviours and has been widely used. It has been found to successfully predict a range of behaviours. For example, Janz and Becker (1984) found that across 18 prospective studies (that is, those in which behaviour was measured later, following an earlier measurement of beliefs) the four core beliefs were nearly always found to be significant predictors of health behaviour (82 per cent, 65 per cent, 81 per cent and 100 per cent of studies report significant effects for susceptibility, severity, benefits and barriers, respectively). Some studies have found that these health beliefs mediate (or explain) the effects of demographic correlates of health behaviour. For example, Orbell, Crombie and Johnston (1995) found that perceived susceptibility and barriers entirely mediated the effects of social class upon uptake of cervical screening. However, the overall evidence for such mediation is somewhat mixed. In addition, the HBM has inspired a range of successful behaviour change interventions. For example, Jones et al (1988) tested an intervention designed to encourage patients visiting an 'accident and emergency' service to make a follow-up appointment with their own doctor. Patients were randomly assigned to a control (i.e. routine care) group or to the intervention group. The intervention involved meeting a nurse who assessed and challenged patients' health beliefs. For example, a patient who did not feel susceptible to reoccurrence of the emergency event (e.g. an asthmatic attack) might be told of the likelihood of reoccurrence without further treatment in order to increase perceived susceptibility. Results of this randomized controlled trial showed that while only 24 per cent of the control group subsequently attended a follow-up, a significantly greater 59 per cent of the intervention group did so.

The main strength of the HBM is the common-sense operationalization it uses including key beliefs related to decisions about health behaviours. However, further research has identified other cognitions that are stronger predictors of health behaviour than those identified by the HBM, suggesting that the model is incomplete. This prompted a proposal to add 'self-efficacy' (see Chapter 8 and below) to the model to produce an 'extended health belief model' (Rosenstock et al, 1988) which has generally improved the predictive power of the model (e.g. Hay et al, 2003).

Protection motivation theory

Protection motivation theory (PMT; Norman et al, 2005) is a revision and extension of the HBM which incorporates various appraisal processes identified by research into coping with stress (see Chapter 3). In PMT, the primary

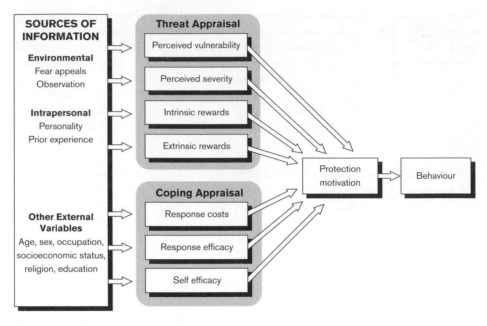

Figure 7.2 Protection motivation theory.

determinant of performing a health behaviour is protection motivation or intention to perform a health behaviour (see Figure 7.2). Protection motivation is determined by two appraisal processes: *threat appraisal* and *coping appraisal*. Threat appraisal is based upon a consideration of perceptions of susceptibility to the illness and severity of the health threat in a very similar way to the HBM. Coping appraisal involves the process of assessing the behavioural alternatives which might diminish the threat. This coping process is itself assumed to be based upon two main components: the individual's expectancy that carrying out a behaviour can remove the threat (response efficacy); and a belief in one's capability to successfully execute the recommended courses of action (self-efficacy).

Together these two appraisal processes result in either adaptive or maladaptive responses. Adaptive responses are those in which the individual engages in behaviours likely to reduce the risk (e.g. adopting a health behaviour) whereas maladaptive responses are those that do not directly tackle the threat (e.g. denial of the health threat). Adaptive responses are held to be more likely if the individual perceives him or herself to be facing a health threat to which he or she is susceptible and which is perceived to be severe and where the individual perceives such responses to be effective in reducing the threat and believes that he or she can successfully perform the adaptive response. So, for example, smokers will try to quit smoking when they believe themselves to be susceptible to smoking-related illnesses which they think to be serious and where quitting smoking is perceived to be effective in reducing the threat and perceived to be something they have confidence they can achieve. The PMT has been successfully applied to the prediction of a number of health behaviours (for recent reviews see Norman et al, 2005).

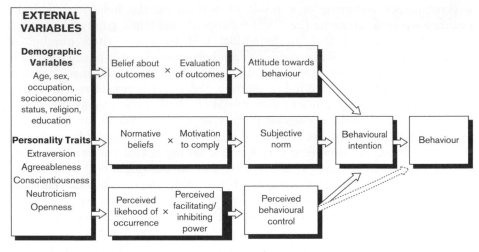

Figure 7.3 Theory of planned behaviour.

Theory of planned behaviour

The **theory of planned behaviour** (TPB) was developed by social psychologists and has been widely applied to understanding health behaviours (Conner and Sparks, 2005). It specifies the factors that determine an individual's decision to perform a particular behaviour (see Figure 7.3). Importantly this theory added 'perceived behavioural control' to the earlier *theory of reasoned action* (Ajzen and Fishbein, 1980) which continues to be applied (Ajzen, 2001). The TPB proposes that the key determinants of behaviour are intention to engage in that behaviour and perceived behavioural control over that behaviour. As in the PMT, intentions in the TPB represent a person's motivation or conscious plan or decision to exert effort to perform the behaviour. Perceived behavioural control (PBC) is a person's expectancy that performance of the behaviour is within their control and confidence that they can perform the behaviour. PBC is similar to Bandura's (1982) concept of self-efficacy used in the PMT.

In the TPB, intention is itself assumed to be determined by three factors: *attitudes, subjective norms* and *PBC*. Attitudes are the overall evaluations of the behaviour by the individual as positive or negative (and so include beliefs about benefits and barriers included in the HBM). Subjective norms are a person's beliefs about whether significant others think they should engage in the behaviour. PBC is assumed to influence both intentions and behaviour because we rarely intend to do things we know we cannot and because believing that we can succeed enhances effort and persistence and so makes successful performance more likely (see Chapter 8). Thus, according to the TPB, smokers are likely to quit smoking if they form an intention to do so. Such an intention to quit is likely to be formed if smokers have a positive attitude towards quitting, if they believe that people whose views they value think they should quit smoking, and if they feel that they have control over quitting smoking.

Attitudes are based on behavioural beliefs, that is, beliefs about the perceived consequences of behaviours. In particular, they are a function of the likelihood of a consequence occurring as a result of performing the behaviour and the evaluation of that outcome (i.e. 'Will it happen?' and 'How good or bad will it be?'). It is assumed that an individual will have a limited number of consequences in mind when considering a behaviour. Thus a positive attitude towards quitting smoking will result when more positive than negative consequences are thought to follow quitting. Subjective norm is based on beliefs about salient others' approval or disapproval of whether one should engage in a behaviour (e.g. 'Would my sexual partner approve?', 'Would my best friend approve?'). These beliefs are weighted by the 'motivation to comply' with each salient other on this issue (e.g. 'Do I care what my sexual partner/best friend thinks about this?'). Again it is assumed that an individual will only have a limited number of referents in mind when considering a behaviour. Thus the more people (whose approval is seen to be important) who are thought to approve of the action, the more positive the subjective norm. Judgements of PBC are influenced by control beliefs concerning whether one has access to the necessary resources and opportunities to perform the behaviour successfully, weighted by the perceived power, or importance, of each factor to facilitate or inhibit the action. These factors include both internal control factors (information, personal deficiencies, skills, abilities, emotions) and external control factors (opportunities, dependence on others, barriers). As for the other types of beliefs it is assumed that an individual will only consider a limited number of control factors when considering a behaviour. So, for example, in relation to quitting smoking, a strong PBC to quit smoking would be expected when a smoker believes there are more factors that facilitate than that inhibit quitting smoking, especially if the inhibiting factors do not have strong effects on the feasibility of quitting.

The TPB has at least two advantages over the extended HBM. First (as in PMT), health beliefs are seen to affect behaviour indirectly, in this case through attitude and intention. Thus the model outlines a mechanism by which particular beliefs combine to influence motivation and action. Second, the model takes account of social influence on action. The TPB has been widely tested and successfully applied to the understanding of a variety of behaviours (for reviews see Ajzen, 1991; Conner and Sparks, 2005). For example, in a meta-analysis of the TPB Armitage and Conner (2001) reported that across 154 applications, attitude, subjective norms and PBC accounted for 39 per cent of the variance in intention, while intentions and PBC accounted for 27 per cent of the variance in behaviour across 63 applications. Intentions were the strongest predictors of behaviour, while attitudes were the strongest predictors of intentions.

The TPB has also informed a number of interventions designed to change behaviour. For example, Hill, Abraham and Wright (2007) employed a randomized controlled trial to test the effectiveness of a TPB-based leaflet compared to a control in promoting physical exercise in a sample of school children. The leaflet condition compared to the control condition significantly increased not only reported exercise but also intentions, attitudes, subjective norms and PBC. Additional analyses indicated that the impact on exercise was mediated (i.e. partly explained) by the increases the leaflet had produced (compared to the control group) in intentions and PBC.

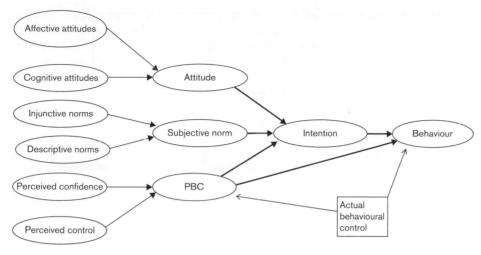

Figure 7.4 The two-factor theory of planned behaviour.

Recent work with the TPB (see Conner and Sparks, 2005) has suggested the value of dividing attitude, subjective norm and PBC each into two components to form the 'two-factor TPB' (Figure 7.4). Attitude is divided into an affective or feeling component and a cognitive or instrumental component. The first concerns beliefs and evaluations about how it will feel to perform the behaviour while the second includes beliefs and evaluation about other consequences. So, for example, quitting smoking might be perceived as both unenjoyable (affective evaluation) but beneficial (cognitive evaluation). As well as subjective norms (defined above), the two-factor model includes descriptive norms. Descriptive norms refer to perceptions of what others are doing ('e.g. all my friends are doing it') rather than beliefs about others' approval of the target individual performing the behaviour. For example, a smoker might believe that important others approved of him or her quitting but those other individuals to have not quit smoking themselves. PBC is divided into perceived control and perceived confidence. So, for example, one might perceive that quitting smoking is within one's control but not feel confident that one can easily quit smoking. The latter factor is most like self-efficacy and has been found to be the stronger predictor of intentions and behaviour (Rodgers et al, 2008).

Social cognitive theory

In social cognitive theory (SCT; Bandura, 1982) behaviour is held to be determined by three factors: goals, outcome expectancies and self-efficacy (see Figure 7.5). Goals are plans to act and can be conceived of as intentions to perform the behaviour (see Austin and Vancouver, 1996; Luszczynska and Schwarzer, 2005). Outcome expectancies are similar to behavioural beliefs in the TPB but here are split into physical, social or self-evaluative depending on the nature of the consequences considered. Thus, in this model, beliefs about others' approval (subjective norms in the TPB) are grouped with beliefs about other consequences. Self-efficacy is the belief that a behaviour is or is not within an individual's control and is usually assessed as the degree of confidence the individual has that they could still perform the behaviour in the face of various

Figure 7.5 Social cognitive theory.

Source: Luszczynska, A., & Schwarzer, R. (2005). Social cognitive theory. In M. Conner & P. Norman (Eds.), Predicting health behaviour: Research and practice with social cognition models. Reproduced with kind permission of the Open University Press Publishing Company.

obstacles. This is very similar to PBC in the TPB and particularly the perceived confidence component in the two-factor TPB. Bandura has recently added socio-structural factors to his theory. These are factors assumed to facilitate or inhibit the performance of a behaviour and affect behaviour via changing goals. Socio-structural factors refer to the impediments or opportunities associated with particular living conditions, health systems, political, economic or environmental systems. They are assumed to inform goal-setting and be influenced by self-efficacy. The latter relationship arises because self-efficacy influences the degree to which an individual pays attention to opportunities or impediments in their life circumstances. For example, self-efficacious individuals intending to exercise might be expected to focus on exercise cues in the environment such as running or cycling routes. This component of the model incorporates perceptions of the environment as an important influence on health behaviours. In overview, the SCT predicts that quitting smoking, for example, is more likely for individuals who have a goal of quitting smoking, who perceive that various positive physical (e.g. health), social (e.g. positive regard from others), and self-evaluative (e.g. feeling good about yourself) outcomes will follow from their quitting smoking, and who perceive they have the confidence to quit smoking in the face of various obstacles.

SCT has been successfully applied to predicting and changing health behaviours. (e.g. Luszczynska and Schwarzer, 2005). However, unlike a number of the other models we have considered, many of the applications of SCT only assess one or two components of the model rather than all components. Self-efficacy and action-outcome expectancies along with intentions have been found to be important predictors of a range of health behaviours in a diverse range of studies (for reviews see Bandura, 2000; Luszczynska and Schwarzer, 2005; see Chapter 8 on changing self-efficacy).

Stage models of health behaviour

The models considered above assume that the cognitive determinants of health behaviours act in a similar way during initiation (e.g. quitting smoking for the first time) and maintenance of action (e.g. trying to stay quit). In contrast, in **stage models** psychological determinants may change across such stages of behaviour change (see Sutton, 2005, for a review). An important implication of the 'stages' view is that different cognitions may be important determinants at different stages in promoting health behaviour. The most widely used stage model is Prochaska and DiClemente's (1984) **transtheoretical model of change** (TTM). Their model has been widely applied to analyze the process of change in alcoholism treatment and smoking cessation. DiClemente et al (1991) identify five stages of change: pre-contemplation (not thinking about change), contemplation (aware of the need to change), preparation (intending to change in the near future and taking action in preparation for change), action (acting to change) and maintenance (of the new behaviour) (see Figure 7.6). Individuals are seen to progress through one stage to the next to eventually achieve successful maintenance. In the case of smoking cessation, it is argued that in the pre-contemplation stage the smoker is unaware that their behaviour constitutes a problem and has no intention to quit. In the contemplation stage, the smoker starts to think about changing their behaviour, but is not committed to try to quit. In the preparation stage, the smoker has an intention to quit and starts to make plans to quit. The action stage is characterized by active attempts to quit, and after six months of successful abstinence the individual moves into the maintenance stage. This stage is characterized by attempts to prevent relapse and to consolidate the newly acquired non-smoking status.

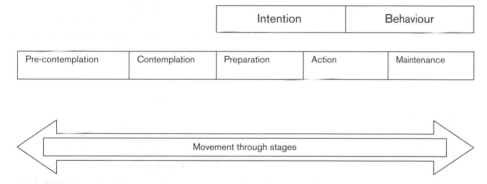

Figure 7.6 Stage components of the transtheoretical model of change.

While the model is widely applied, the evidence in support of stage models and different stages is relatively weak (see Sutton, 2000, 2005). Sutton (2000) concludes that the distinctions between TTM stages are 'logically flawed' and based on 'arbitrary time periods'. Moreover, even Prochaska and DiClemente's own data do not suggest that smokers typically progress through the TTM stages. For example, in one study, Prochaska et al (1991) found that only 16 per cent of participants progressed from one stage to the next without reversals over a two-year period and that 12 per cent moved backwards during the same period! In addition, it has proved especially difficult to support the key prediction that there are different determinants of behaviour change in different stages. The best evidence for stage models would be where we showed that interventions matched to individuals' stage of change were more effective in producing behaviour change than interventions mismatched to an individual's stage (although see also Abraham, 2008). So, for example, in a matched intervention outcome expectancies might be targeted in individuals in the contemplation stage, while self-efficacy was targeted in individuals in the action stage, and this would be reversed in a mismatched intervention. Unfortunately, few such matched–mismatched studies have produced evidence supportive of stage models (see Littell and Girvin, 2002 for a systematic review of the effectiveness of interventions applying the TTM to health-related behaviours). Thus, at present, research findings do not support the added complexity and increased cost of stage-tailored interventions. West (2005) in reviewing stage models has recently suggested that work on the TTM should be abandoned.

It is difficult to usefully categorize people as 'pre-contemplators' or those 'in preparation' because people frequently cycle between such states as their motivation to change shifts. Nonetheless, an individual at a particular time may be more focused on deciding whether or not to act or on ensuring that they act on a prior decision to act (i.e. an intention). This is captured by the terms 'motivational phase' and 'volitional phase', respectively. This two-phase conception of action readiness suggests that health promoters need to think about how they can consolidate people's motivation to act and how they can help people to enact their intentions (see Chapters 8 and 9). In general, the social cognition models considered in this chapter have focused on the former. For example, the TPB does not help us distinguish between intenders who do and do not take action. Thus there is a need to better theorize the processes which determine which intentions are translated into action. As Bagozzi (1993) argues, the variables outlined in the main social cognition models are necessary, but not sufficient, determinants of behaviour. In other words, they can provide good predictions of people's intentions (or motivation) to perform a health behaviour, but not always their actual behaviour. This area of research has been referred to as the 'intention–behaviour gap'.

Focus 7.3

Deciding between social cognition models

Although a great deal of research has been devoted to testing individual social cognition models, little research has compared the relative predictive power of different SCMs. For example, Reid and Christensen (1988) found that while the HBM explained 10 per cent of the variance in adherence among women taking tablets for urinary tract infections to a tablet regimen, the variance explained increased to 29 per cent when cognitions specified by the theory of reasoned action were added.

Another approach to the variety of SCMs is to integrate them. This may be valuable, especially since many include similar cognitions. For example, commentators agree that the key cognitions prominently include intention, self-efficacy and outcome expectancies (or attitudes). An important attempt to integrate these models was made by Bandura (SCT), Becker (HBM), Fishbein (TRA), Kaufen (self-regulation) and

Triandis (theory of interpersonal behaviour) as part of a workshop organized by the US National Institute of Mental Health in response to the need to promote HIV-preventive behaviours. The workshop sought to 'identify a finite set of variables to be considered in any behavioral analysis' (Fishbein et al, 2001: 3). They identified eight variables which, they argued, should account for most of the variance in any (deliberative) behaviour. These were organized into two groups. First were those variables which were viewed as necessary and sufficient determinants of behaviour. Thus, for behaviour to occur an individual must: 1) have a strong intention; 2) have the necessary skills to perform the behaviour; and 3) experience an absence of environmental constraints that could prevent behaviour. The second group of variables were seen to primarily influence intention, although it was noted that some of the variables may also have a direct effect on behaviour. Thus, a strong intention is likely to occur when an individual: 4) perceives the advantages (or benefits) of performing the behaviour to outweigh the perceived disadvantages (or costs); 5) perceives the social (normative) pressure to perform the behaviour to be greater than that not to perform the behaviour; 6) believes that the behaviour is consistent with his or her self-image; 7) anticipates the emotional reaction to performing the behaviour to be more positive than negative; and 8) has high levels of self-efficacy.

Figure 7.7 illustrates this integrated model.

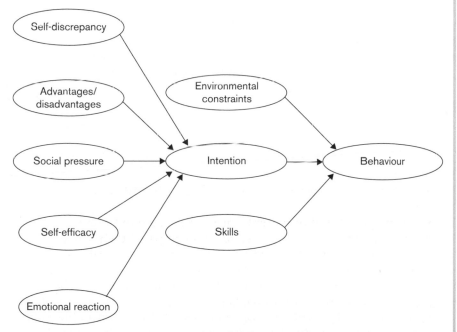

Figure 7.7 The 'major theorists' integrated social cognition model.

If you were trying to identify the determinants of condom use, which cognitions would you focus on? Would this be any different if you were trying to predict smoking cessation?

A critical appraisal of SCMs

The use of SCMs to predict health behaviour has a number of advantages and disadvantages. Below we outline the main advantages of a social cognition approach before considering a range of specific and more general criticisms that have been made of this approach.

There are four clear advantages of using SCMs to predict and understand health behaviours. First, they provide a clear theoretical background to any research, guiding the selection of cognitions and providing a description of the ways in which these constructs combine in order to determine health behaviours. Second, because the models have been repeatedly tested they provide reliable and valid measures of selected cognitions (for example, see Ajzen's website for guidance on developing TPB measures at www.people.umass.edu/aizen/tpb.html). Third, SCMs provide us with a description of the motivational and volitional processes underlying health behaviours. As a result, they add to our understanding of the proximal determinants of health behaviour and, because of this, they, fourth, identify key targets for interventions designed to change motivation (see Chapter 8).

The use of SCMs could also limit our understanding of health behaviour. For example, because SCMs provide clearly defined theoretical frameworks, their use may lead to the neglect of other cognitions. For example, moral norms are not included in the main SCMs but have been shown to be important in behaviours such as blood donation (Godin et al, 2005). Another limitation of SCMs is that while they usefully identify cognition change targets, they commonly do not specify the best means to change such cognitions. Moreover, an over-exclusive focus on SCMs may lead to the neglect of other potentially effective behaviour change interventions, such as increased taxation or legislation, which may not or may not have their effects through the cognitions specified by the SCMs (see Chapter 9).

There has been one widely cited **critique of SCMs** written by Ogden (2003) with a response by Ajzen and Fishbein (2004) (see also Greve, 2001; Norman and Conner, 2005). Ogden's (2003) critique is based on a review of 47 empirical studies published in four main health psychology journals over a four-year period and focuses on the HBM, PMT and TRA/TPB. Ogden raised four issues: use in developing interventions, interpretation of empirical testing, analytical versus synthetic truths and **mere measurement**. Ogden first concluded that SCMs were useful to researchers and '... to inform service development and the development of health-related interventions to promote health behaviors' (Ogden, 2003: 425). However, she also made three key criticisms. First she argued that SCMs cannot be empirically tested, that is, confirmed or disconfirmed. She supported this point by pointing out that researchers do not conclude that they have disconfirmed SCMs when they find that one or more of the theory's constructs do not predict the outcome measure or that the findings do not explain all or most of the variance in intentions or behaviour. Ajzen and Fishbein (2004) highlight that the logic of this argument is unsound. For example in the case of the TPB, numerous descriptions of the theory make clear that the extent to which each of the cognitions predicts intentions or behaviour is a function of the population and behaviour under study. For a specific behaviour and population one or more antecedents may indeed not be predictive, without disproving the theory. For example, social approval may be crucial to some health behaviours but not to others. Thus finding that a particular cognition is not relevant to a particular behaviour does not disconfirm the theory. However, finding that none of the cognitions specified by the theory predicted useful proportions of the variance in intention or behaviour across behaviours would indeed disconfirm the theory. In fact, available evidence suggests that the theory is very useful, explaining on average 40–50 per cent of the variance in intention and 21–36 per cent of the variance in behaviour across studies (Conner and Sparks, 2005).

Ogden also claimed that the theories contain only analytic truths (as opposed to synthetic or empirical truths that are based on evidence) because the correlations observed between measured cognitions are likely to be attributable to overlap in the way the constructs are measured. She claimed that this argument extends to measures of behaviour because these are often based on self-report. This interpretation of the literature has been disputed for two main reasons. First, it is not at all apparent that this explanation would account for the observed patterns of correlations among cognitions that are commonly reported in the literature. Second, high levels of prediction of behaviour are also found with objective measures of behaviour that do not rely on self-report and thus cannot be biased in the way Ogden describes. For example, Armitage and Conner (2001) in their meta-analysis of the TPB showed that intention and perceived behavioural control still accounted for an impressive 21 per cent of variance in behaviour when behaviour was objectively measured across a number of studies.

This examination of the percentage of variance explained by SCMs has discouraged some health psychologists. For example, Mielewczyk and Willig (2007: 818–819) in reviewing this evidence conclude that 'the TPB is therefore unable to account for around 60 per cent of the variance in intentions and for up to almost 80 per cent of that in behaviour. Since the SCM approach is directed purely at providing explanations of variance in outcomes, the extent of that unexplained across such a large body of literature is highly damning'. This pessimism is unfounded for a number of reasons (see Abraham et al, 1998, for a useful discussion). First, as Sutton (1997) notes, the percentage of variance explained by any model, including physiological models of symptom appearance, is directly related to the reliability of the measures employed. The maximum variance that can be accounted for will always be the square root of the product of the two reliabilities. Thus there are inherent measurement limitations on the percentage of variance that any model can explain. Second, when cognition and behaviour measures are not 'compatible' (i.e. do not refer to the identical action, target, time and context), the R^2 will be reduced (Ajzen and Fishbein, 1980). Similarly, if the number of response options used to measure cognitions and behaviour is not equal (e.g. if attitude is measured on a seven-point scale and behaviour on a three-point scale), this will also reduce R^2. Finally, when sampling biases lead to a restricted range in either the independent (cognition) or the dependent (behaviour) variable compared to the actual range in the population (e.g. if the sample drink more alcohol than the sampled population) then the observed R^2 will underestimate the real cognition–behaviour relationship. Thus it is methodologically unrealistic to expect predictive models to explain 100 per cent of the variance in measures of behaviour.

We would claim that explaining 21 per cent of the variance in objectively measured behaviours is 'impressive' (rather than 'damning') because of the potential for behaviour change intervention that this figure represents. Rosenthal and Rubin (1982) translate percentages of explained variance into expected increases in outcome or success rates using their 'binomial effect size display'. This approach indicates that even when 19 per cent of the variance in behaviour is explained we would expect an increase in that behaviour from 28 per cent in a control group to 72 per cent in an intervention group (who had adopted the cognitions that explained the 19 per cent). This would indeed be an impressive finding for any evaluation of a behaviour change intervention (see Godin and Conner, 2008, for an examination of different indices of the intention–behaviour relationship for physical activity). Of course, changing the cognitions specified by the SCMs is a challenging endeavour (see Chapter 9) but the predictive success of SCMs strongly indicates that models such as the TPB can specify change targets that (if successfully changed) could make important differences to the prevalence of health behaviours in the population and, thereby, public health. Consequently, after reviewing available evidence, and providing guidance for behaviour change interventions in the UK National Health Service, the National Institute of Health and Clinical Excellence (2007: 10–11) noted that 'a number of concepts drawn from the psychological literature are helpful when planning ... behaviour change with individuals'. This list included 'positive attitude', 'subjective norms', 'descriptive norms', 'personal and moral norms', 'self-efficacy', 'intention formation' and 'concrete plans'.

Finally, returning to Ogden's critique, she suggested that measuring such cognitions as the TPB suggests prompts their creation rather than simply recording pre-existing thoughts and perceptions. As Ajzen and Fishbein (2004) point out this is a common concern in questionnaire and interview studies. Recent research has in fact supported this concern. The effect has been referred to as the 'mere measurement effect' meaning that measurement by itself prompts cognition and behaviour change. The strongest effects appear to be associated with the measurement of intentions. In Sherman's (1980) original demonstration of the effect, one group of participants was asked to predict how likely they would be to perform a socially desirable or socially undesirable behaviour (volunteering for the American Cancer Society or singing the *Star Spangled Banner* down the phone, respectively) while a second group made no prediction about their behaviour. The results indicated that participants asked to predict their behaviour were more likely to perform the socially desirable behaviour (31 per cent versus 4 per cent) and were less likely to perform the undesirable behaviour (40 per cent versus 68 per cent) compared to control participants making no prediction. Recent research has shown that completing a TPB questionnaire about blood donation led to a 6–9 per cent increase in attendance of blood donation 6–12 months later compared to groups who did not complete such a questionnaire (Godin et al, 2008). However, rather than invalidating the use of SCMs, these findings point to the need for the use of more sophisticated designs to distinguish measurement and predictive effects, e.g.

including conditions without baseline (time 1) questionnaires for comparative purposes. Moreover, these mere measurement effects suggest that SCMs are indeed tapping psychological processes crucial to behaviour change.

The intention–behaviour gap

The intention-behaviour gap refers to the fact that intentions are far from perfect predictors of behaviour. In this section we review two areas of research exploring this gap. The first focuses on the stability of intentions across time while the second examines the volitional processes that might be important in determining whether intentions get translated into action.

Intention stability

In the vast majority of applications of SCMs the predictors of behaviour are measured by questionnaire (at time 1) and then behaviour is measured at a second time point, thereby employing a prospective survey method. One important implication of such a design is that the measured constructs (e.g. attitudes) will remain unchanged between the measurement and the opportunity to act. So, for example, in using the TPB the assumption is that intentions to exercise will remain the same from when the (time 1) questionnaire is completed to the time points at which the respondent has the opportunity to engage in exercise. This is one of the limiting conditions of the TPB. However, cognitions including intentions may indeed change in this time period and such change provides one important explanation of the intention–behaviour gap. Several studies have now demonstrated that the intention–behaviour gap is indeed reduced for individuals with intentions that are more stable over time. For example, Conner, Norman and Bell (2002) found that intentions were stronger predictors of healthy eating over a period of six years when these intentions were stable over a six-month time period. These findings show that intention stability moderates the relationship between intention and behaviour.

A number of other factors have been found to influence the size of the intention–behaviour gap. For example, anticipating feeling regret if one does not perform a behaviour or perceiving a strong moral norm (that is, believing that one is morally obliged to act) have both been found to significantly reduce the intention–behaviour gap (see Cooke and Sheeran, 2004, for a review). Like Conner et al (2002), Sheeran and Abraham (2003) found that intention stability moderated the intention–behaviour relationship for exercising but, more importantly, found that intention stability mediated the effect of other moderators of the intention–behaviour relationship, including anticipated regret. This suggests that the mechanism by which a number of these other moderators may have their effect on intention–behaviour relationships is through changing the temporal stability of intentions. Hence, factors that might be expected to make individual intentions more stable over time would be expected to increase the impact that these intentions have on behaviour and so reduce the intention–behaviour gap.

Implementation intention formation

A variety of factors which affect the enactment of intentions have been investigated including personality traits, self-efficacy and planning. For example, we noted in Chapter 6 that conscientious individuals may possess skills that help them to enact their intentions (see Chapter 8 for more on self-efficacy and Chapter 9 for more on planning). However, another factor may relate to the nature of the intention formed.

Gollwitzer (1993) makes the distinction between goal intentions and **implementation intentions**. While the former is concerned with intentions to perform a behaviour or achieve a goal (i.e. 'I intend to do x'), the latter is concerned with if-then plans which specify an environmental prompt or context that will determine when the action should be taken (i.e. 'I intend to initiate the goal-directed behaviour x when situation y is encountered'). The important point about implementation intentions is that they commit the individual to a specific course of action when certain environmental conditions are met. Sheeran et al (2005: 280) note that "to form an implementation intention, the person must first identify a response that will lead to goal attainment and, second, anticipate a suitable occasion to initiate that response. For example, the person might specify the behaviour 'go jogging for 20 minutes' and specify a suitable opportunity 'tomorrow morning before work'". Gollwitzer (1993) argues that, by making implementation intentions, individuals pass control of intention enactment to the environment. The specified environmental cue prompts the action so that the person does not have to remember or decide when to act.

Sheeran et al (2005) provide an in-depth review of both basic and applied research with implementation intentions. For example, Milne, Orbell and Sheeran (2002) found that an intervention using persuasive text based on protection motivation theory prompted positive pro-exercise cognition change but did not increase exercise. However, when this intervention was combined with encouragement to form implementation intentions, behaviour change was observed (see Gollwitzer and Sheeran, 2006, for a meta-analysis of such studies). Thus implementation intention formation moderates the intention–behaviour relationship demonstrating that two people with equally strong goal intentions may differ in their volitional readiness depending on whether they have taken the additional step of forming an implementation intention. Implementation intention formation has been shown to increase the performance of a range of behaviours with, on average, a medium effect size. Implementation intentions appear to be particularly effective in overcoming a common problem in enacting intentions, that is, forgetting. Provided effective cues are identified in the implementation intention (i.e. ones that will be commonly encountered and are sufficiently distinctive), forgetting appears to be much less likely.

Summary

There is considerable variation in who performs health behaviours. Demographic differences explain part of this variation, although such factors are not easily modifiable. Various modifiable cognitions have been identified which explain differences in who performs health behaviours. Key cognitions include intentions, self-efficacy and outcome expectancies (or attitudes). Cognitions have been incorporated in a number of social cognition models (SCMs) that describe the key cognitions and how they are interrelated in the determination of behaviour. The most important SCMs include the health belief model, protection motivation theory, theory of reasoned action/theory of planned behaviour and social cognitive theory. These models focus on the cognitive antecedents of motivation. Stage models attempt to describe the process of behaviour change from first consideration to maintenance of change but there is limited evidence to suggest that people remain in stable stages of action readiness over time. While SCMs have a number of advantages, criticisms of SCMs suggest the need for further sophistication in the testing of such models. SCMs are limited in their capacity to explain why some intentions are translated into behaviour while others are not. Various factors explaining this intention–behaviour gap have been explored and the important role of the temporal stability of intentions has been identified. Research has also investigated volitional processes which facilitate the enactment of intentions. Implementation intentions, that is, if-then plans situating an intended action in a specific context, have been shown to reduce the intention–behaviour gap.

Key concepts and terms

Critique of SCMs	Self-regulation
Health behaviours	Social cognition models (SCMs)
Health belief models	Social cognitive theory
Implementation intentions	Stage models
Intention–behaviour gap	Theory of planned behaviour
Mere measurement	Transtheoretical model of
Protection motivation theory	change

Sample essay titles

- Critically evaluate the use of social cognition models in understanding health behaviours.

- Compare and contrast the health belief model and the theory of planned behaviour as explanations of why people do and do not perform a range of health behaviours.

- What do we know about the antecedents of intention? Discuss with reference to available empirical evidence.

Further reading

Books

Abraham, C., and Sheeran, P. (2005). 'Health belief model.' In: M. Conner and P. Norman (Eds), *Predicting Health Behaviour: Research and Practice with Social Cognition Models* (2nd Ed.). Buckingham: Open University Press.

Abraham, C., Norman, P., and Conner, M. (2000). 'Towards a psychology of health-related behaviour change.' In: P. Norman, C. Abraham, and M. Conner (Eds), *Understanding and Changing Health Behaviour: From Health Beliefs to Self-Regulation*. Switzerland: Harwood Academic, 343–369.

Conner, M., and Norman, P. (2005). 'Predicting health behaviour: A social cognition approach.' In: M. Conner and P. Norman (Eds), *Predicting Health Behaviour: Research and Practice with Social Cognition Models* (2nd Ed.). Buckingham: Open University Press, 1–27.

Conner, M., and Sparks, P. (2005). 'Theory of planned behaviour and health behaviour.' In: M. Conner and P. Norman (Eds), *Predicting Health Behaviour: Research and Practice with Social Cognition Models* (2nd Ed.). Buckingham: Open University Press.

Norman, P., and Conner, M. (2005). 'Predicting and changing health behaviour: Future directions.' In: M. Conner and P. Norman (Eds), *Predicting Health Behaviour: Research and Practice with Social Cognition Models* (2nd Ed.). Buckingham: Open University Press, 324–371.

Journal articles

Ajzen, I., and Fishbein, M. (2004). Questions raised by a reasoned action approach: Reply on Ogden (2003). *Health Psychology*, 23, 431–434.

Ogden, J. (2003). Some problems with social cognition models: A pragmatic and conceptual analysis. *Health Psychology*, 22, 424–428.

8 Changing motivation

In Chapter 7 we studied cognitions which have been found to differentiate between people who do and do not perform health behaviours. In this chapter we focus on interventions designed to *change cognitions* in order to promote health-related behaviours.

Learning about a health risk can change people's attitudes, intentions and behaviour. Therefore, provision of accessible and easily understood *information* is an important part of health promotion. Information is evaluated by the receiver and if it is judged to be mistaken, personally irrelevant or implying difficult or costly actions it may be ignored. Consequently, health promoters also need to *persuade* individuals and groups to take health-promoting action. Successful persuasion depends on anticipating how recipients will perceive and respond to the persuasive attempt. Successful persuasion is likely to result in *attitude change* and (as we saw in Chapter 7) attitudes provide an important foundation for the motivation to change one's behaviour. However, when people feel they cannot make a change they are unlikely to pursue it. Consequently, ensuring high perceived control and self-efficacy is crucial to maintenance of motivation and the translation of intentions into action. In this chapter we will consider how motivation can be bolstered and changed in five sections: 1) providing information; 2) persuading others; 3) changing attitudes; 4) enhancing self-efficacy; 5) from motivation to behaviour change.

Learning outcomes

When you have completed this chapter you should be able to:

1. Describe how information and advice should be presented to maximize its impact on health-related motivation and action.
2. Explain how social influence techniques can be applied to maximize the impact of health promotion advice on recipients' motivation, in mass media, one-to-one and group communication.
3. Explain how the manner in which messages are processed (i.e. the degree of cognitive elaboration) determines which message features have most impact on attitude change. Use this explanation to provide evidence-based advice on how health promoters can maximize attitude change.
4. Illustrate the importance of self-efficacy to motivation, health behaviour and health and explain how self-efficacy can be enhanced.

Providing information

If people become aware of a health risk from a source they perceive to be trustworthy and they believe they can easily protect themselves, information alone can prompt behaviour change. For example, media coverage about food scares such as bovine spongiform encephalopathy (BSE) can lead to widespread changes in behaviour such as beef purchase (e.g. Swientek, 2001; Tyler, 2001). Inaccurate information can also promote behaviour changes that increase health risk. For example, when a highly regarded medical journal (*The Lancet*) published an article linking the measles, mumps and rubella vaccine (MMR) with autism and inflammatory bowel disease in 1998, MMR vaccination uptake fell and cases of measles increased. Although the validity of the research was subsequently questioned by the journal's editor as well as being denounced by 10 of the 13 original authors and the UK prime minister (see *The Guardian*, Tuesday February 24, 2004), it proved difficult to re-build public confidence in the safety of MMR and raise vaccination uptake to previous levels. Further research found no immunological response differences to MMR in children with and without autism (Baird et al, 2008) but in 2008 national vaccination uptake levels still remained lower than the optimal 95 per cent levels. This example emphasizes the power of a credible source. When scientists and government ministers offer contradictory information or when advice is perceived to serve the interests of the source (e.g. industry), information and reassurance may not be believed. People may interpret, 'there is no cause for concern', as, 'there must be a problem' or, similarly, 'this is dangerous' as 'just more state interference'. Consequently, as well as the ethical imperative for health professionals, scientists and government to ensure that information available to the public is not misleading, there is a need to ensure information is accurate and evidence-based to maintain future credibility.

Source credibility may also be enhanced by presentation of two-sided arguments. Presenting the disadvantages as well as the advantages of a product or recommended action has been found to be more persuasive because two-sided presentations result in greater perceived credibility of the source (e.g. Crowley and Hoyer, 1994; Eisend, 2006). This may be especially true for sceptical audiences. Two-sided arguments may also increase the perceived novelty of the message which, in turn, enhances attention and interest and so may promote positive attitude change (Eisend, 2007). Thus, being open about the costs or side effects of a recommended action may be more effective in changing attitudes and intentions because the audience is more likely to believe that the highlighted benefits are real.

Making information accessible and easy to understand

Information can only change motivation and behaviour if people can access it and understand it. Thus providing accurate information in the right place for the target audience is crucial if information is to affect action. Information providers need to know where and when the target audience will seek information before designing an information campaign. Will the target audience seek information on the web or just before they take their medication or, for example, when they are about to use a sunbed? Preliminary research with the target audience can answer such questions and so help guide effective information provision.

Once the most appropriate context for information presentation is established, information providers must ensure that what they say is easily understood. For example, if patient information leaflets provided with medications are written in tiny writing and include technical terms patients do not understand then they are not likely to enhance adherence. Ease of comprehension is partly determined by what the recipient already knows. If you want to give someone good directions (e.g. in a city) you ideally want to be aware of what landmarks they already know. Yet evidence suggests that health professionals often overestimate patients' knowledge and, therefore, their ability to understand health-related information. For example, Boyle (1970) found that only 20 per cent and 42 per cent of patients, respectively, were able to accurately identify the position of the stomach and heart. Similarly, Hadlow and Pitts (1991) found that while the vast majority of doctors were able to select correct clinical definitions of conditions such as stroke, eating disorder and depression, only 18 per cent, 30 per cent and 32 per cent of patients were able to do so, respectively. Thus prior explanation of medical and unfamiliar terms is required if they are to be used in information designed for the general population.

Text can also be more or less difficult to read depending on how it is written and the words that are used. The level of reading difficulty can be assessed using a variety of measures. For example, the **Flesch Reading Ease measure** (FRE; Flesch, 1948) assesses the average number of syllables in words used and the average sentence length. A score between zero and 100 is generated with higher scores denoting easier texts (e.g. scores of up to 65 are acceptable for literate adults). Media professionals regularly edit text to achieve good readability. For example, the most popular newspaper in the UK is said to have a reading age of nine! Considerable additional effort is required to ensure that health information is readable by the vast majority of the population. For example, in a survey of more than 1000 leaflets provided by palliative care units in the UK and Ireland, Payne et al (2000) found that 47 per cent were printed in less than font 12. Two-thirds had poor readability scores as assessed by the FRE which implied that they would only be understood by 40 per cent of the UK population.

Providing wanted information

Health professionals tend to underestimate patients' desire for information. Even when they are facing bad news and potential terminal diagnoses, evidence indicates that patients want to know as much as possible (e.g. Jenkins et al, 2001) – but what do they want to know? Coulter, Entwistle and Gilbert (1999) reviewed 54 sources of information, including information leaflets, and listened to patients in focus groups to discover what kind of information they wanted. These researchers found that the sources of information they reviewed did not correspond to patients' desires for information. They generated a list of 22 questions that patients commonly want answered (reproduced in Activity box 8.1) and recommended that the patient information resources be written and revised to ensure that they answer these questions.

Activity 8.1

What do patients want to know?

Coulter et al (1999) suggest that patients typically want answers to the following questions.

- What is causing the problem?
- How does my experience compare with that of other patients?
- Is there anything I can do myself to ameliorate the problem?
- What is the purpose of the tests and investigations?
- What are the different treatment options?
- What are the benefits of the treatment(s)?
- What are the risks of the treatment(s)?
- Is it essential to have treatment for this problem?
- Will the treatment(s) relieve the symptoms?
- How long will it take to recover?
- What are the possible side effects?
- What effect will the treatment(s) have on my feelings and emotions?
- What effect will the treatment(s) have on my sex life?
- How will it affect my risk of disease in the future?
- How can I prepare myself for the treatment?
- What procedures will be followed if I go to hospital?
- When can I go home?
- What do my carers need to know?
- What can I do to speed recovery?
- What are the options for rehabilitation?
- How can I prevent recurrence or future illness?
- Where can I get more information about the problem or treatments?

Examine the NHS 'Choices' website (www.nhs.uk/Pages/homepage.aspx). Do you think this website provides the answers to patient questions identified by Coulter et al (1999)? For example, have a look at the body map and the areas it highlights (e.g. head and neck) and/or look at explanations of specific conditions, e.g. 'chlamydia'? How readable is the website? Do you have ideas for improving this website? Note you can send your feedback to the NHS.

Organization of information

In addition to providing easy to understand information that is wanted by the target audience and presented in the right context, information providers can make information easier to understand and remember by organizing it in a manner that is easy to process. Providing information in a logical order facilitates processing. For example, clarifying the cause of an illness before explaining how a treatment works can help a patient understand why the treatment is necessary or why it should be administered as recommended. Telling the audience what

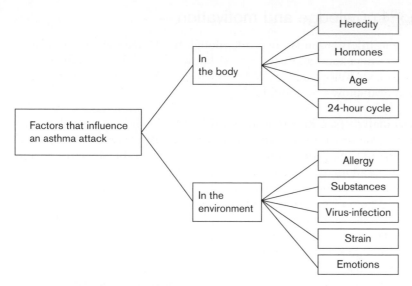

Figure 8.1 Graphic organizers facilitate text comprehension.

Source: Kools, M., Van de Wiel, M.W.J., Ruiter, R.A.C., Crüts, A., & Kok, G. (2006). The effect of graphic organizers on subjective and objective comprehension of a health education text. Health Education & Behavior, 33, 760–772. Reprinted with Permission of SAGE Publications, Inc.

you are about to tell them can also enhance recall. This is often referred to as 'explicit categorization'. For example, a nurse might say 'First, I am going to tell you what I think is wrong, ... now I'm going to tell you about the treatment ... etc.' Highlighting and repeating important points also helps people pay particular attention to them ('This is important so I'm going to say it again'). Finally, when giving advice, it is important to be specific, e.g. 'You need to lose one stone in weight' is much easier to remember and act on than 'You need to lose weight'. Ley et al (1976) wrote a manual for GPs explaining these simple techniques and assessed patient recall for information provided in consultations with four GPs before and after they read the manual. Results showed that recall increased from 52–59 per cent across the four doctors at baseline to 61–80 per cent after the GPs had read the manual. Thus, these five simple presentation techniques (logical order, explicit categorization, specific advice, emphasizing and repeating important points) make information easier to process and recall.

Visual aids can make written materials easier to understand. For example, an experiment conducted by Kools et al (2006) showed that participants who read text describing asthma care extracted from a health promotion leaflet had poorer comprehension of the text than participants who read the same text modified by the addition of **graphic organizers** (including the one in Figure 8.1). Pre-testing of such materials is important to ensure that they are appropriate for the target audience.

The way in which risk information is presented can also determine its impact on motivation and action. As we shall see in Chapter 11, risk information can be more or less persuasive depending on whether it is framed in terms of gains or losses (even when the same information is included).

Information knowledge and motivation

Unfortunately, information is often not enough to change behaviour because even those who understand and have a good knowledge of the consequences of their actions fail to follow advice. Why? Can you think of a health-related behaviour that you know you should change?

Using meta-analysis (see Research methods box 8.1), Sheeran, Abraham and Orbell (1999) examined psychosocial factors associated with heterosexual condom use in 121 empirical studies. **Effect sizes** for 44 separate factors correlated with condom use could be calculated. These analyses revealed an *average weighted correlation* of 0.06 (a small effect size) for the relationship between knowledge and reported condom use. Thus increasing knowledge by itself is unlikely to be enough to promote condom use. By contrast, the average weighted correlations for attitude towards condom use (0.32), others' approval of use (0.37) and intention to use (0.43) were of medium effect size. These findings indicate that changing perceived approval and attitudes towards condoms is much more likely to impact on heterosexual condom use than is changing knowledge. Sheeran et al (1999: 126) concluded that these results 'provide empirical support for conceptualizing condom use in terms of ... an extended theory of reasoned action', and argued that these correlates specify important targets for safer sex promotion. A similar meta-analysis of studies applying the theories of reasoned action (Fishbein and Ajzen, 1975) and planned behaviour (TPB, Ajzen, 1991) to condom use confirmed the utility of these theories as models of cognitive antecedents of condom use (Albarracín et al, 2001). Thus, for many behaviours, changing cognitive elements of *motivation* is critical to behaviour change. This may not be achieved by simply providing good information.

Research methods 8.1

Meta-analysis

Meta-analysis allows researchers to examine the average size of associations (or differences) between two measures or conditions across a series of studies. When combining effect sizes (e.g. the size of an association between two measures) across studies it is important to weight studies for the number of participants because a finding based on 100 participants is likely to be more reliable than one based on 10. For example, if a correlation study found that knowledge and behaviour were correlated at $r = .05$ among a sample of 100 people and another study found the correlation to be $r = .07$ among a similar sample of 100 people then the average weighted correlation (r^+) would be 0.06, across these two studies. However, if the second study had only recruited a sample of 50 then r^+ would be 0.0425. In this way, meta-analyses allow researchers to combine results across studies to calculate average 'effect sizes'. Cohen (1992) has provided guidelines for interpreting the size of sample-weighted average correlations (r) suggesting that $r^+ = .10$ is 'small', $r^+ = .30$ is 'medium', while $r^+ = .50$ is 'large'.

Meta-analyses can also be used to estimate the average impact that behaviour change interventions (see Chapter 9) have on a particular outcome (such as physical activity levels). In this case, the most usual measure is *d* (rather than *r*). *d* is calculated by subtracting the behavioural outcome score of one condition from another (for each study) and dividing this by the standard pooled deviation, that is, the standard deviation for both conditions combined (Hedges and Olkin, 1985). For example, if, at follow-up, those who had received an intervention were found to exercise 3 times a week on average while those in a no-intervention control group exercised only 1.5 times a week on average, and there was an overall standard pooled deviation of 1.5 this would generate a *d* value of 1.0. Cohen (1992) suggests that *d*s of 0.2 are 'small' while *d*s of 0.5 are of 'medium' size and *d*s of 0.8 are 'large' effect sizes. Thus this would be a large and impressive effect size. This is not surprising because in this example the intervention doubled the rate of the target behaviour compared to the control group, indicating an unusually successful intervention.

Persuading others

We have seen that providing information can sometimes be persuasive in itself but that, more often, even when people understand information and have good knowledge of health risks, this may not be enough to motivate change. So how can we overcome resistance to change? How can health professionals move beyond providing information to persuading target audiences to change? Persuasion is *social influence* (one person or group influencing another) and there is a considerable body of research on how social influence works. For example, Pratkanis (2007) lists 107 potentially effective social influence tactics, including being a credible source, being empathetic, using flattery, agenda setting, using metaphor, using story telling, fear appeals and making people feel guilty. Here we will consider some key principles that need to be followed if you want to motivate someone else to change their behaviour.

Message framing

Prospect theory (Tversky and Kahneman, 1981) predicts that people process information differently depending on whether it relates to losses (or costs) or gains (or benefits). Specifically, people tend to be 'risk averse', that is they want to avoid risk, when thinking about gains but, when thinking about potential losses, people tend to be open to taking risks, or risk seeking. Consequently, a behaviour which is not associated with risk may seem more attractive when thinking about gains (because we tend to want to avoid risk when thinking about gains) while a behaviour which is perceived to be risky may be more attractive when people are thinking about losses or costs (when people favour risk). Preventive behaviours including condom or sunscreen use are undertaken to reduce the risk of ill health and so tend to be perceived as low risk. By contrast, detection behaviours such as breast or testicular self-examination are thought to be high risk because, despite the potential long-term benefits, there is an immediate risk of discovering a worrying problem. It has been predicted, therefore, that health promotion information about preventive behaviours will be most effective when it focuses upon potential gains while health promotion information about detection behaviours will be most effective when it focuses upon potential losses or costs (see Rothman and Salovey, 1997). There is some evidence to support this. For example, Detweiler et al (1999) gave people going to the beach messages which either emphasized gains associated with sunscreen use (e.g. 'If you use sunscreen with SPF 15 or higher, you increase your chances of keeping your skin healthy and your life long') or losses associated with not using sunscreen (e.g. 'If you don't use sunscreen with SPF 15 or higher, you decrease your chances of keeping your skin healthy and your life long'). They found that those who read the gain-focused messages were more likely to redeem a coupon to collect sunscreen. Moreover, this (gain-focused) group were more likely to intend to use sunscreen with a sun protection factor of 15 and to intend to apply sunscreen repeatedly.

However, framing effects do not always produce the desired effects on motivation and behaviour. One of the main reasons is that not all preventive behaviours are perceived as low risk and not all detection behaviours are perceived as high risk. For example, consider parents' decisions to have their children vaccinated against measles, mumps and rubella using the combined MMR injection. It is likely that after the publication of the now refuted report linking MMR vaccination with autism and inflammatory bowel disease (see above) parents perceived this preventive behaviour as high risk and therefore, might be more likely to respond to loss-focused messages rather than gain-focused messages. Abhyankar, O'Connor and Lawton (2008) tested this hypothesis and found that, as predicted, a loss-framed message (e.g. 'By not vaccinating your child against mumps, measles and rubella, you will fail to protect your child against contracting these diseases') was more effective in increasing women's MMR vaccination intentions than a gain-focused message (e.g. 'By vaccinating your child against mumps, measles and rubella, you will be able to protect your child against contracting these diseases'). Similarly, when a detection behaviour is perceived to result in a safe or certain outcome, then a gain-focused message is likely to be most effective. A study by Apanovitch, McCarthy and Salovey (2003) found that women who felt safe about the outcome of a HIV test because they considered themselves to be at no risk were more likely to report having the test six months after watching a gain-focused video message compared to those who saw the loss-focused message.

Other factors influence the extent to which messages are processed. For example, the degree to which an individual is involved with an issue has been found to influence the effectiveness of gain- and loss-focused messages. Rothman et al (1993) found that framed messages only worked as predicted for people who were concerned with the target health behaviour (e.g. skin cancer detection). The extent to which a person holds a positive or negative attitude towards the target health behaviour is also important. In a study of intentions to use hormonal male contraception, O'Connor, Ferguson and O'Connor (2005) found that the hypothesized framing effects were only observed in men with a positive attitude towards the behaviour. Thus personal involvement and positive attitude towards the behaviour facilitate framing effects and thereby moderate the relationship between framing and motivation.

Thus framing information and advice in terms of benefits or gains so that this corresponds to how a recommended action is perceived (i.e. low risk behaviours are prompted using gains) can enhance the impact of risk information on motivation and behaviour. However, framing effects should be pre-tested on the target audience and individual characteristics considered before materials are produced.

Social influence motives and principles

Social influence can be understood in terms of the key underlying motives that facilitate cognitive change (Cialdini and Trost, 1998). First, people want to access valid sources of information about their reality. When we see other people looking behind us we sensibly want to turn around to see what is there. This type of influence has been referred to as **informational influence** (Deutsch and Gerard, 1955) and is the basis of expert power (French and Raven, 1960). If we believe that someone else is better informed and better able to predict what will happen to us then they have the potential to exert informational influence over us. Doctors are a good example of experts with informational power in relation to health issues. Second, we are motivated to feel positively about ourselves, that is, to maintain positive self-esteem. Third, we want to have good relationships with other people (sometimes referred to as the 'affiliation motive'). Acceptance by other people is critical to our sense of self-worth so these motivations combine to facilitate **normative influence**. For example, we are reluctant to lose friends' approval so we are willing to do what they want rather than following our own preferences. In doing so we are subject to normative influence.

Research supports a series of principles concerning social influence processes (Cialdini, 1995) which relate directly to these two types of influence. First, as we have seen, ensuring that the message source is perceived to be *credible and expert* enhances persuasive impact. Our perception of a message source also depends on *how we categorize ourselves* in relation to the source (whether this is an individual or group). People seen as similar to ourselves or belonging to the same group are more likely to be liked, viewed positively and able to validate our experiences (Turner, 1991). Therefore, such people have a greater potential to exert normative influence. Consequently, it has been proposed that peers (people belonging to the target audience) are the most persuasive communicators. However, evidence indicates that this is only true if these communicators are also seen to be experts. Those perceived to be expert and whose gender and ethnicity match the target group are most persuasive and helpful (Durantini et al, 2006).

Cognitive dissonance theory (Festinger, 1957) proposes that we are motivated to maintain a consistent view of the world because cognitive inconsistency creates dissonance which is inherently unpleasant. Consequently, when the opinions of others or persuasive messages appear consistent with what we already know and believe, they are more likely to be persuasive. Thus *consistency*, that is, ensuring that a health message does not contradict existing beliefs, commitments or obligations (and thereby generate cognitive dissonance) is an important second feature of communications likely to persuade.

A third, and related, principle is the perception of *consensus*. If a proposed change is supported by everyone (and this emphasizes the importance of not providing contradictory advice) and is adopted by others we are more likely to want to join in. Thus believing that others are performing an action that we are considering (that is holding a positive descriptive norm – Rivis and Sheeran, 2003 – see Chapter 7) is likely to facilitate persuasion and bolster motivation. This may be even more persuasive if we categorize ourselves as belonging to the same group as those adopting the change (e.g. 'Other people like you have already adopted this behaviour') because such identification is likely to enhance the self-worth/validation impact of the message. Thus informational influence (and to some extent normative influence) can be strengthened by three key features of persuasive messages: 1) source credibility and expertise; 2) perceived consistency with current world view; and 3) perceived consensus/identification.

People we like and identify with can exert greater normative influence over us. Thus persuasion is more likely when the source is seen as enjoying a *good relationship or good image* with the target audience. This emphasizes the importance of good social and communication skills among professionals involved in face-to-face health promotion activities and of enhancing the brand value of organizations offering health advice such as the National Health Service (NHS) in the UK. We tend to like those who offer us things of value so people are more open to social influence from those who have provided something for them. Therefore, *reciprocation*, through offering services or products that are seen as valuable, may be a useful way of encouraging a target group to listen to health-related advice. In addition, we value approval so believing that those who are important to us approve of a particular course of action (i.e. holding a positive subjective norm (Fishbein and Ajzen, 1975, see Chapter 7)) is likely to facilitate persuasion and affect motivation. Thus normative influence can be strengthened by three key features of persuasive messages: positive relationships, reciprocation and the approval of valued others.

Persuasion in groups

Both informational and normative influence act on people in groups but persuasion in groups differs depending on whether it is persuasion by the majority (that is, more than half the group), called conformity (Asch, 1952), or conversion to a minority view or action. Majority influence or **conformity** is strengthened by consensus. A large and consistent majority exerts considerable informational and normative influence. By contrast, a minority challenges our usual assumptions and leads us to evaluate the contrast between majority and minority views (Moscovici, 1976; Moscovici and Lage, 1976). **Conversion** to a minority view does not work through consensus influence and is determined instead by how the minority act. If members of a minority group are seen to be consistent, committed, confident and fair they prompt others to think carefully about their alternative position. This systematic consideration and evaluation of the minority view means that, when minorities are persuasive, the attitude change that results from such conversion is likely to be longer-lasting and less subject to counter-persuasion than attitude change due to conformity (Martin et al).

Persuasion and influence in groups have important applied implications because group discussions are regularly used by researchers and health services including the UK NHS. Discussions in focus groups and so-called 'citizen's juries' are regularly used to discover what people want and the results used to draw conclusions about public opinion and popular policy development. One problem associated with this methodology is that the way in which groups are managed and facilitated may affect what people say. For example, the questions posed and choices offered shape responses. Moreover, powerful majorities or confident and committed minorities may limit the number of viewpoints considered through conformity and conversion. Are group discussions the best way of sampling public opinion (see e.g. *The Observer*, Sunday, 30 September, 2007, for comment)?

Obedience and informed decision-making

We have seen how important the source of a message is to persuasion. Holding legitimate authority is an especially powerful attribute in relation to social influence. When people occupy a role in which they accept that another person has the right to direct other people's actions, they are more easily persuaded. This was powerfully demonstrated in Milgram's (1974) experiments in which he showed that people would deliver (what they thought were) electric shocks to others to a much greater extent than was predicted, so long as they accepted the experimenter (ordering the shocks) as a legitimate authority figure. Following this work, Rank and Jacobson (1997) investigated nurses' obedience to an apparent order from a doctor to administer a drug in a too large a quantity, that is to give a patient a drug overdose. They concluded that nurses were less likely to obey the mistaken order if they were familiar with the drug and had time to confer with other nurses. This emphasizes a more general point relevant to all those involved in health care decisions, namely, that being well informed and having time to confer before decisions are made is likely to minimize mistakes, whether the decision makers are managers, doctors, nurses or patients.

Overcoming resistance to change

Persuasion is necessary because often people do not want to change. We do not like others trying to influence us, we often find persuasive communications threatening or unbelievable and we feel it is too difficult to change everyday routines in the face of many competing demands. **Reactance** (Brehm, 1966) is an emotional response to attempts at coercion, prohibition and regulation. Reactance leads people to take the opposite view to that imposed and motivates people to do the opposite of what is recommended. Thus it is important to prepare for and manage the social influence attempts. If a persuasion attempt is insensitive to the needs of the target audience it may have no impact or even be counterproductive.

We have noted the importance of perceptions of the message source and this extends to the way in which the persuasive attempt is delivered. Explicit persuasive attempts may be resisted. For example, it means that tone of voice and non-verbal indicators of power within a relationship can undermine social influence in one-to-one settings. For example, Ambady et al (2002) taped surgeons' consultations with patients and, on the basis of 10-second clips, rated dominance and concern/anxiety in their voices (regardless of content). Higher dominance and lower concern were significantly associated with greater number of previous malpractice claims initiated by their patients! This has important implications for doctor–patient communication which we will consider in Chapter 10.

Governments need to persuade populations that public health legislation is in the public interest before enacting such legislation (e.g. necessitating seatbelt wearing in cars or banning smoking in public places). Otherwise enforcement may be costly and there is a risk that unpopular legislation may be overturned. Thus reassuring a target audience that what is offered is caring advice which is primarily in their own interest is a crucial foundation for persuasion.

Reactance and resistance can be minimized by presenting persuasion attempts as *choices*, by highlighting the ease with which change can be managed and by focusing on what people can do rather than telling them what they should not do (e.g. 'You can choose to be smoke free', 'You can choose to eat a healthy diet and feel and look better') (Knowles and Rinner, 2007). Presenting health advice as choice has been widely adopted by the UK NHS. For example, it has established a 'choices website' described as 'the new service that helps you to make the most of your health and get the best out of the NHS' (www.nhs.uk/pages/homepage.aspx). While the intention here is to promote health behaviour change, the persuasive attempt is presented as offering new opportunities and increasing the recipient's freedom.

Activity 8.2

Design a brief set of arguments that could be used to persuade young people to donate blood, drawing on evidence-based principles of persuasion.

Attitude change

Did you think about a health-related behaviour you feel you should change? Have you not changed because you expect this change to result in negative outcomes? Evaluating action positively, that is, holding a positive attitude towards it is critical to change. Consequently, *attitude change* is a key target for those wishing to persuade others to adopt healthier lifestyles.

Message processing and attitude change

Attitude change is dependent on how a recipient responds to a persuasive message. For example, some evaluative responses are based on superficial impressions while others are the result of systematic consideration. This has important implications for persuasive techniques. Petty and Cacioppo (1986) argue that, although we are all motivated to hold valid attitudes which help us make reliable predictions about our reality (hence the power of informational influence), we can have more or less motivation and capacity to devote to the systematic processing of messages we receive. They refer to the amount of systematic processing devoted to a message as 'cognitive elaboration' and, consequently, their model is known as the 'elaboration likelihood model' (ELM).

The ELM refers to systematic processing of messages as **central route processing** and processing of messages in a superficial manner as **peripheral route processing**. Central route processing involves greater cognitive elaboration and the meaning of the message is critical to persuasion. By contrast, peripheral route processing involves little systematic processing (low cognitive elaboration) and other characteristics of the message are more likely to determine whether or not it is persuasive.

When people are under time pressure, do not understand a message, think that the issue is not relevant to them or are distracted by something else they may evaluate a message on the basis of simple cues rather than considering its meaning in detail. For example, people use simple rules or **decision-making heuristics** to evaluate messages. These include 'expertise = accuracy', that is, she is an expert so what she says must be right, or 'consensus = correctness', that is, if so many people agree they must be right and 'length = strength', that is there are lots of arguments so it must be true. Sometimes situational constraints force people into peripheral route processing. For example, the message may be presented quickly amid distractions as is the case in many television advertisements. In addition, individual differences mean that some people are more or less likely than others to engage in systematic processing. For example, Chaiken (1980) identified people who agreed or disagreed with the length = strength heuristic (using agreement with questionnaire items such as 'The more reasons a person has for some point of view the more likely he/she is correct'). These people were then presented with a message containing six arguments in favour of cross-course, end-of-year examinations for students. However, the message was described to participants as either containing 10 or two arguments (although it always contained the same six arguments). The results showed that those who endorsed the length = strength heuristic were more likely to be persuaded when the message was described as having 10 arguments than were those who did not endorse the heuristic.

Central route (systematic) processing is unlikely among message recipients who do not understand a message. Figure 8.2 shows results from a study by Wood, Kallgren and Mueller Preisler (1985). Among message recipients with poor knowledge, attitude change was almost as likely whether a message contained weak or strong arguments because the ability to engage in systematic, central route processing was compromised by lack of knowledge. These recipients relied on peripheral processing and so failed to differentiate between strong and weak arguments. By contrast, those with good knowledge clearly differentiated between strong and weak arguments and were only persuaded by the former. These results emphasize the importance of knowledge (and, therefore, high quality information) in allowing people to evaluate messages about their health.

When people have time to process messages or make time because they see the message as personally relevant, they are more likely to engage in systematic processing so that the meaning of the message is more important than other

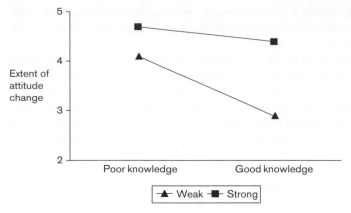

Figure 8.2 Prior knowledge and the effect of argument strength on persuasion.

Source: Journal of Experimental Social Psychology 21, 73–85. Wood, W., Kallgren, C. A., & Mueller Preisler, R. (1985). Access to attitude-relevant information in memory as a determinant of persuasion: The role of message attributes. Reprinted with permission from Elsevier.

characteristics. Figure 8.3 shows how perceiving the message source to be an expert has different effects depending on whether recipients regard a message as high or low in personal relevance. The low relevance participants are strongly affected by perceived expertise and are more persuaded by an expert (rather than inexpert) source whether strong or weak arguments are used. However, for those who see the message as personally relevant (and so engage in systematic processing) only the quality of argument determines persuasion. Strong arguments are persuasive for this group, regardless of source expertise, and even an expert cannot persuade this group with weak arguments. This does not mean that source expertise is unimportant but rather that for those with the ability and motivation to engage in systematic processing poor quality arguments cannot be compensated for by the impression of expertise. In terms of the ELM this means that persuasion does occur through both the central and peripheral routes simultaneously but that one or other route will be dominant depending on factors such as message relevance. Individual characteristics also affect whether people are likely to engage mainly in systematic processing (Briñol and Petty, 2005). For example, some people have a high '**need for cognition**' and so, in general, are motivated to make time for central route processing (Cacioppo et al, 1983).

Figure 8.3 The impact of expertise on persuasion by strong and weak arguments under conditions of low (left) and high (right) personal relevance.

Source: With kind permission of Professor John T. Cacioppo and Professor Richard E. Petty.

Overall then, research suggests that if you do not have strong arguments then you are better discouraging systematic processing and relying instead on numerous arguments, consensus and perceived expertise. Perhaps fortunately, attitude changes resulting from peripheral route processing are less likely to be stable (that is, long lived) and more likely to further change due to counter-persuasion, whereas attitude change resulting from systematic (central route) processing is more likely to be stable and to influence behaviour. Consequently, health promoters should ensure they use strong evidence-based arguments, encourage systematic processing by ensuring appropriate prior knowledge, emphasizing personal relevance, providing distraction-free presentations, using repetition and encouraging confidence in people's own judgement. Having facilitated systematic processing we must ensure that our persuasive messages are easily understood if we are to change attitudes.

Activity 8.3

Identify three television advertisements which illustrate application of evidence-based principles of persuasion.

Enhancing self-efficacy

Perhaps you have not changed the health-related behaviour you thought of earlier because you think it would be too difficult to change. **Self-efficacy** (SE) is the belief that one has the ability and resources to succeed in achieving a goal despite environmental barriers. Perceived behavioural control and SE are important prerequisites of intention (see Chapter 7). SE promotes intention and performance so consideration of SE enhancement bridges our discussion of changing motivation (this chapter) and behaviour (Chapter 9). SE is important to many areas of health psychology. For example, in Chapter 3 we discussed how secondary appraisals determine our experience of stress. When we believe we can competently manage an environmental demand, it becomes a challenge, otherwise it is a stressor. SE can sometimes depend on perceived social support (see Chapter 5), that is, we believe we can competently manage an environmental demand because we know others will help us.

Self-efficacy and performance

SE is correlated with performance across a range of behaviours from academic performance to health-related behaviours (Bandura, 1997). For example, in a meta-analysis (see Research methods box 8.1) of 114 studies of SE and work-related performance, Stajkovic and Luthans (1998) found an equivalent effect size of $d = .82$ which corresponds to an increase of 28 per cent in performance due to higher SE. This is an impressive effect size. Such findings recommend SE-enhancing interventions to improve work performance. However, SE varies across behaviours. For example, DiClemente (1986) noted that the correlation between SE for stopping overeating and quitting smoking was small ($r = .21$) (Bandura, 1997), emphasizing that interventions designed to enhance SE need to be behaviour specific.

While there is little evidence for distinct stages of behaviour change (see Chapter 7), people face different challenges as they progress from adoption (e.g. jogging for the first time) through to establishment of habits (e.g. jogging regularly three times a week). Thus SE-enhancing interventions should target challenges relevant to particular target audiences (Abraham, 2008). To facilitate this, different types of SE measures have been defined. For example, Schwarzer (2008) distinguishes between *action SE* (believing one can succeed in completing a planned behaviour), *maintenance SE* (believing one can maintain the action over time) and *recovery SE* (believing one can adopt the behaviour again after a relapse).

Those who believe they can succeed set themselves more challenging goals. They exert more effort, use more flexible problem-solving strategies and are more persistent *because* they believe they will eventually succeed. By contrast, low SE undermines striving. High SE also minimizes stress (because of favourable secondary appraisals, see Chapter 3) which enhances skilled performance (Bandura, 1997). Moreover, high SE facilitates concentration on the task rather than concerns about personal deficiencies or exaggeration of task demands (Wood and Bandura, 1989) thereby minimizing anxiety during performance. Thus SE affects how people conceptualize a task, how confident they feel during performance, how persistent they are in the face of setbacks, how much effort they invest and how they feel about themselves during performance.

Self-efficacy and health

As well as affecting performance, SE levels affect health directly by moderating the impact of potential stressors on physiological systems. Low SE generates stress which elicits a variety of physiological responses (see Chapter 2). These include the release of catecholamines into the bloodstream, such as adrenaline and cortisol, from the adrenal gland. This, in turn, increases heart rate, blood pressure, sugar levels and blood flow to large muscle groups. SE changes have been found to be associated with catecholamine activation (Bandura, 1997) providing a plausible mechanism by which SE levels alter the physiological impact of environmental demands on the body. It is unsurprising, therefore, that high SE is associated with less down-regulation of the immune system in response to stressors (Wiedenfeld et al, 1990). It has also been argued that intermittent (as opposed to chronic) stress responses may 'toughen' physiological systems by dampening down stress responses over time (Dienstbier, 1989), i.e. periodic increases in sympathetic nervous system arousal train the body to respond less extremely to subsequent stressors. However, this effect depends on these intermittent stressors being perceived as challenges (rather than threats) which, in turn, depends on high SE in relation to actions required by such stressors.

Enhancing self-efficacy

Bandura (1997, 1999) argues that there are four main approaches to enhancing self-efficacy:

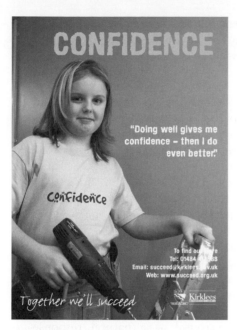

Figure 8.4 Direct experience of success enhances self-efficacy.
Source: With kind permission of Kirklees Council.

1. Mastery experiences.
2. *Vicarious experience*.
3. Verbal persuasion.
4. *Perception of physiological and affective states*.

First, and most powerful, **mastery experiences** (i.e. experience of successfully performing the behaviour) give people confidence that they can tackle new tasks because they know they have previously succeeded with similar challenges. This recommends that teachers and trainers guide learners towards success by identifying manageable tasks and only increasing difficulty as confidence and skill grow, that is by use of **graded tasks** (see Figure 8.4). Moreover, helping someone practise a manageable task and providing feedback can consolidate skills and enhance SE. Failure undermines SE and focusing on past failure can be self-handicapping.

Second, SE can also be enhanced through observation of others' success, especially if we categorize the models as being like ourselves. For example, Bandura (1997) notes that observing failure in a model judged to have less skill than ourselves has little or no impact on SE but observing the same failure in a model judged to have similar skills is likely to undermine SE. Health promoters should conduct preliminary research into when positive and negative models are helpful to people establishing new goals, building SE and acquiring new skills. Positive models (that is, observation of successful others) are likely to be SE-enhancing (e.g. in the case of physical fitness), although in some cases, for example when undesirable body image is salient, negative models (that is, use of models failing to establish physical fitness) may be motivating (Lockwood et al,

2005). Moreover, contrasts between current self and desired or ideal self can be motivating, that is, negative self models (i.e. an undesirable self) may have positive effects on changing motivation when combined with realistic goal-setting opportunities (Oettingen, 1996).

Third, when direct experience and modelling are not available, SE can be enhanced through verbal persuasion. People can be persuaded by arguments demonstrating that others (like them) are successful in meeting challenges similar to their own (thereby changing descriptive norms) as well as persuasion highlighting the individual's own skills and past success. Tailoring communication to enhance persuasiveness (as discussed in this chapter), including, for example, maximizing source trustworthiness and expertise is likely to enhance the effectiveness of such interventions.

Finally, our own physiological reactions and our interpretations of these reactions affect SE. Mood, stress and anxiety during performance can bolster or undermine self-efficacy. For example, although arousal is normal during demanding performances, it can be interpreted as a sign of panic or incompetence. Such interpretations are likely to disrupt and undermine performance. By contrast, acknowledging arousal as a natural response to performance demands may add to excitement and commitment. Thus interventions designed to reduce negative moods and anxiety and to reinterpret destructive interpretations of arousal are likely to enhance SE and facilitate skilled performance.

From motivation to behaviour change

In this chapter we have considered the use of evidence-based techniques to enhance motivation to perform health-related behaviours. In Chapter 7 we noted that motivation alone may not be enough to prompt action. Research on the intention–behaviour gap and implementation intention formation indicates that interventions focusing on post-intentional or volitional processes may be critical to prompting already motivated people to adopt health-promoting behaviours. Thus the challenge for health promoters is to generate the motivation to perform target health behaviours and also to help motivated people develop volitional capacities (e.g. bolstering self-efficacy and prompting implementation intention formation).

In the face of growing health care demands from ageing populations and increasing prevalence of long-term illnesses (see Chapter 10) health services have begun to supplement one-to-one professional-patient models of health care delivery with group and volunteer delivery modes (Whelan, 2002). Such programmes aim to develop health care self-management skills including illness-specific competencies and generic decision-making skills. Evaluations of these interventions have found that they can be both effective in changing behaviour and also cost effective. For example, Lorig, Mazonson and Holman (1993) found that a self-management course for patients with chronic arthritis resulted in increased self-efficacy, reduced pain and a 43 per cent reduction in consultations with doctors. The course was delivered to groups by trained volunteers who were themselves arthritis sufferers. For patients suffering from rheumatoid arthritis, the reduction in health service usage constituted a saving of $162 per patient. Since there are about 386,600 people with rheumatoid arthritis in the UK (Symmons et al, 2002), then, even using 1993 figures with current currency conversion rates, this intervention has the potential to save the UK National Health Services £32 million if it were provided for all sufferers. Other evaluations have identified a variety of health care gains from participation in such group-based self-management training. Barlow et al (2002) reviewed 145 evaluations and concluded that self-management training led to increases in patients' knowledge and SE, better symptom management, adoption of appropriate coping techniques and enhancements in health status. Other studies have found reduced hospitalization (e.g. Lorig et al, 1999a) and enhanced physical and psychological well-being following attendance at such courses (Wright et al, 2003).

Evaluation of health interventions of this kind illustrates one area in which *quantitative and qualitative research* complement each other (see also Chapter 10). Quantitative research is required to assess effectiveness in terms of predefined criteria from health care usage figures, through to attitudes and quality of life using previously validated measures. However, qualitative research, usually using interviews or *focus groups* (where a group discusses a series of questions), can examine the perspective of the user in detail (Payne, 2004). Here the focus is not on the significance of mean differences but on detailed similarities and differences between users' accounts of the intervention. Such research might, for example, reveal which intervention techniques were especially valued or disliked by users and also highlight the range of individual responses in terms of cognition, emotions and behaviour. This could help intervention designers understand why some users respond positively and others negatively and imply modifications to the delivery or content of an intervention. Qualitative analysis of interview data could also reveal positive or negative experiences not previously considered by researchers and, thereby, imply new theoretical advances and/or new outcomes. For example, an intervention targeting motivation change might be found to work for many people through new social relationships and changes in identity. Researchers regularly judge the methodological adequacy of quantitative studies but this is more challenging in the case of qualitative studies. An interesting guide to judging the quality of qualitative studies relevant to health care has been proposed by Daly et al (2007). For a useful introduction see Payne (2004) and for further details on qualitative theory and methods see Murray and Chamberlain (1999) and Smith (2003).

Influenced by the results of quantitative and qualitative evaluation research, the UK Department of Health began to develop the *Expert Patient Programme* (EPP) in 2001. This is a generic self-management training intervention designed to empower patients to effectively manage chronic health conditions and associated symptoms (see Chapter 10). The longer-term aim of the EPP was to facilitate patients becoming key decision-makers in the treatment process and gaining greater control over their lives through improved resourcefulness and self-efficacy, as well as reducing health service demand (Department of Health,

2001). EPP was based closely on the previously evaluated Chronic Disease Self Management Course (Lorig et al, 1999b; see also Bandura, 1999) which developed from the successful interventions with arthritis patients. EPP was implemented throughout the NHS in 2007.

An EPP course comprises six weekly structured self-management training sessions delivered to groups of 6–15 patients with heterogeneous health conditions, led by trained, lay tutors with chronic health conditions. Patients also receive a self-help manual containing further information. The programme includes information provision and cognitive and behavioural modification techniques as well as prompting action planning and problem solving, providing support for taking exercise and eating a healthy diet as well as coping with depression. Course sessions are held in community settings and tutors are volunteers, thus keeping administration costs low. Early evaluations have been encouraging. Barlow et al (2005) observed a number of benefits including increased SE in managing symptoms, reduced fatigue and depressed moods and better communication with doctors. Moreover, benefits were sustained 12 months after attending an EPP course. A randomized controlled trial found improvements in SE and psychological well-being, together with reduced anxiety and greater levels of physical activity, at six-month follow-up (Kennedy et al, 2007).

Summary

Health-related information needs to be accessible, come from a credible source, minimize use of jargon, be easily readable and answer the questions which the target audience are interested in. Simple techniques including logical order, explicit categorization and repetition enhance recall.

Persuasion is a form of social influence which can be understood in terms of underlying motives. We are motivated to access valid sources of information and this facilitates informational influence. We are also motivated to feel positively about ourselves and to have good relationships with others. This facilitates normative influence. Informational influence is strengthened by source credibility and expertise, consistency and consensus. Normative influence is strengthened by positive relationships, reciprocation and approval. Persuasion in groups can be understood in terms of conformity and conversion (in the case of minority influence). Avoiding prohibition and presenting advice as easy-to-implement choices can minimize reactance.

Attitude change based on systematic (or central route) processing is more stable and less susceptible to counter-persuasion than attitude change following from peripheral route processing. Central route processing is more likely when people are informed, motivated (e.g. they think the message is relevant to them) and have the capacity (e.g. distraction-free time to consider arguments) to process messages. During central route processing the meaning or quality of arguments is critical to persuasion.

Self-efficacy is correlated with performance across a range of behaviours but tends to be behaviour specific. SE leads to greater effort, persistence and flexible responding. SE needs to correspond directly to the challenges faced by particular individuals or target audiences. SE can be enhanced by mastery experiences, vicarious experience (i.e. modelling), verbal persuasion and perception of physiological and affective states.

Key concepts and terms

Central and peripheral route processing	Flesch Reading Ease measure
Cognitive dissonance	Graded tasks
Cognitive elaboration	Graphic organizer
Conformity	Informational influence,
Conversion	Mastery experience
Decision-making heuristic	Need for cognition
Effect size	Normative influence
Explicit categorization	Reactance
	Self-efficacy

Sample essay titles

- Information isn't enough: Health psychology research provides a new basis for health promotion. Discuss.

- Attempts to persuade people to avoid unhealthy behaviours often fail. How can health promoters persuade people to look after their health more effectively?

- What lessons can health promoters learn from the psychology of attitude change?

- Why is self-efficacy important to health and health-related behaviour?

Further reading

Books

Cialdini, R.B. (1995). 'Principles and techniques of social influence.' In: A. Tesser (Ed.), *Advanced Social Psychology*. New York: McGraw Hill, 257–281.

Knowles, E.S., and Rinner, D.D. (2007). 'Omega approaches to persuasion: Overcoming resistance.' In: A.R. Pratkanis (Ed.), *The Science of Social Influence: Advances and Future Progress*. New York: Psychology Press, 83–114.

Petty, R.E., and Cacioppo, J.T. (1986). 'The elaboration likelihood model of persuasion.' In: L. Berkowitz (Ed.), *Advances in Experimental Social Psychology*. New York: Academic Press, 19, 123–205.

Journal articles

Bandura, A. (1999). Health promotion from the perspective of social cognitive theory. *Psychology and Health*, 13, 623–650.

Coulter, A., Entwistle, V., and Gilbert, D. (1999). Sharing decisions with patients: is the information good enough? *British Medical Journal*, 318, 318–322.

9 Changing behaviour

Behaviour change is the raison d'être of health promotion and applied health psychology. It is also fundamental to effective health care. A review of the UK National Health Service (Wanless, 2002) concluded that national health services were only affordable if they effectively involved the population in their own health care. As a discussion paper published by the UK Prime Minister's Strategy Unit noted,

> achievement of major policy outcomes, requires greater engagement and participation from citizens – governments can't do it alone ... improvements depend on changes in personal behaviour: for example in health, on better diet and more exercise. (Halpern et al, 2004: 3)

In the UK, the National Institute for Health and Clinical Excellence, which advises on best practice and cost effectiveness in the National Health Service, spent two years drawing up guidance on how to effectively promote health behaviour change (NICE, 2007).

So how can we effectively promote health behaviour change? We saw in Chapter 8 that changing motivation depends on providing accurate information in an accessible form and on using persuasive techniques to promote behaviour-promoting attitudes, normative beliefs and self-efficacy (SE). Yet, while techniques that can prompt and sustain motivational change are essential tools for those wishing to bring about behaviour change, they do not always provide a sufficient toolkit for the task. For example, Sheeran (2002) observed that, across six studies, only 47 per cent of intenders acted on their health-related intention illustrating that, although motivation is prerequisite to action (e.g. Sheeran found only 7 per cent of non-intenders acted), motivation is not always enough.

In this chapter we identify key questions that need to be answered prior to designing behaviour change interventions. We consider how target behaviours may be shaped by social processes beyond individual motivation and self-regulation and emphasize the importance of designing interventions that have their impact at the same level as processes which shape target behaviours. We also discuss the importance of theory in specifying change processes which explain how interventions influence behaviour. Focusing on individual-level interventions, we highlight the importance of precisely defining the target group and then assessing relevant cognitions and skills among that group. We recommend pre-testing intervention materials with the specified target group before investing in intervention. In addition, we examine a range of theory-based behaviour change techniques that can be employed in interventions. Finally, we consider procedures necessary to effectively plan and evaluate behaviour change interventions. The chapter is organized into four sections: 1) specifying behaviours, determinants, target groups and intervention targets; 2) matching materials to change mechanisms; 3) identifying effective behaviour change techniques; 4) designing and evaluating behaviour change interventions.

Learning outcomes

When you have completed this chapter you should be able to:

1. Articulate key questions to be answered by elicitation research prior to intervention design, referring to both the 'social ecological' model of change and the 'information, motivation and behavioural skills' model.
2. Explain how intervention materials can target key behavioural determinants found to be deficient in the target population.
3. Discuss when fear appeals may or may not be effective with reference to protection motivation theory and illustrate the importance of carefully designed theory-based materials.
4. Identify a series of distinct behaviour change techniques and link these to the change mechanisms specified by a range of psychological theories.
5. Critically appraise reports of intervention evaluations in terms of the quality of outcome and process evaluations, as well as the utility and sustainability of the proposed interventions.

Specifying behaviours, determinants, target groups and intervention targets

It is critical, when contemplating behaviour change, to be precise about the definition of *the target behaviour*, e.g. in the case of exercise, how many times a week, for what duration, and at what intensity do we want people to exercise? It is equally important to be clear about *who* exactly an intervention will target. For example, an intervention designed to reduce unwanted teenage pregnancies will not target the average teenager but young men and women who are most likely to have unprotected intercourse at a young age. This is important because subgroups differ in their knowledge, cognitions, motivation and skills, and imprecision in defining the target group may lead to a mismatched intervention which is likely to be ineffective.

Social influences on health behaviours operate at different levels

Psychologists focus on the individual processes involved in behaviour change but behaviour change is embedded in, and must be understood in terms of, social context. Bartholomew et al (2006: 9) advocated a *'social ecological' model of change* which includes individual and social determinants of behaviour and recognizes different levels of intervention (see Figure 9.1).

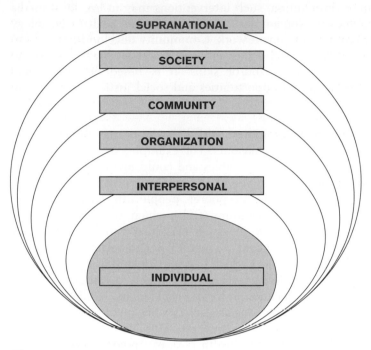

Figure 9.1 Levels of behaviour change intervention.

Source: Adapted from Bartholomew et al, 2006.

We saw in Chapter 4 how relative poverty arising from the distribution of wealth within a country can affect health. The management of taxation and benefit systems has large effects on health and longevity within countries (Wilkinson, 1996) but such change requires action by legislators. Consequently, in certain cases, effective health promotion necessitates lobbying politicians and legislators and presenting the results of research to decision makers in government. This is important work because legislative change can have far-reaching and immediate effects on health. For example, in the UK in 2007, smoking in public places was banned and it became illegal to sell tobacco to people below the age of 18 years. Evaluating a similar legislative change, Sargent, Shepard and Glantz (2004) found that myocardial infarction admissions to a hospital in Montana, USA, fell significantly over six months during a smoking ban in public places, while at the same time, surrounding areas (without a smoking ban) experienced non-significant increases. In some cases, international legislation may even be necessary. For example, while taxation can be effective in reducing smoking, raising the price of cigarettes just in the UK might not be effective because it would encourage cigarette smuggling from neighbouring easily accessible countries where cigarettes are considerably cheaper.

Lack of resources, lack of skills and social norms at community level can also sustain health risk behaviours. Consequently, interventions to promote health behaviours may need to be based in, and engage, communities. This involves meetings and discussion with local people and organizations. It may also entail persuading local government to change policies, enforce existing legislation or provide new resources. In addition, such interventions may utilize local media campaigns and educational programmes. This work merges health psychology practice with community development work. Community development seeks to involve people in identifying local assets and needs and facilitating action to create or acquire new resources and/or skills. It is based on choice and participation and aims to extend opportunities and social justice for people in particular communities.

Community interventions to promote health behaviours may target specific behaviours or a range of related behaviours. For example, such interventions might target buying more fruit and vegetables and could involve campaigns to establish a local fresh produce market and/or the provision of vouchers to make healthier products more affordable to poorer people. In Chapter 8, we considered the UK Expert Patient Programme (EPP), which, while implemented nationally, targets those with chronic illness in particular communities. More comprehensive interventions may target a range of health-related behaviours. For example, the North Karelia Project which began in Finland in 1972 included education on smoking, diet and hypertension using widely distributed leaflets, radio and television slots and education in local organizations. Voluntary sector organizations, schools and health and social services were involved and training was provided for personnel in various contexts. The intervention included education of school students about the health risks of smoking and the social influences which lead young people to begin smoking as well as training for students in how to resist such social influences. This comprehensive intervention was found to be effective on a range of indices including reduction in smoking and serum cholesterol levels. For example, 15 years later, smoking prevalence was 11 per cent lower among intervention participants compared to controls (Vartiainen et al, 1998).

In a review of evaluations of comprehensive community interventions (including the North Karelia Project), Hingson and Howland (2002) found that greater effectiveness was observed when interventions: 1) targeted behaviours with immediate health consequences such as alcohol misuse or sexual risk taking; 2) targeted young people to prevent uptake of health-risk behaviours; 3) combined environmental and institutional policy change with theory-based behaviour change interventions; and 4) involved communities themselves in intervention design.

Organizational rules, norms and resources may create stress (see Chapter 4) and impede health behaviour change. They are, therefore, often targeted both in community interventions and in single-organization worksite interventions. Worksite interventions may aim to integrate physical activity into employees' days including exercise breaks and promotion of walking and stair use or change the availability of healthy food and/or how food is labelled (e.g. Engbers et al, 2005). Worksite interventions focusing on exercise have been found to be effective in increasing physical activity and fitness as well as promoting weight loss among participants (King et al, 1988; Proper et al, 2003).

We have seen the important role that social support can play in moderating stress (in Chapter 5). Interpersonal processes are often critical to prompting and sustaining individual behaviour change. Behaviour change motivation can be undermined when it is disapproved of or resisted by valued others, including family members or opinion leaders. Consequently, additional social support can enhance the effectiveness of interventions both in initiating and maintaining behaviour change. For example, planning how barriers to change may be overcome or the signing of behavioural contracts are change techniques which are facilitated by interpersonal interaction. Moreover, community and worksite interventions (e.g. EPP) may provide social support by establishing buddy systems or support groups in which two or more people work together to support initiation and/or maintenance of behaviour change. Thus establishing how interpersonal processes influence a target behaviour and assessing skills in managing relevant social interactions and available social support is important when designing interventions (e.g. consider the focus on resisting social influence included in the North Karelia Project).

The social ecological model of behaviour change emphasizes that a critical first step in planning individual behaviour change is an assessment of the levels at which social and societal processes shape individual behaviour. Without such assessment, interventions may not target the most relevant or influential antecedents of the target behaviour. These may differ across groups defined, for example, in terms of socio-economic status, age, gender, ethnicity or culture. Such assessments may highlight the need to intervene at interpersonal, organizational, community or national level to change processes that sustain health-compromising behaviours. Thus health psychology practice may include and merge with organizational psychology, community development work and even political lobbying.

Assessing deficits and setting targets

While some health behaviour change interventions may focus exclusively on changing legislation, providing community resources or changing organizational policies, most include change techniques designed to change how individuals perceive and respond to events. At this level, the **information–motivation–behavioural skills model** (IMB; Fisher and Fisher, 1992; see Figure 9.2) provides a useful planning tool. This model acknowledges the potential importance of information provision (see Chapter 8) and encompasses cognitive components of motivation proposed by the theory of planned behaviour (TPB) and social cognitive theory (SCT; see Chapter 7). In addition, this model highlights the importance of skills required to translate motivation into action.

A number of successful behaviour change interventions have been based on the IMB, particularly in relation to HIV-preventive behaviour (e.g. Fisher et al, 1994), and some of these have been evaluated using long-term follow-up (e.g. at 12 months in the case of Fisher et al, 2002). See Focus box 9.1 for an illustration of targets and methods. The IMB model is useful in planning behaviour change interventions both because it emphasizes that a variety of skills are required to translate motivation into behaviour change and because it highlights the need to assess behaviour-relevant deficits among the target group prior to intervention design. According to the IMB model health psychologists need to discover whether the (precisely defined) target group lack any behaviour-relevant

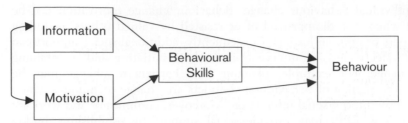

Figure 9.2 The information–motivation–behavioural skills model.

Source: © 1992 by the American Psychological Association. Adapted with permission. Fisher, J.D. & Fisher, W.A. Changing AIDS-risk behavior. Psychological Bulletin, 111, 455–471.

information, whether the key determinants of motivation are in place among this target group and whether the target group lack any skills required to translate motivation into behaviour. Consequently, planning behaviour change interventions depends on prior research examining determinants of the target behaviour (thereby highlighting potential change processes) among the target group and specifying informational, motivational or skill deficits. Such research has been called '**elicitation research**' and often involves interviews and survey studies with the target group. In Chapters 7 and 8 we considered how we can assess and intervene to enhance information and the determinants of motivation.

Behavioural skills

A proposed behaviour change may necessitate a variety of skills which people in the target group may or may not have already developed. Three core classes of prerequisite skills can be defined. The first are *self-regulatory skills*. These are cognitive skills which, for example, help people consider longer-term consequences of current action, evaluate their current behaviour, set new goals, including setting graded tasks, prioritize goals in the face of other demands, plan action before and during goal-relevant experiences and prompt exertion of appropriate effort when opportunities present themselves. Implementation intention formation (i.e. the if-then plans as described in Chapter 7) and SE enhancement (as described in Chapter 8) involve self-regulatory skills of this kind. With this class of skills initial teaching may involve conscious rehearsal of the skill followed by practice over time with a view to longer-term automatic initiation (see Chapter 7) of self-regulatory processes. For example, Schinke and Gordon (1992) describe a culturally-specific intervention including a self-completion book using comic strip characters and rap music verse to encourage effective safer sex regulation among black teenagers. The aim was to develop self-monitoring and planning skills as well as verbal resources which can be used to control and disrupt scripted interaction that could lead to unprotected sex. The acronym SODAS, standing for Stop, Options, Decide, Act and Self-praise, was used in this training. The first step, 'stop', explicitly elicits anticipated regret ('stop and think what these choices could really mean for you today, tomorrow ... and for years to follow' – see Chapter 7) while the fourth step, 'act', involves the reader in generating implementation intentions concerning five types of verbal responses which can be used when they are subjected to social pressure.

Focus 9.1

IMB-based intervention targeting identified deficits

In an intervention designed to reduce the risk of HIV infection among college students, Fisher et al (1996) included intervention components to address deficits in information, motivation and skills identified in elicitation research among US college students. Some of the targets they identified and the methods they used to achieve them are considered below.

Information component

A slide show and large group discussion presented and consolidated information on HIV transmission and prevention, the risk from different sexual behaviours, the effectiveness of condoms, where to buy condoms near campus, safer sex decision-making rules, HIV testing, and facts and myths about HIV/AIDS.

Motivation component

Small group discussions led by a peer educator, followed by large group discussions led by a professional health educator and incorporating a video narrated by HIV-positive individuals were designed to provide persuasive arguments targeting key cognitions. In particular, perceptions of personal susceptibility to HIV and attitudes and subjective norms relating to condom use were targeted.

Skills component

Negotiation self-efficacy was enhanced using peer-led role plays demonstrating safer sex communication. Students were encouraged by educators to practice safer sexual behaviours (e.g. condom handling skills and negotiation role playing) at home. Perceived effectiveness of condom use and self-efficacy in relation to condom use were bolstered by using a video in which peers modelled correct handling and use. In addition, group discussions were used to identify potential problems and reinforce newly learned negotiation skills.

After you finish reading this chapter return to this focus box and think about other change techniques that could have been included in this intervention.

Based on intervention details available on the website for the Centre for Health Intervention and Prevention (University of Connecticut – www.chip.uconn.edu/int_res_int.htm)

New *motor skills* constitute a second class of skills which may be involved in adopting health-related behaviours. For example, correct condom use depends upon a basic understanding of infection control as well as the manual skills involved in opening and using a condom without damaging it. Similarly, before using a gym, people need to be taught to use exercise machines. Certain medication regimens require patients to learn to use devices such as inhalers or needles, and patients and medical staff may need instruction in apparently simple skills such as hand washing as part of infection control in hospitals (Pittet et al, 2000; Pittet, 2002). Thus analysis of any health behaviour targeted in an intervention should involve an assessment of the skills required and the extent to which the targeted recipients are proficient or lacking in these skills. Of course, technological advances can make the skills involved in health behaviours easier to learn. Extra-fine needles make it easier for diabetics to inject themselves, alcohol wipes make hand washing easier and the development of a once-a-day single pill for HIV control makes adherence much easier than if patients have to take 36 pills a day! Thus sometimes skill deficits reveal an important role for organizational or technological change in supporting behaviour change.

Third, we also require *social skills* to manage behaviour and seek others' support for change, for example, the skills to negotiate condom use with a reluctant partner or the skills to explain why we will not engage in alcoholic drinking sessions or eat traditional but unhealthy foods. These social skills required are likely to be determined largely by the target behaviour and the social resources available to individuals planning change. However, assertiveness training (that is, being able to express one's own wants and needs in an honest and non-aggressive manner) and negotiation skills are often prerequisite to managing interactions which arise when individuals begin to change their behaviour.

Whenever skills found to be important to the translation of motivation into behaviour among the target group are identified, interventions should include instruction (which can be provided through a variety of media), opportunities for practice and feedback after practice by someone who is proficient in the required skill/s. These techniques are crucial to the establishment of skilled performance as well as the enhancement of SE (as described in Chapter 8).

Matching materials to change mechanisms

Having considered social processes at different levels affecting a specific behaviour among a precisely defined target group and having decided which determinants and change processes are important (e.g. attitudinal change may be required together with instruction and modelling of a new skill) intervention materials can be designed to correspond to those change processes. While this decision-making sequence may seem obvious (and see section on intervention mapping below), health promotion targeting behaviour change does not always proceed in this manner.

Mismatches between messages and behavioural determinants

Abraham et al (2002) surveyed widely available leaflets promoting condom use in the UK and Germany (gathering leaflets from general practitioners'

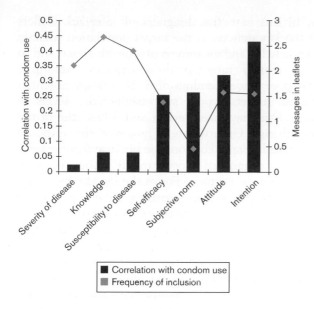

Figure 9.3 Strength of the association between cognitions and condom use and frequency of targeted messages in UK safer sex leaflets.

Source: Halpern, D., Bates, C., Beales, G. & Heathfield, A. (on behalf of the Prime Minister's Strategy Unit, 2004). Personal Responsibility and Changing Behaviour: the state of knowledge and its implications for public policy. (http://www.pm.gov.uk/files/pdf/pr.pdf), HMSO, London. Reproduced under the terms of the Click-Use Licence.

surgeries, clinics for the treatment of sexually transmitted infections and from four of the largest publishers of such materials). The contents of each leaflet, that is the arguments and messages used, were categorized. Few differences in average content were evident between UK and German leaflets. In general, leaflets devoted most content to providing information on the transmission of sexually transmitted infections (STIs), people's risks of acquiring STIs, the effectiveness of condom use and encouraging professional contact. This was judged disappointing because the change targets of these leaflets, for example, knowledge and perceived susceptibility, are weak correlates of condom use. Sheeran et al (1999) report average weighted correlations with condom use of .06 for both measures of knowledge and perceived susceptibility. Even perceived condom effectiveness was found to have an average correlation of only .10 with condom use. Thus the cognitions targeted most frequently by the majority of leaflets were not those found to be those most strongly correlated with condom use. By contrast, cognitions found to be stronger correlates of condom use, such as those specified by the TPB, were targeted less frequently by the leaflets (see Figure 9.3). The researchers identified 20 core messages that corresponded to the cognitive determinants significantly associated with condom use in previous studies. Seventy five per cent of leaflets included less than half of these determinant-matched messages. However, a small number of illustrative leaflets were identified which included between 15 and 18 of the 20 core messages, demonstrating that safer sex promotion leaflets can include a range of messages matched to the cognitive determinants of condom use.

The problem illustrated by this study is that materials are often designed on the basis of assumptions about what kind of intervention is required without adequate elicitation research. In this case the designers of safer sex leaflets seemed to have assumed that the key deficits in the target population (mainly the general population) were knowledge and awareness of a health threat and so the arguments they employed mainly targeted these changes. Among a population in which there was poor understanding of STIs or their potential danger to health, many of these leaflets would successfully raise levels of knowledge and perceived threat. This may have been a useful first step in the context of ignorance of the health risk. Unfortunately, however, this response would be very unlikely to prompt widespread condom use because the messages in the leaflets did not address the cognitions most strongly associated with condom use. Such mismatches are not uncommon. For example, Abraham et al (2007) found that leaflets designed to reduce alcohol consumption (across three European countries) failed, in general, to incorporate the range of research-based messages suggested by prior research into the determinants of risky drinking. It is important, therefore, that persuasive communication (see Chapter 8) used in health promotion is designed to precisely target the determinants of health behaviours, especially those determinants found to be predictive among the target population. Otherwise, even when the incorporated arguments are persuasive, they may fail to generate behaviour change.

Use of fear appeals

Public health campaigns frequently use messages that highlight health risk or threat and recommend protective action. Unfortunately, perceived threat or fear may be less readily translated into behaviour change than is assumed and many **fear appeals** may be ineffective (e.g. Albarracín et al, 2005).

As protection motivation theory (PMT, see Chapter 7) specifies, fear appeals should incorporate threat and efficacy messages emphasizing perceived susceptibility and severity as well as the effectiveness of the recommended protection and SE enhancement (see Chapter 8). Collectively, these messages should prompt protective intentions. Such threat-inducing messages can enhance systematic processing of subsequent messages (as might be expected because of enhanced personal relevance – see ELM in Chapter 8). For example, Das et al (2003) found that fear appeals generated favourable cognitive responses and consequent attitude change *if* participants felt susceptible to the threat (see also Witte and Allen, 2000). However, this approach can be problematic for a number of reasons. Cognitions specified by the PMT may not be the strongest determinants of behaviour so that persuasive fear appeals may have less effect on motivation than, for example, an intervention that effectively changes the cognitions specified by the TPB.

Fear appeals may also fail to persuade. Two types of failure have been identified. First, if people are not persuaded that the threat is relevant to them, this may undermine subsequent intervention and even threaten attitudes towards the recommended preventive action ('If the threat is not personally relevant why bother to take precautions?'). Second, if people do not believe they can protect themselves (i.e. they have low SE) they tend to protect themselves psychologically through defensive cognitive responses (see Chapter 8 on reactance and Chapter 5 on coping). When defensive processing (sometimes called fear control) occurs, then recipients may dismiss the message as untrustworthy – rejecting it altogether – or rejecting its relevance to them (Ruiter et al, 2001). Whether threat-based messages prompt intention formation (as PMT would suggest) or result in undesirable defensive processing depends on the relationship between the perceived threat and efficacy information. When perceived efficacy and SE are more salient than perceived threat (e.g. 'I know I can protect myself against the threat') then positive (danger control) motivational and behavioural change are likely. However, when SE is weak ('It's a threat I cannot manage') then coping is likely to be defensive (see also Chapter 3). Consequently, fear appeals need to incorporate strong and persuasive threat information (to affect subsequent processing) as well as strong efficacy and SE messages if they are to be effective (Witte, 1992; Witte and Allen, 2000). Note too that the framing of risk awareness messages may be crucial (see Chapter 8).

One way of reducing the likelihood that threat messages will encourage defensive processing is to affirm valued images of the self before a threat message. Such 'self-affirmation' reduces the need to defend the self against threat. For example, one might prompt message recipients to think about positive aspects of themselves before receiving threat information. Affirmed participants have been found to be more convinced by threat information and more willing to accept risk or severity of threat (Steele, 1988). For example, in a study conducted by Harris and Napper (2005), male participants in a self-affirmation condition wrote about their most important value, why it was important and how it affected their everyday lives. Participants engaging in health-risk alcohol consumption who had been affirmed in this way reported greater ease of imagining developing breast cancer and higher perceptions of personal risk, suggesting that self-affirmation facilitated acceptance of personal risk (by reducing defensive processing). These high risk, self-affirmed participants were found to have greater intentions to reduce their alcohol consumption at the four-week follow-up compared to controls. In a very similar way, it appears that enhancing SE before presenting threat information can also facilitate acceptance of threatening messages (Floyd et al, 2000).

Two points emerge from our consideration of fear appeals. First, one cannot assume that raising people's awareness of a health threat will promote protective motivation. There may be more important determinants of the target behaviour. More generally, messages based on particular mechanisms of change (such as those specified by PMT) need to be carefully designed to correspond to what is known about these change processes. Poorly designed fear appeals or other messages are likely to be ineffective or even counter-productive (Michie and Abraham, 2004).

Focus 9.2

Promoting smoking cessation

The illustrations below are typical of those used in many anti-smoking campaigns (including those used on cigarette packets). How do these materials correspond to PMT specifications?

Figure 9.4

Source: European Community.

Most smokers want to give up and have tried to quit, so motivation is not usually the main barrier to behaviour change. Instead, most smokers feel low self-efficacy in relation to quitting. The materials shown above do not help bolster smokers' self-efficacy so smokers may dismiss them (e.g. 'That won't happen to me') resulting in no health benefit. Compare these to the 'Get Unhooked' campaign below. This appeal offered

Figure 9.5

Source: © Agency: MCBD, Art Director: Lee Smith, Photographer: Nick Georghiou.

smokers help by first acknowledging how painful and unpleasant quitting might be because of their addiction. Given what you know about fear appeals and smoking, which approach would you invest in pre-testing?

Smoking cessation also illustrates the biopsychosocial nature of health-related behaviour. Evidence suggests that participation in smoking cessation groups which employ verbal persuasion as well as teaching self-regulatory skills increases the chances of successful quitting and abstinence over six months. Moreover, because of the nicotine-based dependency maintaining smoking, use of nicotine replacement therapy Zyban (bupropion hydrochloride which dampens appetite) is also effective. However, the most effective treatment is the combination of behaviour cessation groups and either nicotine replacement therapy or Zyban. This combination increases successful six-month abstinence rates fourfold over that observed without help (West et al, 2000). Thus by taking account of a variety of key cognitive determinants, important self-regulatory and social skills and critical biochemical processes a package of intervention components can be combined to tackle even complex and difficult-to-change behaviours.

Identifying effective behaviour change techniques

We have considered a range of change techniques focusing on various kinds of persuasive communication that might be used to change the determinants of motivation and behaviour. Which of these are most likely to be effective in promoting which behaviours among which target groups? This is an important but challenging question because it depends on reviewing the success and failure of a range of evaluated behaviour change interventions over time.

Which techniques promote condom use for whom?

Albarracín et al (2005) provide a rare example of a systematic review which addresses this question. Using meta-analyses of the results from studies including 354 HIV prevention interventions and 99 control groups, spanning 17 years, these researchers asked which of ten intervention techniques were most effective in promoting condom use among different target groups. The researchers identified five types of persuasive communication which they referred to as 'passive' because these techniques could be employed without active involvement of the recipients (e.g. through a health promotion leaflet). These were provision of: 1) information; 2) arguments designed to change attitudes; 3) arguments designed to change normative beliefs; 4) arguments designed to persuade recipients that they could successfully perform prerequisite tasks, that is, to enhance SE; and 5) threat or fear inducing messages. In addition, the researchers considered five techniques which could be used in interventions involving 'active' or face-to-face interaction with recipients. These included three types of skill training, that is: 6) condom-specific skill training; 7) self-management or self-regulatory skills training; and 8) interpersonal or social skills training. In addition, the researchers considered: 9) provision of condoms; and 10) HIV counselling and testing.

The results showed, perhaps unsurprisingly, that active interventions involving interaction with recipients were more effective in promoting condom use. The most effective interventions provided information, attitudinal arguments, behavioural skills (or SE) arguments and provided self-management (or self-regulatory) skills training. In addition, provision of condoms and HIV counselling and testing enhanced intervention effectiveness. Thus combinations of these techniques should be the preferred approach to generic condom use promotion intervention.

Attitudinal arguments were associated with greater behaviour change (that is, greater condom use) and results also showed that this effect was mediated by changes in attitudes and in normative beliefs (see Focus box 5.2 on mediation and moderation effects). Arguments targeting subjective and descriptive norms were found to promote behaviour change in audiences under 21 years of age but to reduce effectiveness among older recipients (perhaps due to reactance). Thus age moderates the relationship between inclusion of normative arguments and intervention effectiveness. Findings also confirmed that arguments and training designed to teach behavioural skills are successful at changing behaviour for most people (using either passive or active interventions), further emphasizing the importance of self-efficacy enhancement and skills training. However, while self-management skills training was effective for men and women, condom use skills were effective for men but not women. Thus gender moderated the relationship between condom use skills training and intervention effectiveness. Notwithstanding the moderated effect of normative arguments, the findings generally support the IMB, TPB and SCT because the techniques implied by these theories were found to increase the likelihood of a condom promotion intervention being effective and, moreover, their effectiveness was mediated by processes specified by these theories. By contrast, the use of threat-inducing messages did not enhance effectiveness for any audience and had no positive interactions with other techniques. Thus PMT and the threat component of the HBM were not supported by the findings. Note how this further emphasizes the disappointment of the Abraham et al (2002) findings discussed above and shown in Figure 9.3. Note too that this is a good illustration of empirical confirmation (e.g. TPB) and disconfirmation (e.g. PMT) of social cognition models, as discussed in Chapter 7.

Whether the findings of Albarracín et al generalize to other behaviours remains to be confirmed by further analyses but for condom use promotion the results are clear. Interventions involving active participation can be effective and the techniques implied by IMB, TPB and SCT are to be recommended (taking account of particular audience characteristics) while emphasizing risk or threat inducement is not. It is worth noting that given an average d of 0.38 for active interventions and assuming that, on average, 36 per cent of people in a target group use condoms at least sometimes (figures reported by Albarracín et al – see Research methods box 8.1 on d values) then an additional 17 per cent will use condoms at least sometimes following such active interventions. This is a dramatic increase in the number of users following intervention and could have an important impact on STIs and pregnancy rates at a population level.

Focus 9.3

Using cognitive dissonance to promote condom use

Cognitive dissonance theory proposes that we are strongly motivated to avoid and eradicate contradictions in our world views. Consequently, it should be possible to motivate change by generating salient contradictions between beliefs and actions. In an experiment conducted by Stone et al (1994), participants were randomly allocated to one of four conditions: 1) receiving information about condom use (information only); 2) receiving information and giving a talk promoting condom use that might be used in school health education (commitment); 3) being made aware of past failures to use condoms by recalling these failures (failure awareness); and 4) a combination of the commitment and failure awareness conditions. All participants were then given an opportunity to buy condoms cheaply. As Figure 9.6 shows, significantly more people in the combined commitment and failure awareness condition bought condoms (82 per cent) than in the failure awareness condition (50 per cent) or the commitment condition (34 per cent). The study also emphasized that information alone is often not enough to prompt behaviour change because significantly fewer people in the information-only condition bought condoms (44 per cent). This study illustrates how, applying cognitive dissonance theory, a cognitive contrast was created between people's representation of appropriate behaviour (which they were committed to by becoming an advocate of that position for school students) and their own health behaviour. This technique does not rely on a direct appeal, as in the case of persuasive argument designed to change people's perceptions of the outcomes of their action, but depends instead on the power of the salient contradiction between committed beliefs and the person's own past actions. Allowing people to take action that endorses their beliefs adds new cognitions relevant to the salient contradiction and helps resolve it through personal commitment to condom use in the future. Thus the strength of motivation to resolve the contradiction prompts a desirable change in motivation and in key preparatory behaviours (acquiring and carrying condoms).

Figure 9.6 Cognitive dissonance and behaviour change.

Source: Adapted from Stone, J., Aronson, E., Crain, A.L., Winslow, M.P. & Fried, C.B. Inducing hypocrisy as a means of encouraging young adults to use condoms. Personality and Social Psychology Bulletin, 20, 116–128. © Reprinted by permission of Sage Publications, Inc.

Change mechanisms, theory and change techniques

So far, we have focused on information provision, persuasive communication and skills training as key approaches to promoting motivational and behavioural change but there are many other change techniques which intervention designers can employ. A change technique relies on an underlying understanding of change processes. Once we understand such processes we can intervene to prompt change that establishes desired motivation and behaviour. This is directly analogous to intervention in other sciences. For example, once we understand that heat accelerates the oxidization of iron to form iron oxide which lacks the magnetic properties of iron, then we can heat iron filings in a flame, watch the burning process and ascertain that the burnt filings are no longer attracted to a magnet. Here our understanding of oxidation implies the effectiveness of the intervention technique to achieve a desired outcome, namely burning to remove magnetic properties. Similarly, cognitive dissonance theory proposes that salient contradictions in our world view prompt cognitive change (see Chapter 7). So, if we create dissonance (the intervention technique) we can expect to see the predicted cognitive or behaviour change. Focus box 9.3 illustrates how this change underlying mechanism provides the basis for an intervention technique found to effectively promote condom acquisition. Thus the role of theory is to explain the structures (e.g. personality traits – see Chapter 6) and processes (see, e.g., social cognition models in Chapter 7) which, in turn, helps us to understand people's behaviour. The role of behaviour change intervention designers is to employ theory to specify relevant *change mechanisms* and so select intervention techniques that prompt desirable change in psychological systems.

A variety of behaviour change techniques

A list of behaviour change techniques that have been reliably identified across a range of behaviour change interventions was provided by Abraham and Michie (2008) who reviewed previously published lists and categorized the content of interventions included in three reviews including interventions designed to promote exercise and healthy eating. Table 9.1 lists 29 such techniques, providing a brief definition of each and indicating theories which specify change mechanisms on which that technique is based. For example, a variety of theories (TRA, TPB, SCT, IMB, HBM) propose that believing that the consequences of a behaviour will be more positive than negative promotes action, hence use of such arguments (or persuasive communication) is often included in behaviour change interventions. Moreover, Albarracín et al showed that this technique resulted in attitude change and enhanced the effectiveness of condom promotion interventions. By contrast, fewer theories (HBM and PMT) propose that perceived susceptibility and severity prompt action. However, as we have seen, these techniques are often employed in interventions (e.g. see the leaflets reviewed by Abraham et al, 2002) even though there is less evidence to suggest that they are effective (Albarracín et al, 2005). It is important to note here that it is the underlying change mechanisms specified by theories rather than the theories themselves that provide a basis for change techniques. This is one reason why it is useful to integrate theories which propose very similar change mechanisms (see Chapter 7).

Table 9.1 Definitions of behaviour change techniques derived from various theoretical frameworks (based on Abraham and Michie, 2008)

Technique (theoretical framework)	Definition
Provide information about the behaviour–health link (IMB)	General information about behavioural risk, health outcomes or mortality risk in relation to the behaviour
Provide information on consequences (TRA, TPB, SCT, IMB, HBM)	Information about the benefits and costs of action or inaction, focusing on what will happen if the person does/does not perform the behaviour
Provide information about personal susceptibility (HBM, PMT)	Information about negative consequences that are likely to happen to the message recipient rather than people generally
Provide information about severity of health consequences (HBM, PMT)	Information about the seriousness or negative consequence, including that designed to evoke fear responses by emphasizing the risk of dying or serious ill health
Provide information about others' approval (TRA, TPB, IMB)	Information about what others think about the person's behaviour and whether others will approve or disapprove of any proposed behaviour change
Provide information about what others are doing (extended TPB)	Information about what others are doing indicating that a behaviour is common or uncommon among the population or among a specified group
Prompt cognitive dissonance (cognitive dissonance theory)	Create a salient contradiction between belief and action, emphasizing negative consequences of action and facilitating commitment to a belief-confirming action
Prompt intention formation (TRA, TPB, SCT, IMB)	Encouraging the person to decide to act or set a general goal, e.g. to make a behavioural resolution such as 'I will take more exercise next week'
Prompt barrier identification (SCT)	Identify barriers to performing the behaviour and plan ways of overcoming them
Set graded tasks (SCT)	Set easy tasks, and increase difficulty until target behaviour is performed
Provide instruction (SCT)	Telling the person how to perform a behaviour and/ or preparatory behaviours
Model/demonstrate the behaviour (SCT)	An expert shows the person how to correctly perform a behaviour, e.g. in class or on video
Prompt specific goal-setting (CT, GT)	Involves detailed planning of what the person will do including a definition of the behaviour specifying frequency, intensity or duration as well as specification of at least one context, i.e. where, when, how or with whom
Prompt review of goals (CT, GT)	Review and/or reconsideration of previously set goals or intentions
Prompt self-monitoring (CT, GT)	The person is asked to keep a record of specified behaviour/s (e.g. in a diary)

... Continued

Table 9.1 (continued)

Technique (theoretical framework)	Definition
Provide feedback on performance (CT, GT)	Providing data about recorded behaviour or evaluating performance in relation to a set standard or others' performance, that is, the person receives feedback on their behaviour
Provide contingent rewards (OC)	Praise, encouragement or material rewards that are explicitly linked to the achievement of specified behaviours
Teach to use prompts/cues (OC)	Teach the person to identify environmental cues which can be used to remind them to perform a behaviour, including times of day or elements of contexts
Agree behavioural contract (OC)	Agreement (e.g. signing) of a contract specifying behaviour to be performed so that there is a written record of the person's resolution witnessed by another
Prompt practice (OC)	Prompt the person to rehearse and repeat the behaviour or preparatory behaviours
Use follow-up prompts	Contacting the person again after the main part of the intervention is complete
Provide opportunities for social comparison (SCompT)	Facilitate observation of non-expert others' performance, e.g. in a group class or using video or case study
Plan social support/social change (social support theories)	Prompting consideration of how others could change their behaviour to offer the person help or (instrumental) social support, including 'buddy' systems – and/or providing social support
Prompt identification as role model	Indicating how the person may be an example to others and influencing their behaviour or providing an opportunity for the person to set a good example
Prompt self-talk	Encourage use of self-instruction and self-encouragement (aloud or silently) to support action
Relapse prevention (relapse prevention therapy)	Following initial change, identify situations likely to result in re-adopting risk behaviours or failing to maintain new behaviours. Help plan to avoid or manage risk situations
Stress management (stress theories)	May involve a variety of specific techniques (e.g. progressive relaxation) which do not target the behaviour but seek to reduce anxiety and stress
Motivational interviewing	Prompting the person to provide self-motivating statements and evaluations of their own behaviour to minimize resistance to change
Time management	Helping the person make time for the behaviour (e.g. to fit it into a daily schedule)

The list includes four techniques derived from **control theory** (CT, Carver and Scheier, 1982) and *goal theory* (GT, Locke and Latham, 2002). CT was based on cybernetics and proposes that self-regulation depends on monitoring current achievement or performance in relation to a set standard (e.g. a goal) and adjusting behaviour when a discrepancy is detected through feedback about performance (much like a thermostat). This basic sequence of **goal-setting**, **self-monitoring**, **feedback**, **goal revision** and **action planning** to reduce performance–goal discrepancies is a key component of goal theory (Locke, 1991) and other psychological theories concerning goal-directed behaviour (Austin and Vancouver, 1996). Thus behaviour change interventions frequently include goal-setting or intention formation, self-monitoring, feedback on performance (that is, comparing it to a set standard or goal), review and revision of previously set goals and the setting of new goals and specific (or detailed) plans to improve performance.

Four techniques derived from operant conditioning (OC, Skinner, 1938) are also included, that is, providing rewards directly following performance of the target behaviour (i.e. contingent rewards or **reinforcement**), teaching people to use **environmental cues** to prompt behaviour (e.g. placing medication by one's toothbrush), setting up a **behavioural contract** which the individual signs to commit her or himself to undertaking specified behaviours over a period of time and **prompting practice**, that is repeating a newly learned behaviour so that it becomes well learnt and habitual (that is, can be automatically triggered without conscious self-direction). The list also includes four commonly employed sets of techniques, namely **relapse prevention** (Marlatt and Donovan, 2005), **stress management**, **motivational interviewing** (Rollnick and Miller, 1995) and **time management**.

There is limited evidence on the effectiveness of these different behaviour change techniques. Nonetheless, Webb and Sheeran (2006) provide some interesting findings on technique effectiveness. This study focused on the effects of successfully promoting intention (or goal-setting) change on behaviour change. The researchers found that medium-to-large changes in intention change ($d = 0.66$) resulted in small-to-medium change in behaviour ($d = 0.36$ – of a very similar size to those observed in active interventions by Albarracín et al, 2005), thereby endorsing behaviour change interventions which focus on prompting intentions and goal-setting. Table 9.2 shows the average effect size for interventions designed to change a variety of (mostly health-related) behaviours which were found to include the listed change techniques. The number of samples on which these averages is based (k) is also given and it should be noted that in some cases only three samples were available, questioning the reliability of these averages.

The effects for inclusion of information provision and persuasive communication were small to medium and in the range observed elsewhere. Note too that including raising risk awareness was found to be effective across these 31 studies while this technique (threat induction) was not found to enhance the effectiveness of condom promotion interventions. Thus different techniques may be effective for different behaviours and we ideally need to consider effectiveness data on a behaviour-specific basis. Increasing and

Table 9.2 Average effectiveness of behaviour change interventions including various change techniques (from Webb and Sheeran, 2006)

Technique	k	d
Information linking behaviour to outcome	36	0.32
Persuasive communication	16	0.29
Asking questions/quiz	3	0.30
Personalized messages	8	0.26
Enhancing risk awareness	31	0.25
Increasing skills	26	0.27
Rehearsal of relevant skills	15	0.19
Modelling/demonstration by others	14	0.28
Goal-setting	25	0.31
Planning action	4	0.20
Monitoring or self-monitoring	3	0.13
Use of incentives	6	0.58
Social support or pressure	8	0.54

rehearsing skills also had small-to-medium effects as did goal-setting, action planning and self-monitoring. The strongest effects were observed for interventions including the use of incentives and social support or pressure. While these are medium effect sizes they are strong in the context of the usual level of effectiveness observed in evaluations of behaviour change interventions. Thus these findings provide support for use of a variety of behaviour change techniques.

Improving taxonomies of behaviour change techniques

Psychologists have not yet spent as much time as chemists clarifying the relationships between change mechanisms and cataloguing change techniques. Consequently, there is room for improvement in our taxonomies of change techniques (Abraham and Michie, 2008). For example, assuming that increasing risk awareness (Webb and Sheeran, 2006) is the same as threat induction (Albarracín et al, 2005) then, presumably, Webb and Sheeran include attitudinal and normative arguments (as well as those designed to enhance SE) in 'persuasive communication'. Yet these different types of persuasive communication draw upon different change mechanisms and have been shown to have different effects on condom use. Similarly, while we have noted above the importance of various types of skills training (Albarracín distinguished between three types), what techniques should we use to build skills? When 'increasing skills' (Webb and Sheeran, 2006) does not refer to practice (or rehearsal) what does it refer to? Abraham and Michie (2008) suggest that key techniques include providing **instruction** and **modelling**. Similarly, providing condoms, while an effective part of condom promotion interventions, is not a psychological change technique but a behaviour-specific method for providing necessary resources and possibly prompting intention formation (Bryan et al, 1996). Thus there is considerable scope for developing more specific lists of behaviour change techniques which are clearly linked to our understanding of change mechanisms as described in psychological theories.

Designing and evaluating behaviour change interventions

We have considered a variety of theories which identify determinants and change mechanisms involved in motivational and behaviour change. We have noted how intervention designers must explore social processes which shape individual behaviour and how they can select from a variety of individual change techniques based on underlying change mechanisms. This provides a foundation for intervention design.

Structure of interventions

Guidelines such as the **Consolidated Standards for the Reporting of Clinical Trials** (CONSORT, Moher et al, 2001) specify information which should be included in published reports of intervention evaluations and so clarify key methodological points which designers need to consider. Davidson et al (2003) propose that reports of behaviour change interventions should also specify a series of additional characteristics which make it easier for researchers and practitioners to understand and replicate interventions. The list in Table 9.3 specifies ten defining features of behaviour change interventions which, together with the CONSORT guidelines, provide a useful checklist for designers preparing intervention manuals and evaluation reports.

Intervention planning

The process of planning an intervention and managing it from design, through implementation to evaluation is complex. Bartholomew et al (2006) provide a useful guide in six steps which they refer to as '**intervention mapping**' (see too the earlier five-step version in Kok et al, 2004). The first step of this process is a *needs assessment* which involves ascertaining if and how the target group need to change and precisely specifying the target behaviour. As we have noted, this involves elicitation research and identification of motivational and skills deficits.

Table 9.3 Ten defining features of a behaviour change intervention (based on Davidson et al, 2003)

1. The specific behaviour change/s targeted
2. Intervention content (i.e. the change techniques employed – see Table 9.1)
3. Exact materials used (e.g. lesson plans, videos, etc., employed – see Focus box 9.1)
4. Characteristics and qualifications of those delivering the intervention
5. Characteristics of the recipients (i.e. exactly who received the intervention)
6. Setting (e.g. worksite, school)
7. Mode of delivery (e.g. face-to-face, telephone calls, leaflet distribution, etc.)
8. Intensity (e.g. contact time in each session)
9. Overall duration (e.g. number sessions over a given period)
10. Adherence to design (e.g. were lessons/interviews delivered as designed)

The second stage is *setting change objectives*. This involves mapping out the relevant determinants and change mechanisms which could be drawn upon and precisely specifying any targeted changes in cognition or preparatory behaviours (e.g. attitudinal change or changes in carrying condoms) as well as the main behaviour change target. The third stage involves a *theoretical design* linking determinants and change mechanisms to a set of change techniques (scc Table 9.1) most likely to be effective in bringing about the change objectives. The fourth stage is the translation of this theoretical design into a *practical plan*. This will involve reviewing potential materials and methods (videos, leaflets, lesson plans, interview schedules, etc.) to implement the selected techniques in the target setting with the target recipients. It is advisable to consult with potential recipients about materials (e.g. their appropriateness and attractiveness) and to pre-test materials, that is, to run small-scale experiments to see if exposure to the intervention materials has any effect on small groups of representative participants, prior to investing in the intervention as a whole. Once the materials are selected and manuals have been written to describe how the intervention is to be delivered then the intervention is ready for the fifth stage, namely, *implementation*. This involves identifying those who will use the intervention (e.g. teachers in schools or worksite managers) and negotiating its use with them. Note that because users are so crucial it is prudent to involve representative users from stage 3 onwards so that the intervention is developed to meet the needs of those who will adopt and use it because, as we shall emphasize below, if it does not meet users' needs it may never be used! The sixth and last stage is *evaluation*. This involves conducting research to discover whether the intervention really works. Tortolero et al (2005) describe how this intervention mapping approach can facilitate systematic intervention design and planning.

Intervention evaluation

Evaluation involves application of standard psychological research methods but particular applied issues also arise. A few intervention evaluations are included in the recommended reading for this chapter which illustrate many of the points discussed below (Hill et al, 2007; Luszczynska et al, 2007; and see too Michie and Abraham, 2004b).

A key part of any evaluation (and replication) is the availability of accurate detailed descriptions of the intervention. Consequently, it is important that intervention manuals are prepared and available (Abraham and Michie, 2008). Evaluation involves comparison of outcomes between those who received the intervention and those who did not. This may involve a no-intervention control group or another intervention group (as is the case when an intervention is compared to routine care) or both. Typically post-intervention levels of outcome measures are compared, controlling for pre-intervention levels as we expect no difference between intervention and control groups at pre-intervention but a relative post-intervention improvement for the intervention group. Randomization can control for confounding variables but sometimes it is necessary to randomize at group level (e.g. randomizing schools, classes, doctors' surgeries, etc.). In these cases a statistical technique known as **multi-level modelling** can control for systematic biases that might pre-exist between groups (e.g. some classes happen to be more active than others). Where randomization is impossible, matched groups need to be carefully scrutinized to ensure that differences other than exposure to the intervention are not responsible for observed group differences. Note too that inclusion of groups which do not complete pre-intervention measures can control for the mere measurement effect (see Chapter 7).

For successful interventions, an effect size is calculated (e.g. a d value) to indicate how effective the intervention was. Anticipating the likely effect size is important to conducting a pre-evaluation power analysis. This is necessary to ensure enough participants are included to detect any change that the intervention generates. In calculating power and in interpreting observed post-intervention differences, attrition rates (i.e. number of participants who drop out of the study) need to be considered. For example, if an intervention requires persistence and 50 per cent of those in the intervention group drop out, then, even if the intervention is very successful among the remaining 50 per cent (compared to no-intervention controls), the overall impact of this intervention will be limited. **Intention-to-treat analysis** is recommended in such instances. This approach involves all randomized participants in the analyses and counting dropouts as showing no change. Note what a difference this makes when attrition in the intervention group is high.

Validated measures of behaviour are, of course, required to evaluate behaviour change interventions but as well as key behavioural outcomes (e.g. condom use or exercise levels) various other outcomes may be measured pre- and post-intervention. These include psychological determinants assumed to be involved in the change process upon which the design is based (e.g. measures of attitudes, normative beliefs or the extent to which participants engaged in recommended planning). If expected changes in such determinants occur in a successful intervention then the inclusion of these measures allows *mediation analyses* to be conducted, thereby testing whether the assumed change mechanisms account for the success of the intervention. Intervention may be differentially successful for different groups (e.g. men versus women or those high in conscientiousness verses those low in this trait). Such moderation analyses can tell us for whom the intervention was effective but again require appropriate pre-intervention power analysis. Finally, health outcome measures (such as weight loss or STI rates) are valuable to check the hypothesized link between behaviour change and health enhancement. For example, behaviour change interventions focusing on increasing physical activity or promoting a healthy diet may weigh participants in intervention and control groups before and after interventions (e.g. Proper et al, 2003; Luszczynska et al, 2007).

When an intervention is not effective, it is important to know whether it failed because it was not capable of generating the predicted effects (and mediation analyses can help clarify this) or because it was not delivered as designed (e.g. classes were not taught as described in the manual or participants did not read or attend the intervention). To answer this question a process evaluation is required. This involves examining whether the intervention is being delivered as intended *during* the delivery. For example, those delivering and receiving the intervention may be interviewed and surveyed regarding their experience of the intervention. Classes or intervention groups may be observed and examined for fidelity to design, that is, whether those delivering the intervention (e.g. teachers or doctors) are doing what the intervention designers planned during the design phase. If, for example, an intervention is found to have worked for some groups but not others and it is also observed that the difference between groups was fidelity of delivery then it would be clear that the intervention works – but only when delivered strictly according to the prepared manuals. Without a process evaluation we cannot distinguish between failure of impact and failure of delivery.

Evaluating utility and sustainability of interventions

Even well-designed, effective, competently-evaluated interventions may have little impact on health if they are not adopted by their target audience or incorporated into routine care by health care professionals. In order to be adopted, interventions need to be useful to adopters, easy to implement, sustainable and affordable in the setting in which they have been tested. Glasgow et al (2002) and Green and Glasgow (2006) discuss how we can evaluate these intervention features using the **RE-AIM framework** (reach, effectiveness, adoption, implementation and maintenance) (see also Bartholomew et al, 2006).

Reach refers to how many of the target population were involved in an evaluation and how representative they were. For example, if an intervention was evaluated using economically advantaged participants then questions would arise as to whether it would also be effective for economically less advantaged people – or, for example, with those with more severe health problems than the intervention participants. *Effectiveness* relates to the range of effects an intervention might have. For example, even if it changed behaviour, did it enhance overall quality of life or have any unintended consequences (e.g. did participants find it onerous or upsetting)? *Adoption* refers to whether the users (e.g. nurses, teachers, managers, members of the public) are persuaded of the utility of the intervention. This is likely to depend on how easy it is implement, whether they or their clients like it and whether it is compatible with their other main goals (Paulussen et al, 1994). Since cost is important to most people, interventions are unlikely to be used if adopters cannot afford them. Understanding this *adoption and diffusion* process is critical to the overall impact of any intervention (Rogers, 2003). *Implementation* refers to the ease and feasibility of faithful delivery. If an intervention is complex, expensive or requires specialist training or teams of people to deliver it then it is less likely to be sustainable in real-world settings. *Maintenance* refers to the longer-term sustainability of the intervention in real-world settings. For example, if an organization or community does not have the resources to deliver an intervention then, no matter how effective, it will be dropped over time. Similarly, if implementation problems are encountered then, even if the intervention is retained, it may be changed and adapted to the setting which may mean altering or dropping change techniques critical to its initial effectiveness, so rendering it ineffective. These practical, real-world considerations are as important as observed *d* values, if psychologists' work on health behaviour change is to have practical and policy effects.

Research contributions to effective behaviour change and required competencies

We have seen how progress towards behaviour change intervention proceeds from initial testing of predictive models (such as the TPB and PMT – see Chapter 7) to the development of effective and sustainable interventions incorporated in routine practice. Campbell et al (2000) provide a useful five-step framework (referred to as the *Medical Research Council Framework for design and evaluation of complex interventions*) which helps researchers situate their research along this developmental continuum. Initially, key theories need to be developed and tested to establish an understanding of determinants and change mechanism. In this *theory* stage, small-scale experiments and surveys focus on mechanism rather than intervention per se. Then once a clearer idea of mechanism emerges *modelling phase* work begins which involves testing elements of theory and particular change techniques (e.g. the experiment described in Focus box 9.3 might be regarded as a modelling phase study). Once effective techniques are identified then *exploratory trials* can be undertaken (e.g. Hill and Abraham, 2008). If these prove effective then investment in *definitive trials* at national level with detailed, adequately powered outcome and process evaluations is warranted (e.g. Wight et al, 2002). Finally, if these demonstrate effectiveness, then replicating this effect with sustainable interventions in routine practice and everyday use is required to ensure adoption and *long-term implementation*.

Research and implementation of behaviour change intervention is complex and requires skilled work. The UK National Institute for Health and Clinical Excellence has noted that professionals (including psychologists) working in this area need specialist training to attain the required competencies. Thus health psychologists working in behaviour change need these competencies. These include the abilities to competently: 1) identify and assess evidence on behaviour change; 2) understand the evidence on the psychological, social, economic and cultural determinants of behaviour; 3) interpret relevant data on local or national needs and characteristics; 4) design, implement and evaluate interventions; and

5) work in partnership with members of the target population(s) and those with local knowledge. We shall return to this issue of competencies required by health psychologists in Chapter 11.

Summary

A health psychology perspective on changing behaviour involves needs assessment including analyses of the social process affecting a behaviour as well as the motivational and skills resources and deficits of the target population. Theories which specify relevant determinants and change processes are crucial to selection of appropriate change techniques combined in multi-technique interventions. These need to be delivered using audience-appropriate materials and evaluated using outcome and process evaluations to assess theory and effectiveness in promoting health-related behaviour. Effective interventions also need to be useful to adopters, easy to implement and sustainable in the longer term to have an impact on everyday behaviour and health. Behaviour change intervention design and evaluation is skilled work that demands research at different phases of development and a range of professional competencies, requiring specialist training.

Activity 9.1

Illustrative group exercises (e.g. over two class sessions)

- Choose a health behaviour (e.g. exercise) and design an evidence-based intervention to promote this behaviour among a specific target group.
- Draft a plan on how to intervene to enhance fitness among employees in a desk-based organization. Identify the defining features of your intervention (see Table 9.3) and draw upon intervention mapping procedures.
- Select a set of (e.g. 10) published intervention evaluations and try to identify the change techniques they employ. For example, how many of the techniques in Table 9.1 can you identify?
- Select a set of (e.g. 10) published intervention evaluations and assess them in terms of the quality of evaluation and RE-AIM criteria (reach, effectiveness, adoption, implementation, maintenance). On the basis of your analysis, how useful do you think each is in terms of improving health or health care practice?

Key concepts and terms

Action planning	Intention-to-treat analysis
Behavioural contract	Intervention mapping
CONSORT guidelines	Modelling
Control theory	Motivational interviewing
Elicitation research	Multi-level modelling
Environmental cues	Prompting practice
Fear appeals	RE-AIM framework
Feedback	Reinforcement
Goal revision	Relapse prevention
Goal-setting	Self-monitoring
Information–motivation–	Stress management
behavioural skills model	Time management
Instruction	

Sample essay titles

- How can health psychology inform the design of health promotion campaigns?

- What works in health behaviour change interventions? Discuss with reference to empirical research.

- How can behaviour change intervention evaluations help psychology develop better theories of change?

- How can research-based behaviour change interventions have more impact on routine practice in health care settings?

Further reading

Journal articles

Campbell, M., Fitzpatrick, R., Haines, A., et al. (2000). Framework for design and evaluation of complex interventions to improve health. *British Medical Journal*, 321, 694–696.

Green, L.W., and Glasgow, R.E. (2006). Evaluating the relevance, generalization, and applicability of research: Issues in external validation and translation methodology. *Evaluation and the Health Professions*, 29, 126–153.

Hill, C., and Abraham, C. (2008). School-based, randomised controlled trial of an evidence-based condom promotion leaflet. *Psychology and Health*, 23, 41–56.

Kok, H., Schaalma, H., Ruiter, R.A.C., and van Empelen, P. (2004). Intervention mapping: a protocol for applying health psychology theory to prevention programmes. *Journal of Health Psychology*, 9, 85–98.

Luszczynska, A., Sobczyk, A., and Abraham, C. (2007). Planning to lose weight: RCT of an implementation intention prompt to enhance weight reduction among overweight and obese women. *Health Psychology*, 26, 507–512.

5 | Relating to patients

10 Relating to patients

We expect people to consult doctors when they experience symptoms and to follow doctors' advice, especially if the consequences of not doing so are serious. In fact, professional help seeking is not easily predicted on the basis of clinical symptoms and people often do not follow the advice they are given. The patient's own world view shapes their health behaviours, including service usage and adherence. In this chapter we explore what perceptions and beliefs determine health seeking and adherence. We also discuss how doctors and other health care professionals can manage consultations effectively so that they maximize patient satisfaction, empowerment and recovery.

Half the UK population, especially those with long-term illnesses, report having used complementary therapies, making such therapies an important part of health care. We discuss what such therapies offer and consider the challenges involved in integrating them with traditional medical health care. We also examine the nature of placebo effects, their importance in assessing therapeutic effectiveness and what they teach us about the relationship between health and psychological care. Finally, we focus on the needs of people with long-term illnesses and how psychological intervention can help them.

Learning outcomes

When you have completed this chapter you should be able to:

1. Discuss who is most likely to consult health care services (e.g. a doctor) and explain why.
2. Identify key correlates of patient adherence and discuss how adherence can be maximized.
3. Describe key tasks that need to be completed during consultations with patients.
4. Identify key components of patient-centred consultations and discuss the research findings into their effects on patients' well-being and health.
5. Discuss the role of complementary therapies in health care.
6. Define 'placebo effects' and explain how they occur.
7. Discuss the needs of patients with long-term illnesses and illustrate the contribution that psychological interventions can make to caring for these patients.

The chapter is composed of five sections: 1) deciding to consult; 2) adherence and concordance; 3) managing consultations; 4) complementary therapies and placebo effects; 5) managing long-term illness.

Deciding to consult

People frequently experience symptoms but do not consult health services. Estimates vary, but 50–75 per cent of the population experience one or more symptoms of ill health over any two-week period (Demers et al, 1980; Porter, 2004). Yet, as Porter (2004) notes, about one-third of these people do nothing about their symptoms, about one-third self-medicate using over-the-counter medications or use alternative therapies, and only about one-third consult their doctor. Thus, even when health care is free at the point of delivery (as it is in the UK), there is far from a one-to-one correspondence between symptoms and consultation. This is problematic because people who need health care may not seek help and so worsen their prognosis. Moreover, a substantial proportion of those who do consult have only minor symptoms which do not require medical intervention.

Why do people consult?

A number of consultation prompts have been identified (Zola, 1973; Porter, 2004). Symptoms which persist, are perceived to be serious or are perceived to be amenable to treatment are more likely to lead to help seeking. Symptoms which interfere with other goals, for example, by inhibiting activities or reducing attractiveness, are also more likely to lead to consultation. Advice from others is an important additional trigger. Finally, ease of access to services and having time (e.g. away from work or child care) also make consultation more likely. In a study of 1210 people, Berkanovic, Telesky and Reeder (1981) found that 64 per cent reported symptoms over one year. These researchers used multiple regression to discover which of a range of prompts were most strongly associated with consultations following symptom identification. Results showed that respondents who had greater numbers of long-term health problems, were older, had a regular doctor or had greater social support were more likely to consult ($rs = .02$–$.19$). However, consulting was most strongly predicted by advice to consult from a member of their social network ($r = .35$), the degree to which the symptom generated disability ($r = .31$), the *perceived seriousness of the symptom* ($r = .56$) and, especially, the *perceived efficacy of care* (that is, believing that medical intervention could alleviate or eradicate the symptoms, $r = .69$). This study was based on the health belief model (see Chapter 7) but the results also support the theory of planned behaviour emphasizing the role of social norms and the perceived benefits (or efficacy) of acting (that is, positive attitudes towards consulting). The results also emphasize the role of social support in consulting behaviour and the importance of perceptions of medical effectiveness.

Anticipated effectiveness of consultation was also found to be an important trigger in a population study of people with serious breathing difficulties which compared people who had and had not consulted. Controlling for smoking status and perceived relative severity of symptoms, attribution of wheezing to smoking and lower self-efficacy in relation to explaining breathing difficulties to a doctor differentiated between those who did and did not consult (Abraham et al, 1999). The importance of perceived causation was also highlighted by King (1982) who found that understanding of the causes of elevated blood pressure predicted whether or not people attended for screening. Thus causal understanding of symptoms and anticipation of positive and effective interaction with health care professionals are key determinants of health service use.

Symptoms are not always clear, so patients may struggle to understand what they mean. For example, Kendrick et al (1993) found that, for 60 per cent of asthmatic patients, there was no significant correlation between ratings of severity and simultaneous peak flow measurements. This 60 per cent were not characterized by less severe symptoms (as measured objectively by peak flow) or by age or gender. The researchers concluded that a large proportion of asthmatic patients cannot reliably detect changes in their lung function. Similarly, Cantillon et al (1997) found that, for 86 per cent of patients who believed they could predict changes in their blood pressure, there was no significant association between patients' assessments and clinical assessments. Moreover, confidence in the ability to predict was associated with higher anxiety. When symptoms are unclear, emotional responses to their detection are likely to be crucial to the impact that symptom perception has on health behaviour and health service usage.

Interpretation of symptoms

Leventhal and colleagues (e.g. Leventhal et al, 1984, 1997) have identified five broad dimensions within which beliefs about symptoms and illnesses can be categorized. First is *identity*, the way a symptom label is related to our perception of cause, and which has profound implications for how we respond. 'Fatigue' or 'stress' has a very different connotation to 'cancer'. Second, *cause* refers to our understanding of the processes generating symptoms. For example, 'indigestion' has very different implications to 'heart attack' and believing that symptoms are due to one's own behaviour may lead to reduced motivation to seek professional help. Third are beliefs about *consequences*, including the perceived severity of symptoms. Fourth, *timeline*, people's expectations regarding the duration of symptoms and their perceptions of whether symptoms (e.g. of diabetes or asthma) are chronic or acute, can have important implications for help seeking and adherence. Finally, beliefs about *control and treatment effectiveness*, including, for example, perceptions of whether the illness can be cured, strongly affect help seeking. For example, Leventhal et al (1997) found that help seeking is more likely if ambiguous symptoms are detected when someone is also stressed but only if the stress has lasted for three weeks or more. Initially stress may be seen as the cause of a symptom and so it may be expected to be short-lived or to have only minor consequences but if the stress is perceived to be stable, symptoms may be regarded as more serious and long-term. Note how the findings of Berkanovic et al (1981, see above) highlight two of the categories of beliefs proposed by Leventhal and colleagues, namely, perceived symptom seriousness (consequences) and perceived efficacy of care (control-treatment). Note too that these five categories of illness beliefs overlap with beliefs specified by the social cognition models we studied in Chapter 7. For example, the health belief model and the theory of planned behaviour identify beliefs about consequences as important to intention and action and the theory of planned behaviour and social cognitive theory emphasize the importance of perceived control to action. Finally, look back at Activity box 8.1 and compare patients' questions about medication to the beliefs associated with consultation.

Personality and emotional responses affect symptom interpretation

Emotional responses affect symptom reporting and health service usage. For example, Rietveld and Prins (1998) found that negative emotions did not affect objective measures of children's asthma but made it more likely that children would interpret normal exercise-related sensations (e.g. heart pounding and fatigue) as indicating asthma. Those experiencing more negative emotions reported greater breathlessness, regardless of objective symptoms. Patterns of emotional responding are predicted by personality assessments (see Chapter 6) so that, for example, those high in neuroticism report more symptoms (Watson and Pennebaker, 1989). In a study of cold infections, Feldman et al (1999) found that while neuroticism was not related to objective measures of infection, it was associated with symptom reporting among healthy people. Those scoring in the top third of the neuroticism distribution reported more than twice as many symptoms as those in the bottom third. The researchers suggest that this is because higher neuroticism leads to greater attention to somatic experiences and potential symptoms, a conclusion supported by other research (Kolk et al, 2003).

Other personality factors shape symptom detection and perception. For example, while pessimism may be bad for one's health (see Chapter 6), pessimists seem to be more accurate in assessing their health. Leventhal et al (1997) found that self-reported ratings of health were better predictors of mortality five years later among pessimists than optimists. Controlling for age and medical history and comparing those who reported their health to be fair or poor with those who reported their health to be excellent or very good, mortality was 8 times higher among pessimists but only 1.5 times higher among optimists. Here optimism moderates the relationship between self-reported health status and mortality (see Focus box 5.2). More conscientious people tend to detect symptoms earlier because they have a lower threshold for symptom detection and are more concerned with self-protection (Feldman et al, 1999).

Personality traits can affect decisions about service usage and adherence through specific symptom-related beliefs, that is, beliefs mediate the effect of personality on help seeking and adherence behaviour. For example, Skinner, Hampson and Fife-Schaw (2002) found that greater perceived consequences of diabetes symptoms and greater perceived effectiveness of available treatment were both associated with greater self-reported self-care among young people with diabetes. Thus, these beliefs are important both to consulting and adherence (see Berkanovic et al, 1981, and above). Skinner et al found that neuroticism was associated with beliefs about the consequences of diabetes but not with beliefs about the effectiveness of treatment. By contrast, conscientiousness was associated with stronger beliefs in the effectiveness of treatment. The researchers suggested that because conscientious people are more likely to engage in active problem-focused coping (see Chapter 5) they may access more information about their diabetes and its management, which in turn may result in more positive beliefs about treatment effectiveness.

Collectively, then, research suggests that seeking help from health professionals and following their advice is strongly related to people's beliefs about their symptoms or illnesses. Consequently, monitoring and seeking to change such beliefs could lead to more cost-effective use of health services. In particular, promoting accurate beliefs concerning the consequences of symptoms and the effectiveness of treatment appears to have the potential to encourage those who need help to seek it and use it optimally.

Adherence and concordance

Adherence refers to following advice given by health care professionals. This can involve a variety of behaviour changes including taking preventive action (e.g. reducing alcohol consumption or changing one's diet), keeping medical appointments (e.g. screening, physiotherapy or check-up appointments), following self-care advice (e.g. caring for a wound after surgery) and taking medication as directed (in relation to dose and timing). Non-adherence is usually defined as a failure to follow advice to an extent that causes a harmful effect on health or a decrease in the effectiveness of treatment. Most medical interventions rely on patient adherence. Yet about 50 per cent of patients do not take prescribed medications as recommended (Myers and Midence, 1998). This is not new. Thirty years ago Sackett and Snow (1979) reported that only half of patients on long-term medical regimens were adherent. Across behaviours between 15 per cent and 93 per cent of patients do not follow the advice of health care professionals (Ley, 1988) and non-adherence is observed even when its consequences are fatal. In a prospective study of heart, liver and kidney transplant patients, Rovelli et al (1989) found that 15 per cent were non-adherent, with non-adherence leading to organ rejection or death in 30 per cent of non-adherent cases, compared to only 1 per cent among adherent patients. Non-adherence is problematic because it means that when health care professionals make accurate diagnoses of a health problem and prescribe effective treatment their intervention may, nonetheless, be ineffective. Indeed, 10–25 per cent of hospital admissions have been attributed to non-adherence. Thus the potential cost effectiveness of health care services is severely limited by non-adherence.

How can we measure adherence?

Simple self-report measures can provide good estimates of adherence (Morisky et al, 1986) but when self-report measures are compared to objective measures, results indicate that patients tend to overestimate their adherence (Myers and Midence, 1998). Direct indicators such as analyses of urine or blood content and weight change as well as indirect objective measures such as pill counts, refill records and service usage records are also used to track adherence. In addition, indirect measures such as health improvement (e.g. blood pressure or hospitalization) may be employed as measures of adherence (Roter et al, 1988).

Antecedents of adherence

Why do patients not follow advice? Patients are non-adherent for different reasons (Donovan and Blake, 1992). Some patients intend to take recommended actions but forget or find it difficult to do so, resulting in partial adherence. Others suspend medication to test their health or to avoid side effects that might impinge on important social events (Conrad, 1985). Some patients fear medication dependency while others disagree with the doctor's diagnosis or the prescribed treatment and deliberately take more or less than was advised. Knowing why patients do not adhere is important to designing interventions that may promote better adherence. Some key questions that influence patients' decisions to adhere are: Do I really need this treatment? Am I at risk of symptoms without doing what was advised? How effective/beneficial is the recommended action? What side effects will it have? To what extent will adherence conflict with other things I want to do? When consultations do not adequately answer these questions patients may reach their own conclusions and decide against adherence (see Activity box 8.1).

If a patient feels their doctor is not interested in their problem or has not understood it, this will undermine confidence in the doctor's advice. Consequently, **patient satisfaction** is significantly correlated with adherence ($r =$ .26, Ley, 1988). For example, in a well-known study of paediatric consultations, Korsch et al (1968) found that mothers who were very satisfied with their doctor's warmth, concern and communication were three times more likely to adhere than dissatisfied mothers. Satisfaction depends upon the patient's perception of the doctor's sensitivity, concern, respect and competence. Reducing waiting time, taking time to greet the patient in a courteous manner and engaging in friendly introductory exchanges are all likely to increase satisfaction. Asking open-ended questions which cannot be answered 'yes' or 'no' and allowing the patient time to express their worries is also likely to make the patient feel satisfied with the consultation.

Given the importance of patient satisfaction it is interesting to note that doctors' own satisfaction with work is a predictor of patients' adherence. In a two-year prospective study, DiMatteo et al (1993) found that, controlling for adherence at baseline, doctors' satisfaction with their work was a significant predictor of patient's future adherence ($r = .25$). This study also showed that doctors' self-reported willingness to answer all their patients' questions, regardless of the time involved, was positively associated with adherence. Doctors who are happier in their work may be more willing to answer questions and may engender greater satisfaction in their patients. Thus patient satisfaction may mediate the relationship between doctors' job satisfaction and their patients' adherence.

The social context in which people live, including the social support they receive, also affects adherence. Indeed adherence may partially mediate the effect of social support on health. In a meta-analysis summarizing 122 studies reporting associations between social support and adherence, DiMatteo (2004) found that adherence (compared to non-adherence) was 3.6 times more likely among those receiving practical support than among those who did not have such support. Similarly, the risk of non-adherence was 1.35 times higher if patients were not receiving emotional support than if they were. Practical support increases self-efficacy and actual control over adherence behaviours (see the theory of planned behaviour and social cognitive theory – Chapters 7 and 8) thereby rendering recommended changes feasible. A lack of social support may also increase stress levels which may, in turn, allow less priority for adherent goals (DiMatteo, 2004).

Can we improve adherence?

Available evidence suggests that we can improve adherence but that this may require interventions including multiple techniques to change behaviour. For example, in a meta-analysis of 153 studies evaluating the effectiveness of interventions designed to improve patient adherence, Roter et al (1988) found that interventions significantly improved adherence compared to control conditions with small to moderate effect sizes. The researchers reached four conclusions. First, while effect sizes were small, interventions were generally effective. For example, even the smallest effect size on measures of health outcomes translated into a 10 per cent increase compared to no-intervention controls. As the researchers note, a 10 per cent difference between an intervention and control group could 'save considerable cost and suffering' (Roter et al, 1988: 1150). Second, no particular intervention approach worked better than any one other but combinations were more effective than single techniques, especially if they simultaneously targeted education, behaviour change and emotional responses. Techniques targeting adherence behaviour included changing drug packaging, simplifying dose instructions, mailed reminders and skills development approaches. Third, adherence interventions were more effective for some conditions, especially diabetes, asthma, cancer and hypertension, suggesting that it may be easier to increase adherence for some patients than others. Finally, the researchers noted that a broader approach to identifying outcome measures could be beneficial. For example, as well as boosting adherence, interventions may affect patient satisfaction, patient understanding and quality of life. These may be important targets in themselves. This suggestion links to a more general question about the evaluation of health care interventions, that is, who decides what are the appropriate outcome measures? While physical health is very important, is it always the most important outcome? Consider the definition of health we began with in Chapter 1.

In a second meta-analysis, Haynes et al (2005) examined the outcomes of randomized controlled trials which measured adherence to medication and included a clinical or health outcome (i.e. whether people in the intervention condition also showed greater health benefit). For short-term prescriptions they found that 4 of 9 interventions (44 per cent) had an effect on both adherence and at least one clinical outcome while, for longer-term treatment, 26 of 58 (45 per cent) led to improvements in adherence but only 18 interventions (31 per cent) led to improvement in at least one clinical outcome. The researchers concluded that for short-term drug treatments counselling, written information and a personal phone call could boost adherence, but for long-term treatments, no particular technique and only some complex interventions led to

Figure 10.1 Antecedents of adherence.

Source: Adapted from Ley, 1988.

improvements in health outcomes. Those that were successful in improving health included combinations of more convenient care, providing information, counselling, reminders, self-monitoring, reinforcement, family therapy, psychological therapy, crisis intervention, telephone follow-up and additional supervision. Thus it is challenging to improve adherence to long-term medication to the extent that such improvements impact on clinical outcomes. However, while health improvement is a critical outcome it may not be the only one and it is a challenging target for interventions designed to change *behaviour* because even successful interventions (e.g. those generating increases of drug adherence using objective measures) may not make a difference to health.

Although it is sometimes challenging to promote improved adherence, health care professionals can maximize adherence by improving patients' *understanding, recall* and satisfaction. Patients must understand advice before they can follow it and they must remember it beyond the consultation if it is to shape behaviour. Both understanding and recall are associated with patient satisfaction. Consequently, combining these factors, Ley proposed the model of adherence shown in Figure 10.1. Understanding is correlated with adherence ($r = 0.36$; Ley, 1988) and, in Chapter 8, we discussed how health care professionals can enhance patient understanding. Even when information is understood it may be forgotten. For example, in an early study, patients were found to have forgotten around half of the verbal instructions given to them after only five minutes (Ley, 1973). Again, we noted in Chapter 8 how recall could be improved (e.g. see our consideration of logical order, explicit categorization, specific advice and emphasizing and repeating important points).

Adherence can also be maximized by simplifying treatments, for example, reducing the numbers of pills or actions to be taken or simplifying schedules (e.g. once a day is much easier to achieve than three times a day). Providing people with instructions and monitoring devices such as calendars or blister packs with named medication times is also effective. Thus technological advances may play a part in improving adherence.

Strategies that bolster memory for intentions and their subsequent enactment may also be used to increase adherence. For example, **event-based recall** is better than **time-based recall** (Ellis, 1998). So trying to remember 'take antibiotics twice a day' is likely to be less successful than trying to remember 'take antibiotics before breakfast and before dinner'. If one or more intentions have to be recalled, events can be more tightly specified, e.g. 'take blue pill before cereal and red pill with toast at breakfast'. This is very similar to the use of implementation intentions (as discussed in Chapter 7). Memory may also be enhanced by individualized feedback. For patients on long-term treatment medication, adherence can be monitored (e.g. by using electronic pill containers) and combined with individualized recommendations for remembering in relation to specific events (e.g. brushing teeth) that occur when the patient tends to forget their medication. Such interventions have shown some success with blood glucose control in diabetes, nebulizer use in people with obstructive lung disease, psychiatric medication, antiretroviral medication for HIV and oral anti-diabetic tablets (Rosen et al, 2004). Health care professionals can also assess motivation and self-efficacy. For example, patients could be asked if they intend to follow advice and if they see any barriers to doing so (e.g. 'Do you think you will take these tablets four times a day over the next two weeks?', 'Can you think of anything that might prevent you taking the medication?'). Such questions provide a check on the degree to which an agreed plan has been established and its feasibility in the context of the patient's life.

From compliance to concordance

At one time adherence was referred to as *compliance* but this term was discarded because it suggested that patients should do what they were told by doctors and that failing to do so was their responsibility. Patients decide whether the advice they receive is helpful and whether or not they will follow it. Consequently, health care professionals need to collaborate with and persuade patients if they are to shape their health behaviours. It has been proposed that health care professionals should seek to reach '**concordance**', with their patients, that is, a mutual understanding and agreement about treatment and its implementation (Mullen, 1997; Bissell et al, 2004). For example, Bissell et al (2004) used qualitative analyses of interviews with type 2 diabetic patients of Pakistani origin and found that some patients felt they could not discuss emotional, familial and financial factors which undermined their attempts to follow a diet appropriate to their condition. Thus these patients were unable to discuss key barriers to achieving adherence, thereby limiting the possibility that their doctor could offer them advice about how to most closely approximate the recommended diet within the constraints they experienced. If doctors are to ensure that their advice is clearly understood and also consider difficulties the patient may have in following an agreed plan, the consultation must allow time for discussion and negotiation and achieve good levels of concordance.

Managing consultations

Interactions between health care professionals (e.g. doctors and nurses) and their patients have the capacity to affect patient understanding, patient satisfaction, patient adherence and health outcomes. Consequently, the success and cost effectiveness of health care services depends critically on consultation management. Use of good communication skills in consultations has been found to affect a range of health outcomes from emotional well-being to blood pressure

Figure 10.2 Doctor–patient interaction is crucial to patient satisfaction, patient adherence and health outcomes.
Source: Corbis Super RF/Alamy.

and blood sugar concentration (Stewart, 1995). Yet it is all too easy for consultations to go wrong. The Toronto Consensus Statement on Doctor–Patient Communication (Simpson et al, 1991) noted that 54 per cent of patient complaints and 45 per cent of patient concerns were not elicited by doctors and that in up to 50 per cent of consultations the patient and the doctor did not agree on the nature of the main presenting problem. This may be because patients are sometimes interrupted too quickly by their doctors (e.g. within 18 seconds of speaking). Consultations serve different purposes and involve different groups of patients but key principles underlying effectiveness have been identified.

Many models of successful doctor–patient consultations have been developed. For example, after analyzing 2500 taped consultations, Byrne and Long (1976) identified six phases which form the structure of successful consultations. They suggested that the doctor: 1) establishes a relationship with the patient; 2) attempts to discover the reason for the patient's visit; 3) conducts a verbal and/or physical examination; 4) considers the diagnosis with the patient; 5) describes further treatment or investigation; and, finally, 6) ends the consultation. Byrne and Long noted that consultations can go wrong in phase two if the doctor fails to identify the true reason for consulting. Similarly, if the patient fails to understand the diagnosis in phase four this may affect adherence.

The now more widely used **Calgary–Cambridge consultation model** provides a similar guide to structuring consultations (Silverman et al, 2005). Six stages are identified: 1) *initiating the consultation* including establishing rapport (e.g. greetings and introductions) and identifying the reason(s) for the consultation (e.g. asking the patient what they would like to discuss); 2) *gathering information*, including understanding the patient's perspective (e.g. listening attentively without interrupting and using open questions to clarify what has been said); 3) *building the relationship*, including showing interest using non-verbal cues and communicating appreciation of the patient's concerns; 4) *providing structure* including summarizing what has been said; 5) explanation and planning, including providing the correct amount and type of information in a manner which aids recall and understanding and achieves a shared understanding and shared plan; and 6) ending the consultation. Rather than focusing on sequence, Pendleton et al (1984) identified *seven tasks* that need to be successfully completed in a medical consultation. These tasks, listed in Focus box 10.1, overlap substantially with the Byrne and Long and Calgary–Cambridge models and, while developed as a learning aid for doctors, could be applied to many consultations between health care professionals and patients (including those conducted by health psychologists).

Focus 10.1

Seven key tasks in consultations with patients

Pendleton et al (1984) identified seven tasks that need to be successfully completed in a medical consultation.

1. Define the reason for the consultation including the nature and history of the problem, its effects and the patient's concerns and expectations.
2. Consider other problems including risk factors which exacerbate the problem.
3. Choose an appropriate action for each problem in negotiation with the patient.
4. Achieve a shared understanding of the problem(s).
5. Involve the patient in the management of problems and encourage acceptance of responsibility by the patient.
6. Use time and resources appropriately.
7. Establish and maintain a relationship with the patient.

Think about how these tasks relate to how a health psychologist would conduct a consultation with a manager referred because she was suffering serious stress at work (see Chapter 4).

Byrne and Long (1976) contrasted doctor-centred and patient-centred consultations. *Doctor-centred* (or illness-centred) consultations focus on eliciting information necessary for precise diagnosis and prescription of appropriate treatment. The doctor tends to dominate such consultations asking direct, closed questions which demand short factual answers which can clarify details (e.g. 'Where do you feel the pain?'). In such consultations, little time is spent eliciting or understanding the patient's ideas or providing information other than instructions on medical management of the problem. By contrast, in **patient-centred consultations**, doctors ask more open questions which allow the patient to explain their perspective (e.g. 'So what do you think is wrong?'). The doctor also allows time to reflect back what the patient has said to demonstrate understanding and/or show empathy (e.g. 'You're worried about side effects') and to check that any treatment plans are acceptable to the patient. The

Calgary–Cambridge model and Pendleton et al's seven-tasks model both emphasize the importance of patient-centredness in consultations because evidence suggests that patients are less likely to be satisfied and so less adherent following doctor-centred consultations. For example, after observing 865 consultations with general practitioners (or family doctors), Little et al (2001) identified five aspects of patient-centredness: 1) building a partnership, that is, being sympathetic, taking an interest in patients' worries and sharing planning; 2) taking an interest in the patient's life; 3) establishing a personal relationship, that is knowing the patient and their emotional needs; 4) providing health promotion, for example, addressing risk factors in the patient's lifestyle; and 5) taking a positive and definite approach including providing concrete guidance on what was wrong and when it would be resolved. They found that patient satisfaction was related to building a partnership and taking a positive approach. They also found that patients felt more enabled to deal with their problem when doctors had taken an interest in their lives, provided health promotion and adopted a positive approach. Patients also reported fewer symptoms one month after the consultation when doctors adopted a positive approach. Note how such results relate to the finding that doctor's concern/anxiety was associated with malpractice claims (see Chapter 8). It seems that patients expect partnership building and do not appreciate or benefit from doctors airing their uncertainties or concerns.

Does the presenting problem (or illness) moderate the effectiveness of consultation styles? A study by Savage and Armstrong (1990) suggests that it does. In this experimental study 200 patients were randomly allocated to two different consulting styles and followed up one week later. The styles were referred to as 'sharing' ('Why do you think this has happened?', 'What do you think is wrong?', 'Would you like a prescription?', 'What do these symptoms or problems mean to you?') and 'directing' (e.g. 'This is a serious problem', 'You are suffering from X', 'It is essential that you take this medicine', and 'You should be better in X days'). In all cases patients were allowed to complete their explanation of the problem and more than 80 per cent of those receiving each style reported that they had been able to discuss their problem well. Thus phase two in the Byrne and Long model was completed. The researchers found that a 'directing' style was associated with greater patient confidence that their doctor had understood their problem, perception of higher quality explanation by the doctor and greater reported health improvement one week later – but only among patients consulting about a physical problem or receiving a prescription. Among patients with a long-term or psychological illness and among those not receiving a prescription there was no difference between the two consulting styles. These findings mirror those of Little and colleagues emphasizing that, while patients need to be listened to, they expect positive, unambiguous expert advice from doctors reflecting their medical understanding of illness and treatments. However, where the problem has no clear physical diagnosis or cannot be treated using biomedical prescriptions a sharing style is likely to be important to patient satisfaction.

Further insight into which aspects of patient-centredness matter to patients with long-term illness was provided by Michie, Mills and Weinman (2003). These researchers distinguished between measures of the extent to which health care professionals: 1) understand the patient's perspective and acknowledge their beliefs and emotional needs; and 2) empower patients to actively shape the consultation and its conclusions. Thirty studies of consultations with patients who had long-term illnesses were divided into those which measured patient-centredness as *perspective taking* and those which measured patient-centredness in terms of **patient empowerment**. Two of nine studies in the former group found a positive association between patient-centredness and better physical health while nine of ten studies in the latter group found such an association. Thus perspective taking, while important, and perhaps especially important to patients with long-term illness, may not be enough to render consultations more effective in terms of health outcomes. Patient empowerment appears to be crucial.

Patient empowerment

Can we help to empower patients in their interactions with health care professionals? On balance, the evidence suggests that we can. Robinson and Whitfield (1985) gave patients written information before their consultation reminding them that people may regret not asking questions after the consultation, advising them to check their understanding of instructions and the feasibility of those instructions and advising patients to ask about any discrepancies between recommendations made by the doctor and what they had expected. Compared to controls, these patients asked more questions in the consultation and gave more complete and accurate accounts of the recommended treatments after the consultation. Similarly, Cegala et al (2000) found that patients receiving a training booklet designed to enhance patients' communication skills engaged in more effective information seeking, provided more detailed information about their condition to their doctor, and used more summarizing utterances to check information provided by the doctor. Less encouraging results were reported by Kidd et al (2004) who found that an intervention in which patients talked to a researcher about three or more questions they wanted to ask and were encouraged to rehearse these questions did not increase question asking in the consultation. However, the researchers noted that question asking was higher than usual among their control group patients. The intervention did enhance self-efficacy to ask questions but had no impact on health outcomes. In a systematic review of 20 evaluations of interventions designed to increase patients' participation in medical consultations, Harrington et al (2004) found that half of the interventions resulted in increased patient participation with greater effects being observed for clarification seeking rather than question asking. They also noted that a variety of other positive outcomes were observed including perceptions of control over health, preferences for an active role in health care, greater recall of information, better adherence and improved clinical outcomes. Harrington and colleagues suggest that question asking may not be the best measure of whether such consultation empowerment interventions are effective. They note, for example, that patients' perceptions of control over their health and preferences for an active role in their health care were found in all four studies that considered these outcomes. Given the importance of encouraging the general population to take a more active role in preventive health care, further work on such interventions is warranted.

One objection to interventions designed to empower patients during consultations and to patient-centred consultations is that they are likely to be longer and doctors are already hard pressed to see patients who want consultations. Howie et al (1999) examined nearly 26,000 randomly selected adult consultations across 53 medical practices and observed consultation times ranging from less than 5 minutes to more than 15 minutes with a mean of 8 minutes. These researchers administered a patient enablement measure which resembles a measure of consultation-generated, health-related self-efficacy (see Chapter 7). It measured whether patients felt the consultation had made them better or worse at understanding their illness, coping with their illness, keeping themselves healthy and feeling able to help themselves. They found that patient enablement was associated with longer consultations and knowing the doctor better. They concluded that, 'It may be time to reward doctors who have longer consultations, provide greater continuity of care, and enable more patients' (Howie et al, 1999: 738). Longer consultations may not only be associated with greater patient enablement. Reporting on a review of 14 studies, Freeman et al (2002) noted that longer consultations were associated with less prescribing, better recognition and management of psychosocial problems and better clinical care of long-term illnesses. Longer appointments may also be more likely to resolve problems and so reduce follow-up visits for the same problem (Hughes, 1983). Thus a shift to somewhat longer appointments and greater *continuity of care* (that is seeing the same doctor over time) could have beneficial effects on the effectiveness of health services.

Complementary therapies and placebo effects

Poor patient satisfaction and uncertainty about the effectiveness of traditional medicine fosters demand for **complementary or alternative medicine** (CAM). Complementary therapies include a wide range of interventions based on different models of mind and body. The defining feature of such therapies is that they are not understood in terms of the evidence-based models of physiological systems (see Chapter 1). Many also differ from traditional medical care by focusing on the client's overall well-being rather than specific physical problems.

CAM use is widespread in developed countries. It has been estimated that 42 per cent of the US population have used CAM, spending more than $21 billion annually (White, 2000), and two-thirds of those receiving treatment for anxiety or depression report using CAM in the USA (Bassman and Uellendahl, 2003). In Europe, 75 per cent of the French population and 50 per cent of the UK population report having used CAM (Murcott, 2006). Half of UK general practitioners (family doctors) provide CAM and more than 80 per cent of Australian general practitioners have referred patients for CAM (Murcott, 2006). Consequently, CAM has an important role in health care and many patients seen by psychologists will be using CAM.

The House of Lords Select Committee on Science and Technology (House of Lords, 2000) published a report on CAM which distinguished between therapies which do and do not provide diagnoses. Those that do include osteopathy and chiropractic (which are regulated by UK Acts of Parliament), *acupuncture*, herbal medicine and *homeopathy*. Those that do not include aromatherapy, hypnotherapy, reflexology and shiatsu. The Select Committee made a series of recommendations including: 1) therapies which claim to treat specific conditions should have evidence of being able to do so above and beyond the **placebo effect** (see below); 2) if a therapy does gain a critical mass of evidence to support its efficacy the UK National Health Service should provide access to it; 3) training in anatomy, physiology, biochemistry and pharmacology should be included within the education of CAM practitioners likely to offer diagnostic information; 4) CAM therapists should be trained in research methodology and have a clear understanding of the principles of evidence-based medicine; and 5) CAM therapists should encourage patients to see traditional health care professionals. These recommendations highlight the challenges of, on the one hand, providing access to effective treatments based on alternative models of health and, on the other, ensuring that such treatments are indeed effective.

Placebo effects

Placebo effects refer to health or well-being gains observed following administration of pharmacologically inert interventions such as saline injections or sugar pills. In 1955, Beecher found that, across 15 clinical trials, 35 per cent of patients showed health gains in placebo conditions. In contrast, across 114 trials, Hro'bjartsson and Gøtzsche (2001) found that when improvement was measured using a binary outcome (e.g. cured/not cured) placebo treatments had no significant effect on outcome. Placebo conditions also showed no benefit when assessed using objective clinical outcomes. Placebo effects were observed on subjective, continuous outcome measures and in 27 trials assessing pain. Average placebo pain reduction was found to be equivalent to a 6.5 millimetre reduction on a self-report visual analogue scale, measured on a 100 millimetre line. One weakness of such a review is that, if placebo effects are limited to particular types of health gain (such as reduced pain), these effects may not be evident when trials are pooled across conditions (Stewart-Williams, 2004).

Main effects of adherence have also been found in placebo conditions (Epstein 1984). For example, in a trial of beta blockers for women who had had a heart attack, Gallagher, Viscoli and Horwitz (1993) found that 5.6 per cent of those who took 75 per cent of the medication died within 26 months but 13.6 per cent of those who took less than 75 per cent died in the same period. Remarkably, this difference was not noticeably diminished in the placebo condition. In this case, taking beta blockers was not found to be effective above and beyond the placebo effect. However, from a psychological perspective, the interesting question is, 'Why is adherence to placebo treatments associated with improved health outcomes?'.

Placebo effects have raised doubts about a range of treatments. For example, although the UK National Institute for Health and Clinical Excellence (2004) recommended *selective serotonin re-uptake inhibitors* (SSRIs such as Prozac) as the preferred treatment for mild to severe depression, their effectiveness has been questioned because depressed patients in placebo conditions show good levels of recovery (Kirsch and Sapirstein, 1998; Quitkin et al, 2000). Placebo responses raise the possibility that observed treatment effectiveness may not be due, or wholly due, to the pharmacological processes meant to explain the operation of a medication but to psychological changes initiated by beliefs that one is taking an effective treatment which, in turn, lead to health improvement (Moncrieff and Kirsch, 2005).

In trials which only compare a treatment with a placebo condition, numerous factors contribute to an observed 'placebo effect'. Natural fluctuations in physiological functioning mean that, for many conditions, some people spontaneously improve (so called 'spontaneous remission'). This is especially true of long-term conditions when people are likely to seek medical help when their symptoms are most severe. People involved in intervention trials may also change how they assess their symptoms (cf. Norman and Parker, 1996). In addition, they may engage in new behaviours relevant to their treatment. Controlling for such effects necessitates a three-condition design in which treatment is compared to both placebo and a no-treatment control group (e.g. people randomly assigned to a waiting list for trial inclusion). The true placebo effect can then be defined as the additional gain seen in the placebo group over and above the no-treatment condition (Ernst and Resch, 1995). Note too that placebo conditions need to mimic the context in which treatment is administered. These so-called 'non-specific effects' include setting and communication. This is why health care professionals involved in trials should, ideally, be blind to which condition a patient has been allocated.

Explaining placebo effects: Patient expectations and anxiety reduction

Many explanations of placebo effects have been tested and it is likely that multiple processes are involved (see Stewart-Williams, 2004, for a clear summary). For example, placebo analgesic effects have been shown to be mediated by the release of **endogenous opioids** (Levine et al, 1978) demonstrating that some placebo effects have measurable effects on the brain and endocrine system. However, such observations do not explain *how* placebo administration affects physiological systems. This may operate through *patient expectations* and *anxiety reduction*. When a health care professional (perceived to be competent) communicates to a patient that their problem is understood and that they are being prescribed (or advised to undertake) an effective, manageable treatment, the patient will expect their condition to improve. Such expectations may have cognitive, physiological and behavioural effects. For example, believing that the worst is over could liberate the patient to devote time and energy to other life-enhancing pursuits. It could alter coping strategies, perhaps leading to more social support seeking. It is also likely to reduce stress and anxiety. Secondary appraisals (see Chapter 3) will be altered because patients believe they have an important new resource, namely, a treatment that will cure or alleviate adverse symptoms. Anxiety reduction is known to have physiological effects. For example, it is likely to affect endocrine functioning, reducing levels of cortisol and adrenaline in the bloodstream. This, in turn, may have positive effects on blood pressure and immune functioning (see Chapter 2) as well as on cognitive functioning (e.g. memory). Anxiety reduction is also associated with reduced pain because downward neural pathways from the brain can cut off or 'gate' incoming pain signals from peripheral nerves (Melzack and Wall, 1965). Thus a stress reduction explanation based on expectations of treatment efficacy provides a powerful explanation of some placebo effects. This explanation corresponds to Little et al's observation that patients reported fewer symptoms after consultations in which doctors adopted a positive and definite approach including providing guidance on when the problem would be resolved. Moreover, an expectation-based explanation could account for the direct effects of adherence because the more consciously one adheres to the apparently effective treatment the stronger one's expectation of relief or recovery should be. Nonetheless, this explanation does not account for all placebo effects. For example, an objectively assessed bronchodilation placebo effect finding observed by Butler and Steptoe (1986) could not be explained by changes in expectations or anxiety.

Explaining placebo effects: Classical conditioning

Classical conditioning theory may account for some placebo effects. In this model the 'real' drug is the unconditioned stimulus and beneficial physiological changes are the unconditioned response. Similarity of administration of the placebo treatment (e.g. context, nature of treatment, etc.) leads to an association between the placebo treatment (the conditioned stimulus) and the unconditional stimulus. Such effects have been observed in people and animals. For example, Benedetti, Pollo and Colloca (2007) examined the effect of repeated administrations of injected morphine during athletes' training sessions on placebo response. They found that athletes who had had morphine injections during training and who then received a saline injection (which they thought was morphine) showed greater pain endurance and physical performance during competition. This has interesting implications for drug testing in sport because it suggests that after appropriate drug conditioning it may be enough for an athlete to believe they are taking a performance-enhancing drug.

The placebo effect literature strongly emphasizes how important it is to provide patients with expectations of recovery (where it is reasonable and ethical to do so) and to encourage commitment to adherence. The psychological consequences of these processes may greatly enhance the pharmacological processes generated by available drugs. Practitioners able to harness and deliver the psychological and physiological effects evident in placebo responding will maximize the health impact of interventions. This was confirmed by a review of 19 trials. In this review Di Blasi et al (2000) concluded that various contextual factors affected treatment effectiveness and that, in particular, there was evidence suggesting that **cognitive care** (that is managing expectations positively) and **emotional care** (communicating concern for the patient's problems) maximize treatment effectiveness. Thus, to maximize their effectiveness, health care professionals need to be able to deliver such cognitive and emotional care.

Understanding and testing complementary therapies

The assumptions underpinning many complementary therapies are incompatible with scientific findings. For example, some homeopathic treatments are diluted so many times that not a single molecule of the original substance remains. While homeopaths claim that water somehow 'remembers' the original active ingredient, this makes no sense in terms of our understanding of the chemistry of water (Murcott, 2006). Similarly, as the UK NHS website explains, acupuncture is based on the assumption (first made 2000 years ago in China) that health depends on a life force called Qi which flows along 12 bodily meridians. Needles are inserted into the meridians to restore health by unblocking Qi flow. Yet anatomical research has found no evidence of these meridians.

Considerable efforts are devoted to testing the effectiveness of complementary therapies and acupuncture is especially well researched (see Vickers and Zollman, 1999, for a useful introduction to osteopathy and chiropractic). For example, Vas et al (2004) found that combining acupuncture with pharmacological treatment for osteoarthritis of the knee led to greater pain reduction and increased physical functioning one week after treatment, controlling for placebo effects. However, Foster et al (2007) found that adding acupuncture to advice and exercise for osteoarthritis of the knee did not enhance effectiveness. Interestingly, the acupuncture placebo condition involved use of blunt needles which collapse into their handles to give the appearance of penetration to control for contextual effects. The NHS website states that acupuncture 'can be helpful in relieving pain' but also that 'research into the effectiveness of acupuncture treatment for chronic pain has not produced consistent results' and, consequently, 'it is not normally recommended [for chronic pain] unless conventional treatment has failed'. Certainly studies have found that acupuncture enhances the effectiveness of traditional treatment for some conditions but the evidence is less than clear-cut and evaluations of this evidence vary in their conclusions. For example, White (2000) and Bassman and Uellendahl (2003) present fairly positive reviews citing evidence for the effectiveness of acupuncture in treating depression and substance abuse. Murcott (2005) is more pessimistic about the evidence on pain relief noting that there are few studies of longer-term effectiveness. He compares the evidence available for the analgesic effects of aspirin and acupuncture and concludes that evidence for the latter is clearly weaker. Overall, he concludes that evidence for the effectiveness of complementary therapies generally is equivocal. However, here too there is debate about appropriate outcome measures. What if an alternative therapy was found to have no effects on clinical outcomes over and above placebo but was found to have a noticeable effect on patients' reported happiness? Would this constitute effective health care?

Managing long-term illness

In England, 15.4 million people have a *long-term physical illness (LTI)* and this is likely to rise to 18 million by 2025. About 60 per cent of those older than 65 per cent have a LTI compared to 17 per cent of people under 40. People with LTIs are intensive health care users accounting for more than half of general practice appointments and nearly three quarters of inpatient days in hospital. LTIs include hypertension, *asthma*, *diabetes*, coronary heart disease, stroke, *chronic obstructive pulmonary disease (COPD)*, cancer, heart failure, **chronic pain** and epilepsy (Department of Health, 2008).

LTIs affect people's lives in many ways. Sufferers are less likely to be in employment, more likely to be poor, and more likely to need additional care and support from family members and others. With no medical cure in sight it is unsurprising that people with LTIs are also more likely to be CAM users. We have noted that people with LTIs may benefit from self-management interventions (see Chapter 8) and that longer consultations focusing on the patient's beliefs and feelings and prompting patients to take control of illness management may be especially important for these patients (see above). The challenge for people with LTIs is to adapt to their illness, adopt the most effective coping strategies including social support seeking (see Chapter 4) and to maintain high self-efficacy (see Chapter 7) and the best possible **quality of life** (QoL). The extent to which they are able to do this and to enjoy life may predict longevity. For example, Moskowitz, Epel and Acree (2008) found that *positive affect*, including measures of enjoying life, was associated with lower mortality among people with diabetes and people over 65 and especially among those reporting higher levels of stress. The findings suggested that positive affect may buffer stress (see Chapter 3). Consequently, psychological support is crucial to helping this group and some CAM practitioners may be able to offer such support more effectively than health care professionals because they employ longer consultations focusing on overall well-being. A UK Department of Health (2008) report notes that adherence among people with LTIs is poor and that people with LTIs want more health care services delivered in the community and in their homes. The report also notes that providing people with greater control over the services they use is likely to increase adherence, self-efficacy and quality of life.

Cognition and coping is critical to adaptation to LTI. For example, Scharloo et al (2000) found that the five categories of beliefs about symptoms identified by Leventhal and colleagues (as discussed above) predicted coping and *adaptation* in COPD patients, emphasizing the importance of cognitive care and intervention for these patients. Qualitative research can reveal more detailed patterns of illness-related thought. Such studies often reveal the burden that LTIs place on people's *self-image*. For example, Dovey-Pearce, Doherty and May (2007) show how diabetes can affect young people's self-concept, highlighting the desire to be 'normal', the additional adult responsibilities that diabetes places on young people and the importance of peer support. Similarly, Smith and Osborn (2007) illustrated the crushing effect that chronic pain can have on self-concept. Interviewees described how their pain led to social behaviour that they were ashamed of and wanted to distance themselves from their public persona. They expressed nostalgia for a past normal self and were anxious about the self that others attributed to them as a result of their pain-directed behaviour. Patients with LTIs may also find engagement with traditional health services which focus on diagnosis and treatment challenging and alienating. For example, in a qualitative study of stories written by women with chronic pelvic pain, McGowan et al (2007) found that women found consultations unsatisfactory, especially when medical tests failed to validate their experience of pain. The failure to find a physiological explanation left women feeling powerless and devalued and concerned that they were not believed and perceived to be neurotic or depressed by health care professionals. In some cases this led to complete disengagement from health care services, despite ongoing pain.

Behaviour change interventions in long-term illnesses

Behaviour change interventions have much to offer people with LTIs. For example, in a systematic review, Glazier et al (2006) found that 11 of 17 interventions improved diabetes care. Intervention effectiveness was associated with delivery by community educators or lay people, one-to-one interaction with individualized assessment, a focus on behaviour change, provision of feedback, use of 10 or more sessions and a duration of 6 months or more. While such interventions are expensive they are likely to be cost effective because it has been estimated that self-management interventions for people with LTIs could reduce visits to general practitioners by a quarter and hospitalization by a half among this group while also enhancing participants' quality of life (Department of Health, 2008). Note too that behaviour change interventions can prevent some LTIs. For example, Knowler et al (2002) found that a lifestyle change programme including weekly exercise targets was more effective than medication in preventing diabetes onset over a three-year period.

We noted above that clinical evidence of recovery may not always be the most important outcome measure, for example, in relation to interventions designed to increase adherence or patient involvement in consultations. In a classic paper, Kaplan (1990) argued that mortality and quality of life are always the most important outcome measures in health care and, certainly, quality of life improvement is a key measure of success in helping people with LTIs. There are a variety of quality of life and health-related quality of life measures available including one developed by the World Health Organization (WHOQOL Group, 1995) and the Short-Form Health Survey (Ware et al, 1996) which assess the degree to which illness imposes on everyday life and how patients feel about their everyday life.

Managing chronic pain

Chronic pain provides a useful illustration of the importance of psychological theory and intervention to LTI. In a comprehensive review, Gatchel et al (2007) indicate how a biopsychosocial approach to understanding pain emphasizes the role of psychological care in treatment. They note, for example, that anxiety reduction interventions can result in reduced distress and interference with daily living. They also note that enhanced self-efficacy in relation to controlling the impact pain has on everyday living affects the body's opioid and immune systems, reduces pain, improves recovery after surgical procedures and improves overall psychological adjustment. Higher levels of pain-related self-efficacy increase motivation to follow through with goals that become challenging and so reduce activity avoidance and may increase social engagement and support. Consequently these researchers note that 'pain cannot be treated successfully without attending to the patient's emotional state' (Gatchel et al, 2007: 602). Current treatment of pain focuses on *multidisciplinary* programmes, which incorporate a combination of approaches including psychological interventions. Turk and Burwinkle (2000) highlighted the effectiveness and cost implications of such programmes compared to traditional approaches treating chronic pain. They list commonly used measures of pain assessment and show that multidisciplinary programmes are effective, not only in reducing pain but in improving employment status and reducing medication and medical services usage. They also emphasize the role of psychologists both in designing and evaluating interventions within such multidisciplinary contexts.

There are a range of intervention techniques which may be used by psychologists working with patients experiencing pain (see Chapter 2). The *gate-control theory* of pain perception (Melzack and Wall, 1965) clarified how the brain is able to control pain sensation providing a clear pathway for psychological moderation of pain experience. Cognitive intervention techniques involve teaching patients to identify and change cognitions and emotions which increase pain. So, for example, challenging catastrophic or hopeless thoughts may reduce anxiety and enhance self-efficacy. Such interventions have been shown to be effective, especially with chronic pain patients, and can be more effective than pharmacological interventions (Morley et al, 1999; see also Andrasik and Schwartz, 2006). Patients may also be taught new coping strategies including *distraction* (i.e. the patient focuses on a non-painful stimulus in their nearby environment in order to distract attention away from pain), *non-painful imagery* (i.e. the patient focuses on a positive, imagined event/scene unrelated to pain), **pain redefinition** (i.e. the patient learns to redefine negative thoughts about the pain experience using positive self-statements) and *hypnosis* (i.e. the patient experiences less pain while in a relaxed, hypnotic state). Each of these techniques has been found to be effective in reducing the pain experience. However, the evidence is more clear-cut when applied to acute compared to chronic pain (Fernandez and Turk, 1989). Moreover, in certain circumstances (e.g. headache pain), when combined with behavioural techniques, cognitive strategies have been found to be at least as effective as conventional analgesics (Holroyd et al, 1991).

Psychological intervention techniques may also focus directly on pain-related behaviour with a view to enhancing activity and quality of life rather than pain reduction. Application of techniques based on the principles of *operant conditioning* such as *extinction* and *reinforcement* were pioneered by Fordyce (1976). Central to this approach is the assumption that pain behaviours (e.g. withdrawal, lying down, crying, limping, reliance on medication) are learned responses which become conditioned through reinforcement (e.g. receiving attention, sympathy and care in response to pain behaviour and avoiding anticipated pain by taking analgesic medication). Therefore, this approach seeks to:

1. Reinforce adaptive 'well' behaviours such as walking without limping after a minor operation.
2. Encourage family and friends not to attend to or reward pain behaviours.
3. Provide analgesic medication on a fixed schedule (e.g. every 4 hours) and not when the patient requests it or is in pain.

Each of these techniques has been found to successfully reinforce new adaptive behaviour and to extinguish previous maladaptive behaviour (Horn and Munafo, 1997). For example, patients' reliance on medication can be reduced over a short period of time. By providing the medication on a fixed schedule, receiving it becomes independent of their request for it and as a result, reinforcing effects are eliminated. Over a couple of weeks, the dosage of medication can be reduced by mixing it with a flavoured syrup to mask the taste and then gradually reducing the amount of the analgesic in the mixture.

Pain experiences such as headache pain and chronic back pain are caused by changes in physiological processes, which are frequently triggered by stress. Consequently, relaxation and biofeedback techniques are used to help patients manage stress. Typically *progressive muscle relaxation* is used in which patients learn to relax and tighten different muscle groups in a quiet, comfortable environment for approximately 20–40 minutes in weekly sessions over a number of months. Once trained, patients are encouraged to use this technique whenever they feel a painful or stressful episode is developing.

Biofeedback is a technique in which a patient learns to exert control over basic autonomic bodily processes such as blood pressure, heart rate and blood flow as well as learning to gain increased control over voluntary processes such as muscle tension. Feedback is achieved by placing electrodes and transducers on the skin that can detect and convert bodily signals such as temperature, galvanic skin response and blood flow into electrical signals which are then typically transmitted as a tone. Through training and hearing the tone change when a specific muscle group is relaxed, patients can learn to exert control over muscles previously not under their voluntary control. Progressive muscle relaxation and biofeedback have both been found to be effective (e.g. Andrasik and Schwartz, 2006). However, these techniques may have limited impact in patients suffering from severe chronic pain and therefore are often used in combination with other techniques (e.g. Holroyd et al, 2001).

Activity 10.1

Psychological contributions to patient care

Imagine you joined a multidisciplinary clinic for people with LTIs and were asked to draw up a brief report on how application of psychological theory and research could help improve the care the clinic was offering. Make notes for your report.

Summary

Patients are often unable to reliably assess their symptoms. Consequently, beliefs about what symptoms mean and emotional responses to their detection are crucial to the effect they have on health behaviour including consulting health care professionals. Beliefs about symptoms such as perceived seriousness and perceived effectiveness of available treatment mediate the effects of personality (e.g. neuroticism and conscientiousness) on health behaviour including adherence. Most medical interventions rely on patient adherence. Yet non-adherence is high. Patients are non-adherent for different reasons but patients' understanding, recall and satisfaction with health care all predict adherence. Key aspects of relating to patients determine patient satisfaction. Doctors' own satisfaction with their work and patient social support (especially practical support) predict adherence. In general, studies suggest that we can improve adherence although it may be challenging to do so for longer-term treatments to an extent that enhances health outcomes.

Patient satisfaction, adherence and health outcomes are related to consultation management. Reaching an agreed plan with patients is important and referred to as concordance. The Calgary–Cambridge consultation model identifies six key stages while Pendleton et al (1984) identified seven key tasks to be completed in consultations with patients. Patient-centredness and especially listening to patients' concerns is crucial to patient satisfaction. However, a positive direct style communicating expertise is also important, especially for patients with a physical problem that can be treated with medication. For chronically ill patients perspective taking may need to be combined with empowering strategies which help patients take more control of the consultation and their health. Evidence suggests that interventions can be successful in empowering patients' involvement in consultations.

Use of complementary or alternative medicine (CAM) is widespread but doubts remain about the effectiveness of such therapies, especially when placebo effects are controlled for and clinical outcomes are used. Large placebo effects have been observed but the impact of placebo responding on clinical outcomes may be limited to certain health problems including pain relief. A variety of processes underpin observed placebo effects including classical conditioning of drug responses. Patient expectations and stress reduction are likely to play an important role in the psychological and physiological benefits observed in placebo conditions. Adhering to treatment can bolster such expectations which may account for the beneficial effects of adherence to placebo treatments.

People with long-term physical illness tend to be older and to be more intensive users of health care services. The challenge for people with LTIs is to adapt to their illness, adopt the most effective coping strategies and maintain high self-efficacy and a good quality of life. Emotional responses to the illness are likely to affect quality of life and in some cases longevity. Consequently, cognitive and emotional care is critical to efficacious and cost-effective services. Psychological interventions have much to offer. For example, cognitive interventions focusing on cognition and emotion and behavioural interventions focusing on behaviours and quality of life have been found to be effective in pain management.

Key concepts and terms

Adherence
Calgary–Cambridge consultation model
Chronic pain
Cognitive care
Complementary or alternative medicine (CAM)
Concordance
Emotional care

Endogenous opioids
Event-based versus time-based recall
Pain redefinition
Patient empowerment
Patient satisfaction
Patient-centred consultation
Placebo effect
Quality of life

Sample essay titles

- What are placebo effects and can they be used to improve health?

- How can the effectiveness of doctor–patient consultations be maximized? Discuss with reference to relevant research.

- Poor adherence to health promotion and medical advice reduces the effectiveness of health services. How can we improve adherence?

- What is meant by patient-centred consultations and are they effective?

- How can psychologists help people with long-term illnesses?

Further reading

Journal articles

Harrington, J., Noble, L.M., and Newman, S.P. (2004). Improving patients' communication with doctors: a systematic review of intervention studies. *Patient Education and Counselling*, 52, 7–16.

Kaplan, R.M. (1990). Behavior as the central outcome in health care. *American Psychologist*, 45, 1211–1220.

Little, P., Everitt, H., Williamson, I., et al (2001). Observational study of effect of patient centredness and positive approach on outcomes of general practice consultations. *British Medical Journal*, 323, 908–911.

Stewart-Williams, S. (2004). The placebo puzzle: Putting together the pieces. *Health Psychology*, 23, 198–206.

11 Future directions, roles and competencies

We have seen how health psychology research can reveal psychological processes underpinning health and illness and, thereby, suggest changes in health care practice designed to optimize effectiveness. In this chapter we anticipate future directions in health psychology research and consider the contributions that health psychologists can make to health care systems. The chapter consists of two sections: 1) future research directions in health psychology; 2) roles and competencies for health psychologists.

Learning outcomes

When you have completed this chapter you should be able to:

1. Discuss possible future directions in health psychology research.
2. Identify key contexts in which professional health psychologists practise and discuss the competencies they apply.

Future research directions in health psychology

We began by examining the main pathways through which psychological factors impact on physiological functioning and health, in particular, links between the hypothalamic–pituitary–adrenal axis and the sympathetic adrenal medullary system and the cardiovascular system (including effects on blood pressure) and how stress can affect the immune system (e.g. wound healing) and exacerbate pain. Recent research in this area has also considered how stress can result in premature ageing. It appears that stress can literally get under our skin, at a cellular level! For example, Epel et al (2004a) found that psychological stress was associated with increased ageing of our **DNA**. They found that stress shortened the length of important components of our DNA known as **telomeres**. In fact, compared to low stress individuals, the telomeres of individuals with the highest levels of stress were shorter by the equivalent of at least 10 years of additional ageing! It will be interesting to see how such effects relate to differences in health behaviours (see, e.g., the observations of Khaw et al, 2008, discussed in Chapter 1) and whether the stress–telomere relationship is moderated by social support or personality (see Chapters 5 and 6).

As the populations of many developed countries age, the promotion of healthy ageing has become a public health priority (see, e.g., the findings of Yates et al, 2008, in Chapter 1). In this context, understanding the relationship between psychological factors and endocrine functioning has become important. Recent research exploring the daily cortisol profiles of middle-aged women found that the majority had a **'blunted' cortisol profile**, that is lower levels of cortisol in the morning upon awakening, which may act as a marker for psychological and biological vulnerability to adverse health outcomes (Lasikiewicz et al, 2007). Similarly, further research is needed to clarify the impact of other hormones such as testosterone and oestrogen, whose production is known to decline with age, on quality of life outcomes including depression, cognition and sexual health (e.g. O'Connor et al, 2004, 2008b). Further research into physiological functioning is likely to focus on **'metabolic syndrome'**, a relatively new and somewhat controversial condition characterized by obesity, insulin resistance (or type 2 diabetes), high blood pressure, high blood triglyceride levels and low levels of high-density lipoprotein cholesterol. Limited research has thus far indicated that stress-related changes in food intake, if maintained over time, may play a role in increasing risk of developing metabolic syndrome (Epel et al, 2004b; Newman et al, 2007).

In Chapter 3 we examined stress using psychological measures (e.g. life events and daily hassles). Research into stress and individual differences is needed to further clarify why stressors lead to poor health for some but not for others. Scientific advances in genetics offer new opportunities to study the role of specific genes in vulnerability to environmental stressors such as life events (e.g. Caspi et al, 2003). Diary studies of daily hassles have recently been used to help elucidate how stressors influence health behaviours (Johnston et al, 2006; Jones et al, 2007; O'Connor et al, 2008a). Multi-level statistical techniques have resulted in new opportunities for data analysis, opening up avenues for further research in this area. The conservation of resources theory is a promising theoretical framework focusing on protective resources which may help people to be more resistant to stressors while research into stress recovery may help answer the long-standing question of why some people get ill in response to stressors and others do not (Adler and Matthews, 1994). Studies have examined blood pressure and heart rate responses following stressful encounters. Future research could extend this work by examining whether hormonal and immunological parameters take longer to return to normal after stress in vulnerable individuals.

We noted in Chapters 4 and 5 how important context was to the stress–health relationship and how lack of control over work has especially negative impacts on health (e.g. Van der Doef and Maes, 1998). Awareness of workplace stress has increased greatly and requirements on employers to prevent harmful conditions at work are now legally enforceable. Consequently, there is a new impetus for research into stress reduction at work. Most interventions have focused on moderating the impact of stress through counselling and stress management techniques. Further work on stress prevention, including theoretically-based job redesign interventions, is needed. Moreover, research into work–life balance is in its infancy and researchers have only just begun to study positive as well as negative impacts of work on home life (e.g. Carlson et al, 2006).

Health inequalities are a central concern for the UK government and other developed countries. There is some evidence indicating that those with higher socio-economic status may respond more positively to health promotion, thereby widening the health inequalities gap (NICE, 2007). However, there is little good evidence of the moderating effect of social inequalities on health-promoting interventions. Further studies are needed, especially those focusing on how we can empower those from disadvantaged backgrounds to take advantage of and engage with health promotion efforts.

Researchers examining coping have identified many strategies and consistent styles and identified circumstances in which particular approaches are likely to lead to satisfactory outcomes (see Chapter 5). However, further work is needed on how people can proactively cope to avoid future stressors and minimize their impact. There is also a need to identify effective coping with specific stressors (e.g. in medical situations) with a view to developing practice-relevant interventions. Social support is related to health and mortality and has been found to buffer stress–health relationships. New research into the role of web-based social support networks (Kraut et al, 2002) may help clarify how these can be used to optimize positive and minimize negative effects.

Studies have found that people with particular personality traits (e.g. high conscientiousness) not only experience better health but live longer (see Chapter 6). Work in this area is especially impressive because it has often employed objective health measures such as longevity. Further research could clarify the mechanisms by which personality impacts on health. Such understanding is crucial if we are to apply the findings to improve health. For example, work on conscientiousness suggests that its effects are partially mediated by increased health-protective behaviours and decreased health-risking behaviour. Given that personality traits are difficult to change, interventions might need to be targeted at individuals with particular traits (e.g. a focus on improving health behaviours among those low in conscientiousness) and at family dynamics (e.g. Matthews et al, 1996). There is also a need to consider the effects of multiple personality traits simultaneously. For example, little research has attempted to examine the simultaneous influence of the 'Big Five' traits even though they show some degree of intercorrelation.

Several other personality traits have been linked to health outcomes. For example, type D and alexithymia are associated with increased risk of developing cardiovascular disease (e.g. Denollet et al, 1996; Waldstein et al, 2002). Other personality traits may have important implications for health-related communication but have been less thoroughly investigated. *Consideration of future consequences* (CFC) has been identified as being important to people's understanding of health promotion interventions. People high in CFC tend to sacrifice immediate benefits in order to achieve desirable future outcomes, whereas people low in CFC place less value on long-term outcomes and are more concerned with maximizing immediate benefits. It is generally found that low CFC individuals prefer options where gains are immediate and losses occur in the future, while high CFC individuals prefer the opposite, where losses are immediate and gains occur in the future. Recent research has indicated that CFC moderates the persuasive impact of communication messages (Orbell et al,

2004; Orbell and Hagger, 2006). Orbell et al manipulated the time frame in which the costs and benefits of colorectal cancer screening occurred and found that participants low in CFC had greater intentions to participate when the positive consequences were short term and negative consequences long term. The opposite was true for high CFC individuals. Nevertheless, surprisingly little research has examined the role of CFC within the context of conventional health psychological interventions. These findings point to the need to tailor health behaviour interventions to different personality traits. Modern technologies such as the internet and e-mail could be used to achieve this. For example, future research should focus on developing brief, theory-driven, inexpensive, web-based interventions. These should be tailored to individual characteristics, to change health behaviours and to raise awareness of serious health problems (e.g. high blood pressure).

Research into behaviour change has begun to distinguish between *initiation and maintenance of health behaviour* (see Norman and Conner, 2005). Considerable research with social cognition models has focused on the initiation of health behaviour (see Chapter 7). When health benefits are associated with one-off performance (e.g. immunization) this research is immediately relevant to intervention. However, for many health behaviours (e.g. healthy eating, exercise) there is little or no health benefit unless the behaviour is performed and maintained over a prolonged period of time (Conner and Norman, 2005). In such cases initiation is necessary, but not sufficient for health benefits to accrue. Further research on maintenance and habit formation is needed. For example, are the psychological processes which prompt initiation continuous with or distinct from those sustaining maintenance? The evidence is mixed. In a meta-analytic review of the PMT, Floyd et al (2000) reported that response efficacy and self-efficacy showed similar sized effects for both initiation and maintenance, although the number of studies on maintenance was modest. Sheeran et al (2001) showed the TPB to predict attendance at individual screening appointments, but not to predict repeated attendance. In contrast, Conner et al (2002) reported the TPB to be predictive of long-term healthy eating over a period of six years.

Recent theories have focused on the factors that might be different for initiation and maintenance of health behaviours. For example, satisfaction with the outcome of the behaviour (e.g. quitting smoking) may be important in the decision to maintain, but not initiate, a behaviour (Rothman, 2000). In contrast, self-efficacy may be an important determinant of both initiation and maintenance behaviours but may act in different ways (Bandura, 2000). For example, while high expectations may facilitate initiation, these expectations must become more realistic in order that dissatisfaction with outcomes during repeated performance does not inhibit maintenance (King et al, 2002).

There is a need to identify which change techniques are likely to enhance the effectiveness of behaviour change interventions targeting particular behaviours among specified groups (see Chapters 8 and 9). The meta-analytic approach utilized by Albarracín et al (2005) combined data from various studies of condom use interventions, setting new standards in the specification of which techniques enhanced the effectiveness of interventions for particular audiences (e.g. young versus older people). Future research will need to extend use of meta-analysis to other behaviours and to extend the range of techniques considered (see Webb and Sheeran, 2006; Abraham and Michie, 2008). Future trial design could also involve simultaneous tests of interventions with and without particular technique combinations to establish whether the addition of these techniques enhances effectiveness. For example, would the effectiveness of interventions targeting attitudes towards increased exercise (e.g. by focusing on the consequences of exercise behaviours) be enhanced by the addition of incentives and behavioural contracts? By testing two or more versions of interventions (with and without the additional techniques) such questions can be answered.

Interventions to change the participation of patients in consultations have shown some promising results (Harrington et al, 2004; Chapter 10). Further work on the preparation of patients for consultations (e.g. through web-based interventions) has the potential to enhance the health-promotion impact of consultations and thereby increase their cost effectiveness. Similarly, noting the potential effects of placebo treatments (Stewart-Williams, 2004) and evidence that cognitive and emotional care may maximize health benefits (Di Blasi et al, 2000), further work is needed on what type of consultation is most effective for which groups of patients. If health care practitioners can be trained to maximize anxiety reduction and enhance self-efficacy this could improve patient satisfaction, adherence and, thereby, consultation effectiveness. Such benefits may be especially important for patients with long-term illnesses and those for whom there is no obvious pharmacological intervention. For these patients, longer appointments and a greater focus on quality-of-life outcomes may be crucial to effectiveness. Behaviour change interventions have been successful in promoting greater self-care (e.g. Glazier et al, 2006) and in prevention of long-term illnesses (Knowler et al, 2002). Extensions of this work to other areas could be of great benefit to patients while simultaneously enhancing the cost effectiveness of health services.

There is also a need to evaluate policy interventions aimed at behaviour change. For example, how effective is the **food traffic-light labelling** system introduced by the Food Standards Agency (www.eatwell.gov.uk/ foodlabels/ trafficlights/) in shaping consumer choice? How does it compare to other labelling systems? Similarly, the web-based NHS Direct service has been found to elicit 90 per cent satisfaction in public surveys and it is estimated that it recoups half of its running costs by encouraging more appropriate use of NHS services (National Audit Office, 2002). It would be interesting to know, however, whether services like this reduce consultation rates and/or promote health behaviours and whether we can improve their capacity to do so.

Roles and required competencies for health psychologists

We have seen how health psychologists (HPs) have developed and tested theory explaining motivation and behaviour change and applied such theory to the design of interventions to maintain health and prevent illness (e.g. in promoting preventive health behaviours). HPs also study psychological processes involved in causing and sustaining illness including, e.g., responses to stress that undermine psychological and physical well-being. Again this work has direct relevance for interventions both at individual (e.g. stress management) and organizational (e.g. job redesign) levels. In addition, HPs examine processes relevant to the improvement of health care systems, including understanding the effects of interactions between health care professionals and their patients. This work can have direct implications for the training of health professionals.

Research in health psychology tests basic psychological hypotheses in an applied domain as well as addressing applied questions arising from health care practice. Yet in both cases the results often have direct implications for policy and practice at individual, group (e.g. peer and family), organizational, community and national levels. Consequently, health psychology is not only a sub-discipline of the science of psychology, it is also a profession which combines a rich research background of theories and findings with a wide range of research-based practices. Postgraduate professional training courses in HP are offered worldwide (see Michie and Abraham, 2004a, for comparisons between UK training and training offered in a range of other countries) and professional HPs fulfil a variety of practice roles in the UK and elsewhere.

In the UK, *National Occupational Standards* have been developed for a variety of professional roles including psychology. These standards identify the knowledge, skills and levels of competent performance expected after qualification from training programmes and so allow professionals and employers to match acquired skills or competencies against job demands. The 'Key Purpose Statement' from the National Standards for Psychology is as follows:

> *to develop, apply and evaluate psychological principles, knowledge, theories and methods in an ethical and appropriate way (i.e. systematic, evidence-based and reflective) in order to promote work-related issues. This includes the development, well-being and effectiveness of organizations, groups and individuals for the benefit of Society.*
> *(www.bps.org.uk/professional-development/nos/nos_home.cfm)*

This overarching definition of professional practice in psychology is subdivided into six '*key roles*'. Professional psychologists are expected to:

1. Develop, implement and maintain personal and professional standards and ethical practice.
2. Apply psychological and related methods, concepts, models, theories and knowledge derived from reproducible research findings.
3. Research and develop new and existing psychological methods, concepts, models, theories and instruments in psychology.
4. Communicate psychological knowledge, principles, methods, needs and policy requirement.
5. Develop and train the application of psychological skills, knowledge, practices and procedures.
6. Manage the provision of psychological systems, services and resources.

All professional psychologists are expected to attain key roles 1–4 on qualification while it is acknowledged that key roles 5 and 6 may only be attained through experience in practice. Each of these key roles is, in turn, subdivided into many standards of performance. These standards were derived from a series of workshops and consultations that involved a range of applied psychologists across different sub-disciplines. They provide detailed description of the functions and *competencies* that professional psychologists are required to perform and demonstrate once qualified. These standards have been adopted by the British Psychological Society (BPS) in accrediting psychology training courses in the UK and, in broad terms, by the **European Federation of Professional Psychologists Associations** (EFPA) in developing common standards across European psychology training courses (EuroPsyT, 2001). EFPA represents 32 European national psychological associations, including all European Union Member States and has declared that independent practice as a psychologist requires university training equivalent to at least five years of full-time study and at least one year of supervised practice (EFPA, 2006).

The BPS Division of Health Psychology in the UK developed a competence-based qualification in professional health psychology which maps on to the UK National Standards (BPS, 2007). This analysis and definition of health psychology competencies includes 19 core units of competence relating to generic professional competence (which would apply to all psychologists and which corresponds to key role 1 above), consultancy competence (which would map mainly onto key roles 2 and 4), research competencies (which map mainly onto key role 3) and teaching and training competencies (which map mainly onto key role 5). Michie, Johnston and Abraham (2004) provide a useful introduction to this model. UK training in health psychology is currently undergoing change as all UK professional psychologists come under the jurisdiction of the *Health Professions Council* due to changes in national legislation.

A number of key areas of competence which characterize health psychology practice internationally can be identified (see Abraham and Michie, 2005) and mapped onto the core areas of health psychology theory and research discussed in this book. Professional HPs are able to do the following:

1. *Assess*, that is, understand, describe and explain psychological and behavioural processes that result in individual differences, including individual strengths and vulnerabilities. This may involve applying measures to characterize personality, stress levels, attitudes, patient satisfaction, adherence or health behaviours.
2. *Conduct research* including developing theory and methods relevant to health-related behaviour. This could involve applying for research funding, conducting an interpretative analysis of interview data, a systematic review, a meta-analysis, a prospective survey or a randomized controlled trial.
3. *Intervene*, that is, generate changes in psychological and behavioural processes that result in improved health care and health outcomes. This could involve applying learning theory or social cognition theories to design an intervention for an individual in a health care setting, a school class or group of workers in a private company. In Chapter 9 we listed five core competencies which the

UK National Institute for Health and Clinical Excellence recommended for all professionals working in behaviour change, including HPs.

4. *Train and supervise* other health professionals, that is, impart skills of psychological theorizing, assessment and intervention to others. For example, many HPs teach nursing and medical students (e.g. in communication skills) and may also train colleagues in psychological practices, e.g. by running training workshops for teachers or social workers. This will involve designing, delivering and evaluating training using materials appropriate to the audience.

5. *Consult* both with individuals and organizations. This would include being able to manage effective one-to-one consultations as described in Chapter 10 and at the same time being able to accept a commission for a larger piece of work such as evaluating an in-house stress management programme within a company or assisting a local authority with the reduction of unplanned teenage pregnancies. It requires highly developed communication and negotiation skills.

6. *Supervise and manage*, that is guide others with less psychological training or experience in psychological practice. Assessing, training and management are overlapping and complementary skills. Even a newly qualified professional psychologist will be able to monitor, train and report on the design and implementation of psychological research by colleagues with less training in this area. More experienced HPs will be able to manage and supervise teams of fellow HPs.

HPs work in a variety of multidisciplinary settings. Hallas (2004) describes the varied work of HPs in health care demonstrating how the work draws on the full range of competencies outlined above. Hallas notes that HPs may be involved in direct patient care, assessing and enhancing individuals' psychological adjustment to illness and treatment, minimizing distress associated with medical procedures, delivering health education, facilitating patient decision-making, and implementing psychological interventions to promote healthy behaviours. As well as training health care professionals, running stress management courses and advising on job redesign, HPs may investigate whether an attitude change intervention could enhance patient adherence and whether this would have any effects on clinical outcomes. HPs may also work in public health services, e.g. including work on screening and/or shaping environments to facilitate health behaviour uptake at a population level. In addition HPs may work on health service policy by working in government departments for policy development units such as the UK National Institute for Health and Clinical Excellence. Interestingly a position paper from the UK Prime Minister's Strategy Unit, (Knott et al, 2007) outlined a behaviour change framework that draws explicitly on theory and research discussed in this book. The paper emphasizes from the outset the importance of understanding attitudes, values, self-efficacy, intentions and social influence in shaping social change and so emphasizes what a key role HPs have shaping population behaviour change.

Summary

Each area of research we have considered in previous chapters not only provides insights into processes underlying health and illness and effective health care but also raises interesting new questions which only new research can answer. These range from questions concerning fundamental biological processes to questions about coping and personality through to questions about the content and impact of behaviour change interventions and the most effective way in which to manage patient consultations.

Professional health psychologists work in a variety of multidisciplinary settings, including health care settings, organizational settings and government departments. They are trained in a number of key roles and develop a range of competencies through training involving a minimum of five years' full-time-equivalent university training and one year full-time supervised practice. These competencies include research, assessment, intervention training, consultation and management skills.

Key concepts and terms

Blunted cortisol profile
DNA
European Federation of
    Professional Psychologists
    Associations

Food traffic-light labelling
Metabolic syndrome
Telomeres

Sample essay title

- How can health psychologists contribute to the improvement of health care services?

Further reading

Books

Michie, S., and Abraham, C. (Eds) (2004a). *Health Psychology in Practice.* Oxford: Blackwell.

The British Psychological Society (2007). *Qualification in Health Psychology (Stage 2): Candidate Handbook.* Leicester: The British Psychological Society.

www.bps.org.uk/careers/society_qual/qual_downloads$/health_download$.cfm

Journal articles

Turk, D.C., and Burwinkle, T.M. (2000). Clinical outcomes, cost-effectiveness, and the role of psychology in treatments for chronic pain sufferers. *Professional Psychology: Research and Practice*, 36, 602–610.

References

Abhyankar, P., O'Connor, D.B., and Lawton, R. (2008). The role of message framing in promoting MMR vaccination: evidence of a loss frame advantage. *Psychology, Health and Medicine*, 13, 1–16.

Abraham, C. (2004). 'Theory in health psychology research.' In: S. Michie and C. Abraham (Eds), *Health Psychology in Practice*. Oxford: Blackwell, 65–82.

Abraham, C. (2008). Beyond stages of change: multi determinant continuum models of action readiness and menu-based interventions. *Applied Psychology: An International Review*, 57, 30–41.

Abraham, C., and Michie, S. (2005). Contributing to public health policy and practice. *The Psychologist*, 12, 676–679.

Abraham, C., and Michie, S. (in press). A taxonomy of behavior change techniques used in interventions. *Health Psychology*.

Abraham, C., and Sheeran, P. (2005). 'The health belief model.' In: M. Conner and P. Norman (Eds), *Predicting Health Behaviour: Research and Practice with Social Cognition Models*, (2nd Ed.). Maidenhead: Open University Press, 28–80.

Abraham, C., Sheeran, P., and Orbell, S. (1998). Can social cognitive models contribute to the effectiveness of HIV-preventive behavioural interventions? A brief review of the literature and a reply to Joffe (1996; 1997) and Fife-Schaw (1997). *British Journal of Medical Psychology*, 71, 297–310.

Abraham, C., Costa-Pereira, A., du V Florey, C., and Ogston, S. (1999). Cognitions associated with initial medical consultations concerning recurrent breathing difficulties: A community-based study. *Psychology and Health*, 14, 913–925.

Abraham, C., Krahé, B., Dominic, R., and Fritsche, I. (2002). Does research into the social cognitive antecedents of action contribute to health promotion? A content analysis of safer-sex promotion leaflets. *British Journal of Health Psychology*, 7, 227–246.

Abraham, C., Southby, L., Quandte, S., Krahé, B., and van der Sluijs, W. (2007). Identifying research-based persuasive messages in health promotion texts: An analysis of widely available European alcohol-education leaflets. *Psychology and Health*, 22, 31–60.

Ader, R., and Cohen, N. (1975). Behaviorally conditioned immunosuppression. *Psychosomatic Medicine*, 37, 333–340.

Adler, N., and Matthews, K. (1994). Health Psychology: Why do some people get sick and some stay well. *Annual Review of Psychology*, 45, 229–259.

Adler, N.E., Boyce, T., Chesney, M.A., Cohen, S., Folkman, S., Kahn, R.L., and Syme, S.L. (1994). Socio-economic status and health. The challenge of the gradient. *American Psychologist*, 49, 15–24.

Affleck, G., Tennen, H., Croog, S., and Levine, S. (1987). Causal attribution, perceived benefits and morbidity following a heart attack: An eight year study. *Journal of Consulting and Clinical Psychology*, 55, 29–35.

Affleck, G., Tennen, H., Uroows, S., and Higgins, P. (1992). Neuroticism and the pain-mood relation in rheumatoid arthritis: Insights from a prospective daily study. *Journal of Consulting and Clinical Psychology*, 60, 119–126.

Affleck, G., Zautra, A., Tennen, H., and Armeli, S. (1999). Multi-level daily process designs for consulting and clinical psychology: A preface for the perplexed. *Journal of Consulting and Clinical Psychology*, 67, 746–754.

Ajzen, I. (1991). The theory of planned behavior. *Organizational Behavior and Human Decision Processes*, 50, 179–211.

Ajzen, I. (2001). Nature and operation of attitudes. *Annual Review of Psychology*, 52, 27–58.

Ajzen, I., and Fishbein, M. (1980). *Understanding Attitudes and Predicting Social Behavior*. Englewood Cliff, NJ: Prentice Hall.

Ajzen, I., and Fishbein, M. (2004). Questions raised by a reasoned action approach: Reply on Ogden (2003). *Health Psychology*, 23, 431–434.

Ajzen, I., and Fishbein, M. (2005). The influence of attitudes on behavior. In D. Albarracín, B.T. Johnson and M.P. Zanna (Eds), *Handbook of Attitudes and Attitude Change: Basic Principles*. Mahwah, NJ: Erlbaum, 173–221.

Albarracín, D., Johnson, B.T., Fishbein, M., and Muellerleile, P.A. (2001). Theories of reasoned action and planned behavior as models of condom use: A meta-analysis. *Psychological Bulletin*, 127, 142–161.

Albarracín, D., Gillete, J.C., Earl A.N., Glasman, L.R., and Durantini, M.R. (2005). A test of major assumptions about behavior change: A comprehensive look at the effects of passive and active HIV-prevention interventions since the beginning of the epidemic. *Psychological Bulletin*, 131, 856–897.

Alloy, L.B., Abrahamson, L.Y., and Francis, E.L. (1999). Do negative cognitive styles confer vulnerability to depression? *Current Directions in Psychological Science*, 8, 128–132.

Allport, F.H. (1924). Social Psychology. Boston: Houghton Mifflin.

Almeida, D.M. (2005). Resilience and vulnerability to daily stressors assessed via diary methods. *Current Directions in Psychological Science*, 14, 64–68.

Ambady, N., LaPlante, D., Nguyen, T., Rosenthal, R., Chaumeton, N., and Levinson, W. (2002). Surgeons' tone of voice: A clue to malpractice history. *Surgery*, 132, 5–9.

Andrasik, F., and Schwartz, M.S. (2006). Behavioral assessment and treatment of pediatric headache. *Behavioural Modification*, 30, 93–113.

Apanovitch, A.M., McCarthy, D., and Salovey, P. (2003). Using message framing to motivate HIV testing among low-income, ethnic minority women. *Health Psychology*, 22, 60–67.

Armitage, C.J., and Conner, M. (2001). Efficacy of the theory of planned behaviour: A meta-analytic review. *British Journal of Social Psychology*, 40, 471–499.

Asch, S. (1952). *Social Psychology*. Englewood Cliffs, New Jersey: Prentice Hall.

Aspinwall, L.G., and Taylor, S.E. (1997). A stitch in time: Self-regulation and proactive coping. *Psychological Bulletin*, 121, 417–436.

Austin, J.T., and Vancouver, J.B. (1996). Goal constructs in psychology: Structure, process, and content. *Psychological Review*, 120, 338–375.

Bagby, M.R., Taylor, G.J., and Parker, J.D.A. (1994). The twenty-item Toronto Alexithymia Scale–II. Convergent, discriminant, and concurrent validity. *Journal of Psychosomatic Research*, 38, 33–40.

Bagozzi, R.P. (1993). On the neglect of volition in consumer research: a critique and proposal. *Psychology and Marketing*, 10, 215–237.

Baird, G., Pickles, A., Simonoff, E., Charman, T., et al. (2008). Measles vaccination and antibody response in autism spectrum disorders. *Archives of Disease in Childhood*, published online, doi:10.1136/adc.2007.122937

Bandura, A. (1982). Self-efficacy mechanism in human agency. *American Psychologist*, 37, 122–147.

Bandura, A. (1997). *Self-Efficacy: The Exercise of Control*. New York: Freeman.

Bandura, A. (1999). Health promotion from the perspective of social cognitive theory. *Psychology and Health*, 13, 623–650.

Bandura, A. (2000). 'Health promotion from the perspective of social cognitive theory.' In: P. Norman, C. Abraham and M. Conner (Eds), *Understanding and Changing Health Behaviour: From Health Beliefs to Self-Regulation*. Switzerland: Harwood Academic, 229–242.

Bardone-Cone, A.M., and Cass, K.M. (2007). What does viewing a pro-anorexia website do? An experimental examination of website exposure and moderating effects. *International Journal of Eating Disorders*, 40, 537–548.

Barlow, J., Wright, C., Sheasby, J., Turner, A., and Hainsworth, J. (2002). Self-management approaches for people with chronic conditions: A review. *Patient Education and Counseling*, 48, 177–187.

Barlow, J.H., Wright, C.C., Turner, A.P., and Bancroft, G.V. (2005). A 12-month follow-up study of self-management training for people with chronic disease: Are changes maintained over time? *British Journal of Health Psychology*, 10, 589–599.

Barrera, J.M. (1986). Distinctions between social support concepts, measures and models. *American Journal of Community Psychiatry*, 14, 413–445.

Bartholomew, L.K., Parcel, G.S., Kok, G., and Gottlieb, N.H. (2006). *Planning Health Promotion Programs. An Intervention Mapping Approach*. San Francisco, CA: Jossey-Bass.

Bartley, M., Martikainen, P., Shipley, M., and Marmot, M. (2004). Gender differences in the relationship of partner's social class to behavioural risk factors and social support in the Whitehall II study. *Social Science and Medicine*, 59, 1925–1936.

Bassman, L.E., and Uellendahl, G. (2003). Complementary/alternative medicine: ethical, professional, and practical challenges for psychologists. *Professional Psychology; Research and Practice*, 34, 264–270.

Baum, A., and Posluszny, D.M. (1999). Health psychology: Mapping biobehavioral contributions to health and illness. *Annual Review of Psychology*, 50, 137–163.

Beecher, H.K. (1955). The powerful placebo. *Journal of the American Medical Association*, 159, 1602–1606.

Beecher, H.K. (1956). Relationship of significance of wound to pain experienced. *Journal of the American Medical Association*, 161, 1609–1613.

Beehr, T.A., and Newman, J.E. (1978). Job stress, employee health and organizational effectiveness: A facet analysis, model and literature review. *Personnel Psychology*, 31, 665–699.

Belloc, N.B., and Breslow, L. (1972). Relationship of physical health status and health practices. *Preventive Medicine*, 9, 469–421.

Benedetti, F., Pollo, A., and Colloca, L. (2007). Opioid-mediated placebo responses boost pain endurance and physical performance: Is it doping in sport competitions? *Journal of Neuroscience*, 27, 11934–11939.

Benson, H. (1976). *The Relaxation Response*. New York: Morrow.

Berkanovic, E., Telesky, C., and Reeder, S. (1981). Structural and social psychological factors in the decision to seek medical care for symptoms. *Medical Care*, 19, 693–709.

Berkman, L.F., and Syme, S.L. (1979). Social networks, host resistance, and mortality: A nine year follow-up study of Alameda County residents. *American Journal of Epidemiology*, 109, 186–204.

Bissell, P., May, C.T., and Noyce, P.R. (2004). From compliance to concordance: Barriers to accomplishing a re-framed model of health care interactions. *Social Science and Medicine*, 58, 851–862.

Blaxter, M. (1990). *Health and Lifestyles*. London: Tavistock.

Bluen, S.D., Barling, J., and Burns, W. (1990). Predicting sales performance, job satisfaction, and depression by using the achievement strivings and impatience-irritability dimensions of type A behavior. *Journal of Applied Psychology*, 75, 212–216.

Bogg, T., and Roberts, B.W. (2004). Conscientiousness and health-related behaviors: A meta-analysis of the leading behavioral contributors to mortality. *Psychological Bulletin*, 130, 887–919.

Bolger, N. (1990). Coping as a personality process: A prospective study. *Journal of Personality and Social Psychology*, 59, 525–537.

Bolger, N., Davis, A., and Rafaeli, E. (2003). Diary methods: Capturing life as it is lived. *Annual Review of Psychology*, 54, 579–616.

Bond, F.W., and Bunce, D. (2001). Job control mediates change in a work reorganization intervention for stress reduction. *Journal of Occupational Health Psychology*, 6, 290–302.

Boneva, B., Kraut, R., and Frohlich, D. (2001). Using e-mail for personal relationships: The difference gender makes. *American Behavioral Scientist*, 45, 530–549.

Booth-Kewley, S., and Friedman, H. (1987). Psychological predictors of heart disease: A quantitative review. *Psychological Bulletin*, 101, 343–362.

Booth-Kewley, S., and Vickers, R.R. (1994). Associations between major domains of personality and health behavior. *Journal of Personality*, 62, 281–298.

Bosma, H., Peter, R., Siegrist, J., and Marmot, M. (1998). Two alternative job stress models and the risk of coronary heart disease. *American Journal of Public Health*, 88, 68–74.

Bower, J.E., and Segerstrom, S.C. (2004). Stress management, finding benefit, and immune function: Positive mechanisms for intervention effects on physiology. *Journal of Psychosomatic Research*, 56, 9–11.

Boyle, C.M. (1970). Difference between patients and doctors interpretation of some common medical terms. *British Medical Journal*, 71, 286–289.

BPS (2007). *Qualification in Health Psychology (Stage 2): Candidate Handbook*. Leicester UK: The British Psychological Society. (www.bps.org.uk/careers/society_qual/qual_downloads$/health_download$.cfm)

Brehm, J. (1966). *A Theory of Psychological Reactance*. New York: Academic Press.

Breslow, L., and Enstrom, J.E. (1980). Persistence of health habits and their relationship to mortality. *Preventive Medicine*, 9, 469–483.

Briñol, P., and Petty, R.E. (2005). 'Individual differences in attitude change.' In: D. Albarracín, B.T. Johnson and M. Zanna, M. (Eds), *The Handbook of Attitudes*. Mahwah, New Jersey: Lawrence Erlbaum, 575–616.

Brough, P., and Kelling, A. (2002). Women, work and well-being family-work conflict. *New Zealand Journal of Psychology*, 31, 29–38.

Brown, G.W. (1974). 'Meaning, measurement and stress of life events.' In: B.S. Dohrenwend and B.P. Dohrenwend (Eds), *Stressful Life Events: Their Nature and Effects*, London: John Wiley, 217–243.

Brown, G.W., and Harris, T.O. (1978). *Social Origins of Depression: A Study of Psychiatric Disorder in Women*. London: Tavistock Publications.

Brown, J.D., and McGill, K.L. (1989). The cost of good fortune: When positive life events produce negative health consequences. *Journal of Personality and Social Psychology*, 57, 1103–1110.

Bryan, A.D., Aiken, L.S., and West, S.G. (1996) Increasing condom use: evaluation of a theory-based intervention to prevent sexually transmitted diseases in young women. *Health Psychology*, 15, 371–382.

Burke, R.J., Weir, T., and DuWors, R.E. (1980). Perceived type A behavior of husbands and wives' satisfaction and well being. *Journal of Occupational Behavior*, 1, 139–150.

Butler, C., and Steptoe, A. (1986). Placebo responses: An experimental study of psychophysiological processes in asthmatic volunteers. *British Journal of Clinical Psychology*, 25, 173–183.

Byrne, D. (1961). The repression-sensitization scale: Rationale, reliability and validity. *Journal of Personality*, 29, 334–349.

Byrne, P.S., and Long, B.E.L. (1976). *Doctors Talking to Patients*. London: HMSO.

Cacioppo, J.T., Petty, R.E., and Morris, K.J. (1983) Effects of need for cognition on message evaluation, recall and persuasion. *Personality and Social Psychology*, 45, 805–818.

Campbell, M., Fitzpatrick, R., Haines, A., Kinmonth, A.L., Sandercock, P., Spiegelhalter, D. and Tyrer, P. (2000). Framework for design and evaluation of complex interventions to improve health. *British Medical Journal*, 321, 694–696.

Canals, J., Bladé, J., and Domènech, E. (1997). Smoking and personality predictors in young Spanish people. *Personality and Individual Differences*, 23, 905–908.

Cannon, W. (1932). *The Wisdom of the Body*. New York: Norton.

Cantillon, P., Morgan, M., Dundas, R., Simpson, J., Bartholomew, J., and Shaw, A. (1997). Patients' perceptions of changes in their blood pressure. *Journal of Human Hypertension*, 11, 221–225.

Carlson, D.S., Kacmar, K., Wayne, J.H., and Grzywacz, J.G. (2006). Measuring the positive side of the work-family interface: Development and validation of a work-family enrichment scale. *Journal of Vocational Behavior*, 68, 131–164.

Carmody, T.P., Crossen, J.R., and Wiens, A.N. (1989). Hostility as a health risk factor: Relationships with neuroticism, type a behavior, attentional focus, and interpersonal style. *Journal of Clinical Psychology*, 45, 754–762.

Carroll, D., Bennett, P., and Davey Smith, G. (1993). Socio-economic health inequalities: Their origins and implications. *Psychology and Health*, 8, 295–316.

Carroll, D., Ebrahim, S., Tilling, K., Macleod, J., and Davey Smith, G. (2002). Admissions for myocardial infarction and World Cup football: Database survey. *British Medical Journal*, 325, 1439–1442.

Carver, C.S., and Scheier, M.F. (1982). Control theory: a useful conceptual framework for personality–social, clinical and health psychology. *Psychological Bulletin*, 92, 111–135.

Carver, C.S., and Scheier, M.F. (1994). Situational coping and coping dispositions in a stressful transaction. *Journal of Personality and Social Psychology*, 66, 184–195.

Carver, C.S., Scheier, M.F., and Weintraub, J.K. (1989). Assessing coping strategies: A theoretically based approach. *Journal of Personality and Social Psychology*, 56, 267–283.

Carver, C.S., Pozo, C., Harris, S.D., et al (1993). How coping mediates the effects of optimism on distress: A study of women with early stage breast cancer. *Journal of Personality and Social Psychology*, 65, 375–390.

Caspi, A., Begg, D., Dickson, N., Harrington, H., Langley, J., Moffitt, T.E. and Silva, P.A. (1997). Personality differences predict health-risk behaviour in young adulthood: Evidence from a longitudinal study. *Journal of Personality and Social Psychology*, 73, 1052–1062.

Caspi, A., Sugden, K., Moffitt, T.E., Taylor, A., Craig, I.W., Harrington, H., et al. (2003). Influence of life stress on depression: Moderation by a polymorphism in the 5-htt gene. *Science*, 301, 386–389.

Caspi, A., Roberts, B.W., and Shiner, R.L. (2005). Personality development: Stability and change. *Annual Review of Psychology*, 56, 453–484.

Cegala, D.J., McClure, L., Marinelli, T.M., and Post, D.M. (2000). The effects of communication skills training on patients' participation during medical interviews. *Patient Education and Counselling*, 41, 209–222.

Chaiken, S. (1980). Heuristic versus systematic information processing and the use of source versus message cues in persuasion. *Journal of Personality and Social Psychology*, 37, 1397–1397.

Chen, C.C., David, A.S., Nunnerley, H., Mitchell, M., Dawson, J.L., Berry, H., et al (1995). Adverse life events and breast cancer: Case-control study. *British Medical Journal*, 311, 1527–1530.

Chesney, M.A., Eagleston, J.R., and Rosenman, R.H. (1980) The type A structured interview: A behavioral assessment in the rough. *Journal of Behavioral Assessment*, 2, 255–272.

Choosing Health (2004). *Choosing Health: A Consultation to Improve People's Health*. London: HMSO.

Christensen, A.J., Moran, P.J., and Wiebe, J.S. (1999). Assessment of irrational health beliefs: Relation to health practices and medical regimen adherence. *Health Psychology*, 18, 169–176.

Christiansen, A.J., and Smith, T.W. (1995). Personality and patient adherence: Correlates of the five-factor model in renal dialysis. *Journal of Behavioral Medicine*, 18, 305–313.

Cialdini, R.B. (1995). *Principles and Techniques of Social Influence*. In A. Tesser (Ed.), *Advanced Social Psychology*. New York: Mc-Graw Hill, 257–281.

Cialdini, R.B., and Trost, M.R. (1998). 'Social influence: Social norms, conformity, and compliance.' In: D.T. Gilbert, S.T. Fiske and G. Lindzey (Eds), *The Handbook of Social Psychology*, (4th Ed.) New York: McGraw-Hill, Vol. 2, 151–192.

Clow, A. (2001). 'The physiology of stress.' In: F. Jones and J. Bright (Eds), *Stress: Myth, Theory and Research*. England: Pearson Education, 47–61.

Cohen, J. (1992) A power primer. *Psychological Bulletin*, 112, 155–159.

Cohen, S. (2005). The Pittsburgh common cold studies: psychosocial predictors of susceptibility to respiratory infectious illness. *International Journal of Behavioral Medicine*, 12, 123–131.

Cohen, S., and Wills, T.A. (1985). Stress, social support and the buffering hypothesis. *Psychological Bulletin*, 98, 310–357.

Cohen, S., Tyrrell, D.A.J., and Smith, A.P. (1991). Psychological stress and susceptibility to the common cold. *New England Journal of Medicine*, 325, 606–612.

Cohen, S., Frank, E., Doyle, W.J., Skoner, D.P., Rabin, B.S., and Gwaltney, J.M., Jr. (1998). Types of stressors that increase susceptibility to the common cold in adults. *Health Psychology*, 17, 214–223.

Cohen, S., Doyle, W.J., and Skoner, D.P. (1999). Psychological stress, cytokine production, and severity of upper respiratory illness. *Psychological Medicine*, 61, 175–180.

Cohen, S., Miller, G.E., and Rabin, B.S. (2001). Psychological stress and antibody response to immunization: A critical review of the human literature. *Psychosomatic Medicine*, 63, 7–18.

Cohen, S., Doyle, W.J., and Baum, A. (2006). Socio-economic status is associated with stress hormones. *Psychosomatic Medicine*, 68, 414–420.

Coifman, K.G., Bonanno, G.A., Ray, R.D., and Gross, J.J. (2007). Does repressive coping promote resilience? Affective-autonomic response discrepancy during bereavement. *Journal of Personality and Social Psychology*, 92, 745–758.

Conner, M., and Abraham, C. (2001). Conscientiousness and the Theory of Planned Behavior: Towards a more complete model of the antecedents of intentions and behavior. *Personality and Social Psychology Bulletin*, 27, 1547–1561.

Conner, M.T., and Norman, P. (Eds) (2005). *Predicting Health Behaviour: Research and Practice with Social Cognition Models*, (2nd Ed.). Maidenhead: Open University Press.

Conner, M., and Sparks, P. (2005). 'The theory of planned behaviour and health behaviours'. In: M. Conner and P. Norman (Eds), *Predicting Health Behaviour: Research and Practice with Social Cognition Models*, (2nd Ed.). Maidenhead: Open University Press, 170–222.

Conner, M., Fitter, M., and Fletcher, W. (1999). Stress and snacking: A diary study of daily hassles and between meal snacking. *Psychology and Health*, 14, 51–63.

Conner, M., Norman, P., and Bell, R. (2002). The theory of planned behavior and healthy eating. *Health Psychology*, 21, 194–201.

Conner, M., Grogan, S., Fry, G., Gough, B., and Higgins, A. (in press). Direct, mediated and moderated impacts of personality variables on smoking initiation in adolescents. *Psychology and Health*.

Conrad, P. (1985). The meaning of medications: Another look at compliance. *Social Science and Medicine*, 20, 29–37.

Cook, W.W., and Medley, D.M. (1954). Proposed hostillity and pharisaic-virtue scores for the MMPI. *Journal of Applied Psychology*, 38, 414–418.

Cooke, R., and Sheeran, P. (2004). Moderation of cognition-intention and cognition-behaviour relations: A meta-analysis of properties of variables from the theory of planned behaviour. *British Journal of Social Psychology*, 43, 159–186.

Cooper, C.L., and Dewe, P. (2004). *Stress: A Brief History*. Oxford: Blackwell.

Cooper, C.L., Sloan, S.J., and Williams, S. (1988). *The Occupational Stress Indicator*. Windsor: NFER-Nelson.

Cooper, M.L., Wood, P.K., Orcutt, H.K., and Albino, A.W. (2003). Personality and the predisposition to engage in risky or problem behaviors during adolescence. *Journal of Personality and Social Psychology*, 84, 390–410.

Costa, P.T. Jr., and McCrae, R.R. (1980). Influence of extraversion and neuroticism on subjective well-being: Happy and unhappy people. *Journal of Personality and Social Psychology*, 40, 19–28.

Costa, P.T. Jr., and McCrae, R.R. (1987). Neuroticism, somatic complaints, and disease: Is the bark worse than the bite? *Journal of Personality*, 55, 299–316.

Costa, P.T. Jr., and McCrae, R.R. (1990). Personality: Another 'hidden factor' in stress research. *Psychological Inquiry*, 1, 22–24.

Costa, P.T. Jr., and McCrae, R.R. (1992). Four ways five factors are basic. *Personality and Individual Differences*, 13, 653–665.

Coulson, N.S., Buchanan, H., and Aubeeluck, A. (2007). Social support in cyberspace: A content analysis of communication within a Huntington's disease online support group. *Patient Education and Counseling*, 68, 173–178.

Coulter, A., Entwistle, V., and Gilbert, D. (1999). Sharing decisions with patients: Is the information good enough? *British Medical Journal*, 318, 318–322.

Courneya, K.S., and Hellsten, L.M. (1998). Personality correlates of exercise behavior, motives, barriers and preferences: An application of the five-factor model. *Personality and Individual Differences*, 24, 625–633.

Cox, T. (1978). *Stress*. London: Macmillan.

Coyne, J.C., and Gottlieb, B.H. (1996). The mismeasure of coping by checklist. *Journal of Personality*, 64, 959–991.

Creswell, J.D., Lam, S., Stanton, A.L., Taylor, S.E., Bower, J.E., and Sherman, D.K. (2007). Does self-affirmation, cognitive processing, or discovery of meaning explain cancer-related health benefits of expressive writing? *Personality and Social Psychology Bulletin*, 33, 238–250.

Crowley, A.E., and Hoyer, W.D. (1994). An integrative framework for understanding two-sided persuasion. *Journal of Consumer Research*, 20, 561–574.

Crowne, D.P., and Marlowe, D. (1960). A new scale of social desirability independent of psychopathology. *Journal of Consulting Psychology*, 24, 349–354.

Cummings, M.K., Becker, M.H., and Maile, M.C. (1980). Bringing models together: An Empirical approach to combining variables used to explain health actions. *Journal of Behavioral Medicine*, 3, 123–145.

Cunningham, A.J. (1985). The influence of mind on cancer. *Canadian Psychology*, 26, 13–29.

Dakof, G.S., and Taylor, S.E. (1990). Victims perceptions of social support: What is helpful and from whom? *Journal of Personality and Social Psychology*, 58, 80–89.

Daly, J., Willis, K. Small, R., Green, J., Welch, N., Kealy, M., and Hughes, E. (2007). A hierarchy of evidence for assessing qualitative health research. *Journal of Clinical Epidemiology*, 60, 43–49.

Dancey, C.P., Taghavi, M., and Fox, R.J. (1998). The relationship between daily stress and symptoms of irritable bowel: a time-series approach. *Journal of Psychosomatic Research*, 44, 537–545.

Danner, D.D., Snowdon, D.A. and Friesen, W.V. (2001). Positive emotions in early life and longevity: Findings from the Nun Study. *Journal of Personality and Social Psychology*, 80, 804–813.

Das, E.H., de Wit, J.B.F., and Stroebe, W. (2003). Fear appeals motivate acceptance of action recommendations: Evidence for a positive bias in the processing of persuasive messages. *Personality and Social Psychology Bulletin*, 29, 650–664.

Davidson, K.W., Goldstein, M., Kaplan, R.M., et al (2003). Evidence-based behavioral medicine: What is it and how do we achieve it? *Annals of Behavioral Medicine*, 26, 161–171.

Davidson, K.W., Gidron, Y., Mostofsky, E., and Trudeau, K.J. (2007). Hospitalization cost offset of a hostility intervention for coronary heart disease patients. *Journal of Consulting and Clinical Psychology*, 75, 657–662.

Davis, C.G., Nolen-Hoeksema, S., and Larson, J. (1998). Making sense of loss and benefiting from the experience: Two construals of meaning. *Journal of Personality and Social Psychology*, 75, 561–574.

de Lange, A.H., Taris, T.W., Kompier, M.A.J., Houtman, I.L.D., and Bongers, P.M. (2003). 'The very best of the millennium': Longitudinal research and the demand-control-(support) model. *Journal of Occupational Health Psychology*, 8, 282–305.

de Rijk, A.E., Le Blance, P.M., Schaufeli, W.B., and de Jonge, J. (1998). Active coping and need for control as moderators of the job demand-control model: Effects on burnout. *Journal of Occupational and Organizational Psychology*, 71, 1–18.

Deelstra, J.T., Peeters, M.C.W., Zijlstra, F.R.H., and van Doornen, L.P. (2003). Receiving instrumental support at work: When help is not welcome. *Journal of Applied Psychology*, 88, 324–331.

DeLongis, A., Coyne, J.C., Dakof, G., Folkman, S., and Lazarus, R.S. (1982). Relationships of daily hassles, uplifts, and major life events to health status. *Health Psychology*, 1, 119–136.

Demers, R.R., Altamore, H., Mustin, A., Kleinman, A., and Leonardi, D. (1980). An exploration of the depth and dimensions of illness behavior. *Journal of Family Practice*, 11, 1085–1092.

Denollet, J., Sys, S.U., Stroobant, N., Rombouts, H., Gillebert, T.C., and Brutsaert, D.L. (1996). Personality as independent predictors of long-term mortality in patients with coronary heart disease. *Lancet*, 34, 417–421.

Department of Health (2001). *The Expert Patient: A New Approach to Chronic Disease Management for the 21st Century*. London: Department of Health, HMSO.

Department of Health (2008). *Raising the profile of long term conditions care: A compendium of information*. Leeds: Department of Health (www.dh.gov.uk/publications).

Derakshan, N., and Eysenck, M.W. (1997). Repression and repressors: Theoretical and experimental approaches. *European Psychologist*, 2, 235–246.

DeRubeis, R.J., and Crits-Christoph, P. (1998). Empirically supported individual and group psychological treatments for adult mental disorders. *Journal of Consulting and Clinical Psychology*, 66, 37–52.

Detweiler, J.B., Bedell, B.T., Salovey, P., Pronin, E., and Rothman, A.J. (1999). Message framing and sunscreen use: Gain-framed messages motivate beach-goers. *Health Psychology*, 18, 189–196.

Deutsch, M., and Gerard, H.G. (1955). A study of normative and informational social influence upon individual judgment. *Journal of Abnormal and Social Psychology*, 51, 629–636.

Di Blasi, Z., Harkness, E., Ernst, E., Georgiou, A., and Kleijnen, J. (2000) Influence of context effects on health outcomes: a systematic review. *Lancet*, 357, 757–762.

DiClemente, C.C. (1986). Self efficacy and smoking cessation maintenance: A preliminary report. *Journal of Social and Clinical Psychology*, 4, 302–315.

DiClemente, C.C., Prochaska, J.O., Fairhurst, S.K., Velicer, W.F., Velasquez, M.M., and Rossi, J.S. (1991). The process of smoking cessation: An analysis of precontemplation, contemplation, and preparation stages of change. *Journal of Consulting and Clinical Psychology*, 59, 295–304.

Dienstbier, R.A. (1989). Arousal and physiological toughness: Implications for mental and physical health. *Psychological Review*, 96, 84–100.

Digman, J.M. (1990). Personality structure: Emergence of the five-factor model. *Annual Review of Psychology*, 41, 417–440.

DiMatteo, M.R. (2004). Social support and patient adherence to medical treatment: a meta-analysis. *Health Psychology*, 23, 207–218.

DiMatteo, M.R., Sherbourne, C.D., Hays, et al (1993). Physicians' characteristics influence patients' adherence to medical treatment: Results from the medical outcomes study. *Health Psychology*, 12, 93–102.

Dohrenwend, B.P. (2000). The role of adversity and stress in psychopathology: Some evidence and its implications for theory and research. *Journal of Health and Social Behaviour*, 41, 1–19.

Dohrenwend, B.P. (2006). Inventorying stressful life events as risk factors for psychopathology: Towards resolution of the problem of intracategory variability. *Psychological Bulletin*, 132, 477–495.

Dohrenwend, B.P., and Shrout, P.E. (1985). 'Hassles' in the conceptualization and measurement of life stress variables. *American Psychologist*, 40, 780–785.

Dohrenwend, B.P., Link, B.G., Kern, R., Shrout, P.E., and Markowitz, J. (1990). Measuring life events: The problem of variability within categories. *Stress Medicine*, 6, 179–187.

Dohrenwend, B.S., Dohrenwend, B.P., Dodson, M., and Shrout, P.E. (1984). Symptoms, hassles, social supports and life events: The problem of confounded measures. *Journal of Abnormal Psychology*, 93, 222–230.

Doll, R., Peto, R., Wheatley, K., Gray, R., and Sutherland, I. (1994). Mortality in relation to smoking: 40 years' observations on male British doctors. *British Medical Journal*, 309, 901–911.

Donovan, J.L., and Blake, D.R. (1992) Patient non-compliance: Deviance or reasoned decision-making. *Social Science and Medicine*, 34, 507–513.

Dovey-Pearce, G., Doherty, Y., and May, C. (2007). The influence of diabetes upon adolescent and young adult development: A qualitative study. *British Journal of Health Psychology*, 12, 75–91.

Durantini, M.R., Albarracín, D., Earl, A., and Mitchell, A.L. (2006). Conceptualizing the influence of social agents of change: A meta-analysis of HIV prevention interventions for different groups. *Psychological Bulletin*, 132, 212–248.

Eccleston, C., Morley, S., Williams, A., Yorke, L., and Mastroyannopoulou, K. (2002). Systematic review of randomized controlled trials of psychological therapy for chronic pain in children and adolescents, with a subset meta-analysis of pain relief. *Pain*, 99, 157–165.

Edwards, J.R., Baglioni, J.A.J., and Cooper, C.L. (1990). Stress. Type A, coping, and psychological and physical symptoms: A multi-sample test of alternative models. *Human Relations*, 43, 919–956.

EFPA (2006). EFPA Declaration 2006; The European standards of education and training in professional psychology – EuroPsy. www.psykologianopiskelijat.net/EuroPsy2006.pdf

Eisend, M. (2006). Two-sided advertising: A meta-analysis. *International Journal of Research in Marketing*, 23, 187–198.

Eisend, M. (2007). Understanding two-sided persuasion: An empirical assessment of theoretical approaches. *Psychology and Marketing*, 24, 615–640.

Ellis, J. (1998). 'Prospective memory and medicine-taking.' In: L.B. Myers, and K. Midence, (Eds), *Adherence to Treatment in Medical Conditions*. Amsterdam: Harwood Academic, 1113–1132.

Engbers, L.H., van Poppel, M.N.R., Chin, A., Paw, M.J.M., and van Mechelen, V. (2005). Worksite health promotion programs with environmental changes: A systematic review. *American Journal of Preventive Medicine*, 29, 61–70.

Ennis, N.E., Hobfoll, S.E., Schroder, K.E.E. (2000). Money doesn't talk, it swears: How economic stress and resistance resources impact inner-city women's depressive mood. *American Journal of Community Psychology*, 28, 149–173.

Epel, E.S., Blackburn, E.H., Lin, J., Dhabhar, F.S., Adler, N.E., Morrow, J.D., Cawthon, R.M. (2004a). Accelerated telomere shortening in response to life stress. *Proceedings of the National Academy of Sciences*, 101, 17312–17315.

Epel, E., Jimenez, S.Y., Brownell, K., Stroud, L., Stoney, C., and Niaura, R. (2004b). Are stress eaters at risk for the metabolic syndrome? *Annals of the New York Academy of Sciences*, 1032: 208–210.

Epstein, L.H. (1984). The direct effects of compliance on health outcome. *Health Psychology*, 3, 385–393.

Ernst, E., and Resch, K.L. (1995). Concept of true and perceived placebo. *British Medical Journal*, 311, 551–553.

Esterling, B.A., Antoni, M.H., Kumar, M., and Schneiderman, N. (1993). Defensiveness, trait anxiety, and Epstein–Barr viral capsit antigen antibody titers in health college students. *Health psychology*, 12, 132–139.

EuroPsyT (2001). A framework for education and training for psychologists in Europe. www.europsy.eu.com/framework/v5/

Evans, P.D., and Edgerton, N. (1991). Life-events and mood as predictors of the common cold. *British Journal of Medical Psychology*, 64, 35–44.

Evans, P.D., Doyle, F., Hucklebridge, F., and Clow, A. (1996). Positive but not negative life-events predict vulnerability to upper respiratory illness. *British Journal of Health Psychology*, 1, 339–348.

Everson, S.A., Kaplan, G.A., Goldberg, D.E., and Salonen, J.T. (1996a). Anticipatory blood pressure response to exercise predicts future high blood pressure in middle-aged men. *Hypertension*, 27, 1059–1064.

Everson, S.A., Goldberg, D.E., Kaplan, G.A., and Cohen, R.D. (1996b). Hopelessness and risk of mortality and incidence of myocardial infarction and cancer. *Psychosomatic Medicine*, 58, 103–121.

Everson, S.A., Lynch, J.W., Kaplan, G.A., Lakka, T.A., Sivenius, J., Salonen, J.T., et al. (2001). Stress-induced blood pressure reactivity and incident stroke in middle-aged men. *Stroke*, 32, 1263–1270.

Eysenck, H.J. (1967). *The Biological Basis of Personality*. Springfield, IL: Charles Thomas.

Eysenck, H.J., and Eysenck, S.B.G. (1964). *Eysenck Personality Inventory*. San Diego, CA: Education and Industry Testing Service.

Eysenck, M.W., and Matthews, A. (1987). 'Trait anxiety and cognition.' In: H.J. Eysenck and M. Martin (Eds), *Theoretical foundations of Behavior Therapy*. Dordrecht: Kluwer Academic/Plenum, 197–216.

Fawzy, F.I., Fawzy, N.W., Hyun, C.S., Elashoff, R., Guthrie, D., Fahey, J. L., et al (1993). Malignant melanoma. Effects of an early structured psychiatric intervention, coping, and affective state on recurrence and survival 6 years later. *Archives of General Psychiatry*, 50, 681–689.

Feldman, P.J., Cohen, S., Doyle, W.J., Skoner, D.P. and Gwaltney, J.M., Jr. (1999). The impact of personality on the reporting of unfounded symptoms and illness. *Journal of Personality and Social Psychology*, 77, 370–378.

Fernandez, E., and Turk, D.C. (1989). The utility of cognitive coping strategies for altering pain perception: A meta-analysis. *Pain*, 38, 123–135.

Festinger, L. (1957). *A Theory of Cognitive Dissonance*. Palo Alto, CA: Stanford University Press.

Fifield, J., McQuillan, J., Armeli, S., Tennen, H., Reisine, S., and Affleck, G. (2004). Chronic strain, daily work stress and pain among workers with rheumatoid arthritis: Does job stress make a bad day worse? *Work and Stress*, 18, 275–291.

Fishbein, M., and Ajzen, I. (1975). *Belief, Attitude, Intention Theory and Research*. Reading, MA: Addison-Wesley.

Fishbein, M., Triandis, H.C., Kanfer, F.H., Becker, M., Middlestadt, S.E., and Eichler, A. (2001). 'Factors influencing behavior and behavior change.' In: A. Baum, T.A. Revenson and J.E. Singer (Eds), *Handbook of Health Psychology*. Mahwah, NJ: Lawerence Erlbaum, 3–17.

Fisher, J.D. and Fisher, W.A. (1992). Changing AIDS-risk behavior. *Psychological Bulletin*, 111, 455–471.

Fisher, J.D., Fisher, W.A., Williams, S.S., and Malloy, T.E. (1994). Empirical tests of an Information-Motivation-Behavioral Skills model of AIDS preventive behavior. *Health Psychology*, 13, 238–250.

Fisher, J.D., Fisher, W.A., Bryan, A.D., and Misovich, S.J. (2002). Information-motivation-behavioral skills model-based HIV risk behavior change intervention for inner-city high school youth. *Health Psychology*, 21, 177–186.

Fiske, S.T., and Taylor, S.E. (1991). *Social Cognition*, (2nd Ed). New York: McGraw-Hill.

Flesch, R. (1948). A new readability yardstick. *Journal of Applied Psychology*, 32, 221–233.

Floyd, D.L., Prentice-Dunn, S., and Rogers, R.W. (2000). A meta analysis of research on protection motivation theory. *Journal of Applied Social Psychology*, 30, 407–429.

Fogel, J., Albert, S.M., Schnabel, F., Ditkoff, B.A., and Neugut, A.I. (2002). Internet use and social support in women with breast cancer. *Health Psychology*, 21, 398–404.

Folkman, S. (1997). Positive psychological states and coping with severe stress. *Social Science and Medicine*, 45, 1207–1221.

Folkman, S., and Lazarus, R.S. (1985). If it changes it must be a process: Study of emotion and coping during three stages of a college examination. *Journal of Personality and Social Psychology*, 48, 150–170.

Folkman, S., and Lazarus, R.S. (1988). *Ways of Coping Questionnaire Sampler Set: Manual, Test Booklet, Scoring Key*. Palo Alto, CA: Consulting Psychologists Press.

Folkman, S., and Moskowitz, J.T. (2000). Positive affect and the other side of coping. *American Psychologist*, 55, 647–654.

Folkman, S., and Moskowitz, J.T. (2004). Coping: Pitfalls and promise. *Annual Review of Psychology*, 55, 745–774.

Fordyce, W.E. (1976). *Behavioural Methods for Chronic Pain and Illness*. St Louis: Mosby.

Foster, N.E., Thomas, E., Barlas, P., et al. (2007). Acupuncture as an adjunct to exercise based physiotherapy for osteoarthritis of the knee: Randomised controlled trial. *British Medical Journal*, 335, 436 (doi:10.1136/bmj.39280.509803.BE).

Frattaroli, J. (2006). Experimental disclosure and its moderators: a meta-analysis. *Psychological Bulletin*, 132, 823–865.

Freeman, G.K., Horder, J.P., Shah, N.C., et al. (2002). Evolving general practice consultation in Britain: issues of length and context. *British Medical Journal*, 324, 880–882.

French, J.P.R. Jr., and Raven, B. (1960). 'The bases of social power.' In: D. Cartwright and A. Zander (Eds), *Group Dynamics*. New York: Harper and Row, 607–623.

Friedman, H.S. (2000). Long-term relations of personality and health: Dynamisms, mechanisms, tropisms. *Journal of Personality*, 68, 1089–1108.

Friedman, H.S., and Booth-Kewley, S. (1987). The disease-prone personality. *American Psychologist*, 42, 539–555.

Friedman, H.S., Tucker, J.S., Tomlinson-Keasay, C., Schwartz, J.E., Wingard, D.L., and Criqui, M.H. (1993). Does childhood personality predict longevity? *Journal of Personality and Social Psychology*, 65, 176–185.

Friedman, H.S., Tucker, J.S., Schwartz, J.E., et al. (1995). Childhood conscientiousness and longevity: Health behaviors and cause of death. *Journal of Personality and Social Psychology*, 68, 696–703.

Friedman, M., and Rosenman, R.H. (1974). *Type A Behavior and Your Heart*. New York: Knopf.

Friedman, R., Sobel, D., Myers, P., Caudill, M., and Benson, H. (1995) Behavioral medicine, clinical health psychology and cost offset. *Health Psychology*, 14, 509–518.

Frisina, P.G., Borod, J.C., and Lepore, S.J. (2004). A meta analysis of the effects of written emotional disclosure on the health outcomes of clinical populations. *Journal of Nervous and Mental Disease*, 192, 629–634.

Gallagher, E.J., Viscoli, C.M., and Horwitz, R.I. (1993). The relationship of treatment adherence to the risk of death after myocardial infarction in women. *Journal of the American Medical Association*, 270, 742–744.

Gallo, L.C., and Matthews, K.A. (2003). Understanding the association between socioeconomic status and physical health: Do negative emotions play a role? *Psychological Bulletin*, 129, 10–51.

Ganster, D.C., Mayes, B.T., Sime, W.E., and Tharp, G.D. (1982). Managing organizational stress: A field experiment. *Journal of Applied Psychology*, 67, 533–542.

Gatchel, R.J., Bo Peng, Y., Peters, M.L., Fuchs, P.H., and Turk, D.C. (2007) The biopsychosocial approach to chronic pain: Scientific advances and future directions. *Psychological Bulletin*, 133, 581–624.

Geyer, S. (1991). Life events prior to the manifestation of breast cancer: A limited prospective study covering eight years before diagnosis. *Journal or Psychosomatic Research*, 35, 355–363.

Gidron, Y., Davidson, K., and Bata, I. (1999). The short-term effects of a hostility-reduction intervention on male coronary heart disease patients. *Health Psychology*, 18, 416–420.

Giummarra, M.J., Gibson, S.J., Georgiou-Karistianis, N., and Bradshaw, J.L. (2007). Central mechanisms in phantom limb perception: The past, present and future. *Brain Research Reviews*, 54, 219–232.

Glasgow, R.E., Bull, S.S., Gillette, C., Klesges, L.M., and Dzewaltowski, D.M. (2002). Behavior Change Intervention Research in Healthcare Settings: A Review of recent reports with emphasis on external validity. *American Journal of Preventive Medicine*, 23, 62–69.

Glazier, R.H., Bajcar, J., Kennie, N.R., and Willson, K. (2006). A systematic review of interventions to improve diabetes care in socially disadvantaged populations. *Diabetes Care*, 29, 1675–1688.

Godin, G., and Conner, M. (2008). Intention-behavior relationship based on epidemiological indices: An application to physical activity. *American Journal of Health Promotion*, 22, 180–182.

Godin, G., Conner, M., and Sheeran, P. (2005). Bridging the intention-behavior 'gap': The role of moral norm. *British Journal of Social Psychology*, 44, 497–512.

Godin, G., Sheeran, P., Conner, M., and Germain, M. (2008). Asking questions changes behavior: Mere measurement effects on frequency of blood donation. *Health Psychology*, 27, 179–184.

Gollwitzer, P.M. (1990). 'Action phases and mind-sets.' In: E.T. Higgins and R.M. Sorrentino (Eds), *Handbook of Motivation and Cognition: Foundations of Social Behavior*. New York: Guilford Press, Vol. 2, 53–92.

Gollwitzer, P.M. (1993). Goal achievement: the role of intentions. *European Review of Social Psychology*, 4, 142–185.

Gollwitzer, P.M. (1999). Implementation intentions: Strong effects of simple plans. *American Psychologist*, 54, 493–503.

Gollwitzer, P.M., and Sheerna, P. (2006). Implementation intentions and goal achievement: A meta analysis of effects and processes. *Advances in Experimental Social Psychology*, 38, 69–121.

Goodwin, P.J., Leszcz, M., Ennis, M., Koopmans, J., Vincent, L., Guther, H., et al (2001). The effect of group psychosocial support on survival in metastatic breast cancer. *New England Journal of Medicine*, 345, 1719–1726.

Grandey, A.A., and Cropanzano, R. (1999). The conservation of resources model applied to work-family conflict and strain. *Journal of Vocational Behavior*, 54, 350–370.

Grant, K.E., Compas, B.E., Thurm, A.E., McMahon, S.D., and Gipson, P.Y. (2004). Stressors and child and adolescent psychopathology: Measurement issues and prospective effects. *Journal of Clinical Child and Adolescent Psychology*, 33, 412–425.

Green, A.S., Rafaeli, E., Bolger, N., Shrout, P.E., and Reis, H.T. (2006). Paper or plastic? Data equivalence in paper and electronic diaries. *Psychological Methods*, 11, 87–105.

Green, L.W., and Glasgow, R.E. (2006). Evaluating the relevance, generalization, and applicability of research: Issues in external validation and translation methodology. *Evaluation and the Health Professions*, 29, 126–153.

Greenglass, E.R., Schwarzer, R., and Taubert, S. (1999). The Proactive Coping Inventory (PCI): A multidimensional research instrument. Retrieved from http://userpage.fu-berlin.de/~health/greenpci.htm

Greenglass, E., Fiksenbaum, L., and Eaton, J. (2006). The relationship between coping, social support, functional disability and depression in the elderly. *Anxiety, Stress and Coping: An International Journal*, 19, 15–31.

Greenhaus, J.H., and Beutell, N.J. (1985). Sources of conflict between work and family roles. *Academy of Management Review*, 10, 76–80.

Greer, S., and Morris, T. (1975). Psychological attributes of women who develop breast cancer: A controlled study. *Journal of Psychosomatic Research*, 19, 147–153.

Greve, W. (2001). Traps and gaps in action explanation: Theoretical problems of a psychology of human action. *Psychological Bulletin*, 108, 435–451.

Grzywacz, J.G., and Bass, B.L. (2003). Work, family, and mental health: Testing different models of work-family fit. *Journal of Marriage and Family*, 65, 248–262.

Grzywacz, J.G., Casey, P.R., and Jones, F. (2007). The effects of workplace flexibility on health behaviors: a cross-sectional and longitudinal analysis. *Journal of Occupational and Environmental Medicine*, 49, 1302–1309.

Grzywacz, J.G., Jones, F., and Casey, P.R. (in press). 'Workplace flexibility: implications for worker health and families.' In: R.D. Crane (Ed.), *Handbook of Families and Work: Interdisciplinary Perspectives*. Lanham, MD: University Press of America.

Hadlow, J., and Pitts, M. (1991). The understanding of common terms by doctors, nurses and patients. *Social Science and Medicine*, 32, 193–196.

Haefner, D.P., and Kirscht, J.P. (1970) Motivational and behavioural effects of modifying health beliefs. *Public Health Reports*, 85, 478–484.

Haines, V.Y., III, Marchand, A., and Harvey, S. (2006). Crossover of workplace aggression experiences in dual-earner couples. *Journal of Occupational Health Psychology*, 11, 305–314.

Hallas, C.N. (2004). 'Health psychology within health service settings.' In S. Michie and C. Abraham (Eds), *Health Psychology in Practice*. Blackwell: Oxford, 353–371.

Halpern, D., Bates, C., Beales, G., and Heathfield, A. (on behalf of the Prime Minister's Strategy Unit, 2004). Personal Responsibility and Changing Behaviour: The State of Knowledge and its Implications for Public Policy. HMSO, London. www.pm.gov.uk/files/pdf/pr.pdf

Hampson, S.E., Andrews, J.A., Barckley, M., Lichenstein, E., and Lee, M.E. (2000). Conscientiousness, perceived risk and risk reduction behaviors: a preliminary study. *Health Psychology*, 19, 496–500.

Hampson, S., Goldberg, L.R., Vogt, T.M., and Dubanoski, J.P. (2006). Forty years on: Teachers' assessment of children's personality traits predict self-reported health behaviors and outcomes at mid life health. *Psychology*, 25, 57–64.

Hanson, E.K., Maas, C.J., Meijman, T.F., and Godaert, G.L. (2000). Cortisol secretion throughout the day, perceptions of the work environment, and negative affect. *Annals of Behavioral Medicine*, 22, 316–324.

Harrington, J., Noble, L.M., and Newman, S.P. (2004). Improving patients' communication with doctors: a systematic review of intervention studies. *Patient Education and Counselling*, 52, 7–16.

Harris, P.R., and Napper, L. (2005). Self-affirmation and the biased processing of threatening health-risk information. *Personality and Social Psychology Bulletin*, 31, 1250–1263.

Hay, J.L., Ford, J.S., Klein, D., et al. (2003). Adherence to colorectal cancer screening in mammography-adherent older women. *Journal of Behavioral Medicine*, 26, 553–576.

Haynes, C.E., Wall, T.D., Bolden, R.I., Stride, C., and Rick, J.E. (1999). Measures of perceived work characteristics for health services research: Test of a measurement model and normative data. *British Journal of Health Psychology*, 4, 257–284.

Haynes, R.B., Yao, X., Degani, A., Kripalani, S., Garg, A., and McDonald, H.P. (2005). Interventions for enhancing medication adherence. Cochrane Database of Systematic Reviews 2005, issue 4, art. no.: CD000011. DOI: 10.1002/14651858.CD000011. pub2.

Health and Safety at Work Act (1974). London: HMSO.

Heatherton, T.F., Herman, C.P., and Polivy, J. (1991). Effects of physical threat and ego threat on eating behavior. *Journal of Personality and Social Psychology*, 60, 138–143.

Heatherton, T.F., Herman, C.P., and Polivy, J. (1992). Effects of distress on eating: The importance of ego-involvement. *Journal of Personality and Social Psychology*, 62, 801–803.

Hedges, L.V., and Olkin, I. (1985). *Statistical Methods for Meta-analysis*. New York: Academic Press.

Hegel, M.T., Ayllon, T., Thiel, G., and Oulton, B. (1992). Improving adherence to fluid restrictions in makle hemodialysis patients: A comparison of cognitive and behavioural approaches. *Health Psychology*, 11, 324–330.

Helgeson, V.S., Reynolds, K.A., and Tomich, P.L. (2006). A meta-analytic review of benefit finding and growth. *Journal of Consulting and Clinical Psychology*, 74, 797–816.

Herbert, T.B., and Cohen, S. (1993). Depresssion and immunity: A meta-analytic review. *Psychological Bulletin*, 113, 472–486.

Hewitt, P.L., and Flett, G.L. (1996). 'Personality traits and the coping process.' In M. Zeidner and N.S. Endler (Eds), *Handbook of Coping: Theory, Research, Applications*. New York: Wiley, 410–433.

Hill, C., and Abraham, C. (2008). School-based, randomised controlled trial of an evidence-based condom promotion leaflet. *Psychology and Health*, 23, 41–56.

Hill, C., Abraham, C., and Wright, D. (2007). Can theory-based messages in combination with cognitive prompts promote exercise in classroom settings? *Social Science and Medicine*, 65, 1049–1058.

Hingson, R.W., and Howland, J. (2002). Comprehensive community interventions to promote health: Implications for college-age drinking problems. *Journal of Alcohol Studies Suppl* (14), 226–240.

Hobfoll, S. (1989). Conservation of resources: A new attempt at conceptualizing stress. *American Psychologist*, 44, 513–524.

Hobfoll, S. (2001). The influence of culture, community, and the nested-self in the stress process: Advancing conservation of resources theory. *Applied Psychology: an International Review*, 50, 337–421.

Hobfoll, S. (2007). General Resource Evaluation. Retrieved from www.personal.kent.edu/~shobfoll/COR-E.pdf October 2007.

Hochbaum, G.M. (1958) *Public Participation in Medical Screening Programs: A Socio-Psychological Study*. Public Health Service Publication No. 572. Washington, DC: United States Government Printing Office.

Holmes, T.H., and Masuda, M. (1974). 'Life change and illness susceptibility.' In: B.S. Dohrenwend and B.P. Dohrenwend (Eds), *Stressful Life Events: Their Nature and Effects*. London: John Wiley, 45–72.

Holmes, T.H., and Rahe, R.H. (1967). The social readjustment rating scale. *Journal of Psychosomatic Research*, 11, 213–218.

Holroyd, K., Nash, J., Pingel, J., Cordingley, G., and Jerome, A. (1991). A comparison of pharmacological (amitriptyline HCl) and nonpharmacological (cognitive-behavioral) therapies for chronic tension headaches. *Journal of Consulting and Clinical Psychology*, 59, 387–393.

Holroyd, K.A., O'Donnell, F.J., Stensland, M., Lipchik, G.L., Cordingley, G.E., and Carlson, B.W. (2001). Management of chronic tension-type headache with tricyclic antidepressant medication, stress management therapy and their combination. *Journal of the American Medical Association*, 285, 2208–2215.

Horn, S., and Munafo, M. (1997). *Pain: Theory, Research and Intervention*. Milton Keynes: Open University Press.

House of Lords (2000). *Select Committee on Technology and Science, Sixth Report*. London: HMSO. www.publications.parliament.uk/pa/ld199900/ldselect/ldsctech/123/12301.htm

House, J.S., Landis, K.R., and Umberson, D. (1988). Social relationships and health. *Science*, 241, 540–545.

Howie, J.R.G., Heaney, D.J., Maxwell, M., Walker, J.J., Freeman, G.K., and Rai, H. (1999). Quality at general practice consultations: Cross sectional survey. *British Medical Journal*, 319, 738–743.

Hro'bjartsson, A., and Gøtzsche, P.C. (2001). Is the placebo powerless? An analysis of clinical trials comparing placebo with no treatment. *New England Journal of Medicine*, 344, 1594–1602.

HSE (1995). *Stress at Work: A Guide for Employers*. Suffolk: HSE Books.

HSE (2007). The Management Standards. Retrieved on 30 November, 2007, from www.hse.gov.uk/stress/standards/standards.htm

Hughes, D. (1983). Consultation length and outcome in two group general practices. *Journal of the Royal College of General Practitioners*, 33, 143–147.

Jackson, P.R., Wall, T.D., Martin, R., and Davids, K. (1993). New measures of job control, cognitive demand, and production responsibility. *Journal of Applied Psychology*, 78, 753–762.

Jacobs, N., Myin-Germeys, I., Derom, C., Delespaul, P., van Os, J., and Nicolson, N.A. (2007). A momentary assessment study of the relationship between affective and adrenocortical stress responses in daily life. *Biological Psychology*, 74, 60–66.

Janz, N.K., and Becker, M.H. (1984). The health belief model: A decade later. *Health Education Quarterly*, 11, 1–47.

Jenkins, C.D., Zyzanski, S.J., and Rosenmann, R.H. (1971). Progress toward validation of a computer-scored test for the type a coronary-prone behavior pattern. *Psychosomatic Medicine*, 33, 193–202.

Jenkins, V., Fallowfield, L., and Saul, J. (2001). Information needs of patients with cancer: Results from a large study in UK cancer centres. *British Journal of Cancer*, 84, 48–51.

Jex, S.M., Adams, G.A., Elacqua, T.C., and Bachrach, D.G. (2002). Type A as a moderator of stressors and job complexity: A comparison of achievement strivings and impatience-irritability. *Journal of Applied Social Psychology*, 32, 977–996.

John, O.P., and Srivastava, S. (1999). 'The Big Five trait taxonomy: History, measurement, and theoretical perspectives.' In: L.A. Pervin and O.P. John (Eds), *Handbook of Personality: Theory and Research*, (2nd Ed.). New York: Guilford Press, 102–138.

Johnson, B.T., Carey, M.P., Chaudoir, S., and Reid, A.E. (2006). Sexual risk reduction for persons living with HIV: Research synthesis of randomized controlled trials, 1993 to 2004. *Journal of Acquired Immune Deficiency Syndromes*, 41, 642–650.

Johnson, J.V., and Hall, E.M. (1988). Job strain, work place social support and cardiovascular disease: A cross-sectional study of a random sample of the working population. *American Journal of Public Health*, 78, 1336–1342.

Johnston, D.W., Beedie, A., and Jones, M.C. (2006). Using computerized ambulatory diaries for the assessment of job characteristics and work-related stress in nurses. *Work and Stress*, 20, 163–172.

Jones, F., and Bright, J. (2001). *Stress: Myth, Theory and Research*. London: Prentice-Hall.

Jones, F., and Kinman, G. (2001). 'Approaches to studying stress.' In: F. Jones and J. Bright (Eds), *Stress: Myth, Theory and Research*. London: Prentice Hall, 17–45.

Jones, F., Bright, J.E.H., Searle, B., and Cooper, L. (1998). Modelling occupational stress and health: The impact of the demand-control model on academic research and on workplace practice. *Stress Medicine*, 14, 231–236.

Jones, F., Kinman, G., and Payne, N. (2006). 'Work stress and health behaviours: A work life balance issue.' In: F. Jones, R.J. Burke and M. Westman (Eds), *Work-life Balance: A Psychological Perspective*. Hove: Psychology Press, 185–215.

Jones, F., O'Connor, D.B., Conner, M., McMillan, B., and Ferguson, E. (2007). Effects of daily hassles and eating style on eating behavior. *Journal of Applied Psychology*, 92, 1731–1740.

Jones, P.K., Jones, S.L., and Katz, J. (1987). Improving compliance for asthmatic patients visiting the emergency department using a health belief model intervention. *Journal of Asthma*, 24, 199–206.

Kalat, J.W. (2004). *Biological Psychology*. New York: Thomson Wadsworth.

Kalichman, S.C., Benotsch, E.G., Weinhardt, L., Austin, J., Luke, W., and Cherry, C. (2003). Health-related internet use, coping, social support, and health indicators in people living with HIV/AIDS: Preliminary results from a community survey. *Health Psychology*, 22, 111–116.

Kamarck, T.W., and Lovallo, W.R. (2003). Cardiovascular reactivity to psychological challenge: Conceptual and measurement considerations. *Psychosomatic Medicine*, 65, 9–21.

Kaniasty, K.N., and Norris, F.H. (1993). How general is the cost of good fortune? Attempting to replicate Brown and McGill. *Journal of Social Behavior and Personality*, 8, 31–49.

Kanner, A.D., Coyne, J.C., Schaefer, C., and Lazarus, R.S. (1981). Comparison of two modes of stress measurement: Daily hassles and uplifts versus major life events. *Journal of Behavioral Medicine*, 4, 1–39.

Kaplan, R.M. (1990). Behavior as the central outcome in health care. *American Psychologist*, 45, 1211–1220.

Karasek, R.A. (1979). Job demands, job decision latitude and mental strain: Implications for job design. *Administrative Science Quarterly*, 24, 285–308.

Karasek, R.A. (1985). *Job Content Questionnaire and User's Guide*. Lowell, MA: Department of Work Environment, University of Massachusetts.

Karasek, R.A. (1989). 'Control in the workplace and its health related aspects.' In: S.L. Sauter, J.J. Hurrell and C.L. Cooper (Eds), *Job Control and Worker Health*. Chichester: Wiley, 129–160.

Karasek, R.A., and Theorell, T. (1990). *Healthy Work. Stress, Productivity and the Reconstruction of Working Life*. New York: Basic Books.

Kasl, S.V., and Cobb, S. (1966). Health behavior, illness behavior and sick role behavior. *Archives of Environmental Health*, 12, 246–266.

Kendler, K.S., Kessler, R.C., Walters, E.E., Maclean, C., Neale, M.C., Heath, A.C., et al (1995). Stressful life events, genetic liability, and onset of an episode of major depression in women. *American Journal of Psychiatry*, 152, 833–842.

Kendrick, A.H., Higgs, C.M., Whitfield, M.J., and Laszlo, G. (1993). Accuracy of perception of severity of asthma: patients treated in general practice. *British Medical Journal*, 14, 422–424.

Kennedy, A., Reeves, D., Bower, P., et al (2007) The effectiveness and cost effectiveness of a national lay-led self care support programme for patients with long-term conditions: A pragmatic randomised controlled trial. *Journal of Epidemiology and Community Health*, 61, 254–261.

Kessler, R.C. (1997). The effects of stressful life events on depression. *Annual Review of Psychology*, 48, 191–214.

Khaw, K.T., Wareham, N., Bingham, S., Welch, A., Luben, R., and Day, N. (2008). Combined impact of health behaviours and mortality in men and women: The EPIC-Norfolk prospective population study. *PLOS Medicine*, 5, (open access- DOI:10.1371). http://medicine.plosjournals.org/perlserv/?request=get-documentanddoi=10.1371/journal.pmed.0050012

Kidd, J., Marteau, T.M., Robinson, S., Ukoumunne, O.C., and Tydeman, C. (2004). Promoting patient participation in consultations: A randomized controlled trial to evaluate the effectiveness of three patient-focused interventions. *Patient Education and Counseling*, 52, 107–112.

Kiecolt-Glaser, J.K., Marucha, P.T., Malarkey, W.B., Mercado, A.M., and Glaser, R. (1995). Slowing of wound healing by psychological stress. *Lancet*, 346, 1194–1196.

Kiecolt-Glaser, J.K., Page, G.G., Marucha, P.T., MacCallum, R.C., and Glaser, R. (1998). Psychological influences on surgical recovery: Perspectives from psychoneuroimmunology. *American Psychologist*, 53, 1209–1218.

Kiecolt-Glaser, J.K., McGuire, L., Robles, T., and Glaser, R. (2002a). Emotions, morbidity, and mortality: New perspectives from psychoneuroimmunology. *Annual Review of Psychology*, 53, 83–107.

Kiecolt-Glaser J.K., McGuire L., Robles, T.F., and Glaser, R. (2002b) Psychoneuroimmunology. Psychological influences on immune function and health. *Journal of Consulting and Clinical Psychology*, 70, 537–547.

Kiesler, S., and Kraut, R. (1999). Internet use and ties that bind. *American Psychologist*, 54, 783–784.

King, A.C., Carl, F., Birkel, L., and Haskell, W.L. (1988). Increasing exercise among blue-collar employees: The tailoring of worksite interventions to meet specific needs. *Preventive Medicine*, 17, 357–365.

King, C.M., Rothman, A.J., and Jeffery, R.W. (2002). The challenge study: Theory-based interventions for smoking and weight-loss. *Health Education Research*, 17, 522–530.

King, J.B. (1982). The impact of patients' perceptions of high blood pressure on attendance at screening: An extension of the health belief model. *Social Science and Medicine*, 16, 1079–1091.

Kirsch, I., and Sapirstein, G. (1998). Listening to prozac but hearing placebo: a meta-analysis of antidepressant medication. *Prevention and Treatment*, 1, Article 0002a. http://journals.apa.org/prevention/volume 1/pre0010002a.html

Kirschbaum, C., Pirke, K.M., and Hellhammer, D.H. (1993). The 'Trier Social Stress Test' – a tool for investigating psychobiology stress responses in a laboratory setting. *Neuropsychobiology*, 28, 76–81.

Knott, D., Muers, S., and Aldridge, S. (2007). *Achieving Culture Change: A Policy Framework*. London: Cabinet Office, Prime Minister's Strategy Unit.

Knowler, W.C., Barrett-Connor, P.H.E., Fowler, S.E., et al. (2002). Reduction in the incidence of type 2 diabetes with lifestyle intervention or metformin. *New England Journal of Medicine*, 346, 393–403.

Knowles, E.S. and Rinner, D.D. (2007). 'Omega approaches to persuasion: Overcoming resistance.' In: A.R. Pratkanis (Ed.), *The Science of Social Influence: Advances and Future Progress*. New York: Psychology Press, 83–114.

Kok, H., Schaalma, H., Ruiter, R.A.C., and van Empelen, P. (2004). Intervention mapping: A protocol for applying health psychology theory to prevention programmes. *Journal of Health Psychology*, 9, 85–98.

Kolk, A., Hanewald, G.J.F.P., Schagen, S., and Gijsbers van Wijk, C.M.T. (2003). A symptom perception approach to common physical symptoms, *Social Science and Medicine*, 57, 2343–2354.

Koole, S.L., Dijksterhuis, A., and van Knippenberg, A. (2001). What's in a name: Implicit self-esteem and the automatic self. *Journal of Personality and Social Psychology*, 80, 669–685.

Kools, M., Van de Wiel, M.W.J., Ruiter, R.A.C., Crüts, A., and Kok, G. (2006). The effect of graphic organizers on subjective and objective comprehension of a health education text. *Health Education and Behavior*, 33, 760–772.

Korsch, B.M., Gozzi, E.K., and Francis, V. (1968). Gaps in doctor-patient communication: 1. Doctor-patient interaction and patient satisfaction. *Pediatrics*, 42, 855–871.

Krantz, D.S., and Manuck, S.B. (1984). Acute physiological reactivity and risk of cardiovascular disease: A review and methodological critique. *Psychological Bulletin*, 96, 435–464.

Kraut, R., Patterson, M., Lundmark, V., Kiesler, S., Mukopadhyay, T., and Scherlis, W. (1998). Internet paradox: A social technology that reduces social involvement and psychological well-being. *American Psychologist*, 53, 1017–1031.

Kraut, R., Kiesler, S., Boneva, B., Cummings, J.N., Helgeson, V., and Crawford, A.M. (2002). Internet paradox revisited. *Journal of Social Issues*, 58, 49–74.

Kudielka, B.M., Von Kanel, R., Gander, M., and Fischer, J.E. (2004). Effort reward imbalance, overcommitment and sleep in a working population. *Work and Stress*, 18, 167–179.

Kunz-Ebrecht, S.R., Mohamed-Ali, V., Feldman, P.J., Kirschbaum, C., and Steptoe, A. (2003). Cortisol responses to mild psychological stress are inversely associated with proinflammatory cytokines. *Brain, Behavior and Immunity*, 17, 373–383.

Lasikiewicz, N., Hendrickx, H., Talbot, D., and Dye, L. (2007). Exploration of basal diurnal salivary cortisol profiles in middle-aged adults: Associations with sleep quality and metabolic parameters. *Psychoneuroendocrinology*, 33, 143–151.

Lazarus, R.L. (1993). Coping theory and research: Past, present and future. *Psychosomatic Medicine*, 55, 234–247.

Lazarus, R.S. (1966). *Psychological Stress and the Coping Process*. New York: McGraw Hill.

Lazarus, R.S. (1990). Theory-based stress measurement. *Psychological Inquiry*, 1, 3–13.

Lazarus, R.S. (1999). *Stress and Emotion: A New Synthesis*. London: Springer.

Lazarus, R.S. (2001). Conservation of resources theory (COR): Little more than words masquerading as a new theory. *Applied Psychology: An International Review*, 50, 381–391.

Lazarus, R.S., and Folkman, S. (1984). *Stress, Appraisal and Coping*. New York: Springer.

Lazarus, R.S., Kanner, A.D., and Folkman, S. (1980). 'Emotions: a cognitive-phenomenological analysis.' In: R. Plutchik and H. Kellerman (Eds), *Theories of Emotion*. New York: Academic Press, 189–217.

LeShan, L. (1959). Psychological states as factors in the development of malignant disease. *Journal of the National Cancer Institute*, 22, 1–18.

Leventhal, H., Nerenz, D.R., and Steele, D.J. (1984). 'Illness representation and coping with health threats.' In: A. Baum, S.E. Taylor and J.E. Singer (Eds), *Handbook of Psychology and Health*. Hillsdale, NJ: Lawrence Erlbaum, 219–252.

Leventhal, H., Benyamini, Y., Brownlee, S., Diefenbach, M., Leventhal, E.A., Parker-Miller, L. and Robitail le, C. (1997). 'Illness representations: Theoretical foundations.' In: K.J. Petrie and J. Weinman (Eds), *Perceptions of Health and Illness: Current Research and Applications*. Amsterdam: Harwood Academic, 19–45.

Levine, J.D., Gordon, N., and Fields, H.L. (1978). The mechanism of placebo analgesia. *Lancet*, 23, 654–657.

Levy, B.R., Slade, M.D., Kunkel, S.R., and Kasl, S.V. (2002). Longevity increased by positive self-perceptions of aging. *Journal of Personality and Social Psychology*, 83, 261–270.

Ley, P. (1973). Communication in the clinical setting. *British Journal of Orthodontics*, 1, 173–177.

Ley, P. (1988) *Communicating with the Patient*. London: Croom Helm.

Ley, P., Whitworth, M., Skilbeck, C., Woodward, R., Pinsent, R., and Pike, L. (1976). Improving doctor-patient communications in general practice. *Journal of the Royal College of General Practitioners*, 26, 720–724.

Liang, J., Krause, N.M., and Bennett, J.M. (2001). Social exchange and well-being: Is giving better than receiving? *Psychology and Aging*, 16, 511–523.

Linden, W., Rutledge, T., and Con, A. (1998). A case for the usefulness of laboratory social stressors, *Annals of Behavioral Medicine*, 20, 310–316.

Litt, M.D., Tennen, H., Affleck, G., and Klock, S. (1992). Coping and cognitive factors in adaptation to in vitro fertilization failure. *Journal of Behavioral Medicine*, 15, 171–188.

Littell, J.H., and Girvin, H. (2002). Stages of change. A critique. *Behavior Modification*, 26, 223–273.

Little, P., Everitt, H., Williamson, I., et al (2001). Observational study of effect of patient centredness and positive approach on outcomes of general practice consultations. *British Medical Journal*, 323, 908–911.

Locke, E. (1991). Goal theory vs. control theory: Contrasting approaches to understanding work motivation. *Motivation and Emotion*, 15, 9–28.

Locke, E.A., and Latham, G.P. (2002). Building a practically useful theory of goal setting and task motivation. A 35-year odyssey. *American Psychologist*, 57, 705–717.

Lockwood, P., Wong, C., McShane, K., and Dolderman, D. (2005). The impact of positive and negative fitness exemplars on motivation, *Basic and Applied Social Psychology*, 27, 1–13.

Long, B.C., and Flood, K.R. (1993). Coping with work stress: Psychological benefits of exercise. *Work and Stress*, 1, 108–119.

Lorig, K., Mazonson, P.D., and Holman, H.R. (1993). Evidence suggesting that health education for self-management in patients with chronic arthritis has sustained health benefits while reducing health care costs. *Arthritis and Rheumatism*, 36, 439–446.

Lorig, K., Sobel, D., Stewart, et al (1999a) Evidence suggesting that a chronic disease self-management program can improve health status while reducing hospitalization. A randomized trial. *Medical Care*, 37, 5–14.

Lorig, K., Gonzalez, V.M., and Laurent, D. (1999b) *The Chronic Disease Self-Management Workshop Leaders' Manual*. Stanford: Stanford Patient Education Research Center, Stanford University.

Lovallo, W.R. (2005). *Stress and Health: Biological and Psychological Interactions*. Thousand Oaks, CA: Sage.

Lumley, M.A., Tojek, T.M., and MacKlem, D.J. (1999). 'The effects of written emotional disclosure among repressive and alexithymic people.' In: S.L. LePore and J.M. Smyth (Eds), *The Writing Cure*. Washington: American Psychological Association, 75–117.

Luszczynska, A., and Schwarzer, R. (2005). 'Social cognitive theory.' In: M. Conner and P. Norman (Eds), *Predicting Health Behaviour: Research and Practice with Social Cognition Models*, (2nd Ed.). Maidenhead: Open University Press, 127–169.

Luszczynska, A., Sobczyk, A., and Abraham, C. (2007) Planning to lose weight: RCT of an implementation intention prompt to enhance weight reduction among overweight and obese women. *Health Psychology*, 26, 507–512.

Maddux, J.E., and Rogers, R.W. (1983). Protection motivation and self-efficacy: A revised theory of fear appeals and attitude change. *Journal of Experimental Social Psychology*, 19, 469–479.

Major, D.A., and Germano, L.M. (2006). 'The changing nature of work and its impact on the work-family interface.' In: F. Jones, R.J. Burke, and M. Westman (Eds), *Work-life Balance: A Psychological Perspective*. Hove: Psychology Press, 13–38.

Major, V.S., Klein, K.J., and Ehrhart, M.G. (2002). Work time, work interference with family, and psychological distress. *Journal of Applied Psychology*, 87, 427–436.

Manuck, S.B., Kaplan, J.R., and Clarkson, T.B. (1983). Behaviourally induced heart rate reactivity and atherosclerosis in cynomolgus monkeys. *Psychosomatic Medicine*, 45, 95–108.

Manuck, S.B., Kaplan, J.R., Adams, M.R., and Clarkson, T.B. (1988). Studies of psychosocial influences on coronary artery atherogenesis in cynomolgus monkeys. *Health Psychology*, 7, 113–124.

Marlatt, G.A., and Donovan, D.M. (Eds) (2005). Relapse Prevention: Maintenance Strategies in the Treatment of Addictive Behaviors. New York: The Guildford Press.

Marmot, M.G., Davey-Smith, G.M., Stansfield, S., Patel, C., North, F., Head, J., et al (1991). Health inequalities among British civil servants: The Whitehall II study. *Lancet*, 337, 1387–1393.

Martin, R., Hewstone, M., and Martin, P.Y. (2007). Majority versus minority influence: the role of message processing in determining resistance to counter-persuasion. *European Journal of Social Psychology*, 38, 16–34.

Marucha, P.T., Kiecolt-Glaser, J.K., and Favagehi, M. (1998). Mucosal wound healing is impaired by examination stress. *Psychosomatic Medicine*, 60, 362–365.

Mason, J.W. (1971). A re-evaluation of the concept of 'non-specificity' in stress theory. *Journal of Psychiatric Research*, 8, 323–353.

Matarazzo, J.D. (1980) Behavioral health and behavioural medicine: Frontiers for a new health psychology. *American Psychologist*, 35, 807–817.

Matthews, K. (1988). Coronary heart disease and type a behavior: Update on and alternative to the Booth-Kewley and Friedman (1987) quantitative review. *Psychological Bulletin*, 104, 373–380.

Matthews, K.A., and Gump, B.B. (2002). Chronic work stress and marital dissolution increase risk of posttrial mortality in men from the multiple risk factor intervention trial. *Archives of Internal Medicine*, 162, 309–315.

Matthews, K.A., Woodall, K.L., Kenyon, K., and Jacob, T. (1996) Negative family environment as a predictor of boys' future status on measures of hostile attitudes, interview behaviour and anger expression. *Health Psychology*, 15, 30–37.

Matthews, K.A., Katholi, C.R., McCreath, H., Whooley, M.A., Williams, D.R., Zhu, S., and Markovitz, J.H. (2004). Blood pressure reactivity to psychological stress predicts hypertension in the CARDIA Study. *Circulation*, 110, 74–78.

McCabe, P.M., Schneiderman, N., Field, T., and Wellens, A.R. (Eds) (2000). *Stress, Coping, and Cardiovascular Disease*. Mahwah, NJ: Lawrence Erlbaum.

McCrae, R.R., and Costa, P.T. (1987). Validation of the five-factor model of personality across instruments and observers. *Journal of Personality and Social Psychology*, 54, 81–90.

McEwen, B.S. (1998). Protective and damaging effects of stress mediators. *New England Journal of Medicine*, 338, 171–179.

McEwen, B.S. (2007). Physiology and neurobiology of stress and adaptation: Central role of the brain. *Physiological Reviews*, 87, 873–904.

McEwen, B.S., and Stellar, E. (1993). Stress and the individual: Mechanisms leading to disease. *Archives of Internal Medicine*, 153, 2093–2101.

McGowan, L., Luker, K., Creed, F., and Chew-Graham, C.A. (2007). 'How do you explain a pain that can't be seen?': The narratives of women with chronic pelvic pain and their disengagement with the diagnostic cycle. *British Journal of Health Psychology*, 12, 261–274.

McLeod, J., and McLeod, J. (2001). How effective is workplace counseling? A review of the research literature. *Counselling and Psychotherapy Research*, 1, 184–190.

McNeil, A.D., Jarvis, M.J., Stapleton, J.A., Russell, M.A.H., Eiser, J.R., Gammage, P., and Gray, E.M. (1988). Prospective study of factors predicting uptake of smoking in adolescents. *Journal of Epidemiology and Community Health*, 43, 72–78.

Meissner, M. (1971). The long arm of the job: a study of work and leisure. *Industrial Relations*, 10, 239–423.

Melzack, R. (1999). From the gate to the neuromatrix. *Pain*, Suppl. 6, 121–6.

Melzack, R., and Wall, P.D. (1965). Pain mechanisms: a new theory. *Science*, 50, 971–979.

Michie, S., and Abraham, C. (Eds) (2004a). *Health Psychology in Practice*. Oxford: Blackwell.

Michie, S., and Abraham, C. (2004b). Interventions to change health behaviours: Evidence-based or evidence inspired? *Psychology and Health*, 19, 29–49.

Michie, S., Mills, J., and Weinman, J., (2003). Patient-centredness in chronic illness: what is it and does it matter? *Patient Education and Counselling*, 51, 197–206.

Michie, S., Johnston, M., and Abraham, C. (2004). 'Health psychology training: The UK model.' In: S. Michie and C. Abraham (Eds), *Health Psychology in Practice*. Oxford: Blackwell, 9–45.

Mielewczyk, F., and Willig, C. (2007). Old clothes and an older look: The case for a radical makeover in health behaviour research. *Theory Psychology*, 17, 811.

Milgram, S. (1974). *Obedience to Authority: An Experimental View*. New York: Harper and Row.

Miller, S.M., and Mangan, C.E. (1983). Interacting effects of information and coping style in adapting to gynecologic stress: Should the doctor tell all. *Journal of Personality and Social Psychology*, 45, 223–236.

Miller, S.M., Summerton, J., and Brody, D.S. (1988). Styles of coping with threat: Implications for health. *Journal of Personality and Social Psychology*, 54, 142–148.

Miller, T.Q., Turner, C.W., Tindale, R.S., Posavac, E.J., and Dugoni, B.L. (1991). Reasons for the trend towards null findings in research on type a behavior. *Psychological Bulletin*, 110, 469–485.

Miller, T.Q., Smith, T.W., Turner, C.W., Guijarro, M.L., and Hallet, A.J. (1996). A meta-analytic review of research on hostility and physical health. *Psychological Bulletin*, 119, 322–348.

Miller, G.E., Cohen, S., Ritchey, A.K. (2002). Chronic psychological stress and the regulation of pro-inflammatory cytokines: A glucocorticoid resistance model. *Health Psychology*, 21, 531–541.

Milne, S., Orbell, S., and Sheeran, P. (2002). Combining motivational and volitional interventions to promote exercise participation: Protection motivation theory and implementation intentions. *British Journal of Health Psychology*, 7, 163–184.

Moher, D., Schultz, K.F., Altman, D.G., and the CONSORT Group (2001). The CONSORT statement: Revised recommendations for improving the quality of reports of parallel-group randomized trials. *Lancet*, 357, 1191–1194.

Mokdad, A.H., Marks, J.S., Stroup, D.F., and Gerberding, J.L. (2004). Actual causes of death in the United States, 2000. *Journal of the American Medical Association*, 291, 1238–1245.

Moncrieff, J., and Kirsch, I. (2005). Efficacy of antidepressants in adults. British Medical Journal, 331, 155-157.

Morisky, D.E., Green, L.W., and Levine, D.M. (1986) Concurrent and predictive validity of a self-report measure of medication adherence. *Medical Care*, 24, 67–74.

Morley, S., Eccleston, C., and Williams, A. (1999). Systematic review and meta-analysis of randomised controlled trials of cognitive behaviour therapy and behaviour therapy for chronic pain in adults, excluding headache. *Pain*, 80, 1–13.

Moscovici, S. (1976). *Social Influence and Social Change*. London: Academic Press.

Moscovici, S., and Lage, E. (1976). Studies in social influence III: Majority versus minority influence in a group. *European Journal of Social Psychology*, 6, 149–174.

Moskowitz, J.T., Epel, E.S., and Acree, M. (2008). Positive affect uniquely predicts lower risk of mortality in people with diabetes. *Health Psychology*, 27, (Suppl.), S73–S82.

Mullen, P.D. (1997). Compliance becomes concordance. *British Medical Journal*, 314, 691–692.

Murcott, T. (2006). *The Whole Story; Alternative medicine on trial?* (2nd Ed.) Noundsmills, Basingstoke: Macmillan.

Murphy, L.R. (2003). 'Stress management at work: Secondary prevention of stress.' In M.J. Schabracq, J.A.M. Winnubst and C.L. Cooper (Eds), *The Handbook of Work and Health Psychology*, (2nd Ed.). Chichester: Wiley, 533–548.

Murray, M., and Chamberlain, K. (Eds 1999). *Qualitative Health Psychology: Theories and Methods*. London: Sage.

Myers, L., and Abraham, C. (2005). Beyond 'doctor's orders'. *The Psychologist*, 18, 680–683.

Myers, L.B., and Midence, K. (1998) 'Concepts and issues in adherence.' In L.B. Myers and K. Midence (Eds), *Adherence to Treatment in Medical Conditions*. Amsterdam: Harwood Academic Publishers, 1–24.

Myers, L.B., Vetere, A., and Derakshan, N. (2004). Are suppression and repressive coping related? *Personality and Individual Differences*, 36, 1009–1013.

Myrtek, M. (2001). Meta-analyses of prospective studies on coronary heart disease, type A personality, and hostility. *International Journal of Cardiology*, 79, 245–251.

National Audit Office (2002). *NHS Direct in England: Report by the Comptroller and Auditor General*. London: The Stationery Office.

National Institute for Clinical Excellence (2004). Depression: Management of depression in primary and secondary care. Clinical practice guideline No 23. London: NICE. www.nice.org.uk/page.aspx?o=235213

National Institute of Health and Clinical Excellence (NICE) (2007). Behaviour change at population, community and individual levels. Public Health Guidance 6. London: NICE. www.nice.org.uk/guidance/index.jsp?action=byIDando=11868

National Statistics. (2002). The National Statistics Socio-Economic Classification User Manual. Retrieved on 1 December, 2007, from www.statistics.gov.uk/nsbase/methods_quality/ns_sec/downloads/NS-SEC_User.pdf

Nebel, L.E., Howell, R.H., Krantz, D.S., Falconer, J.J., Gottdiener, J.S., and Gabbay, F.H. (1996). The circadian variation of cardiovascular stress levels and reactivity: relationship to individual differences in morningness/eveningness. *Psychophysiology*, 33, 273–281.

Neisser, U. (1967). *Cognitive Psychology*. New York: Appleton-Century-Crofts.

Newman, E., O'Connor, D.B., and Conner, M. (2007). Daily hassles and eating behaviour: The role of cortisol reactivity status. *Psychoneuroendocrinology*, 32, 125–132.

Newton, T.L., and Contrada, R.J. (1992). Repressive coping and verbal–autonomic response dissociation: The influence of social context. *Journal of Personality and Social Psychology*, 62, 159–167.

Nezlek, J.B. (2001). Multilevel random coefficient analyses of event- and interval-contingent data in social and personality psychology research. *Personality and Social Psychology Bulletin*, 27, 771–785.

Niaura, R., Herbert, P.N., McMahon, N., and Sommerville, L. (1992). Repressive coping and blood lipids in men and women. *Psychosomatic Medicine*, 54, 698–706.

Niedhammer, I., Tek, M-L., Starke, D., and Siegrist, J. (2004). Effort-reward imbalance model and self-reported health: Cross-sectional and prospective findings from the GAZEL cohort. *Social Science and Medicine*, 58, 1531–1541.

NIOSH (2004). What is OHP? Retrieved from www.cdc.gov/niosh/ohp.html#whatis

Norman, P., and Conner, M. (2005). 'Predicting and changing health behaviour: Future directions.' In: M. Conner and P. Norman (Eds), *Predicting Health Behaviour: Research and Practice with Social Cognition Models*, (2nd Ed.) Maidenhead: Open University Press, 324–371.

Norman, P., and Parker, S. (1996). The interpretation of change in verbal reports: Implications for health psychology. *Psychology and Health*, 11, 301–314.

Norman, P., Boer, H., and Seydel, E.R. (2005). 'Protection motivation theory.' In: M. Conner and P. Norman (Eds), *Predicting Health Behaviour: Research and Practice with Social Cognition Models*, (2nd Ed.). Maidenhead: Open University Press, 81–126.

Nuttin, J.M. (1987). Affective consequences of mere ownership: The name letter effect in twelve European languages. *European Journal of Social Psychology*, 17, 381–402.

O'Brien, T.B., and Delongis, A. (1996). The interactional context of problem-, emotion-, and relationship-focused coping: The role of the big five personality factors. *Journal of Personality*, 64, 775–811.

O'Connor, D.B., and Ashley, L. (in press). Are alexithymia and emotional characteristics of disclosure associated with blood pressure reactivity and psychological distress following written emotional disclosure? *British Journal of Health Psychology*.

O'Connor, R.C., and O'Connor, D.B. (2003). Predicting hopelessness and psychological distress: The role of perfectionism and coping. *Journal of Counseling Psychology*, 50, 362–372.

O'Connor, D.B., and O'Connor, R.C. (2004). Perceived changes in food intake in response to stress: The role of conscientiousness. *Stress and Health*, 20, 279–291.

O'Connor, D.B., O'Connor, R.C., White, B.L., and Bundred, P.E. (2000a). Job strain and ambulatory blood pressure in British general practitioners: A preliminary study. *Psychology, Health and Medicine*, 5, 241–250.

O'Connor, D.B., O'Connor, R.C., White, B.L., and Bundred, P.E. (2000b). The effect of job strain on British general practitioners' mental health. *Journal of Mental Health*, 9, 637–654.

O'Connor, D.B., Archer, J., and Wu, F.C.W. (2004). Effects of testosterone on mood, aggression and sexual behavior in young men: A double-blind, placebo-controlled, cross-over study. *Journal of Clinical Endocrinology and Metabolism*, 89, 2837–2845.

O'Connor, D.B., Ferguson, E., and O'Connor, R.C. (2005). Intentions to use hormonal male contraception: the role of message framing, attitudes and stress appraisals. *British Journal of Psychology*, 96, 351–369.

O'Connor, D.B., O'Connor, R.C., and Marshall, R. (2007). Perfectionism and psychological distress: Evidence of the mediating effects of rumination. *European Journal of Personality*, 21, 429–452.

O'Connor, D.B., Jones, F., Conner, M., McMillan, B., and Ferguson, E. (2008a). Effects of daily hassles and eating style on eating behaviour. *Health Psychology*, 27, S20–S31.

O'Connor, D.B., Corona, G., Forti, G. et al, the EMAS study group (in press). Assessment of sexual health in ageing men in Europe: Development and validation of the European Male Ageing Study (EMAS) Sexual Function Questionnaire (EMAS-SFQ). Journal of Sexual Medicine.

O'Driscoll, M. Brough, P., and Kalliath, T. (2006). 'Work-family conflict and facilitation.' In: F. Jones, R.J. Burke and M. Westman (Eds), *Work-life Balance: A Psychological Perspective*. Hove: Psychology Press, 117–142.

Oettingen, G. (1996). 'Positive fantasy and motivation.' In: P.M. Gollwitzer and J.A. Bargh (Eds), *The Psychology of Action: Linking Cognition and Motivation to Behavior*. New York: Guilford Press, 236–259.

Ogden, J. (2003). Some problems with social cognition models: A pragmatic and conceptual analysis. *Health Psychology*, 22, 424–428.

Orbell, S., and Hagger, M.S. (2006). Temporal framing and the decision to take part in type 2 diabetes screening: Effects of individual differences in consideration of future consequences on persuasion. *Health Psychology*, 25, 537–548.

Orbell, S., Crombie, I., and Johnston, G. (1995). Social cognition and social structure in the prediction of cervical screening uptake. *British Journal of Health Psychology*, 1, 35–50.

Orbell, S., Perugini M., and Rakow, T. (2004). Individual differences in sensitivity to health communications: Consideration of future consequences. *Health Psychology*, 23, 388–396.

Ormell, J., and Wohlfarth, T. (1991). How neuroticism, long-term difficulties, and life situation change influence psychological distress: A longitudinal model. *Journal of Personality and Social Psychology*, 60, 744–755.

Osterhouse, R.A., and Brock, T.C. (1970). Distraction increases yielding to propaganda by inhibiting counterarguing. *Journal of Personality and Social Psychology*, 13, 334–358.

Ouwehand, C., de Ridder, D.T., and Bensing, J.M. (2007). A review of successful aging models: Proposing proactive coping as an important additional strategy. *Clinical Psychology Review*, 27, 873–884.

Ozer, D.J., and Benet-Martinez, V. (2006). Personality and the prediction of consequential outcomes. *Annual Review of Psychology*, 57, 401–421.

Parkes, K.R. (1991). Locus of control as a moderator: An explanation for additive versus interactive findings in the demand-discretion model of work stress? *British Journal of Psychology*, 82, 291–312.

Paulussen, T., Kok, G., and Schaalma, H. (1994). Antecedents of adoption of classroom-based HIV-education in secondary schools. *Health Education Research*, 9, 485–496.

Payne, S. (2004). 'Designing and conducting qualitative studies.' In: S. Michie and C. Abraham (Eds), *Health Psychology in Practice*. Blackwell, Oxford, 126–149.

Payne, S., Large, S., Jarrett, N., and Turner, P. (2000). Written information given to patients and families by palliative care units: A national survey. *Lancet*, 355, 1792.

Pendleton, D., Schofield, T., Tate, P., and Havelock, P. (1984). *The Consultation: An Approach to Learning and Teaching*. Oxford: Oxford University Press.

Penley, J.A., and Tomaka, J. (2002). Associations among the Big Five, emotional responses and coping with acute stress. *Personality and Individual Differences*, 32, 1215–1128.

Pennebaker, J.W. (1997). Writing about emotional experiences as a therapeutic process. *Psychological Science*, 8, 162–166.

Peterson, C. (2000). The future of optimism. *American Psychologist*, 55, 44–55.

Peterson, C., and Seligman, M.E.P. (1987). Explanatory style and illness. *Journal of Personality*, 55, 237–265.

Peterson, C., Vaillant, G.E., and Seligman, M.E.P. (1988) Pessimistic explanatory style is a risk factor for physical illness: A thirty-five-year longitudinal study. *Journal of Personality and Social Psychology*, 55, 23–27.

Petrie, K.J., Booth, R.J., Pennebaker, J.W., Davison, K.P., and Thomas, M.G. (1995). Disclosure of trauma and immune response to a hepatitis B vaccination program. *Journal of Consulting and Clinical Psychology*, 63, 787–792.

Petrie, K.J., Fontanilla, I., Thomas, M.G., Booth, R.J., and Pennebaker, J.W. (2004). Effect of written emotional expression on immune function in patients with human immunodeficiency virus infection: A randomised trial. *Psychosomatic Medicine*, 66, 272–275.

Petticrew, M., Fraser, J.M., and Regan, M.F. (1999). Adverse life events and risk of breast cancer: A meta-analysis. *British Journal of Health Psychology*, 4, 1–17.

Petty R.E., Cacioppo, J.T. (1986) 'The elaboration likelihood model of persuasion.' In: L. Berkowitz (Ed.), *Advances in Experimental Social Psychology*. New York: Academic Press, 19, 123–205.

Pierce, G.R., Sarason, I.G., and Sarason, B.R. (1991). General and relationship-based perceptions of social supports: Are two constructs better than one? *Journal of Personality and Social Psychology*, 61, 1028–1039.

Pikhart, H., Bobak, M., Siegrist, et al (2001). Psychosocial work characteristics and self rated health in four post-communist countries. *Journal of Epidemiology and Community Health*, 55, 624–630.

Pittet, D. (2002). Promotion of hand hygiene: Magic, hype, or scientific challenge? *Infection Control and Hospital Epidemiology*, 23, 118–119.

Pittet, D.S., Hugonnet, S., Harbarth, P., Mourouga, V., Sauvan, S., Touveneau, and Perneger, T.V. (2000). Effectiveness of a hospital-wide programme to improve compliance with hand hygiene. *Lancet*, 356, 1307–1312.

Pollock, K. (1988). On the nature of social stress: Production of a modern mythology. *Social Science and Medicine*, 26, 381–392.

Popper, K. (1963). *Conjecture and Refutation*. London: Routledge and Kegan Paul.

Porcelli, P., Tulipani, C., Maiello, E., Cilenti, G., and Todarello, O. (2007). Alexithymia, coping, and illness behavior correlates of pain experience in cancer patients. *Psycho-oncology*, 16, 644–650.

Porter, M. (2004). 'Deciding to consult.' In: B. Alder, M. Porter, C. Abraham and E. van Teijlingen (Eds), *Psychology and Sociology: Applied to Medicine*, (2nd Ed.). Edinburgh: Churchill Livingstone, 86–87.

Pratkanis, A.R. (2007). 'Social influence analysis: An index of tactics.' In: A.R. Pratkanis (Ed.), *The Science of Social Influence: Advances and Future Progress*. New York: Psychology Press, 17–82.

Pressman, S.D., and Cohen, S. (2005). Does positive affect influence health? *Psychological Bulletin*, 131, 925–971.

Prime Minister's Strategy Unit (2004). *Personal Responsibility and Changing Behaviour: The State of Knowledge and its Implications for Public Policy*. HMSO, London. www.pm.gov.uk/files/pdf/pr.pdf

Prochaska, J.O., and DiClemente, C.C. (1984). *The Transtheoretical Approach: Crossing Traditional Boundaries of Therapy*. Homewood, IL: Dow Jones Irwin.

Prochaska, J.O., Velicer, W.F., Guadagnoli, E., Rossi, J.S., and DiClemente, C.C. (1991). Patterns of change: Dynamic topology applied to smoking cessation. *Multivariate Behavioral Research*, 26, 83–107.

Prochaska, J.O., DiClemente, C.C., and Norcross, J.C. (1992). In search of how people change: Applications to addictive behaviors. *American Psychologist*, 47, 1102–1114.

Prochaska, J.O., Velicer, W.F., Fava, J.L., et al (2001). Counselor and stimulus control enhancements of a stage-matched expert system intervention for smokers in a managed care setting. *Preventive Medicine*, 32, 23–32.

Proper, K.I., Koning, M., van der Beck, A.J., Hildebrandt, V.H., Bosscher, R.J., and van Mechelen, W. (2003). The effectiveness of worksite psychical activity programs on physical activity, fitness and health. *Clinical Journal of Sport Medicine*, 13, 106–117.

Protheroe, D., Turvey, K., Horgan, K., Benson, E., Bowers, D., and House, A. (1999). Stressful life events and difficulties and onset of breast cancer: Case control study. *British Medical Journal*, 319, 1027–1030.

Quitkin, F.M., Rabkin, J.G., Gerald, J. Davis, J.M., and Klein, D.F. (2000). Validity of clinical trials of antidepressants. *American Journal of Psychiatry*, 157, 327–337.

Rabin, B.S. (1999). *Stress, Immune Function and Health: The Connection*. New York: Wiley.

Ragland, D.R., and Brand, R.J. (1985). Coronary heart disease mortality in the western collaborative group study: Follow-up experience of 22 years. *American Journal of Epidemiology*, 127, 462–475.

Rahe, R.H., and Paasikivi, J. (1971). Psychosocial factors and myocardial infarction: An outpatient study in Sweden. *Journal of Psychosomatic Research*, 8, 35–44.

Randall, R., Griffiths, A., and Cox, T. (2005). Evaluating organizational stress-management interventions using adapted study designs. European *Journal of Work and Organizational Psychology*, 14, 23–41.

Rank, S.G., and Jacobson, C.K. (1977). Hospital nurses' compliance with medication over-dose orders: A failure to replicate. *Journal of Health and Social Behavior*, 18, 188–193.

Reed, G.M., Kemeny, M.E., Taylor, S.E., Wang, H.-Y.J., and Vissher, B.R. (1994). Realistic acceptance as a predictor of decreased survival time in gay men with AIDS. *Health Psychology*, 13, 299–307.

Reid, L.D., and Christensen, D.B. (1988). A psychosocial perspective in the explanation of patients' drug-taking behaviour. *Social Science and Medicine*, 27, 277–285.

Repetti, R.L. (1994). Short-term and long-term processes linking job stressors to father-child interaction. *Social Development*, 3, 1–15.

Repetti, R.L., and Wood, J. (1997). Effects of daily stress at work on mothers' interactions with preschoolers. *Journal of Family Psychology*, 11, 90–108.

Reynolds, J.S., and Perrin, N.A. (2004). Mismatches in social support and psychosocial adjustment to breast cancer. *Health Psychology*, 23, 425–430.

Rhodes, R.E., Courneya, K.S., and Hayduk, L.A. (2002). Does personality moderate the theory of planned behavior in the exercise domain? *Journal of Sport and Exercise Psychology*, 24, 120–132.

Riazi, A., Pickup, J., and Bradley, C. (2004). Daily stress and glycaemic control in Type 1 diabetes: Individual differences in magnitude, direction, and timing of stress-reactivity. *Diabetes Research and Clinical Practice*, 66, 237–244.

Rietveld, S., and Prins, P.J.M. (1998). The relationship between negative emotions and acute subjective and objective symptoms of childhood asthma. *Psychological Medicine*, 28, 407–415.

Rivis, A., and Sheeran, P. (2003). Descriptive norms as an additional predictor in the theory of planned behaviour: A meta-analysis. *Current Psychology: Developmental, Learning, Personality, Social*, 22, 218–233.

Robinson, E.J., and Whitfield, M.J. (1985). Improving the efficacy of patients' comprehension monitoring: A way of increasing patients' participation in general practice consultations. *Social Science Medicine*, 21, 915–9.

Rodgers, W., Conner, M., and Murray, T. (in press). Distinguishing among perceived control, perceived difficulty and self-efficacy as determinants of intentions and behaviours. *British Journal of Social Psychology*.

Roediger, H.L., III, and Karpicke, J.D. (2006). The power of testing memory: Basic research and implication for educational practice. *Perspectives on Psychological Science*, 1, 181–210.

Rogers, E.M. (2003). *Diffusion of Innovations*, (5th Ed.). New York: Free Press.

Rollnick, S., and Miller, W.R. (1995). What is motivational interviewing? *Behavioural and Cognitive Psychotherapy*, 23, 325–334.

Rook, K.S. (1984). The negative side of social interaction: Impact on psychological well-being. *Journal of Personality and Social Psychology*, 46, 1097–1108.

Rosen, M.I., Rigsby, M.O., Salahi, J.T., Ryan, E., and Cramer, J.A. (2004). Electronic monitoring and counseling to improve medication adherence. *Behaviour Research and Therapy*, 42, 409–422.

Rosenberg, M. (1979). *Conceiving the Self*. New York: Basic Books.

Rosenman, R.H., Friedman, M., Straus, R., Wurm, M., Kositchek, R., Hahn, W., and Werthessen, N.T. (1964). A predictive study of coronary heart disease. *Journal of the American Medical Association*, 189, 15–22.

Rosenman, R.H., Brand, R.J., Sholtz, R.I., and Friedman, M. (1976). Multivariate prediction of coronary heart disease during 8.5 year follow-up in the western collaborative group study. *American Journal of Cardiology*, 37, 903–910.

Rosenstock, I.M., Strecher, V.J., and Becker, M.H. (1988) Social learning theory and the health belief model. *Health Education Quarterly*, 15, 175–83.

Rosenthal, R., and Rubin, D.B. (1982). A simple general purpose display of magnitude of experimental effect. *Journal of Educational Psychology*, 74, 166–169.

Roter, D.L., Hall, J.A., Merisca, R., Nordstrom, B., Cretin, D., and Svarstad, B. (1998). Effectiveness of interventions to improve patient compliance: A meta-analysis. *Medical Care*, 36, 1138–1161.

Rothman, A.J. (2000). Toward a theory-based analysis of behavioral maintenance. *Health Psychology*, 19, 64–69.

Rothman, A.J., and Salovey, P. (1997). Shaping perceptions to motivate healthy behavior: The role of message framing. *Psychological Bulletin*, 121, 3–19.

Rothman, A., Salovey, P., Antone, C., Keough, K., and Martin, C. (1993). The influence of message framing on intentions to perform health behaviors. *Journal of Experimental Social Psychology*, 29, 408–433.

Rovelli, M., Palmeri, D., Vossler, E., Bartus, S., Hull, D. and Shweizer, R. (1989). Compliance in organ transplant recipients. *Transplantation Proceedings*, 21, 833–844.

Ruiter, R.A.C., Abraham, C., and Kok, G. (2001). Scary warnings and rational precautions: A review of the psychology of fear appeals. *Psychology and Health*, 16, 613–630.

Ruiter, R.A.C., Kessels, L., Jansma, B.M., and Brug, J. (2006). Increased attention for computer-tailored health communications: An event-related potential study. *Health Psychology*, 25, 300–306.

Rutledge, T., and Hogan, B.E. (2002). A quantitative review of prospective evidence linking psychological factors with hypertension development. *Psychosomatic Medicine*, 64, 758–766.

Sackett, D.L., and Snow, J.C. (1979) 'The magnitude of compliance and non-compliance.' In: R.B. Haynes, D.W. Taylor and D.L. Sackett (Eds), *Compliance in Health Care*. Baltimore: Johns Hopkins University Press, 11–22.

Sapolsky, R.M. (1993). Endocrinology alfresco: Psychoendocrine studies of wild baboons. *Recent Progress in Hormone Research*, 48, 437–468.

Sapolsky, R.M. (1998). *Why Zebras Don't Get Ulcers*. New York: W.H. Freeman.

Sarafino, E. (2008). *Health Psychology: Biopsychosocial Interaction*, (6th Ed.). New York: Wiley.

Sargent, R.P., Shepard, R.M., and Glantz, S.A. (2004). Reduced incidence of admissions for myocardial infarction associated with public smoking ban: Before and after study. *British Medical Journal*, 328, 977–980.

Savage, R., and Armstrong, D. (1990). Effects of a general practitioner's consulting style on patients' satisfaction: A controlled study. *British Medical Journal*, 301, 968–970.

Scharloo, M., Kaptein, A.A., Weinman, J.A., Willems, L.N.A., and Rooijmans, H.G.M. (2000). Physical and psychological correlates of functioning in patients with chronic obstructive pulmonary disease. *Journal of Asthma*, 37, 17–29.

Scheier, M.F., and Carver, C.S. (1987). Dispositional optimism and physical well-being: The influence of generalized outcome expectations on health. *Journal of Personality*, 55, 169–210.

Scheier, M.F., and Carver, C.S. (1992). Effects of optimism on psychological and physical well-being: Theoretical overview and empirical update. *Cognitive Therapy and Research*, 16, 201–228.

Scheier, M.F., Weintraub, J.K., and Carver, C.S. (1986). Coping with stress: Divergent strategies of optimists and pessimists. *Journal of Personality and Social Psychology*, 51, 1257–1264.

Scheier, M.F., Matthews, K.A., Owens, J., Magovern, G.J. Sr., Lefebvre, R.C., Abbott, R.A., and Carver, C.S. (1989). Dispositional optimism and recovery from coronary artery bypass surgery: The beneficial effects of physical and psychological well-being. *Journal of Personality and Social Psychology*, 57, 1024–1040.

Scheier, M.F., Matthews, K.A., Owens, J., et al. (1999). Optimism and rehospitalization after coronary artery bypass graft surgery. *Archives of Internal Medicine*, 159, 829–835.

Schinke, S.P., and Gordon, A.N. (1992). 'Innovative approaches to interpersonal skills training for minority adolescents.' In: R.J. DiClemente (Ed.), *Adolescents and AIDS; A Generation in Jeopardy*. Newbury Park, CA: Sage.

Schneider, G.M., Jacobs, D.W., Gevirtz, R.N., and O'Connor, D.T. (2003). Cardiovascular haemodynamic response to repeated mental stress in normotensive subjects at genetic risk of hypertension: Evidence of enhanced reactivity, blunted adaptation, and delayed recovery. *Journal of Human Hypertension*, 17, 829–840.

Schuler, J.L., and O'Brien, W.H. (1997). Cardiovascular recovery from stress and hypertension risk factors: A meta-analytic review. *Psychophysiology*, 34, 649–665.

Schwartz, G.E. (1980). Testing the biopsychosocial model: The ultimate challenge facing behavioural medicine? *Journal of Consulting and Clinical Psychology*, 50, 1040–1053.

Schwartz, J.E., Neale, J., Marco, C., Shiffman, S.S., and Stone, A.A. (1999). Does trait coping exist? A momentary assessment approach to the evaluation of traits. *Journal of Personality and Social Psychology*, 77, 360–369.

Schwartz, M.D., Taylor, K.L., Willard, K.S., Siegel, J.E., Lamdan, R.M., and Moran, K. (1999). Distress, personality, and mammography utilization among women with a family history of breast cancer. *Health Psychology*, 18, 327–332.

Schwarzer, R. (2001). Stress, resources and proactive coping. *Applied Psychology: An International Review*, 50, 400–407.

Schwarzer, R. (2008). Modeling health behavior change: How to predict and modify the adoption and maintenance of health behaviors. *Applied Psychology: An International Review*, 57, 1–29.

Sears, S.R., Stanton, A.L., and Danoff-Burg, S. (2003). The yellow brick road and the emerald city: Benefit finding, positive reappraisal coping and posttraumatic growth in women with early-stage breast cancer. *Health Psychology*, 22, 487–497.

Segerstrom, S.C., Taylor, S.E., Kemeny, M.E., and Fahey, J.L. (1998). Causal attributions predict rate of immune decline in HIV-seropositive gay men. *Health Psychology*, 15, 485–493.

Selye, H. (1950). Stress and the general adaptation syndrome. *British Medical Journal*, 1, 1383–1392.

Selye, H. (1956). *The Stress of Life*. New York: McGraw-Hill.

Shaw, M., Davey Smith, G., and Dorling, D. (2005). Health inequalities and New Labour: How the promises compare with real progress. *British Medical Journal*, 330, 1016–1021.

Sheeran, P. (2002). 'Intention-behaviour relations: A conceptual and empirical review.' In: M. Hewstone and W. Stroebe (Eds), *European Review of Social Psychology*. Chichester: Wiley, 12, 1–36.

Sheeran, P., and Abraham, C. (2003). Mediator of moderators: Temporal stability of intention and the intention-behavior relationship. *Personality and Social Psychology Bulletin*, 29, 205–215.

Sheeran, P., Abraham C., and Orbell, S. (1999). Psychosocial correlates of heterosexual condom use: A meta-analysis. *Psychological Bulletin*, 125, 90–132.

Sheeran, P., Conner, M., and Norman, P. (2001). Can the theory of planned behavior explain patterns of behavior change? *Health Psychology*, 20, 12–19.

Sheeran, P., Milne, S., Webb, T.L., and Gollwitzer, P.M. (2005). 'Implementation intentions and health behaviours.' In: M. Conner and P. Norman (Eds), *Predicting Health Behaviour: Research and Practice with Social Cognition Models* (2nd Ed.). Maidenhead: Open University Press, 276–323.

Sher, L. (2004). Daily hassles, cortisol, and the pathogenesis of depression. *Medical Hypotheses*, 62, 198–202.

Sherif, M. (1936). *The Psychology of Social Norms*. New York, Harper.

Sherman, S.J. (1980). On the self-erasing nature of errors of prediction. *Journal of Personality and Social Psychology*, 39, 211–221.

Shimuzu, M., and Pelham, B.W. (2004). The unconscious cost of good fortune: Implicit and explicit self-esteem, positive life events, and health. *Health Psychology*, 23, 101–105.

Shipley, B.A., Weiss, A., Der, G., Taylor, M.D., and Deary, I.J. (2007). Neuroticism, extraversion, and mortality in the UK health and lifestyle survey: A 21-year prospective cohort study. *Psychosomatic Medicine*, 69, 923–931.

Siegel, P.A., Post, C., Brockner, J., Fishman, A.Y., and Garden, C. (2005). The moderating influence of procedural fairness on the relationship between work-life conflict and organizational commitment. *Journal of Applied Psychology*, 90, 13–24.

Siegler, I.C., Feaganes, J.R., and Rimer, K. (1995). Predictors of adoption of mammography in women under age 50. *Health Psychology*, 14, 274–278.

Siegrist, J. (1996). Adverse health effects of high-effort/low-reward conditions. *Journal of Occupational Health Psychology*, 1, 27–41.

Siegrist, J. (2002). Effort-reward imbalance at work and health. *Historical and Current Perspectives on Stress and Health*, 2, 261–291.

Siegrist, J. (2005). Effort reward imbalance at work. Institut für Medizinische Soziologie der Heinrich Heine Universität Düsseldorf. Retrieved from www.uni-duesseldorf.de/MedicalSociology/Effort-reward_imbalance_at_wor.112.0.html

Siegrist, J., Peter, R., Cremer, P., and Seidel, D. (1997). Chronic work stress is associated with atherogenic lipids and elevated fibrinogen in middle aged men. *Journal of Internal Medicine*, 242, 149–156.

Silverman, J., Kurtz, S., and Draper, J. (2005). *Skills for Communicating with Patients* (2nd Ed.). Oxford: Radcliffe Medical Press.

Simpson, M., Buckman, R., Stewart, M., Maguire, P., Lipkin, M., Novack, D., and Till, J. (1991). Doctor-patient communication: the Toronto consensus statement. *British Medical Journal*, 303, 1385–1387.

Skinner, B.F. (1938). *The Behavior of Organisms*. New York: Appleton-Century-Crofts.

Skinner, B.F. (1974). *About Behaviorism*. New York: Knopf.

Skinner, E.A., Edge, K., Altman, J., and Sherwood, H. (2003). Searching for the structure of coping: A review and critique of category systems for classifying ways of coping. *Psychological Bulletin*, 129, 216–269.

Skinner, T.C., Hampson, S.E., and Fife-Schaw, C. (2002). Personality, personal model beliefs, and self-care in adolescents and young adults with type 1 diabetes. *Health Psychology*, 21, 61–70.

Sloan, D.M., and Marx, B.P. (2004). Taking pen to hand: Evaluating theories underlying the written disclosure paradigm. *Clinical Psychology: Science and Practice*, 11, 121–137.

Smedslund, G., and Ringdal, I.R. (2004). Meta-analysis of the effects of psychocosial interventions on survival time in cancer patients. *Journal of Psychosomatic Research*, 57, 123–131.

Smith, A., Johal, S., Wadsworth, E., and Britain, G. (2000). *The Scale of Occupational Stress: The Bristol Stress and Health and Work Study.* London: HSE Books.

Smith, J. (Ed.) (2003). *Qualitative Psychology: A Practical Guide to Research Methods* (2nd Ed.). London: Sage.

Smith, J.A., and Osborn, M. (2007). Pain as an assault on the self: An interpretative phenomenological analysis. *Psychology and Health*, 22, 517–531.

Smith, T.W. (1994). 'Concepts and methods in the study of anger, hostility, and health.' In: A.G. Seigman and T.W. Smith (Eds), *Anger, Hostility and the Heart.* Hillsdale, NJ: Lawrence Erlbaum, 23–42.

Smith, T.W., Glazer, K., Ruiz, J.M., and Gallo, L.C. (2004). Hostility, anger, aggressiveness, and coronary heart disease: An interpersonal perspective on personality, emotion, and health. *Journal of Personality*, 72, 1217–1270.

Smyth, J., Ockenfels, M.C., Porter, L., Kirschbaum C., Hellhammer, D.H., and Stone, A.A. (1998). Stressors and mood measured on a momentary basis are associated with salivary cortisol secretion. *Psychoneuroendocrinology*, 23, 353–370.

Smyth, J.M. (1998). Written emotional expression: effect sizes, outcome types, and moderating variables. *Journal of Consulting and Clinical Psychology*, 66, 174–184.

Smyth, J.M., Stone, A.A., Hurewitz, A., and Kaell, A. (1999). Effects of writing about stressful experiences on symptom reduction in patients with asthma or rheumatoid arthritis: A randomized trial. *Journal of the American Medical Association*, 281, 1304–1309.

Snow, H. (1893). *Cancer and the Cancer Process.* London: J. and A. Churchill.

Snyder, C.R., Sympson, S.C., Ybasco, F.C., Borders, T.F., Babyak, M.A., and Higgins, R.L. (1996). Development and evaluation of the State Hope Scale. *Journal of Personality and Social Psychology*, 70, 321–335.

Somerfield, M.R. (1997). The utility of systems models of stress and coping for applied research. *Journal of Health Psychology*, 2, 133–151.

Spiegel, D., Bloom, J.R., Kraemer, H.C., and Gottheil, E. (1989). Effect of psychosocial treatment on survival of patients with metastatic breast cancer. *Lancet*, 2, 888–891.

Staines, G.L. (1980). Spillover versus compensation: A review of the literature on the relationship between work and non-work. *Human Relations*, 33, 111–129.

Stajkovic, A.D., and Luthans, D. (1998). Self-efficacy and work-related performance: A meta-analysis. *Psychological Bulletin*, 124, 240–261.

Steele, C.M. (1988). 'The psychology of self-affirmation: Sustaining the integrity of the self.' In: L. Berkowitz (Ed.), *Advances in Experimental Social Psychology.* San Diego, CA: Academic Press, 21, 261–302.

Steele, G.P., Henderson, S., and Duncan-Jones, P. (1980). The reliability of reporting adverse experiences. *Psychological Medicine*, 10, 301–306.

Steptoe, A., and Marmot, M. (2005). Impaired cardiovascular recovery following stress predicts 3-year increases in blood pressure. *Journal of Hypertension*, 23, 529–536.

Steptoe, A., Hamer, M., and Chida, Y. (2007). The effects of acute psychological stress on circulating inflammatory factors in humans: A review and meta-analysis. *Brain Behavior and Immunity*, 21, 901–912.

Sterling, P., and Eyer, J. (1988). 'Allostasis: A new paradigm to explain arousal pathology.' In: S. Fisher and J. Reason (Eds), *Handbook of Life Stress, Cognition and Health.* New York: Wiley, 629–640.

Stewart, M.A. (1995). Effective physician-patient communication and health outcomes: A review. *Canadian Medical Association Journal*, 152, 1423–1433.

Stewart-Williams, S. (2004). The placebo puzzle: Putting together the pieces. *Health Psychology*, 23, 198–206.

Stone, A.A., Shiffman, S., Schwartz, J.E., Broderick, J.E., and Hufford, M.R. (2002). Patient non-compliance with paper diaries. *British Medical Journal*, 324, 1193–1194.

Stone, J., Aronson, E., Crain, A.L., Winslow, M.P. and Fried, C.B. (1994). Inducing hypocrisy as a means of encouraging young adults to use condoms. *Personality and Social Psychology Bulletin*, 20, 116–128.

Stronks, K., van de Mheen, H., Looman, C.W.N., and MacKenbach, J.P. (1998). The importance of psychosocial stressors for socioeconomic inequalities in perceived health. *Social Science and Medicine*, 46, 611–623.

Sultan, S., Epel, E., Sachon, C., Vaillant, G., and Hartemann-Heurtier, A. (2008). A longitudinal study of coping, anxiety and glycemic control in adults with type 1 diabetes. *Psychology and Health*, 23, 73–89.

Sutton, S. (1997). Predicting and explaining intentions and behavior: How well are we doing? *Journal of Applied Social Psychology*, 28, 1317–1338.

Sutton, S. (2000). 'A critical review of the transtheoretical model applied to smoking cessation.' In: P. Norman, C. Abraham and M. Conner (Eds), *Understanding and Changing Health Behaviour: From Health Beliefs to Self-regulation*. Reading: Harwood Academic Press, 207–225.

Sutton, S. (2005). 'Stage models of health behaviour.' In: M. Conner and P. Norman (Eds), *Predicting Health Behaviour: Research and Practice with Social Cognition Models* (2nd Ed.). Maidenhead: Open University Press, 223–275.

Swientek, B (2001). Let them eat cake: Mad cow disease prevention in Europe. http://findarticles.com/p/articles/mi_m3289/is_1_170/ai_70204304 (accessed 7 June 7, 2007).

Symmons, D., Turner, G., Webb, R., Barrett, E., Lunt, M., Scott, D. and Silman, A. (2002). The prevalence of rheumatoid arthritis in the United Kingdom: New estimates for a new century. *Rheumatology*, 41, 793–800.

Taylor, A.H. (2000). 'Physical activity, anxiety, and stress.' In: S.J.H. Biddle, K.R. Fox and S.H. Boutcher (Eds), *Physical Activity and Psychological Well-Being*. London: Routledge, 10–45.

Temoshok, L., Heller, B.W., Sagabiel, R., et al. (1985). The relationship of psychosocial factors to prognostic indicators in cutaneous malignant melanoma. *Journal of Psychosomatic Research*, 29, 139–154.

Tennen, H., Affleck, G., Coyne, J.C., Larsen, R.J., and DeLongis, A. (2006). Paper and plastic in daily diary research: Comment on Green, Rafaeli, Bolger, Shrout, and Reis. *Psychological Methods*, 11, 112–118.

Terry, D. (1994). Determinants of coping: the role of stable and situational factors. *Journal of Personality and Social Psychology*, 66, 895–910.

The EPIC-Norfolk Prospective Population Study (2008). *PLOS Medicine*, 5, (open access-DOI:10.1371).

Theorell, T., and Rahe, R.H. (1971). Psychosocial factors and myocardial infarction. *Journal of Psychosomatic Research*, 15, 25–31.

Tolman, E.C. (1948). Cognitive maps in rats and men. *Psychological Review*, 55, 189–208.

Tortolero, S.R., Markham, C.M., Parcel, G.S., et al. (2005). Using intervention mapping to adapt an effective HIV, sexually transmitted disease, and pregnancy prevention program for high-risk minority youth. *Health Promotion Practice*, 6, 286–298.

Totman, R. (1975). Cognitive dissonance and the placebo response: The effect of differential justification for undergoing dummy injections. *European Journal of Social Psychology*, 5, 441–456.

Triplett, N. (1898). The dynamogenic factors in pacemaking and competition. *American Journal of Psychology*, 9, 507–533.

Turk, D.C., and Burwinkle, T.M. (2000). Clinical outcomes, cost-effectiveness, and the role of psychology in treatments for chronic pain sufferers. *Professional Psychology: Research and Practice*, 36, 602–610.

Turk, D.C., and Salovey, P. (1986). 'Clinical information processing: Bias inoculation.' In: R.E. Ingham (Ed.), *Information Processing Approaches to Clinical Psychology*. New York: Academic Press, 305–323.

Turk, D.C., Meichenbaum, D., and Genest, M. (1983). *Pain and Behavioural Medicine: A Cognitive-Behavioral Perspective*. New York: Guildford.

Turner, J.C. (1991). *Social Influence*. Buckingham: Open University Press.

Tversky, A., and Kahneman, D. (1981). The framing of decisions and the psychology of choice. *Science*, 211, 453–458.

Twisk, J.W.R., Snel, J., Kemper, H.C.G., and van Mechelen, W. (1999). Changes in daily hassles and life events and the relationship with coronary heart disease risk factors: A 2-year longitudinal study in 27–29-year-old males and females. *Journal of Psychosomatic Research*, 46, 229–240.

Tyler, R. (2001). BSE/'mad cow disease' crisis spreads throughout Europe. www.wsws.org/articles/2001/jan2001/bse-j23.shtml (accessed 7 June, 2007).

Uchino, B.N., Cacioppo, J.T., and Kiecolt-Glaser, J.K. (1996). The relationship between social support and physiological processes. A review with emphasis on underlying mechanisms and implications for health. *Psychological Bulletin*, 119, 488–531.

Vaananen, A., Buunk, B.P., Kivimaki, M., Pentti, J., and Vahtera, J. (2005). When it is better to give than to receive: Long-term health effects of perceived reciprocity in support exchange. *Journal of Personality and Social Psychology*, 89, 176–193.

van dem Knesebeck, O., and Siegrist, J. (2003). Reported nonreciprocity of social exchange and depressive symptoms: Extending the model of effort-reward imbalance beyond work. *Journal of Psychosomatic Research*, 55, 209–214.

Van der Doef, M., and Maes, S. (1998). The job demand-control (-support) model and physical outcomes: A review of the strain and buffer hypotheses. *Psychology and Health*, 13, 909–936.

Van der Doef, M., and Maes, S. (1999). The job demand-control (-support) model and psychological well-being: A review of 20 years of empirical research. *Work and Stress*, 13, 87–114.

van der Klink, J.L., Blonk, R.W.B., Schene, A.H., and van Dijk, F.J.H. (2001). The benefits of interventions for work-related stress. *American Journal of Public Health*, 91, 270–276.

Van Vegchel, N.V., De Jonge, J., Meijer, T., and Hamers, J.P.H. (2001). Different effort constructs and effort-reward imbalance: Effects on employee well-being in ancillary health care workers. *Journal of Advanced Nursing*, 34, 128–136.

Van Vegchel, N.V., De Jonge, J., and Landsbergis, P.A. (2005). Occupational stress in (inter)action: The interplay between job demands and job resources. *Journal of Organizational Behavior*, 26, 535–560.

Vartiainen, E., Paavola, M., McAlister, A., and Puska, P. (1998). Fifteen-year follow-up of smoking prevention effects in the North Karelia Youth Project. *American Journal of Public Health*, 88, 81–85.

Vas, J., Méndez, C., Perea-Milla, E., et al (2004). Acupuncture as a complementary therapy to the pharmacological treatment of osteoarthritis of the knee: Randomised controlled trial. *British Medical Journal*, 329, 1216 DOI:10.1136/bmj.38238.601447.3A

Vedhara, K., and Irwin, M. (2005). *Human Psychoneuroimmunology*. Oxford: Oxford University Press.

Vickers, A., and Zollman, C. (1999). ABC of complementary medicine: The manipulative therapies: Osteopathy and chiropractic. *British Medical Journal*, 319, 1176–1179.

Vollrath, M., Knoch, D., and Cassano, L. (1999). Personality, risky behaviour and perceived susceptibility to health risks. *European Journal of Personality*, 13, 39–50.

Vollrath, M.E. (Ed.) (2006). *Handbook of Personality and Health*. Chichester: Wiley.

Waldron, I. (1988). Why do women live longer than men? *Journal of Human Stress*, 2, 2–13.

Waldstein, S.R., Kauhanen, J., Neumann, S.A., and Katzel, L.I. (2002). Alexithymia and cardiovascular risk in older adults: Psychosocial, psychophysiological and biomedical correlates. *Psychology and Health*, 17, 597–610.

Wanless, D. (2002). *Securing Our Future Health: Taking A Long-Term View*. London: HMSO.

Wardle, J., and Steptoe, A. (1991). The European health and behaviour survey: Rationale, methods and initial results from the United Kingdom. *Social Science and Medicine*, 33, 925–936.

Ware, J.E., Kosinski, M., and Keller, S.D. (1996). A 12-item short-form health survey: Construction of scales and preliminary tests of reliability and validity. *Medical Care*, 34, 220–233.

Warr, P. (1987). *Work, Unemployment and Mental Health*. Oxford: Oxford University Press.

Watson, D. (1988). Intraindividual and interindividual analyses of positive and negative affect: Their relation to health complaints, perceived stress, and daily activities. *Journal of Personality and Social Psychology*, 54, 1020–1030.

Watson, D., and Clark, L.A. (1984). Negative affectivity: The disposition to experience aversive emotional states. *Psychological Bulletin*, 96, 465–490.

Watson, D., and Hubbard, B. (1996). Adaptational style and dispositional structure: coping in the context of the five factor model. *Journal of Personality*, 64, 737–774.

Watson, D., and Pennebaker, J.W. (1989). Health complaints, stress and distress: exploring the central role of negative affectivity. *Psychological Review*, 96, 234–254.

Webb, T.L., and Sheeran, P. (2006). Does changing behavioral intentions engender behavior change? A meta-analysis of the experimental evidence. *Psychological Bulletin*, 132, 249–268.

Weinberger, D.A., Schwartz, G.E., and Davidson, R.J. (1979). Low-anxious, high-anxious, and repressive coping styles: Psychometric patterns and behavioral and physiological responses to stress. *Journal of Abnormal Psychology*, 88, 369–380.

West, R. (2005). Time for a change: Putting the transtheoretical (stages of change) model to rest. *Addiction*, 100, 1036–1039.

West, R., McNeill, A., and Raw, M. (2000). Smoking cessation guidelines for health professionals: An update. *Thorax*, 55, 987–999.

Westman, M. (2001). Stress and strain crossover. *Human Relations*, 54, 557–591.

Whelan, J. (2002). WHO calls for countries to shift from acute to chronic care. *British Medical Journal*, 324, 1237.

White, K. (2000). Psychology and complementary and alternative medicine. *Professional Psychology; Research and Practice*, 31, 671–681.

Whitlock, J.L., Powers, J.L., and Eckenrode, J. (2006). The virtual cutting edge: The internet and adolescent self-injury. *Developmental Psychology*, 42, 407–417.

WHOQOL Group (1995). The World Health Organisation Quality of Life Assessment (The WHOQOL): Position paper from the World Health Organisation. *Social Science and Medicine*, 41, 1403–1409.

Wiedenfeld, S.A., O'Leary, A., Bandura, A., Brown, S., Levine, S., and Raska, K. (1990) The impact of perceived self-efficacy in coping with stressors on components of the immune system. *Journal of Personality and Social Psychology*, 59, 1082–1094.

Wight, D., Raab, G.M., Henderson, M., Abraham, C., Buston, K., Hart, G., and Scott, S. (2002). Limits of teacher-delivered sex education: interim behavioural outcomes from randomised trial. *British Medical Journal*, 320, 1243–1244.

Wilkinson, R.G. (1992). National mortality rates: The impact of inequality? *American Journal of Public Health*, 82, 1082–1084.

Wilkinson, R.G. (1996). *Unhealthy Societies: The Afflictions of Inequality*. Routledge, London.

Wilkinson, R.G. (1997). Health inequalities: Relative or absolute material standards? *British Medical Journal*, 314, 591–595.

Williams, K.J., and Alliger, G.M. (1994). Role stressors, mood spillover, and perceptions of work-family conflict in employed parents. *Academy of Management Journal*, 37, 837–868.

Williams, L., O'Connor, R.C., Howard, S., et al (2008). Type D personality mechanisms of effect: The role of health-related behaviour and social support. *Journal of Psychosomatic Research*, 64, 63–69.

Williams-Piehota, P., Pizarro, J., Schneider, T.R., Mowad, L., and Salovey, P. (2005). Matching health messages to monitor-blunter coping styles to motivate screening mammography. *Health Psychology*, 24, 58–67.

Willis, T.A., O'Connor, D.B., and Smith, L. (2005). The influence of morningness-eveningness on anxiety and cardiovascular responses to stress. *Physiology and Behavior*, 85, 125–133.

Winnubst, J.A.M., Buunk, B.P., and Marcelissen, F.H.G. (1988). 'Social support and stress: Perspectives and processes.' In: S. Fisher and J. Reason (Eds), *Handbook of Life Stress, Cognition and Health*. Chichester: Wiley, 511–528.

Witte, K. (1992). Putting the fear back into fear appeals: The extended parallel process model. *Communication Monographs*, 59, 329–349.

Witte, K., and Allen, M. (2000). A meta-analysis of fear appeals: Implications for effective public health campaigns. *Health Education and Behavior*, 27, 591–615.

Wittrock, M.C., and Alesandrini, K. (1990). Generation of summaries and analogies and analytic-holistic abilities. *American Educational Research Journal*, 27, 489–502.

Wood, R.E., and Bandura, A. (1989). Impact of conceptions of ability on self-regulatory mechanisms and complex decision making. *Journal of Personality and Social Psychology*, 56, 407–415.

Wood, W., Kallgren, C.A., and Mueller Preisler, R. (1985). Access to attitude-relevant information in memory as a determinant of persuasion: The role of message attributes. *Journal of Experimental Social Psychology*, 21, 73–85.

World Health Organization (1948). Preamble to the Constitution of the World Health Organization as adopted by the International Health Conference, New York, 19–22 June, 1946; signed on 22 July 1946 by the representatives of 61 States (Official Records of the World Health Organization, 2, 100) and entered into force on 7 April 1948.

Wright, C.C., Barlow, J.H., Turner, A.P., and Bancroft, G.V. (2003). Self-management training for people with chronic disease: An exploratory study. *British Journal of Health Psychology*, 8, 465–476.

Yates, L.B., Djousse, L., Kurth, T., Buring, J.E., and Gaziano, J.M. (2008). Exceptional longevity in men: Modifiable factors associated with survival and function to age 90 years. *Archives of Internal Medicine*, 168, 284–290.

Zautra, A.J. (2003). *Emotions, Stress and Health*. New York: Oxford University Press.

Zola, I.K. (1973). Pathways to the doctor – from person to patient. *Social Science and Medicine*, 7, 677–689.

Index

A-beta fibres 28
A-delta fibres 28
accident and emergency departments, health belief
        intervention in 141
accident-prone personality 123
accidents 111
achievement-striving 117
ACTH (adrenocorticotrophic hormone) 23
action-outcome expectancies (social cognitive
        theory) 145, 146
action planning 176, 197
action stage (stage model) 147, 148
active interventions 192, 193
active jobs 71
acupuncture 226
adaptation, diseases of (Selye) 44
adaptive responses, protection motivation
        theory 142
additive effects 94
Ader, R., Cohen, N., psychoneuroimmunology 31
adherence to professional advice 213–17, 230–1
    interventions improving 215–17
    long-term illness 227
    placebo effects 223, 225
adoption (in RE-AIM framework) 202–3
adrenal glands 21
adrenaline 21, 23
    common cold and 34
    socio-economic status 68
adrenocorticotrophic hormone 23
aetiological correlates 2–3
affective–autonomic response discrepancy 93
afferent pathways, pain 28
affiliation motive 165
age
    health behaviours 136
    on normative influence 192
    stress recovery 61
ageing
    optimism 113
    research 233–4
    stress 233
agreeableness 126, 127
    hostility and 117
Ajzen, I., and Fishbein, M., on social cognition
        models 150–1, 152
alarm phase, stress response 44
alcohol, on mortality 3
alexithymia 92, 111
    emotional writing 99

allostatic load 44–5, 46 (Fig.)
    on stress recovery 61
alternative medicine, see complementary therapies
anaesthetics, psychological response to surgery 35
analgesics, chronic pain management 229–30
analysis of covariance (ANCOVA) 128
analysis of variance (ANOVA) 128
analytic truths, Ogden on SCMs 151
angina 24
animal studies
    dominance hierarchies 66–7
    stress reactivity 60
anorexia nervosa, negative effects of websites 106
antibody-mediated immunity 32
anticipated regret, intention–behaviour gap and 153
anxiety
    confusion with hassles 54–5
    emotion-focused coping and 90
    reduction, placebo effects from 224–5
    repressive coping 92–3
    on self-efficacy 174
    stress management training on 80
appraisal of situations 52, 88, 96
    as confounding variable 54
    perceived social support 100, 101
    positive reappraisal 97–9
    secondary 88, 224
    threats, protection motivation theory 142
arousal levels
    coping styles and 93–4
    self-efficacy and 174
arthritis
    self-management course 174–5
    see also rheumatoid arthritis
assertiveness training 186
assessment, professional competencies in 239
assessment of needs, intervention mapping 199
asthma, patients' assessment of symptoms 211
atherosclerosis 24
athletes, placebo effects 225
attitudes
    change 168–71
    message framing and 164, 192
    theory of planned behaviour 143–4, 145
attributional styles
    hostility 117
    optimistic 114
attributions, optimism vs pessimism 112–13
attrition rates, research on behaviour change
        interventions 201

authority 167
autonomic nervous system 20, 36
average weighted correlations, knowledge *vs* condom
    use 162
avoidance coping 91
axons 18

B-lymphocytes 32
behaviour 10
    see also health behaviours
behavioural contracts 197
behavioural pathways 3–4, 16
    eating behaviour 56
behavioural skills 184–6, 199
    condom use 192
behaviourism
    origins 5
    see also classical conditioning; operant
        conditioning
beliefs
    about symptoms 211–13
    see also health belief model
benefit finding, in coping 97–9
benefits of stress 43, 48
    at work 68
bereavement
    gender on effects 100
    positive affect and 96–7
beta blockers, placebos *vs*, mortality 223
Big Five Taxonomy, personality types 110
binomial effect size display, SCMs 152
biofeedback 79, 230
biopsychosocial model 6, 15–38
blood circulation 21–2
blood donation, mere measurement effect on
        volunteering 152
blood pressure 22
    stress recovery 61
    see also hypertension
blunting (coping style) 93–4
body-self neuromatrix 30
books
    Health Psychology 9–11
    learning from 6–7
brain 16–18, 36
breast cancer
    internet use 105
    life events 51
    optimism 113
    self-examination for 163–4
    social support 102
    see also mammography
breathing difficulties, prompts for consultations
        210–11

British Psychology Society 239
    Division of Health Psychology 6, 239
bronchodilation, placebo effect 225
buffer hypothesis
    job demand–control model 72
    social support 102
buffers 95
Byrne, P.S., and Long, B.E.L., on doctor-patient
        consultations 218, 219–20

C-fibres 28
Calgary–Cambridge consultation model 218–19, 220
CAM, *see* complementary therapies
cancer
    emotional writing interventions 99
    internet use 105
    life events 46, 51
    personality prone to 111
    social support 102, 104
    socio-economic status 67
Cannon, W., work on stress 43
cardiovascular disease
    socio-economic status 67–8
    stress 4, 24, 60
    see also coronary heart disease
cardiovascular system 21–2
caregivers, wound healing in 35
catastrophizing 80
    chronic pain 229
catecholamines 21
causal understanding of symptoms, prompts for
        consultations 211
causation
    correlations and 128–9
    direction 128–9
    theories and models 69
cell-mediated immunity 32
central nervous system 18–20
central route processing (elaboration likelihood
        model) 169, 176
cerebellum 18
cerebrospinal fluid 20
cerebrum 16–17
cervical screening, socio-economic status on
        uptake 141
    challenges, threats *vs* 172
change
    health behaviours
        long-term illness 228
        models 139, 147
        motivation 157–78
        NICE on 152
        techniques promoting 179–206
        in workplace 80–1

resistance to 167–8
theory of 194
children
life events scales 50
MMR vaccination 158, 164
work stress on mothers 75
choices, presentation of persuasion attempts as 168
'Choices' website, National Health Service 160, 168
cholesterol, North Karelia Project 182
chronic bronchitis, socio-economic status 67
chronic pain
management 228–30
on self-image 227
circulation of blood 21–2
citizens' juries, see focus groups
classical conditioning 5
immunosuppression 31
placebo effects 225
classification systems, research on coping 90–1
clinical psychology 2
cluster analysis, social support for cancer
sufferers 102
cognitions
of health 135–56
interventions to change 157
see also 'need for cognition'; social
cognitive theory
cognitive appraisal, see appraisal of situations
cognitive behavioural skills training 79, 80
benefit finding in 97
hostility reduction 118
cognitive care 225
long-term illness 227
cognitive dissonance 165, 195 (Table)
condom use 193
cognitive elaboration 169
see also elaboration likelihood model
cognitive maps, rats 5
Cohen, S., stress and common cold 33–4
colorectal carcinoma screening, consideration of
future consequences (CFC) and 236
common cold
neuroticism, symptom interpretation 212
stress and 31, 33–4
communication
doctors with patients 167–8, 217–18
vs adherence to professional advice 214
see also consultations
skills for patients 221
community level, behaviour change intervention
181–2
compensation hypothesis, work vs home life 75
competencies, health psychologists 237–40
for research 203–4

complementary therapies 222–3, 225–6, 231
long-term illness 227
compliance 217
diary studies 54
concordance 217
conditioned immunosuppression 31
conditioning, see classical conditioning; operant
conditioning
condom provision 199
condom use
effective behaviour change techniques 191–3
leaflets on 186–9
meta-analysis of studies 236–7
motivation 162
skills teaching 185–6
threat induction 192, 197
see also safer sex regulation
confiding relationships 101
conflict, work–life 76
conformity 166
confounding factors 128
appraisal of situations as 54
conscientiousness 109, 123–6, 126, 127,
129, 235
mediated effects 125, 130
symptom interpretation 212
consensus 166
conservation of resources theory 58–9, 62, 234
work–family conflict 76
consideration of future consequences (CFC) 235–6
consistency, messages 165
Consolidated Standards for the Reporting of Clinical
Trials (CONSORT), guidelines 199
constitutional vulnerability model, hostility 119
consultations, professional competencies in 240
consultations (doctor–patient) 231
duration 222
future work on 237
management of 10–11, 217–22
reasons for 210–13
contemplation (stage model) 147, 148
contingent rewards 196 (Table), 197
continuity of care 222
contracts, behavioural 197
control 78
perceived, theory of planned behaviour 145
perceived behavioural (PBC) 143
see also empowerment; job demand–control
model
control groups, research on behaviour change
interventions 201
control theory (CT) 195 (Table), 196 (Table), 197
conversion to minority view 166
Cook–Medley hostility scale 117

COPE (questionnaire) 89–90, 91
  positive reappraisal in 97
coping 10, 87, 88–99, 235
  chronic pain 229
  long-term illness 227
  neuroticism and 96, 121
  personality and 128
  transactional theory 52
coping appraisal, protection motivation theory 142
Coronary Artery Risk Development in Young Adults
    (CARDIA) study 60
coronary heart disease
  daily hassles *vs* life events 57
  hostility and 116, 117–18
  placebos and mortality 223
  type A personality 115–16
  type D personality 120
corpus callosum 16
correlations 69
  causation and 128–9
cortex, cerebral 17
corticotrophin releasing factor 23
cortisol 21, 23, 33
  ageing on profiles 234
  daily hassles 57
  reactivity 57
  socio-economic status 68
  Trier Social Stress Test 26
costs of illness 3
  saving by volunteer and group health care 175
counselling, employees 80
covariance, analysis of 128
credibility of information 158
cross-sectional methods 128
  stress measurement 53
crossover, work *vs* home life 75
cues to action (prompts) 196 (Table), 197
  for consultations 210
  health belief model 140–1
culturally-specific intervention, safer sex
    regulation 184
cyberspace, *see* internet
cynicism 117, 118
cytokines 32
  common cold and 34
  stress on 33
cytotoxic killer cells 32

d values, meta-analysis 163
daily stress measurements 52–7
debates, transactional approach to stress *vs*
    conservation of resources theory 59
decision-making heuristics 169
defensive processing of fear appeals 188–9

defensiveness, measure 93
definitions
  health (WHO) 1–2
  health behaviours 136
  health psychology 1–4
  self-regulation processes 139
  stress 42–3
    resource-based 58
  stress process (transactional model) 88
demand, *see* job demand–control model
dendrites 18
denial 90
depression
  daily hassles and 54–5, 57
  optimism *vs* pessimism 113
  placebo effects 223–4
  social support and 101
descriptive norms, theory of planned
    behaviour 145
detection behaviours, as high-risk 163–4
diabetes mellitus
  daily hassles 57
  emotion-focused coping and 90
  prevention by behaviour change
    interventions 228
  self-image 227
diagnostic correlates 2–3
diaries, stress measurement 52–7
diastolic blood pressure 22
diathesis, *see* stress diathesis model
diencephalon 16, 17
differential exposure hypothesis, socio-economic
    status 67
differential vulnerability hypothesis, socio-economic
    status 67
Diogenes of Oenoanda, wall etching 4
direct pathways 4, 15–38
  coping and social support 94
'directing' *vs* 'sharing', consultations 220
direction of causation 128–9
dispositional coping styles 91
  see also individual difference models
dissonance, cognitive 165, 195 (Table)
  condom use 193
distraction, chronic pain 229
distress
  breast cancer, *vs* mammography
    attendance 125–6
  confusion with stress 54
  type D personality 120
divorce
  cardiovascular disease 24
  parental, Terman study 124
doctor-centred consultations 219

doctors
  communication with patients 167–8, 217–18
    vs adherence to professional advice 214
    see also consultations
  complementary therapies and 222
  satisfaction with work 214
dominance hierarchies 66–7

eating behaviour
  daily hassles and 55–6
  stressors on snacking 56, 57
effect sizes
  binomial display, SCMs 152
  meta-analysis 162
  research on behaviour change interventions 201
effectiveness (RE-AIM framework) 202
efferent pathways 28
effort–reward imbalance (ERI) model 73–4, 82
ego-threatening stressors, on eating behaviour 55
elaboration likelihood model (ELM) 169
  peripheral route processing 169, 176
elderly people
  health behaviours on mortality 3
  social reciprocity lack 74
'electric shock' experiment 167
elicitation research 184
emotion-focused techniques, stress management 79, 88, 89–90
emotional care 225
emotional eating 56
emotional support 102
emotional writing interventions 98–9
empirical papers 7–8
employee assistance programmes 80
employers, legal requirements 77
empowerment of patients 221–2
enacted social support 102
endocrine system 20–1
endorphins (endogenous opioids) 28, 224
engineering approach, *see* stimulus
enhancement and enrichment (work–family facilitation) 76–7, 79
environmental cues 197
Epicurus 4
epidemiological transition 66
essay writing 8–9
European Federation of Professional Psychologists Associations 239
European Health Psychology Society 6
event-based *vs* time-based recall 216
event-contingent diary studies 54
examinations (academic)
  coping with failure 88
  on wound healing 35

exercise
  common cold and 34
  diabetes mellitus prevention 228
  on mortality 3
  TPB-based leaflet on 144
  in workplace 80–1, 182
exhaustion phase, stress response 44
expectations
  initiation *vs* maintenance of health behaviours 236
  placebo effects 224, 225
experiments 128–9
  on obedience 167
Expert Patient Programmes (EPP) 175–6, 182
experts 170
  influence 165
explicit categorization, information provision 161
explicit self-esteem 49, 50
extinction (operant conditioning), chronic pain and 229
extraversion 109, 122–3, 126, 127, 129
  hostility *vs* 117

facilitation, work–family 76–7, 79
families
  hostility and parent-son discussions 119
  in social hierarchy 67
  work–life conflict 76
  work stressors on 75
family–work facilitation 76–7, 79
fear appeals 188–9, 195 (Table)
  condom use and 192, 197
  quitting smoking 190–1
feedback, performance of health behaviours 196 (Table)
fight-or-flight reaction 43
Finland, North Karelia Project 182
fitness, physical 80–1
  see also exercise
Flesch Reading Ease measure 159
flexible working 79
focus groups 167
  on self-management health care 175
Folkman, S., transactional approach to stress 42–3
food labelling, questions 237
football, cardiovascular disease 24
forebrain 16–17
forgetting
  implementation intentions countering 154
  professional advice 216
frameworks 69
framing effects 163–5, 192
frontal lobe 17
functional approach, research on social support 100
future consequences, consideration of (CFC) 235–6

future directions of research 233–7
future-oriented coping 99

gain spirals 58
gains *vs* losses, risk-taking and 163–5
gate-control theory of pain 27–9, 36, 229
    placebo effects 224–5
gender
    behaviour change interventions, condom use 192
    giving *vs* receiving support 103
    health behaviours 136
    as moderator of stress 95
    social support 100
    socio-economic status and mortality 67
general adaptation syndrome (Selye) 43–4
genetics, stress diathesis model 51, 234
giving *vs* receiving support, gender 103
glucocorticoids 21, 23
goal theory (GT) 195 (Table), 196 (Table), 197
goals
    measure of pursuit 112
    revision 197
    setting 197
    social cognitive theory 145
    see also implementation intentions
graded tasks 173
graphic organizers 161
gross national product, life expectancy *vs* 66
group delivery modes, health care 174–5
groups
    persuasion in 166–7, 191
    see also focus groups

Hallas, C.N., on work of health psychologists 240
hand-held computers, diary studies 54
Hassles and Uplifts Scale 52–7
HBM (health belief model) 139–41, 148, 195
    (Table), 211–12
health, definition (WHO) 1–2
Health and Safety at Work Act (1974) 77
health behaviours 2, 136–8
    conscientiousness and 125
    health cognitions and 135–56
    on health outcomes 138
    hostility and 119
    initiation and maintenance 236
    mismatches with messages 186–91
    on mortality 3
    motivation on 174–6
    neuroticism and 121–2
    promoting change 179–206
        design and evaluation of techniques 199–204
        identifying effective methods 191–9
        long-term illness 228
    taxonomy of techniques 198–9
    in workplace 80–1
    see also motivation; persuasion
    relationships with intentions 126, 148, 153–4, 197
health belief model (HBM) 139–41, 148, 195
    (Table), 211–12
health cognitions, health behaviours and 135–56
health motivation 141
    see also motivation
Health Professions Council 239
health psychologists, competencies required
    237–40
    for research 203–4
heart 21
heuristics, for decision-making 169
hierarchical linear modelling 56
hierarchies 66–7
higher-order categories, research on coping 90–1
hindbrain 18
Hippocrates 4
historical aspects, stress research 43–4
HIV infection
    IMB-based prevention 185
    internet use 105
    tests for, gain- *vs* loss-focused messages 164
    see also condom use
Hobfoll, S., conservation of resources theory 58–9
Holmes, T.H., and Rahe, R.H., social readjustment
    rating scale 48
home life, work stressors on 65, 74–7
homeopathy 225–6
hope 112
hormones 20
hostility 109, 117–19, 126, 127, 130
    attributional style 117
    coronary heart disease 116, 117–18
    reduction 118
House of Lords Select Committee, on complementary
    therapies 222–3
Huntington's disease, internet social support 105
hypertension 60
    on mortality 3
    stress 22
hypnosis, chronic pain 229
hypothalamic–pituitary–adrenal (HPA) axis 21, 22,
    23, 36
    daily hassles 57
hypothalamus 17

identity disruption model (Brown and McGill)
    49–50
imagery, non-painful 229
IMB model, *see* information–motivation–behavioural
    skills model

immune system 31–7
    intermittent stress responses 172
    neuroticism 122
immunosuppression, conditioned 31
impatience, type A behaviour 117
implementation (RE-AIM framework) 203
implementation intentions 154
implicit self-esteem 49, 50
impulsivity 123
income distribution, Japan vs England 66
indirect pathways, see behavioural pathways
individual difference models
    social support and 103–4
    stress measurement 55, 57, 59–61, 234
    see also dispositional coping styles
individual level, health behaviour change
        interventions 183–4
inequality, social 66–7, 235
influence
    normative 165, 192
    social 163, 165–6, 180–3, 195 (Table)
influenza, interleukin-6 and 34
information
    before consultations 221
    desire for 159–60
    message evaluation 169, 170 (Fig.)
    organization 160–1
    provision 158–63, 185, 195 (Table), 198 (Table)
information–motivation–behavioural (IMB) skills model
        183–4, 195 (Table)
    condom use 192
informational influence 165
informational support 102
    internet 105
initiation of health behaviours 236
injunctive norms, theory of planned behaviour 145
injuries, unintentional 111
ink blot test (Rorschach) 123 (Fig.)
instrumental support 102
intention to treat analysis, behaviour change
        interventions 201
intentions
    formation 195 (Table)
    of implementation 154
    relationships with behaviour 148, 153–4, 197
        conscientiousness and 126
    stability of 153
interactional-appraisal approach to stress, see
        transactional approach to stress
interleukin-1 32
interleukin-1β, wound healing 35
interleukin-2 32
interleukin-6, infections and 34
intermittent stress responses 172

internal representation, by rats 5
international legislation 181
International Personality Item Pool 121
    on conscientiousness 124
internet
    health behaviour interventions via 236
    NHS Direct service 237
    paradox 105
    social support 104–6
    see also websites
interval-contingent diary studies 53
intervention mapping 199–200
interviewing
    motivational 196, 197
    Western Collaborative Group Study 115
irritability, type A behaviour 117
irritable bowel syndrome, daily hassles 57

Japan, income distribution 66
Jenkins Activity Survey 116
job content questionnaire 72
job demand–control (JDC) model 70–3, 82
    effort–reward imbalance model vs 74
jobs, redesign 72
jogger's high 28
journals
    health psychology 6
    see also empirical papers

Karasek, R.A., job demand–control model 70–3
key roles
    competencies and 239
    psychologists 238–9
Kiecolt-Glaser, J., stress and wound healing 34–5
killer cells, cytotoxic 32
knowledge, health behaviours and 137, 162
Kuopio Heart Study 4, 60

laboratory test, stress 25–6
lagged effects of stress 53
    hypertension 60
'larks' (morningness), on stress reactivity 60
Lazarus, R., transactional approach to stress 42–3,
        52–7
leaflets
    on condom use 186–9
    on exercise 144
    with medication 159
learning 6–9
legislation
    behaviour change 181
    persuasion and 168
'length equals strength' heuristic 169
letters of name, implicit self-esteem 49

Leventhal, H., on professional help-seeking 211
life change unit scores 48
life events 46–51, 62
    daily hassles vs 57
    social support on effects 101
Life Events and Difficulties Schedule (LEDS) 51
life expectancy
    gross national product vs 66
    health behaviours on 3
    optimism on 113
    see also mortality
lifestyle change interventions, in workplace 80–1
limbic system 17
Linguistic Inquiry and Word Count (software) 99
lobbying 181
local government, behaviour change intervention
        181–2
long-term illness 226–30, 231
long-term treatments, adherence to professional
        advice 215–16
longevity, see life expectancy; mortality
longitudinal studies 128
    intention–behaviour gap 153
loss spirals 58
losses vs gains, risk-taking and 163–5
lung cancer, socio-economic status 67
lymphocytes 32

macrophages 32
maintenance
    of health behaviours 236
    of interventions (RE-AIM framework) 203
majority influence 166
maladaptive responses, protection motivation
        theory 142
mammography
    conscientiousness on attendance 125–6
    messages matched to coping styles 94
Management Standards, work stress and 77
Marlowe–Crowne measure of social
        desirability 93
marriage
    base for social readjustment scale 48
    gender on benefits 100
mastery experiences 173
Matarazzo, J.D., definition of health psychology 2
McEwen, B.S., allostatic load 44–5
meaning of pain 26–7
measles, mumps and rubella (MMR) vaccine 158
    gain- vs loss-focused messages 164
measurement
    artefact of
        personality vs health outcomes 127
        see also mere measurement effect

of stress 52–4
    diaries 52–7
    Hassles and Uplifts Scale 52–7
    individual difference models 55, 57, 59–61, 234
mediated effects
    conscientiousness 125, 130
    of coping 94–5, 96
mediation analyses, behaviour change interventions
        201–2
medication, information leaflets 159
medico-physiological approach to stress 42
meditation 79
medulla oblongata 18
Melzack, R., see gate-control theory of pain
memory, treatment advice 216–17
meninges 20
mere measurement effect 152
    see also measurement, artefact of
messages
    framing 163–5, 192
    mismatches with behavioural determinants 186–91
    personal relevance 170–1, 195 (Table)
    processing, attitude change 168–71
meta-analyses 162–3
    studies on condom use 236–7
metabolic syndrome 234
metencephalon 18
midbrain 18
Mielewczyk, F., and Willig, C., on SCMs 151
mineralocorticoids 21
minority influence 166
mistrust 117
modelling
    building self-efficacy 173–4
    hierarchical linear 56
    multi-level 201, 234
modelling phase studies 203
models 69
moderated effects
    conscientiousness 125–6
    of coping and social support 95
monitoring (coping style) 93–4
moral norms 150
morningness-eveningness, on stress reactivity 60
morphine, placebo effects and 225
mortality
    conscientiousness on 124
    extraversion 122
    health behaviours on 3
    long-term illness 227
    neuroticism 122
    non-adherence to professional advice 213
    optimists vs pessimists 212
    placebos and 223

social support on 100
socio-economic status 67
type A personality 116
type D personality 120
see also life expectancy
mothers, work stress on 75
motivation
adherence to treatment 217
behaviour change from 174–6
condom use 162
interventions to change 157–78
safer sex 185
see also persuasion
motivational interviewing 196, 197
motivational phase, self-regulation processes 139, 148
multi-level modelling 201, 234
myelencephalon 18
myocardial infarction 24
smoking legislation on incidence 181
myocardium 21

name-letter effect, implicit self-esteem 49
National Health Service
'Choices' website 160, 168
costs of illness 3
NHS Direct service 237
self-care and 179
National Institute for Health and Clinical Excellence
(NICE), on psychology and behaviour
change 152
National Occupational Standards 238
National Standards for Psychology, Key Purpose
Statement 238
'need for cognition' 170
needs assessment, intervention mapping 199
negative affect, see neuroticism
negative effects
anorexia nervosa websites 106
self-injury message boards 106
negative emotions, symptom interpretation 212
negotiating skills, behaviour change 186
nerve fibres 27, 28
nerves 16
nervous system 16–20, 36
extraversion and 129
networks, social 100, 103, 104–5
neuromatrix 30
neuromatrix theory of pain 29–30, 36
neurons 18
pain fibres 27, 28
neuroscience 6
neurosignatures 30
neuroticism 109, 120–2, 126, 127, 129, 130
coping and 96, 121

hostility vs 117
symptom interpretation 212
neurotransmitters 18
NHS Direct service 237
nicotine replacement therapy 191
nociceptors 28
non-adherence, to professional advice 213
non-painful imagery 229
'non-self', immune system 31
noradrenaline 21, 22–3
common cold and 34
socio-economic status 68
normative influence 165, 192
North Karelia Project, Finland 182
note-making 7
nurses, 'overdose' experiment 167

obedience 167
obesity, on mortality 3
objectivity
conservation of resources theory 58
stress measurement 54–5
occipital lobe 17
occupational health psychology 68–74
see also work
OCEAN model, personality types 110
Ogden, J., critique of social cognition models
150–1, 152
openness 110, 126
operant conditioning (OC) 5, 196 (Table), 197
chronic pain 229
optimism 97, 109, 111–15
mortality 212
optimistic attributional style 114
organization of information 160–1
organizations, professional, health psychology 6
outcome expectancies, social cognitive theory
145, 146
outcome measures, behaviour change interventions
201, 202
long-term illness 228
overcommitment 73
'overdose' experiment on nurses 167
overeating, quitting, self-efficacy 171
overlap of measures, Ogden on SCMs 151
'owls' (eveningness), on stress reactivity 60

pain 26–30, 36
acupuncture 226
cardiovascular disease 24
chronic
management 228–30
on self-image 227
placebo effects 223, 224–5

pain redefinition 229
paper-and-pencil diaries 54
papers, empirical 7–8
parasympathetic nervous system 20
parent-son discussions, hostility and 119
parietal lobe 17
passive interventions, behaviour change 192
passive jobs 71
patient-centred consultations 219–21
patients
    empowerment 221–2
    enablement (Howie) 222
    expectations, placebo effects 224, 225
    information desired 159–60
    satisfaction, *vs* adherence to professional
        advice 214
pattern theory, pain perception 27
peers
    IMB-based interventions 185
    influence 165, 195 (Table)
Pendleton, D., tasks in consultations 219, 220
perceived behavioural control (PBC) 143
perceived confidence and control, theory of planned
        behaviour 145
perceived social support 100, 101
percentage of variance (social cognition models)
        151, 152
perfectionism 59
    coping styles on effects 96
performance-enhancing drugs, placebo effects
        and 225
peripheral nervous system 20, 36
peripheral route processing (elaboration likelihood
        model) 169, 176
personal relevance of messages 170–1, 195 (Table)
personality 10, 109–31, 235
    coping styles 94–6
    susceptibility to stress 59
    on symptom interpretation 212–13
    see also specific types; individual difference models
personalizing 80
perspective taking, patient-centredness as 221
persuasion 157, 163–8, 176, 199
    groups 166–7, 191
pessimism
    on health 113
    symptom interpretation 212
phantom limb pain 29–30
physical fitness 80–1
    see also exercise
physical stressors, on eating behaviour 55
physiological reactivity, *see* stress reactivity
physiology, response to stress 4–5
pituitary gland 21

placebo effects 223–5, 231
planned behaviour, *see* theory of planned behaviour
PMT, *see* protection motivation theory
pons 18
Popper, K., on theories 70
positive affect 96–7
    long-term illness 227
    optimism and 113–14
positive life events 48, 49–50
positive reappraisal 97–9
pre-contemplation (stage model) 147, 148
preparation (stage model) 147, 148
preventative approaches
    coping 96
    as low-risk 163
prevention
    diabetes mellitus 228
    HIV infection 185
        see also condom use
    work stressors 77–81, 234
primary appraisal 88
Prime Minister's Strategy Unit, on citizen
        participation 179
proactive coping 99
problem-focused coping
    positive affect 97
    stress management 79–80, 88, 89
process evaluations, behaviour change
        interventions 202
progressive muscle relaxation 79, 230
prompting practice 197
prompts, *see* cues to action
prospect theory 163–5
prospective studies, *see* longitudinal studies
protection motivation theory (PMT) 141–2, 154, 195
        (Table)
    condom use 192
    fear appeals 188
    initiation *vs* maintenance of health behaviours 236
psychology
    health *vs* clinical 2
    origins 5
psychoneuroimmunology 31–5
psychophysiological pathways 4, 15–38
psychophysiological reactivity, *see* stress reactivity
psychosocial vulnerability, hostility and 119
public health legislation
    behaviour change 181
    persuasion and 168
public health programmes, ancient Greece 4
public opinion 167

Qi (life force) 226
qualitative studies 175

quality of life, long-term illness 228
quantitative studies 175
questionnaires
  Conservation of Resources Evaluation 58
  COPE 89–90, 91
    positive reappraisal in 97
  effort–reward imbalance model 73–4
  intention stability 153
  Jenkins Activity Survey 116
  on job content 72
  reliability on social support 102
  Ways of Coping 88–9
  see also self-report measures

r values, meta-analysis 162
radon, smoking and 126
randomization 201
rats, cognitive maps 5
RE-AIM framework 202–3
reach (RE-AIM framework) 202
reactance 167
reactivity, *see* stress reactivity
reading difficulty, information text 159
reasoned action, theory of 143, 195 (Table)
recall of advice, adherence and 216–17
receiving *vs* giving support, gender 103
reciprocation, persuasion and 166
reciprocity, lack in effort–reward imbalance
    model 73–4
recovery, *see* stress recovery
references, in essays 9
regret, anticipated, intention–behaviour
    gap and 153
reinforcement
  chronic pain and 229
  see also contingent rewards
relapse prevention 196 (Table)
relationships (interpersonal), quality 100–1
relative poverty 66
relaxation training 79
  for chronic pain 230
relevance, personal, of messages 170–1, 195 (Table)
reliability
  life-event research 50
  questionnaires on social support 102
remission, spontaneous 224
repressive coping 91–3
research
  on behaviour change interventions 199, 200–4
  competencies in 203–4
  empirical papers 7–8
  experiments 128–9
  future directions 233–7
  professional competencies in 239

on self-management health care 175
  see also meta-analyses; science; trials
resistance phase, stress response 44
resistance to change 167–8
resource-based models, *see* conservation of
    resources theory
resource caravans 58
response-based approach to stress 42
response efficacy, protection motivation theory 142
rewards
  contingent 196 (Table), 197
  see also effort–reward imbalance model
rheumatoid arthritis
  daily hassles 57
  volunteer-delivered group health care 175
rich–poor divide, Japan *vs* England 66
risk information, presentation 162
risk-taking
  gains *vs* losses and 163–5
  optimism and 114
role models 196 (Table)
Rorschach ink blot test 123 (Fig.)

safer sex regulation 185–8
  culturally-specific intervention 184
  see also condom use
satisfaction with outcomes, initiation *vs* maintenance
    of health behaviours 236
Schwartzer, R., on resource-based models 59
science 69
SCM, *see* social cognition models
SCT, *see* social cognitive theory
secondary appraisal 88, 224
sedentary lifestyle, on mortality 3
segmentation hypothesis, work *vs* home life 75
selective serotonin reuptake inhibitors, placebo
    effects 223–4
'self', immune system 31
self-affirmation, in fear appeals 189
self-affirmation writing, cancer 99
self-efficacy 145, 176–7
  adherence to treatment 217
  on chronic pain 228
  consultations and 221, 222
  enhancing 171–4
    in fear appeals 188
  health belief model and 141
  initiation *vs* maintenance of health
      behaviours 236
  protection motivation theory 142
  social cognitive theory 145–6
self-esteem
  identity disruption model and 49–50
  social support and 103

self-image, long-term illness 227
self-injury message boards 106
self-management training 174–6
    long-term illness 228
self-monitoring 184, 195 (Table), 198 (Table)
self-motivation 196 (Table)
self-regulation
    processes 139
    skills 184
self-report measures
    neuroticism and 121, 127, 130
    see also questionnaires
self-talk 196 (Table)
Selye, H., work on stress 43–4
sentient neural hub 30
sexually transmitted diseases, see condom use; safer
        sex regulation
'sharing' vs 'directing', consultations 220
shellshock 42
short-term treatments, adherence to professional
        advice 215
signal-contingent diary studies 54
situational coping 91, 96
skills
    behavioural 184–6, 199
        condom use 192
    see also communication
Skinner, E.A., on literature on coping 90–1
sleep habits
    common cold and 34
    on mortality 3
smoking
    common cold and 34
    health cognitions and 137
    legislation 181
    on mortality 3
    neuroticism 122
    North Karelia Project 182
    quitting
        fear appeals 190–1
        self-efficacy 171
        stage model 147
    radon and 126
snacking, stressors on 56, 57
social causation hypothesis 67
social cognition models (SCM) 137–53, 155
    criticisms 150–3
    integration of 148–9
social cognitive theory (SCT) 145–6, 195 (Table)
    condom use 192
social drift hypothesis 67
social ecological model, behaviour change 180–3
social inequality 66–7, 235
social influence 163, 165–6, 180–3, 195 (Table)

social networks 100, 103, 104–5
social psychology 5
Social Readjustment Rating Scale 47 (Fig.), 48
social skills, negotiating behaviour change 186
social support 87, 100–7, 235
    on adherence to professional advice 214–15
    behaviour change promotion 182–3, 196 (Table)
    direct effects 94
    in job demand–control model 72
    mediator of effects on stress 95
    negative effects 103
    proactive coping and 99
    prompts for consultations 210
socio-economic status 65, 66–8, 82, 235
    on uptake of cervical screening 141
socio-structural factors, social cognitive theory 146
SODAS (acronym) 184
soldiers, wound pain 26
somatic nervous system 20
source credibility 158
specificity theory, pain perception 27
spillover hypothesis, work stress 75
spinal cord 18
spirals, of loss or gain 58
spontaneous remission 224
stability of intentions 153
stage models 139, 147–9, 172
statistics 9
    behaviour change interventions 201
    cluster analysis 102
    meta-analyses 162–3
    SCMs 151
    use of diaries 53
stimulus, stress and 42
strain, job demand–control model 71
    hypothesis 72
stress 9–10, 16, 36
    chronic pain from 230
    direct, mediated and moderated effects on 95–6
    hypertension 22
    on immune system 31, 33–5
    laboratory test 25–6
    management 88, 89, 196 (Table)
    management training 79–80
    neuroticism and 121
    personality and 128
    physiological response magnitude 4
    positive affect on 227
    research on 41–63, 233, 234
    response 4–5, 22–6
    self-efficacy vs 172
    symptoms and 211
    on telomeres 233
    work, see work, stressors

stress diathesis model 51, 59
stress reactivity 60, 129
  cortisol 57
  hostility 119
  type A personality 117
stress recovery 60, 61
strokes 24
structural approach, research on social support 100
subjective norms, theory of planned behaviour 143,
    144, 145
substance P 27
substantia gelatinosa 27
sunscreen, gain- vs loss-focused messages 164
supervision of health professionals,
    competencies in 240
surgery, psychological response on wound
    healing 35
survival of cancer, social support 104
sympathetic adrenal medullary response system
    22-3, 36
sympathetic nervous system 20
symptoms
  interpretations 211-13
    personality on 212-13
  prompts for consultations 210-11
synapses 18
systolic blood pressure 22

T-lymphocytes 32
targeting health interventions 180
tasks in consultations (Pendleton) 219, 220
taxonomy of health behaviour change
    techniques 198-9
technology
  for health behaviours 186
  for treatment adherence 216
telencephalon 16
telephone counselling, employee assistance
    programmes 80
telomeres, stress on 233
temporal lobe 17
Terman Life-Cycle personality cohort study 124
terminal illness, social support 104
Terry, D., on coping 96
testicular cancer, self-examination for 163-4
tests (academic), learning from 6-7
thalamus 17
theories 69, 70
  of change 194
theory of planned behaviour (TPB) 143-5, 195
    (Table), 212
  condom use 192
  initiation vs maintenance of health behaviours
    236

theory of reasoned action (TRA) 143, 195 (Table)
third variable problems 129
threat induction, condom use and 192, 197
threats
  appraisal, protection motivation theory 142
  challenges vs 172
  perceptions
    health belief model 140
    see also fear appeals
three-condition design, trials with placebos 224
time-based vs event-based recall 216
time management 196 (Table)
Toronto Alexithymia Scale 92
touch sensation, nerve fibres 28
TPB, see theory of planned behaviour
TRA (theory of reasoned action) 143, 195 (Table)
training (professional)
  complementary therapy practitioners 223
  professional competencies in 240
  psychologists 238, 239
trait anxiety, emotion-focused coping and 90
transactional approach to stress 42-3, 52-7, 62
  coping 88
  debate vs conservation of resources theory 59
  hostility and 119
transcendental meditation 79
transmission cells, pain 27-8
transtheoretical model, behavioural change
    139, 147
trends, stress 61-2
trials
  acupuncture 226
  of behaviour change techniques 203
  future trends 237
  placebos in 224
Trier Social Stress Test (TSST) 25-6
tropisms, personality and health outcomes 127
two-factor theory of planned behaviour 145
two-sided arguments, source credibility 158
type A personality 109, 115-17, 127
type C personality 111
type D personality 120

understanding of advice, adherence and 216
understanding of symptoms, prompts for
    consultations 211
uplifts (Hassles and Uplifts Scale) 52-7
users, testing behaviour change interventions
    with 200

vaccination 31
  see also measles, mumps and rubella (MMR)
    vaccine
validity, life-event research 50

variance
    analysis of 128
    percentage of, SCMs 151, 152
vegetables, consumption on mortality 3
vicarious experience, *see* modelling
visual aids 161
volitional phase, self-regulation processes
        139, 148
volunteer delivery modes, health care 174–5
vulnerability
    psychosocial, hostility and 119
    see also differential vulnerability hypothesis

wall etching (Diogenes) 4
war wounds, pain 26
Ways of Coping questionnaire 88–9
websites
    'Choices' (NHS) 160, 168
    harmful 106
    theory of planned behaviour 150
Western Collaborative Group Study 115
Wilkinson, R.G., on relative poverty 66

work
    interventions for behaviour change at 182
    social support at 103
    stressors 42, 65, 68–77, 82
        cardiovascular disease 24
        on eating behaviour 55–6
        objectivity of studies 54
        prevention and reduction 77–81, 234
    type A behaviour 117
work–family facilitation 76–7, 79
work–life balance 75, 82
work–life conflict 76
World Health Organization, definition of health 1–2
wounds
    healing, stress and 34–5
    pain, soldiers *vs* civilians 26
written emotional disclosure interventions 98–9
Wundt, W. 5

yoga 79

Zyban (bupropion) 191